Defining Duty in the Civil War

CIVIL WAR AMERICA
Gary W. Gallagher, Peter S. Carmichael, Caroline E. Janney,
and Aaron Sheehan-Dean, editors

This landmark series interprets broadly the history and culture of the Civil War era through the long nineteenth century and beyond. Drawing on diverse approaches and methods, the series publishes historical works that explore all aspects of the war, biographies of leading commanders, and tactical and campaign studies, along with select editions of primary sources. Together, these books shed new light on an era that remains central to our understanding of American and world history.

Defining Duty
IN THE CIVIL WAR
*Personal Choice, Popular Culture, and
the Union Home Front*

J. Matthew Gallman

The University of North Carolina Press   Chapel Hill

© 2015 The University of North Carolina Press
All rights reserved
Manufactured in the United States of America
Set in Miller by Tseng Information Systems, Inc.
The paper in this book meets the guidelines for permanence and durability
of the Committee on Production Guidelines for Book Longevity of the Council on
Library Resources. The University of North Carolina Press has been a member
of the Green Press Initiative since 2003.

Cover illustrations: "A Fancy Soldier" (Courtesy of the Library
Company of Philadelphia) and "The Draft" by T. F. G. Miller (Courtesy of
the Henry E. Huntington Library, San Marino, Calif.)

Library of Congress Cataloging-in-Publication Data
Gallman, J. Matthew (James Matthew)
Defining duty in the Civil War : personal choice, popular culture,
and the Union home front / J. Matthew Gallman.
pages cm. — (Civil War America)
Includes bibliographical references and index.
ISBN 978-1-4696-2099-2 (cloth : alk. paper) — ISBN 978-1-4696-2100-5 (ebook)
1. United States—History—Civil War, 1861–1865—Social aspects.
2. National characteristics, American—History—19th century. 3. Nationalism—
United States—History—19th century. 4. Patriotism—United States—History—19th
century. 5. Northeastern States—Social conditions—19th century. 6. Political culture—
United States—History—19th century. 7. Political culture—Northeastern States—
History—19th century. 8. Duty. 9. Duty. I. Title.
E468.9.G36 2015
973.7'1—dc23
2014047576

Contents

Defining Duty in the Civil War

Only Bread and the Newspaper
We Must Have

In early 1863 Philadelphian Charles Janeway Stillé published a pamphlet titled *How a Free People Conduct a Long War*.[1] It seemed a good time to ask the question. The Civil War had been dragging on for nearly two years and gave little sign of ending. The previous September the Union forces under General George McClellan had managed to turn back the audacious invasion north by the Army of Northern Virginia at Antietam Creek, but there was little to celebrate in a bloody day of fighting that produced more than fourteen thousand Federal casualties and saw Confederate general Robert E. Lee escape the battlefield and return south to regroup. In the 1862 elections, Abraham Lincoln's Republican Party had lost twenty-two seats, offering eloquent testimony to the war weariness on the northern home front.[2]

Stillé, a prominent lawyer and member of the United States Sanitary Commission, drew on the historic example set by the British during the Napoleonic Wars to explain how free people of goodwill should respond to a long war. In essence, he called on his readers to stick with the war even though things seemed difficult. In times of adversity a free people must endure hardships to achieve worthy goals. This message struck a nerve among prowar northerners. Stillé's pamphlet went through multiple printings and sold as many as a half million copies.[3] *How a Free People Conduct a Long War* was just a single contribution to a complex and multi-layered northern war culture that helped define what it meant to be a citizen of the United States in wartime. In the midst of national crisis, this Union war culture offered advice to people who had every reason to feel confused about their duty. This is a study of the printed advice patriotic northerners sought and received during the American Civil War.[4]

■ Let me begin with three large observations about the North during the Civil War. The first is that northerners, even prowar northerners, were not as homogeneous a group as we sometimes imagine. As students of the war, we are—I believe—too quick to think in terms of simple binaries. At the most basic level, the familiar distinction is between "the North" and "the South" (or, if we are a bit more precise, between "northerners" and "white southerners"). A more nuanced analysis recognizes that both the Union and the Confederacy were divided nations, each with its own dissenters. In the North, vigorous dissent came from the peace wing of the Democratic Party, who became known as "Copperheads." Others, both Republicans and Democrats, generally supported the war although they might have opposed particular war measures. These distinctions are useful, and they become even more valuable when we consider regional distinctions within the northern and border states. The levels and vigor of dissent varied substantially from state to state, and from community to community. Some northerners opposed the Civil War, either from the outset or with the passage of time. Some of these wrote passionate partisan speeches or pamphlets, others rioted in the streets in opposition to the draft, a few left the country altogether, and others presumably sat home and quietly stewed, voting Democrat on election day.[5]

My contention is that these widely recognized lines of political difference still leave us with a vast body of undifferentiated northerners who remained fundamentally in favor of the Union war effort and certainly never embraced Copperheadism. At one end of the spectrum were the very passionate prowar patriots. They enlisted at the first opportunity, spoke at recruiting rallies, ran voluntary societies, preached patriotic sermons, volunteered as nurses, attended meetings, wore ribbons, and in many cases became almost obsessed with acquiring the latest news from the front. Others were less demonstrative, and perhaps more ambivalent about the war. Some of these might have been unhappy with the Lincoln administration for specific measures. Many had no enthusiasm for emancipation, even if they accepted the Emancipation Proclamation as a wise war measure. Most probably grumbled at one time or another about one thing or another. When the elections of 1863 and 1864 rolled around, some of the men in this group might have voted for Democratic candidates in state and national elections, even while they continued to support the war. But whatever their differences in belief and behavior, these prowar northerners—male or female, white or black, native-born or immigrant—shared a common characteristic: they wanted the Union to win the Civil War. If you stopped them on the street or engaged them in conversation in their shop or office, they would agree that they hoped for Union victory. And, perhaps as emphatically, they wanted to see the Confederacy defeated.[6]

My second observation is simply this: Americans in 1860 had no reason to know how to behave in the midst of a war of this magnitude. The American Revolution had been a tremendously long war, requiring huge sacrifices from citizens and soldiers, but that conflict had ended eighty years earlier. Moreover, the scale of the armies in the field during the Revolutionary War (or the War with Mexico) would be dwarfed by the size of Civil War armies. The War of 1812 and the Mexican-American War had resulted in roughly 4,000 American combat deaths. A long list of military conflicts with Native Americans and the Barbary Pirates during the nineteenth century had cost the United States armed forces roughly 800 or so combat deaths scattered over sixty years. In sum, the United States military had suffered fewer than 5,000 combat deaths in the six decades before the Civil War. In a single day at the Battle of Antietam, roughly 3,600 Americans (2,100 Union soldiers) died in combat. During the Overland Campaign in May and June 1864, the Federal armies under the command of Ulysses S. Grant suffered somewhere between 6,500 and 7,500 killed in action in about six weeks.[7]

There is no need to belabor the point. The Civil War presented Americans with a conflict of unparalleled size. At all levels of society, individuals and institutions were asked to raise, outfit, and organize armies of unheard-of scale, while civilians encountered massive personal challenges in coming to terms with the conflict even if they never confronted an invading army.[8] Yet despite its magnitude, the Civil War presented prowar northerners with no obviously recognized roadmap dictating how they should behave. Although circumstances certainly forced many northerners into action, most northern civilians faced complicated choices, not unambiguous mandates. My goal is to consider how northerners came to understand what was expected of them in this national crisis. I wish to uncover how ordinary people knew how to exhibit their patriotism if they were not going to make major personal sacrifices. And how did their neighbors decide whom to respect and whom to spurn? This public conversation offered yardsticks to measure appropriate wartime behavior. The answers to these questions were hardly obvious in April 1861.

This leads to my final observation. When faced with a war of unprecedented scope, unknown duration, and unclear expectations, northerners turned to their larger community for guidance. Much of this guidance came from a mass outpouring of popular publications. As we shall see, some of this flood of advice was, like Stillé's popular pamphlet, explicitly didactic. Other cultural messages came from popular fiction, biting satire, political cartoons, and all manner of printed material. My goal is to unravel what northerners found when they consumed the wealth of printed materials produced during the war.

◼ When we study the United States during the Civil War era, it is commonplace to see the antebellum decades as shaped by crucial debates over expansion and the future of slavery, and the chain of events that led to secession and war. But these distinctly partisan and sectional political developments amounted to only one strand in the complex narrative that shaped the first half of the nineteenth century. The main lines of that broader history are familiar. In brief, during the decades between 1800 and 1860 the population of the northern states grew at a spectacular pace, fueled by an impressive natural population increase[9] and substantial immigration from abroad, particularly in the 1840s and 1850s. Meanwhile, the pace of economic production outstripped this rapid population increase, as producers became increasingly embedded in regional, national, and international markets, and all sectors of the economy expanded their reliance on technology, thus enhancing productivity. As the population and economy grew, it also shifted geographically. According to the United States census, in 1800 the "mean center of population of the United States" was just north of Washington, DC. Sixty years later that imaginary population midpoint had moved west into southern Ohio.[10] Meanwhile, in 1790 roughly 7 percent of Americans outside the southern states lived in urban areas, where "urban" meant communities of over twenty-five hundred people; on the eve of the Civil War, roughly a quarter of northerners lived in urban places.[11]

In myriad ways the decades of the mid-nineteenth century introduced Americans to unfamiliar challenges and circumstances. Many moved into new environments, with unique obstacles and expectations. Others, particularly those who shared in the emergence of a vast middle class, saw shifts in cultural expectations that accompanied changes in status.[12] Even those who remained firmly rooted in the agrarian communities of their forebearers found that changes in markets, technology, and communication all produced new dimensions to familiar experiences. And as they moved into new settings, Americans faced a plethora of unfamiliar decisions, both large and small, as they struggled to acquire and maintain the elusive state of respectability in uncertain times. Although their experiences were remarkably diverse, one response to these waves of newness seemed almost universal: Americans turned to printed materials for advice on how to proceed.

Some of the more challenging, and subtle, transitions in cultural expectations concerned the changing notions of appropriate gender roles. Political, economic, religious, and cultural shifts that dated to the late eighteenth century produced a world of evolving expectations for both women and men, particularly in those parts of the country profoundly affected by the market revolution. In one of the foundational texts in American women's history, the historian Barbara Welter examined a diverse array of published materials—short stories, poems, sermons, advice manuals, and so on—published in the antebellum Northeast and identified what she called a "Cult of True Womanhood," portraying an idealized notion of how a proper "true woman" was expected to behave.[13] Readers—largely young, white, middle-class women—turned to these prescriptive sources for both edification and entertainment. In some cases the cultural message appeared as explicit rules for behavior, but in other cases the reader read about characters making mistakes and suffering misfortunes.[14]

Victorian Americans—and especially young men—who ventured into the emerging American cities turned to a lively advice literature, offering guidance on how to behave, who to avoid, and generally which paths to select in this foreign environment. As the scholar Karen Halttunen has noted, this literature warned of the dangers and temptations of the "confidence man" and the "trickster." Guides instructed the youthful innocents venturing into the urban landscape to be vigilant about thieves, gamblers, con artists, and men and women on the make who were not what they appeared to be. In a culture that valued purity of mind and simplicity of spirit, the clever hypocrite constituted the greatest of threats.[15] While Halttunen's study considered publications aimed at the middle classes, poor immigrants from Ireland and Germany turned to comparable volumes devoted to providing advice and caution to those destined for US ports. Here again the advice often amounted to avoiding strangers who were not as they seemed, including disreputable "runners" who prowled the wharves in search of easy marks.[16]

In her study of American manners, C. Dallett Hemphill considered how etiquette manuals, sermons, and other prescriptive literature offered antebellum Americans direction as they navigated a changing world where the familiar rules of deference and patriarchy were giving way to a newly democratized society. Once again, Hemphill's crucial insight is that when confronted with unfamiliar terrain, Americans consulted published sources for guidance.[17] In his study of antebellum New York City, David M. Henkin takes this analysis a step further and in a somewhat different direction, arguing that newcomers to the nation's cities had to learn how to read the city's many public texts—newspapers, bulletin boards, signs, broadsides—in order to understand urban life.[18]

As this discussion suggests, several strands came together in the antebellum decades, producing this flood of prescriptive literature. First, the pace of change left many Americans uncertain about decisions to be made and steps to take. Second, there appeared to be a broad consensus that answers could be found in printed materials. Certainly advice manuals, published sermons, and popular fiction did not replace family and community conversation, but the unfamiliar nature of society's new challenges prompted readers to turn to new answers. Finally, and crucially, the nation's technological capacity to produce and distribute cheap printed materials drove this explosion in prescriptive literature.

Here we drift onto another vast topic, where certain core points are worth noting. First, the literacy rate in the northern states during the Civil War was extremely high. Although degrees of literacy are difficult to assess, the overwhelming majority of northerners were comfortable around the printed word, and thoroughly accustomed to books, pamphlets, newspapers, and so on. Moreover, it was commonplace for antebellum Americans to read aloud to friends, coworkers, and family members and to discuss what they were reading in conversations and correspondence. Thus when we consider the actual circulation of texts, those figures will invariably understate the overall consumption of the printed sources. Second, the rate of publication of all sorts of materials was growing rapidly, and generally much faster than the population. By 1860 there were more than four thousand newspapers and journals published in the United States. Many of these publications had modest circulations and spoke to local audiences, and the disproportionate number were produced in New York and the other major East Coast cities.[19] But the reductions in printing costs and the expansion in the federal mail system had paved the way for a steady growth in specialized journals and publications aimed at national readerships.[20]

As we consider what northerners were reading during the Civil War, the timing of the conflict becomes significant, both because of the technological and institutional capacity to distribute printed materials quickly and because of the array of new journals being published. Several of the North's more popular and widely circulated journals had only recently begun publication. *Harper's Monthly Magazine*, which would become one of the nation's leading literary magazines, began operations in 1850; *Arthur's Home Magazine*, a Philadelphia monthly aimed largely at women, ran its first issue in 1852; Boston's *Atlantic Monthly*, which would produce some of the crucial commentaries on the Civil War, started publishing in 1857. The nation's two great illustrated weeklies, *Frank Leslie's Illustrated Newspaper* and *Harper's Weekly*, began publishing in 1855 and 1857, respectively. Each of these two fierce competitors boasted circulations of over one hundred thousand during the war years. The decade before the Civil War also saw an explosion in new comic newspapers, producing a combination of highbrow and quite lowbrow humor. These included *Yankee Notions* (1852), *Nick Nax* (1856), *Frank Leslie's Budget of Fun* (1859), and *Vanity Fair* (1859).[21]

■ For nearly all northerners, the Civil War presented challenges and choices rather than circumstances that allowed for only a single path. Although the United States mobilized a huge army to fight the Civil War, that mobilization—through vigorous recruiting, attractive financial offers, and federal conscription—only lured a portion of able-bodied men into uniform, especially in the war's first year.[22] Many men who could have fought chose not to. Others served only for short stints. And others still watched from the sidelines for many months or years before finally volunteering.[23]

The numbers here are so large as to feel overwhelming, yet they are also instructive. The Union army's official records contain nearly 2.5 million enlistments by white men, but that number includes men who enlisted for a short time early in the war and then later reenlisted for three years. The best estimates are that roughly 2.1 million white men served in the Union military, including those who only served in short-term emergency regiments. The 1860 census of the United States described "military age" as between ages eighteen and forty-five. Just over 5 million northern white men fell in that age range at some point between 1861 and 1865. If we make some adjustments for southern white men who enlisted in the Union army and immigrants who arrived after 1860 and volunteered, it is probably fair to say that roughly 40 percent of white men who lived in the loyal states in 1860 and were between eighteen and forty-five at some point during the war served in uniform.[24] This is certainly a huge percentage, even though the Confederacy mobilized military-aged white men at roughly twice that rate.[25]

The observation that roughly two in five military-aged men in the North volunteered (or were drafted and held to service) supports two complementary points at the heart of this study. First, military-aged men who supported the Union war effort surely must have felt pressure to enlist when so many northern citizens were volunteering. But unlike southern white men in much of the Confederacy, men in the northern states would not necessarily be social outliers if they chose not to enlist. This was particularly true for older northerners. The median age of enlistment in the Union army was about 23.5; two-fifths of all new recruits were twenty-one or younger.[26] The economic historian Robert Fogel concluded that 55 percent of all Union volunteers were born in the eight years between 1837 and 1845. In fact, over 55 percent of young men in each cohort born between 1840 and 1845 (between ages sixteen and twenty-one in 1861) were accepted for military service; four out of five men born in 1843 were examined and approved for service. By contrast, only a third of men who were between twenty-five and twenty-nine in 1861 were accepted for service, and roughly one in five men who were in their thirties when the war began.[27]

What does this flurry of numbers mean? The short answer is that an extremely large number of northern men chose to serve in the Union army, but the majority of these volunteers were young men in the early stages of life. Popular histories and scholarly studies often portray a world where legions of married men marched off to war, leaving behind wives and children. These family breakups certainly happened in thousands of northern homes, but in 1860 the mean age of marriage for men was about twenty-five, or two years older than the median age of enlistment.[28] It is probable that no more than a third of Civil War volunteers were married at the time of enlistment, and many of those had not yet started families. Here again we have a huge number: that estimate would still leave us with roughly seven hundred thousand married Union volunteers. But the fact remains that when married men contemplated enlisting, they did so in a world where the majority of their married peers were staying home.

This raises a complex question: if voluntarily donning a uniform was an acknowledged sign of patriotism, how did northern society assess those able-bodied men who chose to remain in civilian garb? What were the cultural yardsticks used to assess the citizenship and manhood of male civilians who had not enlisted? And, perhaps more important, how did individual men who felt committed to the Union war effort weigh their own decisions? These discussions of individual decisions occurred against the backdrop of an expanding middle class, and a huge new army of citizen-soldiers who embodied this new world. As the Civil War historian Russell Weigley explained, this was the "first occasion in the modern history of Western civilization when not only officers drawn largely from the upper social classes and rank-and-file soldiers crimped from the lowest rungs

Introduction

of the socioeconomic ladder went to war, but also in many thousands the sons of the middle classes." The men in the ranks of this new Union army were remarkably representative of the folks back home, including scores of men from the emerging middle class. They and their loved ones contemplated events at home and news from the battlefield from a perspective shaped by intertwined notions about family, class, and nation.[29]

■ We began this discussion with Stillé's pamphlet, which is a good example of the war's explicitly didactic publications. By the mid-nineteenth century, the privately printed publication had a long history. Independent authors had debated public affairs in pamphlets in the years leading up to the American Revolution, and again as the nation debated the terms of the US Constitution.[30] During the Civil War, several groups in the northern states formed to print and distribute pamphlets. The three central players in this ongoing war of printed words were the Democratic Society for the Diffusion of Political Knowledge, founded in New York City in February 1863; the Unionist Loyal Publication Society, also established in New York; and the Board of Publications, operating out of Philadelphia's Union League. The somewhat smaller New England Loyal Publication Society soon joined the fray. The Loyal Publication Society (LPS) distributed an estimated 900,000 copies of 90 different publications, including Stillé's pamphlet; Philadelphia's Union League's Board of Publication published over 4 million copies of 104 different titles.[31]

The elite members of the North's urban Union leagues devoted much of their money and energy to encouraging an enhanced sense of nationalism, stressing that citizens owed their country loyalty in times of war. Boston's Edward Everett Hale made the case in his anonymously published story "The Man without a Country," which introduced the tragic Philip Nolan. According to Hale, in his youth Nolan had gotten mixed up in Aaron Burr's treasonous conspiracy, and when brought before the court Nolan declared, "Damn the United States! I wish I may never hear of the United States again!" The furious—and quite clever—judge sentenced Nolan to a lifetime aboard navy vessels, with orders that he never again set foot on land or ever hear a word about his native country. Fifty years later, Nolan is visited at his deathbed, in a cabin surrounded by symbols of the nation he had abandoned and the identity he had lost in the process. Hale originally published his tale in the *Atlantic Monthly*, and it was quickly reprinted and sold a half million copies during the war.[32] This emphasis on unquestioning loyalty to the nation remained a central theme in political pamphlets and published sermons. The celebrated Unitarian minister Henry W. Bellows made this the centerpiece to his 1863 sermon *Unconditional Loyalty*, which quickly became another best-selling LPS pamphlet.[33]

The explicitly partisan pamphlets produced by the LPS and the Society for the Diffusion of Political Knowledge and other smaller groups fall outside the central concerns of this study. Their authors either concentrated on shaping the political behavior of readers or weighed in on more abstract constitutional or legal issues. Stillé and a handful of the other pamphleteers interest me because they were not focused on how the reader should vote or what he or she should believe but, rather, on how the pro-Union reader should *behave*. Stillé's main point was that just wars sometimes take time and require patience and endurance on the home front. With the war dragging into its third year, the author was telling his audience to "hang in there" despite frustrating news from the front and a general sense that the future seemed cloaked in uncertainty. He was not speaking to those northerners who opposed the war effort.

Political pamphlets were only the top layer of a large stack of wartime publications offering messages on how citizens should—and should not—respond to the war. Northern ministers did not abandon their pedagogical role once the shooting started. Religious leaders delivered hundreds of sermons aimed at explaining the nature of Christian duty in wartime, many of which were reprinted in local newspapers or as privately distributed pamphlets. Newspaper editors across the political spectrum weighed in on government policies and individual responsibilities. These materials combined to offer another layer of this vast public conversation.[34]

These overt efforts to shape public opinion and behavior were part of a much broader cultural story. Much as scholars have found cultural messages about expected gender and class roles embedded in diverse antebellum publications, the wartime debate about citizenship and civic obligation found its way into all sorts of publications.[35] Novelists set plots in home front communities, constructing characters facing the same sort of challenges that vexed their readers. The North's popular journals, aimed at various levels of readership, began publishing short stories featuring families struggling with enlistment, young women volunteering as nurses, and soldiers home on furlough. Amateur poets flooded the national press with verse about wartime dramas and dilemmas. Entrepreneurial publishers found a ready market for new song sheets and songbooks about Civil War themes. Meanwhile, recruiters produced and distributed a new sort of patriotic art: the recruiting poster.

Quite a few of these novels, short stories, and poems used the war as a setting for popular romanticized tales, following well-established literary patterns and often including unmistakable prescriptive messages. In addition to these fairly serious, often rather maudlin, tales of love and loss, northern readers were entertained by all sorts of humor and satire.[36] Most newspapers and journals published short humorous "squibs" either as part of a regular column or as useful filler to finish columns of print. During the war, these little jokes and short news items routinely mocked the war's cowards and fools. The new illustrated weekly newspapers and comic journals ran hundreds of cartoons depicting characters that soon became familiar parts of the wartime popular culture. Satirical drawings also circulated in popular "valentines," commonly featuring a caricature accompanied by a bit of doggerel verse. Other humorists turned their talents to song, writing parodies of popular lyrics to poke fun at the war's more ridiculous characters. The war years also saw the invention of the patriotic envelope. These envelopes, which included a patriotic or humorous drawing in the upper corner, quickly became collectors' items in the North.[37]

The war years produced a cohort of extremely popular humorists, who collectively created a distinct American genre, populated by wonderfully ridiculous satirical characters like Artemus Ward (created by Charles Farrar Browne), Petroleum Nasby (David Locke), Orpheus C. Kerr (Robert Henry Newell), and the Disbanded Volunteer (Joseph Barber). These characters, all written in heavy phonetic prose, portrayed satirical extremes. They were commonly horrible or silly in their behavior, but the reader was invited to find humor in their absurdity. On occasion, the character served as an innocent—and completely unaware—observer, describing the appalling behavior of others without recognizing what the reader sees clearly.[38] Much of the war's comic energies focused on partisan politics, mocking the enemy, or poking fun at either military officers or the lowly enlisted man. But the clever satirists also turned to the foibles around them on the home front.[39] The best of this genre was widely read, and often shared. In one famous example Abraham Lincoln, a fine humorist in his own right, enjoyed entertaining his cabinet and personal secretaries with readings from the latest from Orpheus Kerr or Artemus Ward.[40]

The war also spawned a wealth of magazines and novels aimed at young northern readers. In many senses the story of these publications meshes with the larger narrative. Before the Civil War this was already a vibrant literature, with an enthusiastic youthful audience. With the outbreak of war, the children's magazines continued to prosper, and new publications appeared. Some editors shifted their content to become more patriotic and even political, training young readers in their roles as wartime citizens. And much like the writers of romantic fiction aimed at adult readers, the children's authors used the war as a backdrop to revisit familiar moral and ethical themes in new surroundings. Youthful readers learned to support the Union war effort, while also being reminded that the national crisis made good manners and filial devotion that much more important.[41]

■ These printed materials—both words and images—constitute the core evidence in this book. Although individual authors and publications differed in their perspective and intended audience, clear patterns emerge. The wartime messages built on patterns that had been established in the antebellum decades, but the war presented unique challenges for ordinary citizens, producing a distinctive war culture. Throughout the first half of the nineteenth century, Americans—and particularly middle-class white northerners—had turned to advice manuals, etiquette books, published sermons, and popular literature for advice on how to respond to unfamiliar personal problems. Young women and men learned lessons about how to behave toward each other in public. Aspiring members of the middle class read pointers on how to entertain guests. Even parents purchased advice manuals on how to parent and educate children for a changing world.[42] Newcomers to a city found advice about which strangers should be trusted. Agricultural journals reported on new innovations to improve crop output. The range of issues addressed by these new publications was vast, but they shared the conviction that expertise was there for the reading and that wise consumers should and would seek such counsel.

The war literature shared much in common with these antebellum publications, but the questions differed in a fundamental way. During the Civil War the North's readers struggled with their individual roles within a broader national context. The questions posed by the war were not about strategies for individual success, but about how the individual should understand his or her role as part of a national cause. In this sense their shared commitment to the Union framed the conversation about individual behavior. Individually and collectively, northerners struggled with the meaning of duty in the midst of a bloody civil war, even while they remained deeply conscious of their continuing duties to family.[43]

This focus on how individuals should behave as parts of a nation at war also broadened the published advice beyond concerns about individual interactions. The antebellum urban guides that warned of the unscrupulous "confidence man," for instance, intended to warn individual readers of the traps that such characters might set for the unsuspecting farm boy. The wartime discourse pointed out similarly shady characters, but now the danger was to the national cause—the Union—rather than the individual reader's well-being. The concern shifted from "Who should I distrust?" to "Who should *we* distrust?" These tales of wartime villains illustrated the implications when civilians failed to properly understand their wartime duties. Popular essays, pamphlets, and cartoons directed loyal citizens to be vigilant in uncovering those frauds who threatened the national cause.

Here the cultural conversation about wartime behavior also drew on broader understandings about the nature of leadership and the proper character of public men. As many scholars have demonstrated, Americans in the first decades of the nineteenth century embraced an evolving set of values that collectively defined a distinct "republican ideology." The core values—which commonly transcended class and party—celebrated public virtue and honesty, while insisting on constant vigilance against corruption and excessive power in the hands of leaders. At its heart, those who embraced these republican values worried about threats to the public as much as they celebrated the possibilities for the future. By the eve of the Civil War these inherited values had to a great extent given way to broader notions of liberalism, with its greater emphasis on the strength of democracy, the power of the market, and possibilities of future progress. But popular suspicions about dishonesty, duplicity, and outright corruption remained a part of the nation's cultural consciousness.[44]

The multiple messages emerging from hundreds of stories, poems, cartoons, pamphlets, and other wartime sources fall into a handful of readily identifiable topics, which give this book its structure. The three chapters in part 1, "Fools, Hypocrites, and Scoundrels," are dominated by the war's satirists, humorists, and cartoonists. Arranged in a loose chronological order, these initial chapters consider how northern popular culture responded to the war by constructing a handful of exaggerated stereotypes, each describing the sort of character civilians could safely mock and revile.

Chapter 1 begins with a brief consideration of communities bracing for war. The patriotic "War Meetings" that sprang up in the days and weeks after the firing on Fort Sumter were ripe for gentle satire, although in the initial patriotic fervor few observers had the perspective—or inclination—to mock their fellow citizens. Once the war had begun in earnest, regiments had been mustered in and headed for the front, and civilians at home had started to mobilize, northerners on the home front began to take stock. Cartoonists and satirists took aim at society's most empty-headed, who blithely glided through their lives without grasping the war's significance. Young male dandies, who flitted from party to party with no thought of the war, and self-centered young women, who thought only of soirees and beaus, made easy targets. These men and women were viewed as a source of amusement, and at least in the war's first year they usually earned gentle treatment. Readers who recognized the war's magnitude could rest easy in the knowledge that they were not so oblivious as these fools and swells.

Before long, northerners began pointing their fingers at the hypocrites and frauds who had found ways of taking advantage of the Civil War for personal gain. Chapter 2 considers the rising public outrage at the North's "shoulder straps," those men who lounged around bars and fashionable parties proudly sporting officers' uniforms but never actually going into the field. The anger directed at these men was not that they were too cowardly to actually fight, but that they were dishonestly basking in the glory earned by those men who were bravely serving in uniform. Chapter 3 turns to a more complicated form of wartime misbehavior: the "shoddy aristocracy." Fraudulent war profiteers were initially scorned because they were literally selling shoddy merchandise to the military. But with the passage of time the critique shifted to those war profiteers who did not seem to deserve their riches.

Both the shoulder straps and the shoddy aristocracy emerged as subjects of satire and serious public commentary by 1862, as citizens on the home front began to recognize that certain people in the North were capable of behaving badly even while others suffered. The specific transgressions differed, but both chapter 2 and chapter 3 deal with the construction of stereotypes attacking men and women who had exploited the national emergency for their own ends. Dishonesty and duplicity, not inaction or selfishness, earned disapprobation.

Taken together, the chapters in part 1 map out a set of popular types that defined the actions marking some northerners as poor citizens. To a great degree these were exaggerated portraits of real characters. These were the wartime versions of the prewar "confidence men," whom wise readers knew not to trust. But whereas the antebellum confidence man, with his duplicity and charm, threatened the unwary individual, these wartime rogues threatened the national cause. Their personal decisions responded to the profit-maximizing goals of the free market, which may have been fine in the antebellum years, but they failed the test of patriotic duty and thus illustrated the dangers of unchallenged selfishness, or even self-interest, in wartime.

The satirical types in part 1 also imposed a sort of cultural continuity on a world in flux. Portraits of silly women who failed to understand the war reinforced familiar gender stereotypes about women's political acumen even while implicitly rewarding those who were not so oblivious. The recurring portrayal of "Shoddy" families as Irish bumpkins tripping over their newfound wealth bespoke a society that would not tolerate ethnic and class transgressions, even in wartime.

These extreme caricatures illustrated how patriotic civilians should not behave, but in so doing they sometimes appeared to suggest that ordinary people's actions that were not quite so bad were perhaps acceptable. War contractors who profited from the Union's vast mobilization could sleep easy if they had avoided the excesses of the Shoddy Aristocracy. Middle-class women who enjoyed an evening on the town could do so free of guilt so long as they also kept abreast of war news. Civilian men who lounged around bars or saloons talking about the war had no cause for shame if they were not impersonating officers. By constructing a shared understanding of the wrongdoers—real or imagined—northern authors and readers came to a mutual understanding that the vast majority of prowar northerners were probably living acceptable lives, generally supportive of the Union war effort. The important marker defining the bad citizen was hypocrisy or raw dishonesty.

Part 2 shifts the focus from these types whose actions illustrated *unacceptable* wartime behavior, to the more challenging decisions with which ordinary civilians wrestled as the war progressed. As we move into part 2 we turn from the wartime version of the antebellum visitor's guides, warning of dangerous characters, to a wartime etiquette manual, offering guidance on how to behave in unfamiliar circumstances. But now that advice covered not merely how to "succeed" in a changing world, but how to be a good citizen in a nation at war.

Chapters 4 and 5 examine the ongoing debate about duty in wartime and the obligations of individual men and women in support of that war effort. Chapter 4, "Our Duty," considers the many published voices that sought to offer the nation's civilians specific guidance on the nature of duty in wartime. The discussion did not hinge on matters of cowardice and bravery; rather, it turned on honesty and respect for society's rules. A man who chose not to serve faced little public sanction so long as he weighed his decisions honestly and his behavior did not reveal core hypocrisy. Chapter 5 moves the narrative into 1863, while emphasizing the rising public hostility toward the war's unapologetic cowards. At midwar the terms of discussion shifted when the federal government turned to conscription. Now the question was not simply "What should a good citizen do in wartime?" It became "How must a good citizen respond to conscription?" The federal draft, surely serious business from any perspective, spawned waves of humorous commentary in editorials, cartoons, and small newspaper squibs. In many senses the cartoons portraying draft evaders recalled the satirical tones of the images of shoddy merchants or silly swells, but these new images contained a more threatening message: if drafted men acted like cowards and hypocrites, they risked public scorn.

The discussions of duty and cowardice in chapters 4 and 5 are often deeply interwoven with gendered notions of manhood, although ideas about masculinity only rarely provided clear guidance. Young men might enlist in response to the direct appeals to their masculinity, and true cowards risked emasculating cultural sanctions. But between the extremes individual decisions remained murky, largely because the obligations of manhood suggested contradictory messages. In the eyes of some, domestic obligations trumped the lure of martial finery, and familiar gender codes provided unclear answers when men were drawn to the excitement of battle but were also perpetually reminded of duties closer to home.[45]

In chapter 6 we turn to a more extended analysis of the prescribed roles of wartime women. Quite a bit of romantic fiction and poetry, particularly in the national women's magazines, included tales of women as the mothers, wives, and sweethearts of soldiers or potential enlistees. Other stories featured women as nurses or volunteers, or as individuals who declined to engage in war work. The prescriptive messages in these works of popular fiction were joined by pamphlets, speeches, and editorials aimed at shaping the behavior of prowar northern women. A century earlier, notions of patriotism—linked as they were to broader ideas about political engagement—fell largely within a male domain. Women were presumed to experience patriotism largely as reflected through, and directed by, the men in their lives.

As we shall see, from the very early moments of the Civil War white northern women engaged in their own public conversations about how they should respond to the crisis, and both women and men wrote essays and tracts aimed directly at female audiences. Patriotic women were urged to be supportive when men wished to enlist, but beyond calls to maintain their public enthusiasm for the conflict, the cultural message remained quite flexible. Women at home could choose to devote their energies to the war effort, but there was little indication that they were duty-bound to sacrifice for the cause. They were, however, expected to give up their men freely and even eagerly. Here the female patriot wrestled with obligations rooted in her own individual relationship to the nation, as they conflicted sharply with her personal and familial obligations and commitments. Domesticity and nationalism clashed in fiction and prose, producing complicated choices.

The final chapter shifts the focus in multiple ways by considering the wartime debate about the Civil War within the African American community. If northern whites were essentially asking what a patriotic citizen owed to the nation in wartime, black northerners wondered how to respond when neither side fully recognized their citizenship or even their personhood. These were vibrant discussions within the free black community, but free black characters were largely invisible within novels and periodicals written for predominantly white audiences. Chapter 7 considers familiar questions from different perspectives, while mining somewhat different sources. Rather than playing out personal decisions in romantic fiction, the northern black community wrestled with wartime decisions in editorials, letters to newspapers, allegorical poems, and impassioned public oratory. The resulting discussion illuminates how African Americans responded to these wartime challenges, while also offering a different viewpoint on the discussions of the meaning of citizenship within the white community. Even if most of the North's free blacks agreed that they preferred a Union victory, there was far less consensus about whether this was truly their war. And whereas white northerners commonly wrestled with an individual's responsibility to the nation, black northerners were far more likely to frame that question in communal terms. Rather than asking, "What should I do?" they debated, "What should *we* do?" Still, although the questions were framed in collective terms, the decisions remained up to individual contemplation and choice.

This final chapter, then, discusses a distinctive debate within a community that made up a relatively small—and marginalized—portion of the North's population. But that separate black public conversation also places the more substantial discussion within the dominant white population in a new light. As we shall see, the emphasis on individual choice and obligation appears different when set against the vigorous black debate about collective responsibility and opportunity.

■ The reader will encounter hundreds of voices in the chapters to come. Nearly all of the authors and cartoonists will be unfamiliar. Some were well known in their time; others published the occasional novel or short story but had no larger reputation. In some cases, poems and stories were published anonymously, often submitted by loyal readers. My goal is to capture the essence of a larger national conversation, rather than to dissect the motivations of individual authors. In this sense, stories, poems, and novels appeared within a popular marketplace, where editors made decisions with subscribers in mind. Often those publication decisions were not about ideology—they were about audience. Several of the national journals seemed intent on including a geographic mix in their fiction; others published with a regional audience in mind. Some of the New York–based cartoonists concentrated on local targets; others sought universal themes. Several of the popular satirists came from the Midwest and created midwestern alter egos and communities, but they spoke to national readerships.

The wartime editors—of journals, newspapers, and publishing houses—were crucial players in this ongoing public conversation, selecting stories and images that fit editorial agendas and the interests of particular readerships. Even within a universe of generally prowar publications, their perspectives on many issues fell across a fairly wide political spectrum. But on the issues that are central to this study, the points of consensus are quite strong. The ardent Republican and the passionate War Democrat could find common ground in attacking the war profiteer, even if they had differing perspectives on the political forces that produced such scoundrels.

The cluster of new humor magazines that had emerged just before the war faced particular challenges when political tensions gave way to horrific violence. If the political satirist was generally comfortable expressing an oppositional voice, how must he proceed in times of war? New York's *Vanity Fair* faced such a test. Founded by conservative Democrats, who had little enthusiasm for Abraham Lincoln and even less interest in abolitionism or racial equality, the ostensibly nonpartisan humor magazine adopted a stance that supported the war effort while ridiculing Republican excesses. The result was a highly popular weekly with a notorious reputation for racism. Edited for a time by Charles Farrar Browne, who first published many of his popular Artemus Ward pieces there, *Vanity Fair* managed to maintain both its oppositional satirical voice and its prowar stance by unleashing a regular stream of cartoons and humorous essays skewering the war's hypocrites, scoundrels, and cowards. There the Union Democrat found common ground with the staunch Republican.[46] *Frank Leslie's Budget of Fun*, another humor magazine founded in 1859, initially adopted a similar—although more partisan—political stance, supporting the war effort while critiquing the administration. But whereas the antiabolitionist *Vanity Fair* folded in 1863, *Frank Leslie's Budget of Fun* shifted to a more pro-Lincoln stance and continued to thrive.[47]

One novelist stands out in this larger conversation, both as an author

Introduction

who will appear in several chapters and as a useful illustration of this political observation. New Jersey Democrat Henry Morford wrote and published three home front novels during the four years of the Civil War.[48] Morford was a clerk of the court, a dedicated member of Tammany Hall (New York's Democratic political machine), and an enthusiastic amateur author. He authored long poems in honor of Tammany Hall's annual meetings as well as a book of verse.[49] After the war he published a popular guide to European travel, various other novels and books of poetry, and at least one opera.[50] Morford's three novels are set almost exclusively in the northern states.

Each of Morford's long books included dozens of characters, a rich tapestry (or muddled mess) of subplots, and a wealth of political and romanticized messages illustrating many of the key themes that defined home front conversations during the war. Thus one novel tackles "shoddy" and the corruption surrounding war contracting, a second targets the fraudulent "shoulder straps" who paraded around northern cities, and the final book offers a subtle discussion of the real meaning of "cowardice" in wartime. The Democrat Morford—not unlike *Vanity Fair*—had little confidence in either the Lincoln administration or the Union military hierarchy, but he was unwavering in his support for the Union cause. The sinners he sought to unmask were defined not by their political partisanship or ideology, but by their character deficiencies.[51]

Largely forgotten today, Morford's books circulated widely in the North during the war and were the subject of dozens of reviews in contemporary journals. We do not know precisely how many copies he sold or how many people read each book, but there is substantial evidence that the novels were well known and frequently recognized for their broad-based appeal. *Shoulder Straps*—the first of the three home front novels—went through five editions, suggesting that the demand exceeded Philadelphia publisher T. B. Peterson's initial expectations.[52] When *Shoulder Straps* first appeared, one Ohio newspaper ran a lengthy excerpt and declared that "it is emphatically the novel of the year, and is creating a great sensation everywhere."[53] The *Philadelphia Press* praised the book as "the first attempt of any importance to produce a novel out of the war."[54] After the publication of *The Days of Shoddy* near the end of 1863, the effusive *Press* ran several separate reviews and multiple notices declaring that Morford had surpassed his fine first novel.[55] A year later the *Cleveland Morning Leader* marked the publication of *The Coward* with a long review, noting that Morford was "well known as the author of *Shoulder Straps* and *Days of Shoddy*" and that this new volume "is emphatically the novel of the year, and is creating a great sensation everywhere."[56] A half-column advertisement in Philadelphia's *Daily Evening Bulletin* called *The Coward*—the third novel—"the most charming book of the summer season."[57] Immediately after the war *Frank Leslie's Illustrated Newspaper* reviewed Morford's first postwar effort and reminded readers of "the large editions sold of 'Shoulder Straps,' 'The Days of Shoddy,' 'The Coward,' etc."[58]

Not all reviewers were equally impressed, but all seemed to acknowledge Morford's broad appeal. The reviewer for *Harper's New Monthly Magazine* complained that *Shoulder Straps* "pretends to be a story of the war, but . . . this is a false pretension." But following a detailed dissection of the book's confusing plot, *Harper's* concluded that "on the whole the book is entertaining, in spite of its many faults." Washington, DC's *Evening Star* found *The Coward* to be "a terrible hodgepodge of careless writing of the sensational sort," but the reviewer acknowledged that Morford's story-telling kept the reader's attention.[59] Editors and reviewers across the country seemed to agree that Morford's novels were popular, provocative, and sometimes a bit amateurish.[60]

This book argues that the thousands of diverse publications appearing in the North during the Civil War produced a set of coherent cultural messages that were absorbed by a large portion of northern society. That is not to say that American culture—even northern prowar culture—was homogeneous, or that the publications consulted here are a perfect reflection of that culture. After all, a disproportionate number of wartime books and journals were published in New York, Boston, or Philadelphia, and some of the urban journals had an unapologetically provincial approach to both humor and news.[61] Moreover, despite technological developments, even the cheaper newspapers and journals were not accessible to all potential readers, and their content reflects this fact. Nonetheless, there are various reasons to believe that the popular publications examined here reflect quite broad northern cultural patterns.

In his study of nineteenth-century American culture, Lawrence Levine argues that to a surprising extent antebellum Americans enjoyed a "shared culture" that spanned both geography and class. Levine found, for instance, that Americans across the country and from all walks of life enjoyed Shakespeare, even if traveling troupes might adjust their performances to meet different audiences. Midcentury Americans embraced the Italian opera with similar enthusiasm. When Jenny Lind—the famed "Swedish Nightingale"—toured the country in 1852, the singing sensation appealed to Americans from all walks of life. As Levine sees it, the great national divide between "highbrow" and "lowbrow" culture did not really emerge until late in the century.[62] The scores of traveling speakers who traversed the nation before and after the war illustrate the same point. Thanks to improvements in railroad travel, and the enthusiastic energies of various speaker bureaus, dozens of popular lecturers and entertainers found their way to towns across the country. And when they arrived in small towns in distant states they found enthusiastic audiences who already knew of their fame from newspapers and other publications.[63]

As we have seen, American print culture was in particular flux on the eve of the Civil War, and in many ways the impact of these recent changes also reduced the importance of distance. Although many books came from eastern publishing houses (or were imported from abroad), improved transportation and postal services and reduced printing costs had made inexpensive novels available across the nation.[64] The publishers of the major monthly journals and the new illustrated weekly newspapers aimed for national audiences to complement their local readerships. Frank Luther Mott, the great historian of American periodicals, argues that on the eve of the Civil War journals such as *Harper's*, *Putnam's*, and the *Atlantic Monthly* all targeted national readerships, as did the two leading women's magazines, *Peterson's Magazine* and *Godey's Lady's Book*.[65]

The Civil War drew the nation's newspapers and journals even more fully into a single public discourse. As jurist Oliver Wendell Holmes famously proclaimed, "We must have something to eat, and the papers to read. . . . Only *bread and the newspaper* we must have, whatever else we do without." Holmes was reflecting on the popular obsession with the latest war news. All across the nation, civilians had become desperate for reports from the front, even if that news was distorted or at best a partial truth. Holmes, always fascinated by the battlefield as a furnace that tests manhood, believed that "war not only teaches what man can be, but it teaches also what he must not be."[66] Holmes's essay, published in the *Atlantic Monthly* only months after the war had begun, captured the national fascination with war reporting that produced an abrupt leap in the demand for newspapers. But he understated how broad that obsession with the printed word would become, and the stakes at hand. Not content to report from the battlefield, northern periodicals wrestled with behavior at home. Throughout the North, newspapers and journals increasingly became part of a shared national discourse, much of which centered on what men *and* women could be, and what they "must not be."

As the patriotic conversation became national, wartime newspapers increasingly took to reprinting stories from periodicals in other cities. Humorous and outrageous anecdotes about the war's cowards and cheats cropped up all over the country. One story about Connecticut draftees who had reportedly chopped off their trigger fingers to avoid the draft appeared in newspapers in Connecticut, Ohio, Illinois, Wisconsin, Oregon, and California within a month. Multiple publications reprinted the same poems mocking war contractors.[67] The major new humorists quickly developed national reputations as newspapers and journals across the country reprinted their essays.

Consider the publication strategies of San Francisco's *Golden Era*. The weekly newspaper began publication in 1852; by the outbreak of the Civil War it already had the largest circulation in the Far West. Some of the paper's material had a distinctly western flavor, but the editors also borrowed liberally from newspapers published in eastern cities.[68] The *Golden Era* also made regular use of humorous articles from New York publications, offered extended commentary on the latest issues of *Atlantic Monthly* and other eastern journals, and routinely reprinted satirical material from Mark Twain, Artemus Ward, and Orpheus Kerr. This borrowing was not a one-way exchange. In one 1862 issue the editors observed wryly that the latest packet of Philadelphia newspapers included no fewer than eight stories "stolen" from the *Golden Era*.[69] Northerners from coast to coast who only read local newspapers were regularly reading material that originated in other publications across the country.

The distribution of New York's *Vanity Fair* is a good illustration of this phenomenon. Although the weekly humor magazine only began publication in 1859, by 1861 newspaper editors across the country had taken to reprinting poems, humorous essays, and clever one-liners from the irreverent weekly. The digital collection "Nineteenth Century U.S. Newspapers" (a Gale Publication) offers scans from an eclectic assortment of wartime newspapers from across the nation. The collection includes roughly thirty northern newspapers published during the life of *Vanity Fair* with ten or more scanned issues; twenty-four of those newspapers reprint stories from the humor magazine or cite it in some similar fashion. Where the newspaper runs in the collection are especially complete, *Vanity Fair* crops up dozens of times.[70]

Readers who enjoyed the latest poem or joke from a distant publication had ample opportunity to purchase the full issue. In Cleveland, local book dealers Hawk and Brothers ran a regular ad in the *Daily Cleveland Herald* announcing the latest arrivals from the eastern press. These notices almost always mentioned *Vanity Fair*, the new home of popular local writer Artemus Ward, as well as other New York humor magazines, including *Phunny Phellow* and *Frank Leslie's Budget of Fun*. Washington,

DC's *Daily National Intelligencer* routinely published a long ad from a local bookseller that listed nearly every weekly and monthly journal cited in this book, and quite a few more. Newspaper and journal editors published regular features where they offered capsule commentaries on the latest new publications to arrive in the city. Certainly the national periodicals did not find their way into every home across the land, but interested readers in distant towns could acquire copies of even the more specialized publications.

Even a casual glance at the personal writings of ordinary civilians suggests that Americans across the nation were aware of fairly distant publications and regularly shared and discussed the latest periodicals.[71] Writing from near Chambersburg, Pennsylvania, diarist Rachel Cormany reported that although she read the *Philadelphia Inquirer* for regular news, "my Harpers Weekly keeps me posted on general war news."[72] Mary Vermillion lived in both Indiana and Iowa during the war, while her husband—William—was off fighting for the Union. Mary was an energetic reader, and her letters often mention how she was reading several newspapers, including the *New York Tribune*. On one occasion she received four novels from Chicago, and on several other occasions she referred to stories in the Chicago newspapers. In late November 1863, after Mary had returned to Iowa, a Mrs. Paschal visited her home with a social invitation. As Mary explained it to Will: "She is making a club for Peterson's Magazine, and she came to get me to subscribe. I didn't do it. I told her I didn't care much for ladies magazines while the war lasts, and then there are others that I would much rather have than Peterson's. I hope she will get her club though, for she is a very good, amiable woman. Everyone who gets a club for a good magazine or newspaper is a good public benefactor." Even though Vermillion was no particular fan of *Peterson's Magazine*, the Philadelphia-based literary magazine, her Iowa neighbors were apparently enthusiastic readers and anxious to discuss each new issue.[73] Frances Peter's diary records the tumultuous life of a Unionist in Lexington, Kentucky, as she endured both Rebel occupation and Union triumph. Always desperate for news, Peter's diary mentioned reading at least a dozen different newspapers from Kentucky and Ohio, which in turn reprinted news from dozens of other papers.[74]

Much of this shared national wartime culture reflected the impact of market forces on publishing decisions. As Americans became absorbed by war news, wise local editors borrowed material from distant publications to appeal to their own readers, often without attribution.[75] Once southern markets closed or became less accessible, some savvy publishers adopted a more explicit pro-Union voice. On occasion these forces of cultural homogeneity were more intentional. In October 1862, California Republican Thomas Starr King wrote to James T. Fields, the editor of the *Atlantic Monthly* and the coproprietor of an influential New York publishing house, describing his ongoing project to bring northeastern culture to his adopted home. "The State must be Northernized thoroughly by Schools, Atlantic Monthlies, lectures, N.E. preachers, Library Assoc[iations]— in short Ticknor & Fields-ism of all kinds," King effused. King, a transplanted New Englander, made sure that a steady stream of authors, artists, and lecturers crossed the continent to reach California audiences.[76]

The letters home from Union soldiers tell a similar story. Men in the field had irregular access to a host of newspapers, both sent from home and picked up along the way, and they often discussed the news with their loved ones. New Jersey general Robert McAllister regularly wrote home to his wife, Ellen, about the latest news from an assortment of New York and New Jersey newspapers. Writing from Petersburg in July 1864 he urged Ellen to read an essay on "shoddy" in the latest issue of *Harper's Magazine*, adding, "You ought by all means to take one of these monthlys. If not Harper's, then take the Atlantic Monthly."[77] In his letters home, Vermont private Wilbur Fisk sometimes mentioned New England newspapers, but he also occasionally commented on papers from New York and Philadelphia.[78] Soldiers on the march, even more so than civilians, received their news from a wide array of print sources.[79]

If these sources indeed capture a conversation that spanned the entire North, did it also encompass all northerners? Most importantly, this book focuses on materials written by and to northerners who were essentially in favor of the war, even if they had doubts about Abraham Lincoln and some of his policies. Insofar as the collective conclusions took aim at the North's worst hypocrites and frauds, they did so from the perspective of those who wished for Union victory.

The publications described here involved both men and women, although not always in equal numbers or in the same conversation. Some short stories, novels, and pamphlets were written by women and aimed at female readers; other material spoke specifically to the particular challenges facing military-aged men. It is not always possible to know how, and to what extent, specific texts were read by both men and women. *Peterson's Magazine* and *Godey's Ladies' Book*, for instance, were surely aimed at a female audience, but one can wonder whether a short story about men and women debating the merits of enlistment might have been read aloud or discussed at dinnertime.

It is less clear how far these discussions in print reached poorer working-class readers and recent immigrants. Although literacy rates were high, and improvements in technology had made newspapers and some books inexpensive, it is not always apparent whether members of the working class were reading the texts discussed here, or even wrestling with the same issues. The evidence is mixed. Taken as a group, the home front stories and satires portray an economically diverse world. Many stories describe communities with characters coming from all levels of economic life. The main figures in the sentimental wartime fiction are rarely of the wealthy elites, living in mansions with squadrons of servants. But few of the home front stories take members of the true working classes as their main subjects, and they only occasionally feature characters wrestling with economic struggles.[80] The very wealthy and the very poor appear more frequently in the wartime cartoons, but in most cases they are the subject of satire, not the intended audience. As we shall see, Irish immigrants were periodically the targets of indignant commentary in response to claims of improper war profiteering. But wartime literature rarely spoke directly to recent immigrants.[81] This was largely a cultural conversation that emerged from, and spoke to, the North's vast middle class.[82]

Although the imagined world constructed by these home front authors reflected substantial geographic and economic diversity, it was a world populated almost exclusively by white characters. African Americans figure in cartoons and political commentary, but usually these are slaves or "contrabands" from the Confederate states, not free blacks living in the North. Very few stories and novels set in the northern states include African American characters, and there is no indication that these authors were attempting to capture the particular issues facing free blacks in the North. The literature aimed at white readers had little to say to or about black northerners.[83] On the other hand, a substantial network of African American newspapers, and abolitionist newspapers with both black and white readerships, spoke directly to the distinctive debates within the African American community. These sources provide the foundation for chapter 7.

■ On July 4, 1861, President Abraham Lincoln delivered a message to Congress in special session. "This is essentially a Peoples' contest," he explained. He went on to add that "this is the patriotic instinct of the plain people. They understand, without an argument, that destroying the government, which was made by Washington, means no good to them."[84] Although directed by that federal government, the Civil War was a war fought by citizen-soldiers, supported by the voluntary energies of civilians on the home front. Despite four years of bloody conflict and intense public dissent, the Union staged local, state, and federal elections as scheduled, in an impressive testimony to the power of democracy. And despite the significant wartime expansion of executive powers and the growth of large centralized institutions dedicated to prosecuting the war, the success of the Union war effort depended on the voluntary decisions of individual men and women. In stark contrast with modern conflicts, those individual decisions were made with almost no propaganda interventions by the federal government.[85] These individual decisions were not made in a vacuum, nor were they deeply informed by past experience. They were decisions made by people who wished to do their duty but who were often unsure about precisely what that meant. Much of the time, patriotic men and women found themselves weighing duty to nation against duty to family. Sometimes they simply contemplated their own personal limitations and wondered how they should proceed.

This book is an exploration of the vast cultural conversation that informed tens of thousands of individual wartime decisions. These decisions, in turn, became the basis for the Union's ultimate victory in the People's Contest.

PART ONE

On Fools,

Hypocrites,

and

Scoundrels

Striped Pants and Empty Heads

The Fools, Swells, and Jesters of the Civil War

WAR MEETINGS

In the first months of the Civil War, patriotic war meetings were a staple in both the Union and the Confederacy. In the days after the fall of Fort Sumter, communities across the North held remarkably similar enthusiastic meetings. Local political leaders and newspaper editors would denounce the southern attack on federal property and call on young men to step forward and avenge the assault on the nation. Uniformed veterans or members of the militia would second the martial call. Often clergymen joined these leaders on the platform, affirming that the conflict was indeed a just war. Local women attended these early gatherings, generally playing nonspeaking roles in the public dramas, and then they immediately set to work sewing battle flags for the local troops.

An observer who stumbled upon any of these gatherings would have come away with a very clear sense of what the nation's patriotic citizens should do, at least in those first days of the war. Only a few months before, many northern voices had called for caution and compromise, but once the shooting started the weight of public opinion tilted dramatically toward unreflective military fervor. In fact, the war enthusiasm in those heady first days after Fort Sumter was so great that available regiments filled in many communities before all the eager young men could get into uniform.[1]

As the Union first mobilized for war, northern newspapers and journals muted any impulse toward humor in the face of war fervor. But before long, the silly and overblown targets proved too delicious for some satirists, while a few other pundits saw a bigger—and less appealing—picture. In May, the New York–based humor journal *Vanity Fair* ran a short piece titled "The Flag Mania," in which an "Enthusiastic Patriot" accosts a man on Broadway, demanding to know if the stranger had "the Star Spangled

Banner on [his] person." When the man admits that he does not happen to be carrying a flag with him, the Enthusiastic Patriot stabs the unfortunate man and *"walks quietly away,"* leaving it to the local police to remove the corpse.[2] *Vanity Fair* played this little story for humor, but it was a black humor with more than a little bite. In the first days after the outbreak of war, overzealous patriots in many cities indeed threatened citizens who failed to show the flag.[3] Essayist Mary Abigail Dodge, writing as "Gail Hamilton," supported the war effort but saw little virtue in the war's early "Mob Patriotism," suggesting that to her the patriotic mobs of the North were indistinguishable from the proslavery mobs in southern communities. "If a man is a traitor at heart, is he any less a traitor because a motley crowd forces him to raise the Red, White and Blue?" she asked.[4] Threats of violence hardly constituted an effective prescription.

In "Hurrah for the War!" the Democratic-leaning *Vanity Fair* reported that "all over the North" men and women "have risen at last and gone at the business of battle in right earnest." But despite this enthusiasm, the editorial noted, "we do not as yet half know what War means." These fervent patriots were pleased to punish the South and perhaps to strike a blow against slavery, but they had no notion of what they were getting themselves into.[5] A few months after the war began, *Arthur's Magazine* commented on the "war fever" that had left young men so absorbed with the conflict that they found themselves unable to read or write or think about anything else. While other journalists embraced an excitement that seemed to belie the war's fundamental dangers, this editorial described a cohort of young men who awoke each day "from peaceful unconsciousness to a sense that there is something wrong . . . which, like some evil bird, seemed to have flown away, but which sits waiting for us on its perch by our pillow, in the gray of the morning."[6] But such notes of caution were rare in those early days.

Eventually, northern humorists began to recall these heady weeks in April 1861 through a new—more cynical—lens. In the one-act farce *Off to the War!*, playwright Benjamin Edward Woolf introduced the blustering Bostonian Mr. Doddlewobble, a patriot who was not attending war meetings but who was immersed in the feverish wartime press. As the scene opens, Mr. Doddlewobble sits in his drawing room, surrounded by newspapers. He is annoyed because the various reports contradict each other, leaving him unsure what to believe. When Mrs. Doddlewobble enters the room, her befuddled husband declares, "I don't believe that there's any army, any war, any navy, or anything but newspaper extras." She accuses him of being hostile to the military, to which he responds, "Haven't

I been a colonel in my time?" We learn that Mr. Doddlewobble had indeed served in the peacetime military, but as soon as the war began he abandoned his commission and became a civilian. He insists that this was not a decision born of cowardice, but a selfless act on his part to make room for other men who were more anxious to go to war. When Mrs. Doddlewobble asks him to think of the honor that he could have brought home had he served in the Union army, Mr. Doddlewobble replies: "Think of the honor of coming home full of holes!" In his ridiculous Mr. Doddlewobble, Benjamin Edward Woolf lampooned those northern men who pored over the latest newspapers, claiming to support the war effort while finding every excuse to stay home.[7]

Charles Farrar Browne, who wrote under the pseudonym Artemus Ward, rose to prominence as one of the war's leading satirists. Browne began his career as a journalist in Ohio, but shortly before Abraham Lincoln's election he moved to New York City, where he took a position with *Vanity Fair.* The Artemus Ward columns reappeared in newspapers across the nation and became so popular that in the spring of 1862 Browne published his first book of essays. *Artemus Ward, His Book,* sold forty thousand copies and was republished in expanded editions three times in the 1860s.[8]

In one of his earliest wartime essays, Ward described events in the fictional town of Baldinsville, Indiana. At first the locals in the isolated town knew nothing of the brewing conflict, but Ward explained that "the newspapers got along at last, chock full of war, and the patriotic fever fairly bust out in Baldinsville." Ward, a captain in Baldinsville's militia company, quickly noticed "a gineral desire on the part of young men who are into the crisis to wear eppylits." Thus he "detarmined to have my company composed excloosviely of offissers, everybody to rank as Brigadeer-Ginral." Ward, like Benjamin Edward Woolf, saw the early war press as complicit in producing an irrational war hysteria. And the men of Baldinsville, like Boston's Mr. Doddlewobble, equate officers' stripes with military valor.

Bedecked in his new uniform, Ward went to the weekly war meeting, where he was pleased to find "a choice collection of young ladies, who was standin near the church door a-seein the sojer boys come up," although the assembled women had a laugh at his expense when he tripped over his own sword. The next day, Ward's company of officers set about training for war, and he reported that "we've got all the tackticks at our tongs' ends, but what we particly excel in is restin muskits. We can rest muskits with anybody." With this short piece, the wry humorist got in a few gentle swipes at the men who were excited to play soldier (so long as they wore officer's stripes), as well as the women who were thrilled at the men in uniform. Here and elsewhere, Ward casts the women of Baldinsville in dual roles. On the one hand, they are the subject of satire for becoming swept up in the same early war silliness that absorbed their men. But on the other hand, the women of Baldinsville are the observers of events who—like Ward's readers—could laugh at the worst excesses. Yes, they showed up to watch the uniformed company of faux officers drill, but they also laughed when the bumbling Ward nearly fell over his sword. And whereas Ward's character seemed proud of how well his men could "rest muskits," we assume that the women shared a chuckle with the reader.[9]

In October 1862, with communities pushing to fill enlistment quotas in advance of the coming draft, Ward's "A War Meeting" described Baldinsville's response to the new military challenge. When the town gathered to address the crisis they elected Mr. Slinkers, the editor of the local newspaper, as their official "Cheerman." Mr. Slinkers promptly "got up and said the fact could no longer be disguised that we were involved in a war. 'Human gore,' said he, 'is flowin'. All able-bodied men should seize a musket and march to the tented field. I repeat it sir, to the tented field.'" When a member of the audience asked why Slinkers did not enlist himself, the editor explained that his position in the press made him too valuable at home. Slinkers was followed to the podium by Mr. Hinkins, a "Softmore" at the local college, who spoke enthusiastically about the cause before adding, "'I regret I can't mingle in this strife personally.'" Next came the minister, who claimed that he was willing to enlist, although no one considered it a good idea.

Finally, as the assembled men were about to vote on a series of resolutions supporting the war, Ward's bellicose wife burst into the room with a group of women "carryin' guns" and declared, "You men air makin' fools of yourselves. You air willin' to talk and urge others to go to the wars, but you don't go to the wars yourselves. . . . We want you able-bodied men to stop speechifying, which don't 'mount to the wiggle of a sick cat's tail, and to go fi'tin'; otherwise you can stay to home and take keer of the children, while we wimin will go to the wars!" With these threats hanging in the air, the men of Baldinsville stepped up and met their enlistment quota. Here again Ward seems to have cast the town's women—and especially Artemus's own wife—in dual roles. They are there to speak harsh truths to the male leadership, who have shown more bluster than bravery. For women to stand up and challenge men in a public meeting calls into question the masculinity of the men of Baldinsville. But at the same time, Ward satirizes this feminine public outburst. Mrs. Ward's spoken words seem silly on the printed page, even if her point is sound. And the satirical point really turns on the ridiculous notion of "wimin" who "will go to the wars!" The very idea makes the "War Meeting" a subject for ridicule.[10]

In these two short pieces Artemus Ward used the language and symbol of gender to make his larger points about home front foolishness. But his targets are the war's hypocrites: the silly soldier who revels in his officer's shoulder straps but has no intention of fighting, the warmongering editor who will bluster but not serve, the budding intellectual who celebrates war in the abstract, the sweetly naive minister who does not really understand what he is saying. Ward often directed his biting satire at those men whose actions contradicted their words. Hypocrisy, not simple cowardice, earned ridicule in these early days of the war.

Novelist Mary J. Holmes captured the atmosphere of those early war meetings in *Rose Mather: A Tale*. The tone of Holmes's text differed dramatically from that of Ward's short humorous pieces, but some of the same themes emerged. Set in the small, fictional New England town of Kockland, the novel—published shortly after the war—begins just as the nation is reeling from news of the firing on Fort Sumter, forcing it to "rise from its lethargic slumber and shake off the delusion with which it had so long been bound." Although many locals had sympathized with the South, the outbreak of hostilities brought all together in a common cause. In the first pages of the novel, the residents of Kockland gathered in a "dense and promiscuous crowd" at "the old brick church." The men found seats in the church center, while their "wives and mothers" huddled near the entrance, watching the proceedings with trepidation. Like the women of Baldinsville, they observe while the men act, for better and for worse.

As the men and boys step forward to volunteer, Holmes recounts the scene from the perspective of these women. Some adopt a brave, impassive stance. Others respond with near hysteria. One elderly woman watches a poor townswoman's cries and mutters that the woman's sons "nough-sight better be shot than hung." In the midst of this emotional scene, the beautiful and elegant Rose Mather—a recent arrival from Boston and wife of the town's richest man—enters the church and takes a seat. Rose Mather does not make a good first impression on her new neighbors or on the reader. When a friend reports that Rose's husband Will has enlisted, Rose is flabbergasted. "Such people as Will don't go to the war," she declares. "It s a very different class, such, for instance, as that one going up to sign. Upon my word, it's the boy who saws our wood!" Unbeknownst to Rose, the boy's widowed mother sits nearby quietly weeping. A few moments later Rose announces that no husband who truly loved his wife would leave her to join the army, pushing poor Annie—another central character whose loving husband had just enlisted—into new paroxysms of tears.[11]

In this opening scene, Holmes recalled the April 1861 war meetings as a time of almost universal masculine patriotism, but also a time when women of all ages recognized the dangers that lay ahead. The women of Kockland seem to come together in a shared crisis. But the shockingly oblivious Rose Mather illustrates the class distinctions that threatened to divide even the small New England town. As the book unfolds, Rose evolves in predictable ways, and the personal chasm created by class and circumstance is bridged in the war's various melodramas, but in those first few pages the reader is left with a terrible sense of the novel's wealthy heroine.

Holmes's war meeting is far different in tone from Ward's Baldinsville gathering. Kockland's men are anxious to serve, while Baldinsville's residents seem content to talk. Yet the scenes are similar in that the men in both villages are full of hope and patriotic fervor, and more than a little bluster. The women in both scenes are cast as observers. Unlike many political gatherings, when women would have been excluded as a matter of course, these "promiscuous crowds" welcome the presence of females as silent observers bearing witness to masculine bravery. In both Baldinsville and Kockland, the women observe with a clear-eyed sense of the true stakes at hand. When Ward's women break convention and speak harsh truths, they earn their own satirical ridicule. Holmes's female characters whisper and weep, but—in April 1861—remain as observers.

The war meetings immediately after the firing on Fort Sumter, and the patriotic gatherings across the North in the months to come, captured the overwhelming enthusiasm for the Union cause in the minds of northern citizens, when war weariness and Copperheadism had yet to take their toll. The satirists who portrayed these early assemblies found much to mock, particularly in the hypocrisy of flowery orators and puffed-up patriots who embraced the war but seemed to be a bit thin on promises of personal sacrifice. Or, like Artemus Ward, they ridiculed observers—both women and men—who were thrilled by the excitement without demonstrating any comprehension of the march of events. These themes would mark much of the critical commentary in the months to come. Prowar northerners had little tolerance for blustering hypocrites, and not much more patience for the ignorant fools and the helplessly self-absorbed.

When the war first began, civilians on both sides anticipated a short—and perhaps glorious—military conflict. Before long, northerners grew restive with the slow progress of the Union army in the field and reports of corruption at home. As we shall see in the next several chapters, various

On Fools, Hypocrites, and Scoundrels

unsavory characters emerged in the wartime literature to exploit opportunities, avoid duties, and display their gifts for hypocrisy and dishonesty when the times called for patriotic duty and moral purity. Authors of fiction, editorials, and satire attacked these rogues, marking their behavior as outside the bounds of proper wartime citizenship. But before the true scoundrels became a familiar part of northern print culture, other character types came in for more lighthearted ridicule.

These were the war's silly fools. They stumbled their way through the war, especially in that first year, without fully grasping the horrors that had beset their nation. Unlike the jester of English courts or Shakespearean comedies, these men and women—at least the adults—were not providing harsh truths under the guise of harmless idiocy. They were simply honest fools, happily unaware of their own ignorance. The fictional swells and fools of the war's first year provided everyday citizens with a reassuring message: the nation might be undergoing unprecedented tumult, but engaged readers—sitting at home surrounded by newspapers and journals—are playing their proper roles as part of an informed citizenry. You might be a noncombatant, the message seemed to read, but you are on solid patriotic ground because you are not an ignorant fool!

SWELLS

One of the favorite figures for cartoonists was the urban "swell." The young male swell of the late nineteenth century was a popular character on the burlesque stage as well as on the fashionable streets of New York City. As the literary scholar Michelle Durden explains, "The swell is recognisable from his highly fashionable and affected appearance. He is generally depicted wearing an evening jacket, kid gloves, walking stick, monocle, and top hat." On the stage, the swell exhibited a "'drawling talk,' [and] an 'affected walk' or 'mincing gait.'" Some swells were portrayed as hard-drinking rowdies, but Durden notes that the more foppish sort "avoids physical confrontations with others because he is afraid of spoiling his good looks." These burlesque characters represented caricatured versions of the true young dandies who populated urban clubs and elite colleges, adopting exaggerated modes of dress and speech. Durden argues that in their burlesque form, the swells were mocked in sexual terms, with double-entendres about their "gay" lives. In practice, the swells were fashion-conscious dandies who appeared effeminate to some observers, even if their sexuality was unclear.[12]

Only a few years old when the Civil War began, *Vanity Fair* stood atop the vibrant world of comic journals, known for "skewering folly wherever it was to be found."[13] To *Vanity Fair*'s editors and cartoonists, the city's young wartime swells made an irresistible nonpartisan target.[14] In a June 1861 cartoon two extremely well-dressed young men are relaxing in an office stacked with books and files. Bill is congratulating Charley for having promised to purchase uniforms for an entire company of volunteers. Charley, bedecked in a vest and jacket, a monocle on a long chain, and a pair of extraordinarily billowy pants with thin vertical stripes, deflects the compliment, noting that outfitting a military company "only takes as much as it does to make me three pairs of pants."[15] In the same issue, the humor magazine published "A Little Ballad," purported to be a submission for a competition for a new national hymn. Dedicated to "those young gentlemen who are about to leave for Europe," the poem mocked the sons of the North's elite classes who were heading across the Atlantic just as other young men were marching off to war. "Double quick is not so gay; / As flaning in Paris far away," the poem declares. The "Young Arthur" of the verse is teased gently at first, but the poem ends with a bite, declaring, "We really think he'd better stay, / 'Over in France and far away.'" The swell in this poem found that "no manly ardor fired his clay," thus he took the first opportunity to tour Europe rather than the battlefields of Virginia. The reader is left with little respect for the wealthy swell and with no particular objection to the swift departure of such a fundamentally useless fellow.[16]

A month later, *Vanity Fair*'s "Scene in a Fashionable Hotel" showed two young and well-dressed scions of wealthy families discussing current events and how the war might intrude on their lives. Charlie asks Fred if his "Governor [has] given his consent to your joining the army." Fred replies, "The old gentleman says I must stay at home, and protect the family in case of invasion." The viewer is left doubting that either fellow has any real interest in enlistment. Other swells actually seemed inclined to volunteer, but they showed no sense of the implications. In an October 1861 cartoon a man with a carefully manicured mustache, debonair hat, cane, and flashy checked vest approaches a recruiting station, where several tough-looking gentlemen are accepting applications. The recruiter seems skeptical at his appearance, but the swell responds: "Don't you want to recruit a fine, manly person, something in this style, for an officer; say a lieutenant-colonel, or colonel, or any little position of that kind?" This swell, like Ward's men of Baldinsville, is willing to enlist only with the promise of an officer's commission. And, like Ward's yokels, this urbane recruit's claim to "manliness" seems in question.[17]

SCENE IN A FASHIONABLE HOTEL.

1st Swell.—Ah! Fwed; has your Governor given his consent to your joining the Army?

2d Swell.—Well, no, Charlie; the old gentleman says I must stay at home, and protect the family in case of an invasion.

This cartoon, published only three months after the fall of Fort Sumter, shows two young "swells" discussing why they will not be enlisting. Note the lisping spelling of "Fwed." Although the war is in its very first months, both these young men are sporting what appears to be military-like kepis, but neither has any intention of ever serving in a real uniform. *Vanity Fair*, July 20, 1861, 36. Courtesy of HarpWeek.

In the widely reprinted "The Swell's Soliloquy on the War," a lisping young man declares, "I don't appwove this hawid waw" and whines, "Why don't the pawties compwaamise?" The speaker complains that "the vulgah crowd" are "spawting uniforms in cullaws so extremely loud," while the charming young ladies have been absorbed with silly war talk. The poor swell finally reaches his limit when he visits the home of "Miss Mawy Hertz," only to discover that the fashionable female patriot had been busily sewing "the weddest kind of flannel shirts!" Apparently the flannel was just too much: the swell springs for the door, asking once again, "Why don't the pawties compwamise?" In this poem we see the swell in all his ridiculous glory. He objects to the war as a noisy distraction and as an affront to his fashion sense. And all the while he demonstrates no understanding of—or interest in—the conflict's larger stakes. "The Swell's Soliloquy" has a particularly clear gendered aspect. The foppish fellow is completely effeminate in his dress and sensibilities, making it clear that his rejection of the war reflects his own lack of manhood.[18]

Although military uniforms might not have been deemed particularly stylish when worn by the nation's rank and file, in the first months of the war military wear found its way into high fashion and deft satire. One cartoon showed a well-dressed man, wearing a top hat, approaching his friend who is sporting a military-looking kepi. "Why Fwed!" he lisps, "You haven't joined the army have you?" "Fwed" explains that of course he has not really enlisted. "This kind of thing, you know, is all the go now," he explains. Whereas the North's "shoulder straps" wore officers' uniforms as a way of winning undeserved respect, Fred and his friends just saw the uniform as the latest fashion statement. In another cartoon, the portly "Hamilton Brown" takes the new fashion a step further, appearing on the streets with enormous striped pants and a shirt festooned with stars, thus producing his own "star spangled banner suit." The caption explains that the outfit allows him to "show that though he suffers no wounds" for his country's defense, he still can "wear stripes in her behalf." Another drawing portrayed a pear-shaped gentleman sporting a military kepi, a billowing jacket, and huge pants; he explains, "If you want a uniform that will show off your figure to advantage, what can be neater than this?" Each of these cartoons mocks the men who embraced the war as an opportunity to adopt a new fashion, while failing to recognize the somber circumstances that had produced the sporty uniforms.[19]

Sometimes the laugh was on the swell's failed pursuit of patriotic fashion. A cartoon in *Frank Leslie's Budget of Fun*—another quite new and irreverent magazine—portrayed Mr. August White, a fancily dressed gentleman from Fifth Avenue's upper crust, who took great pride in his flowing locks. Mr. White, to his horror, has had his head shorn by his barber, who explains that he has given him a military "Zouave" cut. A drawing in *Yankee Notions*, another popular new humor paper, played on a similar theme, as a young swell orders an outfit "suitable for" the wedding dinner he is to attend, only to discover that the tailor—who was perhaps making a point—has sent him a Zouave uniform. The soldier's mustache often proved compelling to the home-bound swell. In "Prepared to Dye for his Country," a young "light haired individual" visits his sweetheart and explains, "I consider it the duty of every man, in a crisis like this, to prepare himself to do military style of thing, you know." His plan, he declares, is to "have my moustache dyed to-morrow!" A cartoon in *Comic Monthly*

WHY FWED! YOU HAVEN'T JOINED THE ARMY HAVE YOU?

Fwed.—AW! NO, NOT EXACTLY—THIS KIND OF THING, YOU KNOW, IS ALL THE GO NOW.

"Fwed," the mustache-twirling swell, sports a military kepi, prompting his well-dressed friend to ask whether he has enlisted. But he has only adopted fashionable faux military garb. At this early stage in the war, the cartoonist gives no indication that the young woman in the drawing is disturbed by the conversation, but the sign in the background declaring "Volunteers Wanted" reminds the reader of the real war that is under way. *Vanity Fair*, October 26, 1861, 198. Courtesy of HarpWeek.

showed poor Jack at a party, sporting a new mustache in a "war like fashion," only to find that the ladies still declined to give him the time of day.[20]

Whereas many of the early war commentaries portrayed the swells as so naive that they seemed almost innocent of any wrongdoing, some—even in the war's early months—were tougher on the self-absorbed civilians. One cartoon in *Yankee Notions* showed "Jones" asking "Nibbs" why he had not enlisted. Nibbs explained that he was going to enlist, but it

MR. AUGUSTUS WHITE (of Fifth avenue, who prides himself upon his glossy and flowing locks)—" *Told you to cut it fashionable ! Certainly ; but you shaved me ! What style do you call this ?*"
BARBER—" *Zouave, sir ; all the go now with the firemen !*"

The wealthy Mr. Augustus White went to his barber for a "fashionable" new haircut. His barber, revealing a taste for irony, has cut his hair like one of the local firemen who has enlisted in the Zouaves. New York's Zouaves were celebrated Union soldiers, often drawn from volunteer fire departments and known for their colorful uniforms. Mr. White found himself wearing a fashion he had no interest in adopting. *Frank Leslie's Budget of Fun* (October 1861): 5. Courtesy of HarpWeek.

dawned on him that he might get shot in the face and his "looks would be spoiled forever." Besides, he added, "the women folks wouldn't listen to the proposition anyhow!" Thus the satirist portrays Nibbs as particularly afraid of losing his looks rather than his life. Moreover, the suggestion is that adoring women are really responsible for keeping him from uniform. The angry poem "The Sweet Little Man" attacked the North's swells with no hint of jest. Speaking directly to those men "with the terrible warlike moustaches" who keep company with lovely ladies while criticizing the men who ran at Bull Run, the poem mocks the "Stay at Home Rangers." The title and many verses take direct aim at the manhood of the "Sweet Little Man" who would let women, armed with broomsticks, protect him from harm.[21]

A November 1862 cartoon called "An Appetizer" adopted a similarly angry tone. The drawing shows two gentlemen sitting down for a leisurely dinner at a fine restaurant. A uniformed drummer boy with a bandaged leg approaches them and offers to "show you my sore leg" for a dime. The thought of the boy's wound brings on a flood of nausea in one fellow. The two swells are essentially no different than they had been a year before, but their ignorance and indifference to terrible events becomes less benign when the wounded boy is added to the frame. The following year a cartoon in *Comic Monthly* depicted a soldier in uniform, identified simply as "one of the right sort," confronting a bearded man, sporting a top hat and cane—"One of the Wrong Sort"—to ask him why he is not drilling with the men. "Haw," the swell explains, "fact is I'm genewally engaged—some evening party or dinner party every night, you know; but I shall come next year, you know, when that sort of thing is all over." The cartoon is like those of two years earlier, with the swell navigating his own social calendar while barely recognizing that there is a bloody war under way, but the presence of uniformed soldiers in the image makes the contrast more dramatic, and the swell's excuses ring hollow. Even civilians on the home front had seen enough of the war's destruction to judge him harshly.[22]

With the advent of the draft, the North's satirists would have much to say about those men who bent the rules to avoid service, but what of the ridiculous swells who failed to comprehend the draft? In July 1862 *Vanity Fair* pictured two "elegant young men" lounging in a well-appointed study, discussing the upcoming draft. "The ideaw of drafting fellars like you and me!" an exasperated man sporting a flowing mustache declares. "Why can't they raise an army out of idle men?" The artist, who called the cartoon "Opinion of an Overworked Man," meant to poke fun at these silly members of the elite, but the tone is ambiguous. Perhaps these privileged

Nibbs explains to Jones that he had considered enlisting, but he feared that he might get shot in the face and disappoint the womenfolk. Although the swells are often portrayed as lisping, seemingly unmanly characters, they are also often presented—even in the same cartoons—as accomplished ladies' men. *Yankee Notions* 10 (July 1861): 206. Courtesy of HarpWeek.

Jones.—WHY, NIBBS, HOW D'YE DO? I HEARD THAT YOU HAD ENLISTED.

Nibbs.—I DID HAVE AN IDEA OF DOING SO, BUT YOU SEE I WAS AFRAID OF GETTING SHOT IN THE FACE, AND THEN, YOU KNOW, MY LOOKS WOULD BE SPOILED FOREVER; AND BE-SIDES, THE WOMEN FOLKS WOULDN'T LISTEN TO THE PROPOSI-TION ANYHOW!

men simply do not fathom the world in which they live, making them fair game for humor but almost too stupid to be worth serious outrage. The following month, cartoonist Howard Del drew an "elegant young man" visiting a United States Recruiting Office. The young dandy brought with him a petition signed by five hundred women, "praying that he may be exempted from military duty, as drafts do not agree with my constitution." "The New 'Social Evil'" featured a "Small Swell"—sporting a top hat and cane—chatting with a tall fellow who looks like a farmer. The swell complains: "Dweadful boaw, this Dwaft. Dwags a fellah from the boozum of his Club!" In "Dodging the Draft—A Swell's Strategem" a lisping "Broadway Swell" appears before the Committee on Exemptions dressed as a

On Fools, Hypocrites, and Scoundrels

ONE OF THE RIGHT SORT.—" Why don't you come to drill, man ?"
ONE OF THE WRONG SORT.—' Haw, fact is I'm genewal'y engaged—some evening party or dinner party every night, you know ; but I shall come next year,
you know, when that sort of thing is all over."

A soldier is trying to convince a swell to enlist, but the civilian—of the "wrong sort"—has too many parties on his schedule to volunteer at the moment. Note how the tone toward the swell has shifted since the beginning of the war. *Comic Monthly* (September 1863): 10. Courtesy of HarpWeek.

THIS ELEGANT YOUNG MAN PRESENTS TO THE RECRUITING COMMITTEE A PETITION, SIGNED BY 500 LADIES, PRAYING THAT HE MAY BE EXEMPTED FROM MILITARY DUTY, AS DRAFTS DO NOT AGREE WITH HIS CONSTITUTION.

This cartoon, published shortly after the start of the first state militia draft, portrays a foppish fellow presenting a petition to the recruiting office, signed by "500 ladies, praying that he may be exempted from military duty." Here is another swell being portrayed as unmanly, but also as a favorite of the ladies. *Vanity Fair*, August 9, 1862, 70. Courtesy of HarpWeek.

laborer and accompanied by an elderly woman posing as his widowed mother and an infant playing the role of his dependent child. "Dangers of the Park" returns to the sartorial theme, as a Union recruiter confronts a well-dressed swell and urges him to enlist and avoid the draft, thus earning "a hundred an' fifty dollars an' clothes!" This cartoon inverts the familiar theme of the oblivious swell, as the unaware Union corporal badly misjudges what might induce the wealthy and impeccably dressed young man to enlist.[23] Each of these cartoons from the war's second year portrayed

On Fools, Hypocrites, and Scoundrels

DODGING THE DRAFT—A SWELL'S STRATAGEM.

MR. NOB DE SNOB (a Broadway Swell, as he appeared before the "Committee on Exemptions.")—"*Aw—these persons are me mothaw and me Orphaun infawnt, aw. I suppaut them by aw—manual labah.*"

Here the "Broadway swell" has attempted to disguise himself as a manual laborer and the sole supporter of an aged mother and "orphaun infawnt." He appears ridiculous with his armload of tools, and he does not seem to grasp how the exemption system works. Of course his lisping upper-class accent is a dead giveaway. The juxtaposition of the wealthy draft-dodger and the working-class woman posing as his mother underscores the class tensions that had become part of home front life. *Frank Leslie's Illustrated Newspaper*, September 19, 1863, 420. Courtesy of HarpWeek.

familiar swells responding to conscription, as they had responded to the outbreak of war, with an oblivious and self-centered attitude. On the one hand, the introduction of conscription had changed the stakes, making all military-aged men potential recruits, including the swells. On the other hand, in those early months of the draft the satirists still seemed to find humor in their confusion.

In the war's final years, as the North's manpower shortages grew more dire, the satirists lost patience with the lisping and unaware swells. In October 1864, *Frank Leslie's Budget of Fun* pictured a classic swell—with a trimmed beard, a stylish cap, and striped pants—entering a city street-car, only to find a wounded soldier on his way home from the front, with his feet propped on the only open seats. The "Languid Swell"—upset about finding no seat—declares, "I wish I was a soldier, coming home from the wars." The angry wounded soldier replies, "I dare say you do, you coward, for you wouldn't like to go—that's sure." Unlike the silly swell who had been put off by the wounded drummer boy two years earlier, this fellow provokes true anger.[24] A few months later, *Yankee Notions* returned to the theme of the clueless swell, but with a twist. In the cartoon called "Sympathy," a classic northeastern "miserable little swell" is chatting with a tall returning veteran. The soldier had lost an eye and arm at Gettysburg, but fought on until he lost a leg at the Battle of the Wilderness. The swell seems fascinated by his tale, then notes, "You look a little thinner than when I saw you last. . . . When," he asks, "are you going back?" After nearly four years of war, this swell is unchanged. He is as oblivious as he had been in April 1861. But now the cartoonist has created a caricatured veteran, missing two limbs and an eye, to make it clear how unacceptable this sort of unapologetic home front ignorance had become.[25]

THE PRESS BATTALION

Humorists and cartoonists also delighted in poking fun at themselves and their fellow members of the press who "went off to war" but really only experienced the conflict from a safe distance. These intrepid reporters became another familiar satirical theme in the early months of the war. In some senses these portrayals mirrored the teasing of the swells: silly civilians coexisting alongside the serious trauma of war. But in this case the clever cartoonists were enjoying their own ironies. They were "off to war" without experiencing the real war, but their humor demonstrated to readers that they were cleverly self-aware.

In October 1861 *Frank Leslie's Budget of Fun* ran a series of cartoons on

TRUE FOR ONCE.

LANGUID SWELL (who can't get a seat)—"*I wish I was a soldier, coming home from the wars.*"
WOUNDED SOLDIER—"*I dare say you do, you coward, for you wouldn't like to go—that's sure.*"

The foolish swell, such a popular satirical target early in the war, reappeared in this 1864 cartoon titled "True for Once," but in a less innocuous form. Here the well-dressed civilian is complaining because the wounded soldier has taken up an extra seat. The soldier has no use for the selfish coward. By placing the wounded soldier and the swell together in the same frame, the artist underscores the latter's ethical failures. *Frank Leslie's Illustrated Newspaper*, July 16, 1864, 272. Courtesy of HarpWeek.

the adventures of the "Press Battalion." In the first, a motley assortment of reporters have reported for their "Undress Drill," where they demonstrate absolutely no facility for military marching. Their frustrated captain tells them that their reward will be to hear him read his new poem, "'The Hero's Grave.'" The cartoon mocks the peculiar inversions produced by warfare, where journalists march off to war and military captains pen poetry. The next drawing shows the Press Battalion parading in their "Grand Review."

Sympathy.

Miserable little swell (to old acquaintance).—HA! LOST YOUR EYE AND ARM AT GETTYSBURGH, AND YOUR LEG AT THE BATTLE OF THE WILDERNESS. YOU LOOK A LITTLE THINNER THAN WHEN I SAW YOU LAST. HEM! WHEN ARE YOU GOING BACK?

Like "True for Once," this cartoon—published in the final year of the war—reflects a society that has had its fill of the foolish swells. Here the "miserable little swell" can see that the soldier has lost two limbs and an eye in battle, yet asks him, "When are you going back?" The civilian who is so unaware of the true realities of war is no longer seen as simply silly. *Yankee Notions* 14 (January 1865): 15. Courtesy of HarpWeek.

A half dozen portly or excessively skinny reporters appear dressed in misshapen uniforms preparing to head for the front. The final image shows this same motley assortment of writers "routing" the Confederate army with a battery of overblown newspaper reports and editorials.[26] Thus the cartoonist gets jabs in at these ridiculous journalist-noncombatants while also making fun of the excessive rhetoric of war reporting.

A few months later, *Ballou's Dollar Monthly Magazine*—a small-circulation journal—ran a similar twelve-part series, "Sketches of the

On Fools, Hypocrites, and Scoundrels

Grand Review of the Press Battalion. Their talented captain compliments them upon their unequalled proficiency.

The wartime cartoonists loved joking about their own colleagues in the press, who headed off to war without any sense of military bearing. Here we see the "Grand Review of the Press Battalion": a motley crew of out-of-shape scribes. *Frank Leslie's Budget of Fun* (October 1861): 16. Courtesy of HarpWeek.

War," documenting the experiences of "the artist" after "receiving a commission to sketch at the seat of the war." On arriving at the front, the artist is confronted by a rebel picket and "displays his bravery" by fleeing in terror. But in the next frame the artist's official "sketch of the affair" shows him disarming the rebel with a sword. In the following pair of images the cartoonist first sketches himself in "'the thickest of the fight,'" and the companion image portrays the reality: he sat at a safe distance and watched the battle through a spyglass. Finally the intrepid artist is sent home, undamaged by his short stint at war.[27]

These cartoons differ from the portrayals of the northern swells in that the men of the press corps are self-consciously mocking their own quasi-military exploits. As representatives of the home front, sent off to observe the world of the soldier, the cartoonists seem to question the notion that men armed with pens and notebooks could ever capture the true war. Unlike the swells, they get that they are a bit silly. At the same time, they parodied the mysterious world of soldiers' drills and military terms, so foreign to life back home. Much like the satirical commentary on the swells, these

BALLOU'S DOLLAR MONTHLY MAGAZINE.
THE CHEAPEST MAGAZINE IN THE WORLD.

He blunders upon the rebel lines, is fired upon by a picket, and displays his bravery.

His sketch of the affair.

His sketch of a battle, in which he is present in the "thickest of the fight."

The fact of the case.

His heroic exertions affect his health, and he gets permission to return home.

He brings home a cargo of trophies captured with his own sword.

This cartoon, in twelve images, follows the intrepid artist as he heads off to war and then revises his own history in his battlefield sketches. In the first several sketches the artist is rather like the new military recruit, sporting his military equipment as well as his artist's tools. But as soon as the firing begins, he makes himself scarce. When things settle down, the artist produces a version of the battle where he is the hero "in the thickest of the fight," thus demonstrating how events on the battlefield are redefined in the retelling. *Ballou's Dollar Monthly Magazine* (January 1862). Courtesy of the American Antiquarian Society.

SKETCHES OF THE WAR.

Delight of our artist on receiving a commission to sketch at the seat of war.

He purchases the necessary equipments.

He starts for the seat of war.

On arriving, he finds it necessary to dispense with some of his "duds."—He starts on a sketching tour.

Finds a rebel battery, and proceeds to sketch it.

Is fired upon—appearance of his unfinished sketch.

ironic portrayals of reporters and cartoonists at war largely appeared in the first year of the Civil War, when the whole adventure was new and unfamiliar. As the casualties mounted, joking around about marching and battles lost its appeal.

SILLY WOMEN

The urban swells and idle journalists who paraded through the early months of the war, happily unaware of the horrors of the battlefield and the far worse horrors to come, had their satirical counterpart in the silly ladies of cartoons and comic prose. These caricatured women also looked at national events through the lens of their own self-interest, even while they gave every indication that they supported the war effort and hoped for Union victory. In all sorts of settings they demonstrated a charming inability to comprehend the realities of warfare. Like the commentary on the swells, and the self-effacing joking by the wartime journalists, the satirized women seemed harmless enough, and the jokes had little bite, at least at first. Instead, their example once again provided northern readers with a sort of positive reinforcement, underscoring their own comparative military savvy.

Immediately after Fort Sumter, patriotic women—and particularly those of the leisurely classes—leapt into action, forming sewing circles, rolling bandages, and preparing all sorts of packages to be sent to the front. These efforts were quite real, and this sort of spontaneous wartime voluntarism proved valuable in supporting the war effort while also giving citizens—both women and men—on the home front the conviction that they were contributing to the Union cause. Still, this early flurry of enthusiastic activity left the door open for the satirists. Only a few months after Fort Sumter, *Vanity Fair* ran an essay titled "The Luxury of Giving" by a contributor who signed himself "The Corporal." The humorous piece teased women for inundating infantrymen with luxury items that no man could carry with him on the march. "A soldier is not, properly speaking, a rheumatic or bilious maiden of advanced age. Nor an infant afflicted with flatuency," the author advised. "Don't continue to offer him bundles of boneset, peppermint, and fennel. . . . Urge him not to put loaf cakes and elderberry wine in his knapsack!"[28] A cartoon that August mocked "Fanny"—who saw herself as "very like Florence Nightingale"—as she packed up a large box of wines and preserves "for the dear volunteers." Another cartoonist portrayed a "naïve country girl" giving a soldier from the Twenty-First Regiment a ham to be delivered to her cousin in the Twenty-

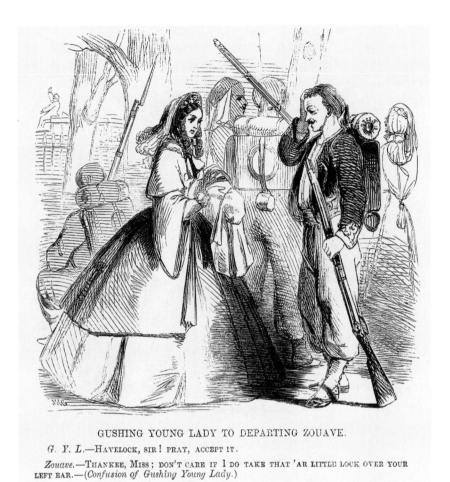

GUSHING YOUNG LADY TO DEPARTING ZOUAVE.

G. Y. L.—Havelock, sir! pray, accept it.

Zouave.—Thankee, Miss; don't care if I do take that 'ar little lock over your left ear.—(*Confusion of Gushing Young Lady.*)

This sweet cartoon from the war's first months plays on both the misplaced enthusiasm of the young woman and the confusion of the smitten young soldier. She has made him a havelock (a piece of headgear not really suited to this war), and he thinks she is offering him a lock of her hair. *Vanity Fair*, June 15, 1861, 274. Courtesy of HarpWeek.

Second, since the sequential regiments must surely be camped near each other. As the men came home on furlough, the enthusiastic female volunteers took pains to make them welcome. In September 1862 a New York cartoonist portrayed an overweight Private Smith reporting for duty after his furlough, explaining sheepishly that he was unable to resist the temptations provided by New York's ladies. *Vanity Fair* remarked on the great demand for lemons from eligible women who hoped to use the thirst-quenching fruit to woo young soldiers home on leave.[29]

The satirists loved commenting on the scores of women who threw

WHY SHOULDN'T HE?

Naïve Country Girl.—Volunteer, will you please take this ham to my cousin; he belongs to the 21st Regiment. You are from the 22nd—it is quite near.

Obliging Zouave.—Oh yes; certainly—of course!

In the first months of the war, satirists often returned to the theme that civilians—and particularly women—had little understanding of military matters. Here a "naïve country girl" hopes that a soldier from the Twenty-Second Regiment can bring a ham to her cousin in the Twenty-First, since presumably the regiments must be camped in numerical order. The obliging Zouave is happy to take the ham! *Vanity Fair*, August 17, 1861, 78. Courtesy of HarpWeek.

themselves into sewing work. As the war's first winter approached, one poet published doggerel verse about the "fifty thousand maids and matrons, and widows a hundred score," all gathering for the "Knitting of the Socks!," while another penned a celebration of the North's "Army of the Knitters."[30] A cartoon in *Frank Leslie's Illustrated Newspaper* featured a young woman proudly displaying fancy men's "drawers"—resplendent with lace and other finery—that she had been sewing "to send off to the poor soldiers."[31] In the imagined community of Baldinsville, Artemus Ward's wife enjoyed attending the local "sowin' circle" because "she and the wimin folks was havin' a pleasant time slanderin' the females of the OTHER sowin' circle (which likewise met that arternoon, and was doubtless enjoyin' theirselves ekally well in slanderin' the fust-named circle)." "I allus like to see people enjoy theirselves," he added.[32]

Union soldier Orpheus C. Kerr, the pen name of popular humorist Robert Henry Newell, had great fun with these patriotic women in a November 1861 essay. "Ah, woman! what should we do without thee!" he wrote. "All our patriotism is but the inspiration of thy proud love, and all our money is but the few shillings left after thou hast got through buying new bonnets. Oh! woman—thoughtful woman! the soldier thanks thee for sending him pies and cakes that turn sour before they reach us; but for heaven's sake, don't send us any more havelocks, or there'll be a crisis in the linen market."[33] Kerr and other satirists routinely took aim at professional soldiers, contractors, and politicians who had failed to perform their expected tasks, but in this passage the tone is quite different. These female volunteers had stepped forward with no professional role or expectation. Here the joke was not that these women were cynically using their wartime roles to feather their own nests but, rather, that their honest actions in the name of the war effort were largely misguided if not counterproductive.

Often the point was that patriotic women, despite their best intentions, had no understanding of military affairs. A *Vanity Fair* cartoon showed a young man patiently trying to explain military strategy to his aunt, who appears pleasantly befuddled. Another found "Arabella" chiding her civilian husband because the officers at the party had such good stories about Bull Run. "Oh, how I do wish you were a major—or captain—or something 'nice,'" she exclaims. For most of the war it was routine for captured prisoners to be "exchanged" for prisoners held by the other side. A short squib in the *Chicago Tribune* played on this notion, telling the tale of a young bride who grew upset when she learned that her husband was to be exchanged, since she wanted to keep the original.[34]

Arabella, (who adores the defenders of our Union.)—Oh! Augustus, how eloquently Col. de Shann describes the action at Bull-Run, and with what modesty he speaks of himself on that occasion. Oh, how I *do* wish you were a major—or captain—or—or something 'nice.' "

A few months after the First Battle of Bull Run, Colonel de Shann is regaling party guests with tales of the action. Arabella wishes that her husband was "a major—or captain—or—or something 'nice.'" Arabella clearly knows nothing of military ranks. Meanwhile, the colonel is almost certainly embellishing his own adventures. *Vanity Fair*, October 5, 1861, 160. Courtesy of HarpWeek.

Another popular topic concerned the notion that the North's girls and young women could not see past their own romantic ambitions. In "A Fashionable War Epistle," *Frank Leslie's Budget of Fun* showed a young girl writing to her best friend, bemoaning the decline in her social life with all the eligible men away at war. Soon enough men would start trickling home on furloughs or other leaves, providing new possibilities. In a May 1862 cartoon in *Nick Nax*, a young girl at a fancy ball is literally snagged by a soldier when her dress catches on a piece of his uniform. Another cartoon showed Clara and Laura chatting at a party. Clara had been engaged to an upstanding merchant, but on further reflection she had concluded that "epaulets and gilt buttons" were to be preferred over a "plain black coat." Later, as more and more eligible men went off to war, cartoonists drew angry "spinsters" at home, robbed of potential husbands. But when talk turned to drafting bachelors while excusing married men, those same spinsters enjoyed a new "Ray of Hope," as even the homely woman of advancing age had hopes of marriage if it protected her intended from conscription.[35]

Other humorists played with the idea that women were in fact adept at military maneuvers, but they applied those skills to affairs of the heart. In the poem "Drilling," "Sweet Amy" decides that she wants to learn to "drill" Charley as his captain does. The pair moves through a series of increasingly romantic military maneuvers, until in the final verse:

Charles "ordered arms," without command,
She smooth'd her rumpled hair,
And pouted, frown'd, and blush'd, and then
Said softly—"As you were!"

Author Allie Allyn's humorous essay "Generalship," in the February 1864 issue of *Godey's Lady's Book,* considered the same theme from the perspective of a more mature woman. Presented as a guide to being a successful wife, Allyn explains to her readers how she uses the strategies of the successful general to manipulate her husband.[36]

Periodically the innocent and fundamentally unaware woman was used as a vehicle to mock those men who remained at home. Not long after the First Battle of Bull Run, *Vanity Fair* ran a cartoon showing a young woman at a party chatting with a civilian man. The pair overhear a Union colonel regaling listeners with tales from the battle, prompting the young woman to tell her friend that she wished he was more like the entertaining colonel. Her comment does not seem to be pressuring him to enlist, yet he could hardly avoid the conclusion that a uniform would enhance his chances with her.[37]

On occasion, even in the early months of the war, the portraits of these seemingly oblivious women appeared less generous. In one lengthy piece in *Yankee Notions,* "Polly Snoofles" goes on about her "patriotic experiences" watching the local soldiers head off to war. When her daughter breaks into tears at the departure of her beau, Polly reassures her: "Even if Ichabod should git shot, there is Rewben Skrabble left; he ain't goin." A cartoon in

"Ruling Passion, &c."

CLARA—*Why, how is this! FRED JONES turns his back upon you!! I thought you were engaged!*

LAURA—*Well, so I was last winter; but I'm not going to throw myself away upon the son a merchant when there are so many opportunities in the army. No, I am sick of a plain black coat. The epaulette and gilt buttons now takes precedence.*

Dozens of wartime cartoons played on the war's impact on romantic possibilities. As we shall see, many suggested that patriotic women would insist on dating men in uniform. In this May 1862 cartoon we see two women at a party. One had been engaged, but she has abandoned her civilian lover because "there are so many opportunities in the army." The cartoonist seems to be mocking flighty women who are enraptured by uniforms, while also suggesting that men on the home front who wish to win such women should enlist and earn a uniform. *Nick Nax* (May 1862): 5. Courtesy of HarpWeek.

A RAY OF HOPE.

Sanguine Spinster.—" No more single men to be appointed to the Police; how fortunate! Wait till they come to draft the bachelors, and then !—"

Cartoonist Howard Del plays on the unintended consequences of new rules making it more difficult for unmarried men to avoid military service. Here an unattractive "spinster" feels "a ray of hope" at the prospect that new conscription rules might encourage more men to get married. The cartoon comments on the impact of the draft, while also underscoring familiar gender stereotypes about husband-hungry women. *Vanity Fair,* August 23, 1862, 87. Courtesy of HarpWeek.

Frank Leslie's Budget of Fun played on similar dark themes, as a woman at a party compliments her friend's new black dress, noting that it will serve as an ideal mourning outfit should her soldier husband fall in battle. "An Object of Interest" shows a woman listening as a returned soldier explains that he "lost his health" in the war, to which the young lady gushes, "How very interesting!" This idea that northern women came to see men as little more than interchangeable potential suitors took on a new twist with the emergence of conscription legislation. In June 1863 cartoonist Penfield-Bross drew a couple at dinner as a new draft day approached. The man is worried that he might get drafted, and his dinner companion tells him not to worry because she can easily find a substitute.[38]

These cartoons and other bits of humor played on the idea that some northerners on the home front were unmindful of the true nature of the war. Both the swells and the clueless women were self-absorbed egoists, viewing events through the lens of their own interests and aspirations while blithely ignoring the war's horrors. The early war cartoonists and satirists usually presented these civilians as harmless creatures, good for a chuckle. Even those men and women who had little knowledge of military matters could enjoy these cartoons with the confidence that they were not the sort who would be the subject of such mocking.

And like the jokes about the swells, these critiques of empty-headed women have a powerful gendered component. Often the point was that silly women are ignorant when it comes to manly military matters. In other cases it was not ignorance, but selfishness, that earned criticism. The humorists seemingly drew on a palette of popular gender stereotypes in making fun of these women. And it is noteworthy that this gendered satire did not appear in women's magazines. But the cartoons and jokes were almost never about woman's essential nature, only about particular women—embodying belittling stereotypes—who failed to grasp the war's meaning. The larger point was that their excesses or shortcomings placed them outside the bounds of True Womanhood, at least as it should exist in time of war, much as the lisping swells represented a failure of proper masculinity during wartime. Women and men who did not recognize their own behavior in these portraits could take pleasure in the satirized images.

CHILDREN: INNOCENT OBSERVERS

This brings us to a final category of charmingly innocent wartime observers: children. A few cartoonists used the vehicle of young children to make similar points about the wartime behavior of adults. In these cases the fact that children failed to grasp the war's larger import is used by the cartoonists to point a finger at adults who should know better. Children on the home front heard much about the war, but they processed what they heard through their own distinctive perspectives. Moreover, from the standpoint of the humorist, children had a wonderful tendency to speak their minds unfiltered by social convention. When the drummer boy in "An Appetizer" offers to show his wound to a cowardly swell for a dime, the boy is not trying to show the well-dressed civilian up as a coward, but the reader sees the drama in those terms.

The journal *Yankee Notions* regularly used cartoons of children to make larger points about the war. In "Women Are All Alike," a small boy complains because his young girlfriend has taken to following around soldiers in uniform, while ignoring his intentions. Another cartoon portrayed a very young girl, presumably a maid, explaining to her employer that her beau was going off to war and thus she intended to sign on as a nurse.[39] Many cartoonists had fun with the scores of boys on the home front who became absorbed in playing war, even while adult men were marching off to their death. In "Patriotic Mother," an exasperated mother offers to send her young son—and his loud drumming—off to the real war.[40] By contrast, a November 1861 cartoon in *Yankee Notions* featured a mother beaming at "the display of patriotism" exhibited by her noisy sons, while her guest—a Mr. Tibbs—glowers in the corner. Here the boys are happily playing soldier, and the mother is proud of her sons' patriotic enthusiasm, but the reader is focused on the civilian Tibbs, whose failure to serve is highlighted by the children's games.[41] The following month *Yankee Notions* returned to the same theme in a cartoon of a "patriotic son" sporting a toy rifle, talking to his mother as his sedentary father looks on. The boy declares that he wishes he "was as big as pa." His mother asks him why he feels that way, and he explains that then he could "volunteer and fight the rebels!" The boy seems happily unaware of the implications of his wish, but the annoyed father immediately tells his wife to "put that child to bed."[42] Each of these images in the first year of the war used a "patriotic" boy to unwittingly ridicule adult men who had declined to enlist. By putting the commentary in the voices of boys, the cartoonists skirted the broader political and cultural issues. Did these men have some legitimate reason to stay at home while others enlisted? Perhaps. But whatever considerations kept these men on the home front were too nuanced to resonate with these patriotic lads.

In February, *Yankee Notions* shifted the terrain a bit, portraying a boy and a girl in intense conversation. The boy, sporting a kepi and a stick (perhaps serving as a toy rifle), is explaining to his sweetheart that she must not beg him to stay at home, for "how can a fellow of my age remain at home and see his country's flag trampled on by traitors[?]" Here again the cartoonist shows children acting out the sort of patriotic conversa-

Wartime humorists often used small children to convey their satirical messages. Here a young boy is upset because his girlfriend has wandered off after a man in uniform. His response speaks for those hapless civilian men who watched as women on the home front gravitated toward men in uniform. *Yankee Notions* 10 (August 1861): 252. Courtesy of HarpWeek.

Women are all Alike.

Boy.—How strange it is that the women folks run after those soger chaps so. Now, there's Maria, she never took no notice of me at all, and we've been engaged goodness knows how long.

tions that their elders—or at least their patriotic elders—were having. The suggestion is that this is what patriotic adults would be saying if they had these children's purity of spirit.[43]

Of course, children were also the target audience for wartime magazines and novels aimed at youthful readers. These stories often celebrated the virtues of patriotism, with young characters supporting the war at home or finding opportunities to exhibit bravery in the field (as drummer boys or in other roles). No doubt these books and stories produced actual awkward conversations between bellicose boys and their fathers who re-

Had him there.

Patriotic son.— I wish I was as big as pa, mother.
Mother.— What would you do, my son?
Son.— Why, I'd volunteer and fight the rebels!
Father (angrily.)—Mother, put that child to bed.

Once again, the cartoonist uses the child to poke fun at adults. Here the "patriotic son" with his toy rifle declares that he wishes he was "as big as pa" so that he could enlist to "fight the rebels!" Pa, who is sitting comfortably, reading *Yankee Notions*, is not amused. The artist is playing on the bellicose spirit that had absorbed the attentions of young boys on the home front. *Yankee Notions* (December 1861): 357. Courtesy of HarpWeek.

mained at home. While that literature praised a sort of engaged stoicism in children left behind when their fathers went off to war, it is not clear that the young readers were taught to expect that their relatives would enlist. They were, however, expected to recognize that the Civil War was an important event that required attention of readers large and small.[44]

■ Through characters such as oblivious swells, foolish journalists, silly women, and innocent children, northern cartoonists and other satirists commented on the fundamental gap between the horrors of "the real war" and the seemingly harmless pageantry imagined by the nation's citizenry who were safely ensconced at home. The caricatures were so outrageous or silly that they perhaps left readers with a sense of satisfaction that although they, too, lived far from the seat of war, they were nowhere near as unaware as these absurd characters. The home front patriots read accounts of real battles, and even if they had not experienced the war first-hand, they could rest assured that their understanding of the national crisis far exceeded that of these caricatures. The first duty of the good citizen was to be informed and aware, even if also safe and sound. The greater satirical bite, and the most powerful literary indictments, would be reserved for those men and women on the home front who were guilty of hypocrisy and dishonesty, not mere silliness.

Don't You Think It Is Time You Took Off That Uniform?

Shoulder Straps and Faux Soldiers

OUR COUNTRY NOW AND OUR COUNTRY FOREVER!

In the first paragraphs of Henry Morford's *The Days of Shoddy: A Novel of the Great Rebellion in 1861*, a New York newsboy known as "Coffee Joe" rushes across Broadway, headed for the Astor House, loaded down with the latest newspapers. This "modern Mercury" carries news of the surrender of Fort Sumter and the start of the Civil War. Along the way he stops to sell a paper at the offices of "Charles Holt & Andrews," cloth importers and traders. Burtnett Haviland, the clerk who first grabs the paper, scans the news and breaks into sobs "over the degradation of his country." Immediately the talk turns to war as the office full of adult businessmen, bellicose clerks, and excited errand boys discuss how they shall respond to the crisis. Burtnett declares that he will be one of the first volunteers as soon as the call comes. But the "gray-haired and prudent" Mr. Wales reminds the eager clerk that he has a young family to support. "'Can you afford to leave them?'" he asks. "'God help me! I had forgotten them!'" Burtnett replies, as he immediately backs off from his bold declarations. It would, he concludes, be impossible to support his wife and young child on a soldier's pay. Overhearing this discussion, Charles Holt—the establishment's owner—steps forward and promises to continue Burtnett's salary should he choose to enlist, adding that he will also see to the needs of his clerk's family should Haviland fall in battle.[1]

In these opening pages Morford captured something of the fervor that swept over Americans in both the North and the South in April 1861. In cities and towns across the country, civilians rushed to newspaper offices for the latest news. Within days, Abraham Lincoln would call for seventy-five thousand ninety-day volunteers to put down the rebellion. Union recruiting posters printed in those first few weeks stressed the appeals of patriotism and martial excitement. "Our Country Now and Our Country Forever!" declared one Pennsylvania poster distributed only days after the fall of Fort Sumter. Below these bold words a bald eagle clutched a banner proclaiming "Union and Liberty." The rest of the poster promised the opportunity to avenge the gross insult to "THE AMERICAN FLAG," while the fine print assured recruits that they would leave for the seat of war as soon as possible. Military recruiters had no difficulty finding willing recruits in those first days after Fort Sumter. The artists who designed the early recruiting posters knew their audiences. The images featured flags, eagles, horses, and dashing men in fine uniforms. The texts celebrated Union and promised vengeance.

The scene Morford described was replayed across the country. Tens of thousands of patriotic young men like Burtnett Haviland read news of the fall of Fort Sumter and resolved to have a hand in the fight before it was over. They responded to the multiple appeals of patriotism, Union, masculinity, vengeance, and the promise of martial excitement.[2] In many communities, the chief concern was that the available places would be filled before the volunteer could add his name to a regimental roster. The men who stepped forward earned the esteem of their peers, the respect of society, and—in many cases—admiring looks from eligible young women.

Morford also captured several larger truths in the novel's first pages. Although Burt is caught up in war enthusiasm, Mr. Wales quickly brings him back to earth by reminding the clerk that he has a young bride and a small child to support. He concludes that he cannot enlist because a soldier's pay could not support his family. This is his personal response, but it appears to be shared by his employer and coworker: family obligations trumped patriotic impulses. Meanwhile, Charles Holt is not really too old for military service, but there is no suggestion that he would or should consider enlisting. Instead, the wealthy importer offers to support the war effort by paying his clerk while he is off defending the Union. In sum, the news of Fort Sumter propelled many men to want to do something. They felt a duty to act, but how they acted was dictated by personal circumstances and inclinations rather than by legal constraints or the overwhelming dictates of patriotic citizenship. Moreover, the men who enlisted in those first few months understood military service more as a grand opportunity than as an obligation that exceeded all others.

■ For well over a year the Union army relied entirely on volunteers to fill the ranks. Long before the original three-month enlistments expired,

Abraham Lincoln had called for five hundred thousand new recruits for three-year service. Like the initial recruits—many of whom opted to join new three-year regiments—these volunteers answered appeals to their patriotism, coupled with challenges to their masculinity and in many cases promises of spots in celebrated regiments under popular officers. Recruiting posters continued to feature flags and eagles, as well as men on horseback. Increasingly, recruiters targeted ethnic groups to fill particular regiments. "Arouse! Arouse! Arouse!" a poster for New York's Garibaldi Regiment screamed out, aiming specifically at "Italians, Hungarians, Germans, and French Patriots of All Nations."[3]

On the home front, northern society embraced the Union soldier. Popular lithographs portrayed the war's heroes and fallen martyrs. Poems and songs celebrated the North's fighting man going off to war. Patriotic envelopes portrayed patriotic slogans and military imagery. Newspaper accounts traced the exploits and travails of Union regiments in the field. Small-town papers followed the exploits of the local boys in the field. Meanwhile, new photographic technology made *cartes de visite*—small photographic portraits—available to northerners. Ordinary infantrymen could visit a photographer's studio and come away with a stack of pictures glued to 2½-by-4-inch card stock. Friends, family members, and loved ones purchased leather-bound photograph albums—yet another innovation—to fill with *cartes de visite* of young Union soldiers in uniform. Entrepreneurial photographers, led by the famed Mathew Brady and his colleague Edward A. Anthony, took to marketing *cartes de visite* of the Union's military heroes, including Elmer Ellsworth—one of the war's first martyrs—and Colonel Robert Anderson, who had gained national celebrity when he surrendered his command at Fort Sumter. Northerners in blue had earned widespread respect, even while events on the battlefield gave little cause for enthusiasm.[4]

Popular columnist Fanny Fern approved of the changes that accompanied the northern war spirit, as "sectional prejudices" had given way to "the noble qualities of the men of the North." Nowhere was this sense of shared sacrifice and commitment more apparent than when soldiers from the front returned to northern streets. "A military cap and a crutch are the surest passports at present to the universal heart," Fern wrote, "so tenderly does it throb for those who have rallied for and suffered in the defense of our common rights." As northern citizens embraced the war's true heroes, they grew increasingly intolerant of those frauds and con men who sought to profit from this collective goodwill.[5]

LIBERTY AND UNION, NOW AND FOREVER.

For right is right, since God is God,
And right the day must win,
To doubt, would be disloyalty,
To falter, would be sin.

The Civil War saw an explosion in personal correspondence as young men went off to war, leaving behind long lists of friends and loved ones. The war, and the patriotic impulses that accompanied it, generated a thriving business in the printing of patriotic envelopes. More than fifteen thousand different designs appeared during the war years, mostly in the northern states. The first envelope features classic patriotic imagery: Lady Liberty holding an American flag. The second envelope has a similar visual message, although this time featuring a uniformed soldier, but it adds a short verse that ends, "To doubt would be disloyalty, / To falter, would be sin." This message encourages readers to erase their "doubts," but not necessarily to act in any particular way. Courtesy of the Library Company of Philadelphia.

In July 1862, Nathaniel Hawthorne—writing under the pen name "A Peaceable Man"—published a highly critical, satirical essay titled "Chiefly about War-Matters" in the *Atlantic Monthly*. The essay described his travels across the East, including visits to military camps and the seat of war. Along the way the Peaceable Man leveled barbs at the North's military and political leaders. Hawthorne was not happy about the progress of the war, and even less happy with the men charged with prosecuting it. The massive increase in the military, and in the scores of men who insisted on some sort of higher rank, boded ill for the future. "Even supposing the war should end to-morrow, and the army melt into the mass of the population within the year, what an incalculable preponderance will there be of military titles and pretensions for at least half a century to come!" he wrote. "Every country-neighborhood will have its general or two, its three or four colonels, half a dozen majors, and captains without end. . . . Military merit, or rather, since that is not so readily estimated, military notoriety, will be the measure of all claims to civil distinction." If Hawthorne disdained superfluous military officers in the field, he reserved his most acerbic remarks for those officers who wore the uniform but somehow never seemed to find their way to the battlefield. He found the nerve center for these characters in Washington's Willard's Hotel. "It is the meeting-place of the true representatives of the country," he reported. "You exchange nods with governors of sovereign States; you elbow illustrious men, and tread on the toes of generals; you hear statesmen and orators speaking in their familiar tones. You are mixed up with office-seekers, wire-pullers, inventors, artists, poets, prosers (including editors, army-correspondents, attachés of foreign journals, and long-winded talkers), clerks, diplomatists, mail-contractors, railway-directors, until your own identity is lost among them."

Hawthorne devoted several pages to the crowd at Willard's. In many senses the old men, reliving past glories, dominated the Willard's scene. Among the younger men, "A Peaceable Man" found many who sported military uniforms. "The bulk of the army had moved out of Washington before we reached the city," he reported, "yet it seemed to me that at least two thirds of the guests and idlers at the hotel wore one or another token of the military profession. . . . Many of them, no doubt, were self-commissioned officers, and had put on the buttons and the shoulder-straps, and booted themselves to the knees, merely because captain, in these days, is so good a travelling-name. The majority, however, had been duly appointed by the

President, but might be none the better warriors for that." Amid those military posers Hawthorne noted only the occasional "veteran among this crowd of carpet-knights," who had earned true military decorations from some past conflict.

Although a patriot, Hawthorne's "Peaceable Man" was no supporter of the generals and politicians in charge of the war. America's republican values had long included a healthy skepticism about the overly powerful, especially when bedecked in military finery. But the New Englander's portrait of the drinking crowd at Willard's also captured two particular sorts of hypocrites who fell outside the realm of accepted wartime behavior. The first he deftly labeled the "self-commissioned officers." These were the imposters who had donned uniforms and adopted military titles but were complete frauds, with no military position at all. The second group could perhaps claim some military rank, but the presence of a rank—as reflected by the omnipresent "shoulder straps"—really meant nothing. They were soldiers, but in name only. These were the war's new breed of confidence men, now operating under the guise of the Union cause rather than the banner of individualism.[6]

Hawthorne's essay captured a crucial point that attracted much home front commentary in the first eighteen months of the war. Many observers—both Republicans and War Democrats—criticized individual officers and politicians even though they supported the ultimate goals of the Union war effort and the citizen-soldiers in the ranks. But if professional incompetence and cynical careerism drew the wrath of prowar northerners, they saved their greatest outrage—and creative satire—for the hypocrites who displayed the uniform over brandy and cigars, while never straying into harm's way. These were the war's fraudulent "shoulder straps."

Democratic editor and politician Benjamin Wood captured a very similar scene in his novel *Fort Lafayette*, published in 1862. In one chapter Wood, a Copperhead, describes the bar in a fashionable New York hotel, full of uniformed officers drinking to excess. These "embryo Napoleons . . . wore their shoulder straps with a killing air," for "their tailors had made them heroes, every one," Wood wrote. As the drink flowed, one colonel regaled his colleagues with the story of "a party of Congressmen" who had visited camp and proceeded to get royally drunk with the officer of the day and his buddies. Wood used the scene to get in digs at both the nation's political leadership and its faux shoulder straps. Later in the same chapter a drunken colonel loses his money gambling and recoups his losses by selling a captaincy to another man for five hundred dollars, revealing another layer of corruption. Shoulder straps, it seemed, sometimes went to the higher bidder.[7]

The popular critiques of these shoulder-strapped hypocrites began shortly after the outbreak of war. *Vanity Fair* took regular digs at the members of the local Home Guard, who proudly displayed their uniforms while avoiding real military service. Barely a month after Fort Sumter, the New York journal ran a piece on these fellows. "Quite a number of very estimable young persons are actively engaging themselves, just now, in the pleasing if not exhilarating occupation of organizing soldier-companies to stay at home during the war," *Vanity Fair* reported. These developments had effectively—if oddly—"exploded" the familiar notion that "a young, able-bodied man not hampered by the necessity of getting bread for his family, has no excuse for turning a deaf ear to the call of his country." Moreover, the comic essay continued, the military uniforms and officers' titles were every bit as impressive to the city's young women as those displayed by real soldiers.[8] The following month the humor weekly featured a cartoon showing a bedraggled member of the Home Guard dragging himself up the stairs to his home, exhausted from a day's drilling and drunk from an evening's partying. In July 1861, as both sides anxiously awaited the war's first major battle, *Vanity Fair* portrayed another Home Guard soldier, surrounded by fawning women, explaining how he knew much more about military matters than the professional soldiers.[9] New York, like Ward's Baldinsville, seemed full of men who loved fancy uniforms, and women who loved those men.

The poem "The Song of the Home Guard," published in August 1861, mocked those men who "volunteered" to stay home. Written in the voice of a Home Guard soldier speaking to his comrades in arms, the verse begins:

"Let dogs delight to bark and bite,"
I have no taste for war;
In cannon's roar and bullet's flight
And nasty pools of gore.

However, he goes on to explain:

I love the drums' and trumpets' crash,
The uniforms and things;
The sunlight sabre's glittering flash
(When all unused to human hash!)
To me a pleasure brings.

NOT USED TO IT.

Home Guard.—Well—'swonderful howerdrill wearsout a m'ran's legs—fearf'lly f'tiguing.

As true soldiers were drilling for war and going to bed exhausted from their exertions, this cartoon mocks the "Home Guard" soldier who is dragging himself home after a long evening of drinking. *Vanity Fair*, June 1, 1861, 253. Courtesy of HarpWeek.

But he has less enthusiasm for the grim realities of war, leading him to the wise decision:

> Let others fight, let others fall,
> Let others wear the bays,
> But at the military ball
> Let me alone adorn the festive hall,
> Where gimp and buttons blaze.

And, finally, the fake soldier concludes:

> So now, brave boys, I move that when
> The war has drained our land,
> Of good and valiant fighting men,
> Should we be called, I move that then
> We instantly disband.[10]

Vanity Fair often used Delmonico's, a fashionable New York restaurant, as a setting for commentary on the "shoulder straps." In May it ran two images of "A Member of the Seventh Regiment Dining." In the first cartoon the new recruit is eating at Delmonico's, while in the second he is in uniform sitting under a tree at camp in Annapolis. This pair of cartoons seemed to be pointing out that even the sons of New York's elites were in uniform, but six months later *Vanity Fair* had changed its tune, running a series of six cartoons titled "The Defenders of Fort Delmonico," featuring uniformed men enjoying lovely—and safe—meals at the restaurant's elegant tables. In the first image, two drunk young soldiers stand at a table before a toppled bottle of wine, declaring that they will "place Delmonico in a thorough state of defense." The next frame shows the two men manning a makeshift perimeter outside the restaurant, behind crates of wine. In the third, a cluster of men are sharing a toast, promising to "never leave" their favored restaurant, but in the next image they are all leaving for a moment—surrounded by handsome women—in order to "recruit." In the fifth picture they have returned with more recruits, who now lie about the dining room surrounded by empty bottles. The final image finds the faux soldiers facing a "grand charge" in the form of their enormous bill; the restaurant's owner suffers a terrible loss when the men skedaddle without paying their tab.[11]

The barbs aimed at the home front warriors continued throughout the war's first year. In a short piece dated "Broadway, December 10, 1861" Artemus Ward imagined a letter from the young Henry Adolphus to his worried (and wealthy) parents: "Dear Father and Mother—We are all getting along very well. We mess at Delmonico's. Do not repine for your son. Some must suffer for the glorious Stars and Stripes, and dear parents, why shouldn't I? Tell Mrs. Skuller that we do not need the benefits that she so kindly sent to us, as we bunk at St. Nicholas and Metropolitan. What our brave lads stand most in need of now is Fruit Cake and Waffles. Do not weep for me."[12] In a comic song based on a popular verse, "Jeannette" bemoaned the fact that her beloved "Jeannot" was bound for the war, "with those straps upon your shoulders and that sabre by the side." But in fact, Jeannot explains, "I simply wear this uniform to promenade Broadway" for the Home Guard. "Do you think to save the Union, I Delmonico's would leave?"[13] Whether enjoyed by New Yorkers or by readers in distant corners of the nation, Delmonico's had become the symbol of extravagant privilege, unmindful of patriotic obligation.

Frank Leslie's Budget of Fun, another popular humor magazine with a large national following, also enjoyed having fun at the Home Guard's

THE DEFENDERS OF FORT DELMONICO.

1. A Prominent member of Le Jeunesse Doré addresses a few youthful patriots—"Yes! we will place Delmonico in a thorough state of defence"—

2. Delmonico's—Garrisoned

3. The Oath—they swear never to LEAVE it—

4. But occasionally they go out recruiting

5. "We are rapidly filling up."

6. Terrific engagement—Grand Charge—utter rout of the F. D. D's with great loss————to the landlord.

Cartoonists for New York–based *Vanity Fair* enjoyed ridiculing the local elites who paraded around in uniforms but spent much of their time dining at the city's fashionable Delmonico's restaurant. This series of six drawings plays on the idea that these faux soldiers are engaged in defending "Fort Delmonico," down to the "Grand Charge" at the end of the evening. *Vanity Fair*, November 23, 1861, 232. Courtesy of HarpWeek.

5. *They have a dress parade. Colonel Tug compliments them on their splendid appearance, and confidentially informs them that "all is quiet on the Potomac, the enemy having departed." They receive the news with ecstacy, and in the warlike enthusiasm of the minute demand to "be led there." Their colonel promises them that "the battle shall be short and desperate."*

This is from a series of six cartoons that traces the military adventures of "Mr. Tobias" and his buddies as they form a military company, elect all members as officers, have their portraits taken, and finally are overwhelmed by a gaggle of angry geese. Even a year into the Civil War, home front readers were willing to chuckle at the thought of grown men playing soldier. Notice how this New York cartoon featured a military company that shared much in common with Artemus Ward's men from Baldinsville. *Frank Leslie's Budget of Fun* (June 1862): 5. Courtesy of HarpWeek.

expense. In a series of six cartoons the reader meets "Mr. Tobias," a clerk at a dry goods store. Early in the war Mr. Tobias is so swept up in war fever that he gets all the young men in his boardinghouse to form a regiment. They immediately elect "Tug" as their colonel, and the rest all claim roles as captains or other officers. (Like Ward's Baldinsville men, none intend to be a mere private.) Tug celebrates his new position by going to the photographic studio to have his portrait taken in his new Zouave uniform. The men then gather and drill, complimenting each other on their performance. In the final scene these home front soldiers are surrounded by angry geese who threaten to overwhelm the men and drive them from the field.[14]

In some respects, the silly men of the Home Guard are reminiscent of the urban swells. Both caricatures portrayed privileged young men enjoying the good life at home while other men were off at war. But whereas the swells seemed almost unaware of the realities of war, the men who ate at Delmonico's or drank at Willard's in their fancy uniforms enjoyed the benefits of their shoulder straps while intentionally avoiding battle. Their hypocrisy was a greater affront to northern society, because these uniformed men—unlike the swells—had some awareness of the war's realities, yet chose to adopt a fraudulent role. Like the swells, these frivolous urban young men were both wealthy and almost always presented as New Yorkers. Thus both class and place set these stereotyped characters apart from other northerners, and readers nationwide could take pleasure in seeing familiar antebellum regional hostilities revisited in a wartime setting. Wealth and privilege, it seemed, enabled some to profit from the war without risk.

Another recurring character in the printed commentary was the unethical colonel who hung around the home front, ostensibly recruiting men for a new regiment. In September 1861 one such fellow appeared in a *Frank Leslie's Budget of Fun* cartoon as a mustachioed colonel reclining on a hammock with a cigar in his mouth, a bottle of brandy at his side, and cans of meats and anchovies—no doubt stolen from military stores—on a shelf behind him. His clerk sits at a desk, recording the names of new recruits. "Bill, you must put thirty more names at least on the roll," he instructs. "It will be impossible to drink and smoke cigars on our pay, without we have a few dummies in each company." This, the cartoonist explains, is why there are "so many missing men after a battle": unscrupulous officers were stuffing regimental rolls with fake names and profiting from their lies. In January 1862 the *Chicago Tribune* adopted a less playful tone, remarking at all the partially filled regiments that crowded the city's camps, waiting to complete their numbers and head for the front, while "thousands of wearers of shoulder straps [were] loitering about in various parts of the country, ostensibly recruiting, but in reality living at ease on the people's money."[15]

As Hawthorne noted, some of the more reprehensible characters were those who intentionally donned fake uniforms in order to earn admiration or to reap other rewards. In October 1861 *Vanity Fair* published a satirical editorial in the form of a letter to a certain "young gentleman in Broadway" who had no military position but had taken to parading the streets in a flashy uniform shortly after Fort Sumter fell. In those first days, the author recalled, "pretty women peeped at you from underneath drooping eyelids," while men were quick to "take you by the hand because they

COLONEL.—" *Bill, you must put down thirty more names at least on the roll.   It will be impossible to drink and smoke cigars all day upon our pay, without we have a few dummies in each company.   Put down a dozen Smiths, and half a dozen Browns, Joneses and Robinsons.*"
ORDERLY—" *All right, colonel—I know my duties.*"
[This fully accounts for the missing men after a battle.]

Reports of long lists of men "missing" after battles prompted this cartoonist to suggest that colonels were padding their regiments' ranks and pocketing the pay of nonexistent soldiers. In a single image, the cartoonist managed to get digs in at the false colonels and the war's unethical war profiteers. *Frank Leslie's Budget of Fun* (September 1861): 16. Courtesy of HarpWeek.

thought you were going to give your aid to the country." But now, after a half year of posturing on Broadway, "you are regarded in a manner not wholly unconnected with contempt." So, in conclusion, the biting letter asked: *"Don't you think it is about time you took off that uniform?"* [16]

Boston's *Ballou's Monthly Magazine* had fun with these miscreants in a twelve-part cartoon called "Effects of the War on M. De Laine . . ." M. De Laine, a hapless dry goods clerk, loses his job during the war-induced

Effects of the War on M. De Laine, a fashionable Dry Goods Clerk.

He is informed by his employer that, owing to the depressed state of business, his services will not be wanted in future.

He tries in vain to procure a situation, grows desperate, curses the war and his luck

Has at first some idea of joining the army—but finding he would be obliged to go as a common soldier, he is disgusted and gives it up.

Funds getting low, and his landlady being anxious for her bill, he concludes to step out, and thus rid himself of her troublesome demands.

MONEY LOANED

Now hard up, he is determined to have some money, and pawns his watch to a friendly broker.

Being in funds again, he attends the opera, hoping some rich lady will fall in love with him; he attracts the attention of a lady, and resolves to accompany her home.

This series of twelve cartoons follows the adventures of dry goods clerk M. De Laine. Having determined that he does not wish to enlist as a mere infantryman, M. De Laine makes a series of progressively foolish decisions, until he finds himself posing as a soldier who he believes is safely off at the front. In the final frame his irate double appears to break up M. De Laine's fake marriage. *Bailou's Monthly Magazine* (March 1862). Courtesy of the American Antiquarian Society.

Imagine his surprise to find it is his landlady, who, seeing him at the opera, thinks she will take the opportunity to get her little bill.

He hits upon a new idea—he will represent an officer in the army of his name; he procures a uniform, and goes into society.

Thinking he must have something to create a sensation, he sets his cap up, and discharges his revolver at it, and completely riddles it with balls.

The dodge takes; he is made a great lion of; every one has heard of his brilliant deeds on the field of battle; he captivates a rich and dashing widow.

Preparations are made for a wedding on a grand scale—the city is alive with excitement—they proceed to the cathedral, to be joined in happy bonds for life.

Just as the ceremony begins in rushes the real Captain De Laine of the United States army; the bride faints, and our hero leaves for parts unknown.

economic downturn. He considers enlisting, but rejects the idea when he learns that he would have to enter service as a mere infantryman. So he pawns his watch and goes to the opera in hopes of snagging a rich woman's attentions. When this plan fails, he purchases a military uniform and adopts the identity of a real Union officer who shares his name. To make the impression more dramatic, M. de Laine takes a revolver and fires several bullets into his cap. This dodge works, as the counterfeit war hero wins the heart of a wealthy widow and they are soon to wed. But on the day of the wedding the real Captain de Laine returns from the field, the anguished widow faints, "and our hero leaves for parts unknown."[17]

As civilians on the home front became more familiar with the realities of real military service, reactions to fraud grew more acerbic. In April 1862 *Vanity Fair* reviewed the recently published *New York State Army List*. The entire column was devoted to how this official list would be an excellent resource for uncovering those "swaggering persons who have been traveling upon sword and spurs for some time past," accepting free drinks and meals as fraudulent soldiers. A few weeks later, the journal reprinted a story warning hotel owners and tailors about scam artists who had been in the city claiming to be naval officers. *Vanity Fair* also reported that similar confidence men in uniform had been cheating people in Washington. And whereas in October 1861 the journal simply mocked the uniformed man who had been parading on Broadway, in May 1862—after many months of hard fighting—*Vanity Fair* published a no-nonsense commentary, attacking "the blue-and-gold, shoulder-strapped shams who dawdle about our streets," under a familiar title: "Young Man! Take Off That Uniform!"[18]

Similar messages found their way into comic valentines that entertained northerners. One such "valentine" depicted "A Fancy Soldier" with this verse:

> Your swashing gate and vacant stare,
> Pleased fools in times of peace;
> But since afraid to go to war,
> Put off the duds and cease.

It was one thing to wear military finery in peacetime, but a very different matter in times of war.[19]

When manpower shortages led to new calls for recruits and talk of conscription, the satire about the men of the Home Guard grew less amused and more hostile. In "The Home Guard's Complaint"—published in June 1862—an anonymous poet portrayed one such soldier declaring,

A FANCY SOLDIER.

Your swashing gate and vacant stare,
Pleased fools in times of peace;
But since afraid to go to war,
Put off the duds and cease.

Comic valentines were a particularly popular comic art form in the mid-nineteenth century, and especially during the Civil War. This drawing mocks the men on the home front who parade around in uniforms without going to war. Courtesy of the Library Company of Philadelphia.

You command me to go, when I hoped to remain.
My buttons are bright, and my uniform is gay,
And I only desired at soldier's to play.[20]

Much as patience for the silly swells eventually wore thin, this poem published during the war's second year is unambiguous in attacking those Home Guard soldiers who merely wish to "play" at war.

With men beginning to return home on furlough, the faux soldiers found a new opportunity to exploit. The poem "The Soldier on Leave" described uniformed men who were appearing on city streets claiming to be wounded heroes, when in fact they had never seen a battlefield. The narrator concludes:

Some call me a coward; that isn't polite;
For how can you think a poor sick man to fight?
And then Generosity's very sublime . . .
Aren't you willing a Coward should have a good time?[21]

In a cartoon titled "Self Respect," *Vanity Fair* showed a combat veteran wearing an unmarked overcoat over his real uniform to avoid being confused for a member of the Home Guard.[22] Just as the images of wounded soldiers placed in cartoons alongside home front swells had presented readers with a sharp contrast, the return of furloughed veterans weary from the battlefield ensured that the North would no longer wink at dishonest shoulder straps.

SHOULDER STRAPS

In his second home front novel, *Shoulder Straps*, Henry Morford took on these false soldiers with a vengeance. Set in New York in the first eighteen months of the war, the novel features a complex cast of characters. In an early chapter we meet the charming and clever Josephine "Joe" Harris, who is close friends with Richard Crawford, an invalid suffering from some undisclosed illness. Joe feels very protective of Richard and makes it clear that she believes Crawford's cousin, Egbert, is up to no good. Egbert is a colonel in the army, but Joe mutters about how he "strut[s] about with his shoulder-straps and red sword belts," hinting that even his military rank is suspect.[23]

The next chapter introduces Emily Owen, a young woman of quick wit and modest means who is being pressured into an arranged marriage with the wealthy financial speculator John Broadley Bancker. She prefers Frank Wallace, a humble printer. Bancker is a colonel in the army and makes much of the fact that he is busy recruiting a regiment, but Emily scoffs at his efforts, referring disparagingly to his "shoulder straps" the first time we meet the pair. Before long both suitors are at Emily's home, competing for her affections. Frank tries to bait Bancker into a fight by suggesting that despite his fine uniform the colonel is really a coward and his regiment a fiction. As the two men leave the Owen residence, they see a runaway carriage flying down the street. As if to confirm Frank's claims, Bancker cowers in fright while the young printer leaps into the street to stop the carriage and save the day.[24]

This episode underscores several points. Bancker, the braggart with the flashy uniform, is revealed as a hypocrite and a coward. The reader

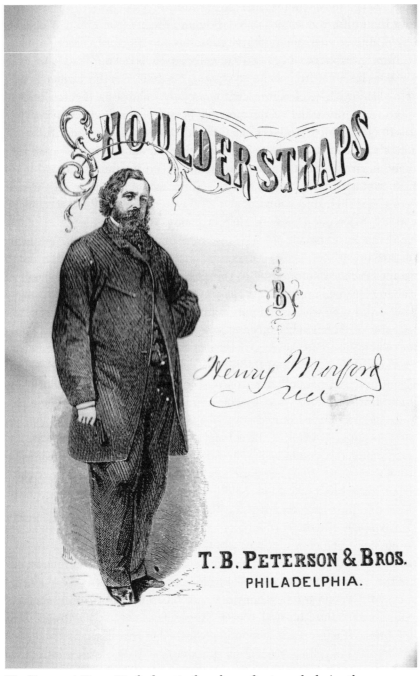

SHOULDER-STRAPS

BY

Henry Morford

T. B. PETERSON & BROS.
PHILADELPHIA.

War Democrat Henry Morford wrote three home front novels during the war years. *Shoulder Straps*, Morford's first novel, took on the faux soldiers who paraded around eastern cities. The flyleaf of Morford's novel included a picture of the author. Author's personal collection.

does not yet know whether he is really recruiting a regiment, but we learn that the uniform does not make the man. Meanwhile, Frank Wallace is brave, able-bodied, and unmarried. Nothing in Morford's descriptions of the printer explains why he has not enlisted. He is not opposed to the war, nor does he suffer from some mysterious disability. Yet this civilian is presented as both a heroic figure and the proper romantic partner for Emily.[25]

Morford shifts the scene to Long Island, where Egbert Crawford's 200th New York Volunteers is supposed to be encamped and drilling.[26] Despite much flattering newspaper commentary about the fine new regiment, it turns out that Egbert has failed to recruit a full roster, and those men who are in camp are a rowdy and undisciplined lot, while the officers spend their time drinking at a local watering hole. These revelations confirm Josephine Harris's earlier suspicions that Egbert is a man of low character. Sure enough, she soon discovers that Egbert has been poisoning his cousin with some mysterious substance as part of an elaborate plot to acquire Richard's property.[27] In this fashion, Morford yokes misdeeds in a character's personal life with failures to act as a proper wartime citizen. The sort of man who would poison his cousin is precisely the sort of citizen who would fail in his duty as a soldier.[28] This discovery opens up a long and complex subplot, where Joe cleverly thwarts Egbert and saves the day.

Along the way, Joe and Emily meet, and Emily reveals that she loves Frank but that her father keeps pushing Colonel Bancker on her. Joe orchestrates a clever charade where Frank comes to Emily's home disguised as a wounded war veteran. In that role, Frank regales everyone in the household—including the colonel—with horrific tales of the war. The poor "colonel" becomes so agitated that Frank gets him to admit that he has no regiment and is a complete fraud. Frank lunges for Bancker, pulling off his wig and revealing a balding head. All share a hearty laugh at the miserable "shoulder strapped" fraud.[29]

This is quite an extraordinary scene in a wartime novel. Frank, the masculine hero who is destined to win the heroine, is a civilian posing as a wounded soldier in order to unveil Bancker, the fraud who is pretending to be an officer. Frank's talk of bloody battles provides the powerful contrast between the false and the real, much as the cartoons showing veterans encountering swells throws the evils of the latter into sharp relief. Frank's final lunge at his competitor further reveals that Bancker is a balding fellow, calling his supposed masculine virility further into question. But notice that this is a scene with no real soldiers. Like characters in a Shakespearean comedy, people are not always as they appear to be.

On Fools, Hypocrites, and Scoundrels

But whereas Bancker's uniform and wig indicate deceit, Frank only temporarily wears a disguise to uncover his rival's fraud.

Shoulder Straps ends with a long chapter that picks up the book's many threads. Bancker stops wearing his uniform and wig and never returns to the Owens' home. Frank continues to date Emily, but without her father's approval. The subject of Frank's enlisting in the army never comes up. Free of Egbert's poisons, Richard Crawford is quickly restored to full health and marries. He also does not consider enlisting. Joe falls in love with Tom, the central figure in an entirely separate narrative thread (he is also not a soldier). The 200th is combined with another regiment, and Egbert—humbled by his many personal and professional sins—volunteers to be aide-de-camp for General Hooker. In the book's final pages Egbert dies while leading a small cavalry charge at Antietam, effectively erasing his earlier sins.[30]

Shoulder Straps was a quite popular, widely reviewed novel.[31] As such, it is a useful window into public sentiments midway through the war. The core message is hardly subtle. Morford, like the cartoonists at *Vanity Fair*, Nathaniel Hawthorne in the *Atlantic Monthly*, and any number of other northern commentators, was setting his sights on the war's con men: the scores of shoulder-strap-wearing frauds and hypocrites produced by the national crisis. Egbert Crawford had secured a military office and reaped the social benefits of his position, while failing to do his job or prepare his men for combat. John Bancker bought a uniform and a wig and tried to profit from the sacrifices of other men.[32] Both men attempted to parlay their false military finery into undeserved romantic success. Each of them illustrates the worst sort of home front citizen, as well as how the personal and the patriotic became intertwined. Characters who fake their patriotism are not to be trusted in their personal relationships. But if the disreputable men are the ones who flaunt their false uniforms for personal gain, the reverse is not necessarily the case. The extensive cast of *Shoulder Straps* includes a few soldiers, but nearly all of the heroic men, including Frank Wallace, are not soldiers and in fact never discuss enlisting.

Lest his plot leave readers unconvinced, in the middle of the novel Morford injected a long chapter offering broader commentary on the war and home front society as things stood in June and July 1862. "Half of the New York regiments," he claimed, "had originally been officered by men who had no intention of fighting, and who merely took commissions and spent a few weeks in camp or in the field of inactive operations, in order that they might have 'Colonel,' or 'Major,' or Captain attached to their names."

Then there was "the other class—those who had never intended to go at all—those who had no heart in the cause . . . and who had merely assumed the regulation uniform to feed *vanity* or their *pocket*." These men could be found strutting on Broadway, visiting the theater, or "creat[ing] sensations at the watering-places." Barely a year into the Civil War, men on the home front were apparently free to live and love as happy civilians, so long as they did not claim the cultural rewards of the uniform.

OUR DEPARTED BRAVES

By the summer of 1862, Union army commanders had begun to take action to drag military officers from cushy hotels back to the seat of war. In May, H. C. Whitney, the paymaster for the US Army, announced that in future officers in the volunteer army could not receive their pay if they were absent from their regiments. The *Chicago Tribune* thought this a splendid idea, noting that it was a "timely hint to gentlemen fond of displaying their shoulder straps in civic circles" while "depriving the camps of the light of their buttons and gold lace."[33]

On July 7 General Ambrose Burnside issued General Orders No. 2 to crack down on the widespread practice of officers resigning their commissions "from caprice or fancied wrongs." In future, Burnside warned, any officer who attempts to abandon his position "while his brothers are daily expecting orders to march against the enemy, will not be accepted, and will remain only as a record of disgrace against him as one who, from an unworthy personal motive, is willing to commit moral treason."[34] The *Wisconsin Daily Patriot* celebrated Burnside's order, noting that it had become commonplace for officers in the Army of the Potomac to give up their fighting commands and then turn around and accept military positions recruiting men for the home "*defence of Washington*."[35]

Only a few weeks after he took over the newly formed Army of Virginia, General John Pope issued a strongly worded order, creating a pass system to regulate the movements of officers and men in his command, and particularly to stop the practice of officers leaving the army for junkets into Washington. Officers caught away from their posts after July 22 would be "arrested and tried for disobedience of orders."[36] The Washington press reported that by July 21 General Pope's order had already "had a visible effect in the hotels, saloons and other public resorts in the city" and that "shoulder straps have been few and far between."[37] The following month Pope further ordered that mounted patrols "shall scour the whole country for 5 miles around their camps at least once every day . . . to bring into their respective commands all persons absent without proper authority."[38] The next day, Major General John E. Wool added a General Order from the Eighth Army Corps in Harrisburg, Pennsylvania, in response to reports that "scarcely an officer is found in the Camp attending to his business of preparing men for departing to Washington." In future, officers would only be allowed to leave camp on official business. The *Philadelphia Inquirer* praised this move, noting that of late "our military officers sport their tinseled uniforms and blazing shoulder-straps on promenade; sleeping at the 'best hotels,' and enjoying costly liquors and wines, while their men have been neglected."[39]

In early November—only days after Abraham Lincoln removed General George McClellan from command—Major General Henry Halleck issued a short Special Order directing all officers in the Army of the Potomac to return to their commands or risk being removed from military service.[40] It almost seemed as if the Union leadership had decided to heed the words of Hawthorne's "Peaceable Man." *Vanity Fair* marked the occasion with a humorous poem dedicated to "Our Departed Braves." Where, the poet asked, were those soldiers, "So trim, so debonair, / So affluent of hair" who had so recently "beautified our streets and cut such swells / On the front stoops of all of our big hotels." Thanks to Halleck's "rude dispatch" these uniformed dandies had "left our maids and widows quite *distrait* / And taken all the shine out of Broadway." Meanwhile, the poem continued, the "Men of the swordless fist" were now wondering, "shall I enlist," and claim the vacated spots in hotels and on street corners? "We might not have to go, / Into the fight you know."[41]

"The Discarded Lieutenant's Lament," sung to the tune of the popular "The Irish Emigrant's Lament," targeted Union officers who lost their commissions after Halleck's order. The lieutenant mourns the lost days when he "roamed at large through Willard's bar," sharing war stories with his "brother-heroes of the war." But in November, "Col. Halleck me foreswore," and before long the provost marshal had broken up his happy life. Even though the lieutenant had given up his stripes, he had not lost hope "while Politics do reign." With any luck at all "my Congressman will me array with shoulder-straps again!"[42] Although the discarded lieutenant remained hopeful for the future, by the close of 1862 the terrain had shifted. Civilians on the home front would no longer tolerate officers displaying their shoulder straps in bars while their comrades were dying in the field. Moreover, after a year and a half of warfare the Union army had evolved into a highly organized professional army, with no room for fraudulent officers.

THE DISCARDED LIEUTENANT'S LAMENT.

AIR.—"The Irish Emigrant's Lament."

I'M laid upon the shelf, MARY,
  My heart is very sore;
One cold November morn, Mary,
  Old HALLECK me foreswore.
Once, flush of chinky—so to speak—
  My lark soared loud and high,
Pale brandy's bloom upon my cheek,
  The dew-drop in my eye.

I roamed at large through WILLARD'S bar,
  Where I was wont to meeet
My brother-heroes of the war,
  And tales of blood repeat.
No more "refreshments" now, I ween,
  Nor slings nor cocktails rare,
Nor spree till with gray morning's sheen
  Came Provost-Marshal's care.

Farewell to all—the drum, the fife,
  The army's blissful ease!
Where late I lapped of sparkling life
  I now absorb its lees:
But hope forbids me to give way
  While Politics do reign,
My Congressman will me array
  With shoulder-straps again!

This satirical song plays on the popular song "The Irish Emigrant's Lament." In this case, the speaker is one of the lazy shoulder straps who had happily hung around Willard's Hotel. Now new regulations and a newly energetic Provost Marshal's Office have destroyed the life he once loved. The lyrics illustrate the specific point about the North's unsavory shoulder straps, while also demonstrating how political topics quickly found their way into popular verse. *Vanity Fair*, December 13, 1862, 286. Courtesy of HarpWeek.

Meanwhile, new federal measures punished civilians who paraded around in uniforms with no connection to real military service. One newspaper reported that three hundred of these frauds had been detained in Washington by late November, including various local "gamblers and blacklegs" who had been passing themselves off as Union officers. The *Tribune* praised these efforts in the East, but urged federal officials to enforce the same rules in Chicago in order to round up the local "gang of villains" who still masqueraded as Union soldiers.[43]

Even with the military crackdown on shoulder straps and deserters, the occasional problems persisted, and reports of these disreputable men periodically found their way to all corners of the Union. In September 1862 the *Baltimore American* reported on the "multitudinous shoulder straps" in Washington, DC. "On the Avenue, one man out of every three you meet wears shoulder straps, and in the corridors, public rooms and billiard saloons of the hotels, their number is still preponderating."[44] Across the country, the *San Francisco Bulletin* ran a lengthy "Letter from Philadelphia" on January 10, 1863. The author caught the West Coast readers up on all sorts of goings-on in the City of Brotherly Love, including comments on the federal draft and an extended discussion of the city's shoulder-strap problem: "Notwithstanding the recent stringent orders of the War Department, in regard to officers absent from their commands, there are still a good many loafing about this city, delighting the hearts of silly girls with their attentions and 'shoulder straps'; and disgusting every true patriot. . . . They ought to be stripped of their trappings and put in a hen-coop."[45] A few weeks later the *Wisconsin Daily Patriot* published an encouraging report, noting that recent congressional action "providing for reducing all absent officers to the ranks" seemed likely to "cause a rattling among the brass buttons and shoulder straps."[46]

The problems of absentee officers and imposters in uniform wandering the streets and watering holes never completely disappeared during the Civil War, but the northern focus on these disreputable types reached its apex in the war's first eighteen months. These were the months when volunteers stepped forward fairly readily and civilians on the home front expressed admiration for patriotic citizen-soldiers. The public conversation—in novels, cartoons, and editorials—initially mocked those men who seemed to want to bask in the reflected glory of the real soldiers. But when tales of battlefield carnage found their way to the home front, the satire became more pointed. The message was clear. Northern society seemed willing to accept that some men would choose not to enlist for various reasons, but they soon turned on those men who attempted to impress by donning fake uniforms. As the federal military effort became more professionally organized, it became more difficult for men to profit from the war effort while staying out of harm's way. Or, at least, they could not take advantage of the war merely by putting on a blue uniform and a set of shoulder straps.

In the world of northern public discourse, the "shoulder straps" had a close cousin in the "commission seeker." If the former was a glory-seeking fraud, the latter was equally focused on claiming public admiration, although with somewhat less dishonesty. These men, who cropped up regularly in fiction, cartoons, and satire, seemed willing to enlist and go to war, but they had definite conditions. The commission seekers would enlist only if they were guaranteed a military commission befitting their perceived rank in society and their clear—although heretofore untapped—military talents. Some, like the cartoon "swells," seemed to be honestly unclear about the qualifications required of officers, but others believed that they were too good to sign up as mere enlisted men. In so doing, they contemplated enlistment—an ostensibly patriotic act—only as mediated by the expectations of their class.

In March 1862, *Vanity Fair* took on the "place-hunting petitioners" who had no military background but for some reason had "an insane desire to be appointed to some nice, easy, military office, such as that of Brigadier General."[47] A few months later, the humor weekly ran a long letter from "Macarone," who described an ambitious young man who wanted to join the cavalry but insisted that despite his utter lack of experience, he should be at least a lieutenant.[48] As we saw in "The War Fever in Baldinsville," Artemus Ward's fellow citizens in the imagined Indiana town insisted that if they must serve, they should all be officers.[49] In a later story, Ward mocked the ambitious "Mr. Flambeau," who protested that his high level of patriotism would best be served by putting him in some well-paid political appointment rather than as a humble private.[50] Joseph Barber's Disbanded Volunteer wrote from Washington's National Hotel, which he found crowded with anxious office seekers and men in search of undeserved military commissions. "Ef thar was the same paytryiotic competishin for places in the ranks, a millyun of men mought be razed in six weeks without a cornskripthin," he declared.[51]

The authors of romantic fiction made the same point by celebrating characters who resisted such crass motivations. One short story in *Peterson's Magazine* featured a humble Union recruit who is teased by his friends for enlisting without a commission, but he wins respect and advancement on the battlefield and returns home to marry his sweetheart.[52] In her serialized *Breaking Hearts*, Mary A. Howe constructs a complex plotline where a character initially negotiates for a military commission as a condition of enlisting, but ends up volunteering as a private and moving through the ranks based on his own valor.[53] In these and other wartime stories one type of manly hero was the character who refuses to claim a commission, but instead earns his shoulder straps on the battlefield.

Both the faux shoulder straps and the cynical commission seekers deserved public distain because they actively sought to exploit the national crisis for their own glory. It was their dishonesty and self-aggrandizement that set these men outside the bounds of acceptable behavior, making them targets for both satirists and authors of popular fiction. Meanwhile, able-bodied men who simply went about their own business without donning a uniform seemed to attract little public scorn in the home front literature. As we shall see in the next chapter, those who found economic profits during the war's first years provoked an entirely different conversation about citizenship, ethics, and wartime, but in its essence the issues were quite similar: northern society rejected those people who acted fraudulently or hypocritically, or who seemed to enjoy undeserved benefits in the midst of war.

CHAPTER THREE

Your Diamonds May Flash Gaily, But There's Blood on Them

A Shoddy Aristocracy

In the previous chapter we saw the first scenes in Henry Morford's *The Days of Shoddy*. News of the fall of Fort Sumter arrives in New York, and enthusiastic clerk Burt Haviland resolves to join the Union army, supported by the patriotic assistance of his employer, Charles Holt. But much as Morford's villainous characters in *Shoulder Straps* revealed their true nature by exploiting the war for personal gains, Charles Holt was not the selfless patriot and philanthropist that he seemed in those first few pages. Within hours of learning that war had begun, Holt was writing to his partner—in Europe on business—urging him to buy up all the cloth he could in anticipation of the upcoming demand for uniforms. Soon we discover that Holt's generosity to Burt was merely a ruse to get his clerk out of the way so that he could attempt to seduce the lad's lovely and naive young wife, Mary. In this fashion, Morford links the morality of the sexual predator to that of the cynical war profiteer. Despite his best efforts, Holt fails to seduce Mary, and after a complex series of events he is captured by Confederate troops who believe—incorrectly—that he is a Union spy. In the novel's final chapter, Holt's estranged Rebel wife is walking down the street in Richmond and sees her husband in the window of Libby Prison. She tells a soldier that the man in the window is trying to escape and offers him a gold coin to shoot the culprit. The soldier complies, blowing off the top of Holt's head with a single shot.

Holt's violent death seems to be the ultimate prescriptive message, warning readers of the price of despicable behavior. The clothier's attempts to ruin Mary and destroy his clerk's marriage are personal failings that are central to the narrative, but Morford concludes his volume by returning to Holt's sins against the nation. "Men of the stamp of Charles Holt," he warns, "will still attempt to outrage every precept of honor and virtue, . . . and they will not think it beneath them, while they are taking advantage of the absence of patriotic men in the public service, to destroy the peace of homes once happy,—to buy and sell a few rotten satinets, shoddy clothes, shoes with glued soles, muskets without vents and tents made of six-cent muslin, and all other army supplies of a corresponding character, to maintain or increase ill-won fortunes, or to furnish themselves with the means of indulging the costlier luxuries and vices." In this discussion Morford slipped seamlessly from indicting the personal immorality of Holt's ilk to the economic immorality and patriotic failings of men who sold shoddy merchandise to the army. He went on to predict that those who grow suddenly wealthy in wartime will suffer dire consequences: "The wealth suddenly acquired by knavery is sure to curse its holder with ridicule, if it brings with it no worse punishment. The wife of the shoddy millionaire will buy diamonds that she can neither appreciate nor value and wear them so unfitly and ungracefully that every gem will cast a new ray of light on the splendid misery of her position. The shoddy millionaire himself will struggle for places in social life and public employment, for which he is no more fitted than desired; and every upward step which he succeeds in taking will but make him a more shining mark for covert ridicule or open detestation."[1]

In these two long editorial interludes, Morford was describing different sorts of economic sins and seemingly conflating all the perpetrators under the same "shoddy" label. Some contractors were truly guilty of selling shoddy merchandise. The term "shoddy" originally described cheap cloth made by pressing together textile scraps. Such material might look fine on casual inspection, but it would not stand up to hard marching or heavy wear. During the Civil War, Americans used the term much more broadly, while keeping with the same general definition. Shoddy merchandise was of poor quality, usually sold under false pretenses. Burnt coffee or undersized tents threatened the soldier's creature comforts, but the greater outrage was reserved for cheap shoes, poorly made uniforms, faulty ammunition, or anything that was liable to put the fighting man at risk.

The second long passage shifts attention from the shoddy material to the purveyors themselves. The contractor whose sudden riches outstripped his capacity to spend with the proper style and dignity deserved public sanction. The wives who wore their new rings "unfitly" had tried to climb beyond their station. By the midpoint of the war, these newly wealthy people—perhaps as much as the true crooks who sold shoddy merchandise—would became the object of widespread public scorn, regardless of the quality of their goods.

On Fools, Hypocrites, and Scoundrels

Morford's Charles Holt bridged those two shoddy types, while not quite matching either. He was not guilty of selling the army shoddy goods. His sin was that he exploited the emergency for his own gains, thinking about individual profits while others thought only of national patriotism. He was also not really one of the war's newly wealthy. He had wealth when the war began, and did his best to make more. In this malevolent character, Morford stitched together Holt's sexual and patriotic immorality, while using lengthy interludes to point a broader finger at the Union's war profiteers. His readers knew that Holt was a bad guy because of his personal transgressions, but it would be up to northern society to decide when wartime profits called for social sanction.[2]

THE DREAM OF THE ARMY CONTRACTOR

Reports of unscrupulous war contracts selling shoddy merchandise to the military began to crop up almost as soon as the Civil War began. The fact that there were such problems early in the war should come as no surprise. Before the war began, the Union army totaled little more than sixteen thousand men. By January 1862 the North had over seven hundred thousand men in uniform. The logistical challenges involved in arming and outfitting such a huge fighting force in such a short period of time were almost overwhelming. Quartermasters scrambled to acquire the equipment to get their regiments armed and into the field; independent manufacturers competed for war contracts while desperately trying to find the raw materials and labor to meet their deadlines; federal officials established a network of regional arsenals for manufacturing military goods. For a time things were fairly chaotic, as each of the participants in this emerging war-contracting system learned his or her job. No doubt people of goodwill sometimes bought and sold inferior products. It was also an ideal moment for profiteers and con men to exploit the opportunities.[3]

Popular outrage over shoddy uniforms and sleazy war profiteers soon prompted a series of government investigations. In June, Pennsylvania governor Andrew G. Curtin named a committee to investigate charges of fraud within the state. Their report, published in August, failed to identify any outright fraud, but the committee had harsh words about poor management and unpatriotic war profiteering. New Yorkers soon learned of scandals involving faulty uniforms contracted by Brooks Brothers.[4] Several other reports and published investigations followed. In July 1861 the House of Representatives named a five-man select committee, initially chaired by New York congressman Charles Van Wyck, to investigate contract fraud nationwide. The New York and Pennsylvania reports certainly interested the committee, but some of the biggest revelations came out of investigations of General John Frémont's Western Department, headquartered in St. Louis. The Van Wyck Committee issued a preliminary report in December, which included more than a thousand pages of testimony on fraud and wrongdoing. The committee—later under the chairmanship of Elihu Washburn—published a second interim report in July 1862 and its final report the following March.[5] These congressional reports, which combined to exceed three thousand pages, became the subject of widespread debate and controversy, providing the backdrop to much of the public conversation about shoddy contractors.[6]

Although reports of fraud and war profiteering would persist throughout the Civil War and the products of official investigations and court cases would trickle out for years, the Union army had begun to solve the worst problems by the war's second year. In January 1862, Abraham Lincoln replaced his ineffectual secretary of war, Simon Cameron, with Edwin M. Stanton, who immediately took measures to clean up war contracting. Meanwhile, the Quartermaster's Department, under the able leadership of Montgomery Meigs, evolved into a much more organized and efficient organization. These developments did not remove fraud, but they certainly limited the worst offenses.[7]

Like the public responses to the "shoulder straps," the earliest printed commentary on the shoddy contractors tended to be light satire. Philadelphia engraver George Wevill published a pair of cards, titled "Before" and "After," showing the impact of the highly publicized inquiries. In the first, the fat-cheeked war contractor is pleased to have made "a few thousand off my Contract for supplying the Volunteers." In the second, the same man's hair is blown back and his glasses are in flight as he learns that the "Grand Jury have found a true bill" and the volunteers intend to tar and feather him when they return to town.[8] In June 1861, *Vanity Fair* published a poem, "War Contractors!," decrying the bad meat and flimsy uniforms that these scoundrels had been foisting on the army, concluding that when they reach the gates of heaven they will find a sign announcing "No Jobbing Contractors Admitted."[9] A month later, as news of shoddy uniforms from Philadelphia's Girard House began circulating in the press, *Vanity Fair*'s cover cartoon depicted a gathering of Pennsylvania soldiers wearing hopelessly frayed uniform pants, as a sergeant orders the men to "close up" so that the approaching ladies would not be embarrassed by the gaps in their attire.[10]

Joseph Barber's Disbanded Volunteer commented extensively on the

This comic two-sided card, created by engraver George Wevill, shows a fat and happy contractor on one side, and the same man after he was charged with contract fraud by the Grand Jury on the other side. Courtesy of the Library Company of Philadelphia.

state of affairs in July, noting that sutlers and quartermasters "continnees to swindl the poor sojers as ushil." And when he spoke with a noted clothing contractor about the recent government investigations, he claimed, the man simply laughed in his face. The following year the Disbanded Volunteer devoted several of his weekly letters to tales of corruption and shoddy merchandise, directing choice (and largely incoherent) words at the "horseflesh hounds, shoddy swindlers, beef bandity, riful raskills, provishin pirits, blankit belzebubs, and the gallus birds of that fether."[11]

In August, *Vanity Fair* ran a particularly bitter poem, "The Dream of the Army Contractor," by Charles Graham Halpine (unattributed). The poem begins with "Old Hucklebury," a wealthy war contractor, sitting in his comfortable chair after a sumptuous meal and bottles of fine wine. "Old Hucklebury" drifts off to sleep and has a horrible nightmare where he is visited by the skeleton of a Union soldier who makes him drink a poisonous liquid. In the last line, the terrified "old fellow woke with a yell!"

This *Vanity Fair* cover is commenting on the recently published reports of shoddy uniforms having been produced by the Girard House contractors in Philadelphia. The uniforms are in such tatters that they are no longer suitable for the company of ladies, forcing the men to "close up" to maintain their dignity. *Vanity Fair*, July 6, 1861, cover. Courtesy of HarpWeek.

The journal illustrated the poem with a drawing of a terrifying skeleton, dressed in shoddy rags, holding a goblet over a cowering Hucklebury. Four years later, shortly after the end of the war, the *Comic Monthly* would reprint the same poem, perhaps to remind its readers—and the shoddy contractors—of this dark chapter.[12]

"Song of the Shoddy," published only five months after the fall of Fort Sumter, tells the tale of shoddy in the alternating voices of the officer, the quartermaster, and the tailor. The "Song" illuminated how shoddy uniforms and faulty buttons had been undermining the Union war effort.

> Regiments of gallant fellows,
> In a pauper garb bedecked;
> Rippling seams and jackets ripping
> Pantaloons completely wretched?

Following the long and troublesome accounts of uniformed men marching into battle with the worst sort of shoddy uniforms, *Vanity Fair* seemed to have already lost its stomach for clever satire.[13]

Other humorists noted the role of corrupt government officials in the shoddy trade. One artist portrayed an inspector bending over a large barrel of stinking pork, while accepting a fifty-dollar bill to approve the rotten meat. The accompanying verse announced: "He's a curse to his kind— his country's worst bane, / Deserving the noose on the hangman's line."[14] Another small image, perhaps by the same artist, depicted a bearded "war contractor" with the caption: "Its not after glory you pant, / Its only after dollars and cents you want."[15]

As public attacks on the war contractors continued, the press took pains to educate its readers about the new challenges to military preparedness. In October, *Scientific American,* in response to "the charges, so extensively circulated against a portion of our army clothing contractors," published a brief tutorial on the true meaning of the word "shoddy."[16] The *New York Herald* explained that shoddy "is a counterfeit cloth made of pulverized old rags" that "dissolves under a soaking rain." But having offered a technical definition, the anti-Republican newspaper went on to portray Republican mayoral candidate George Opdyke as "the shoddy candidate," thus contributing to the expansion of the term's meaning in popular conversation.[17]

Shoddy remained a subject of occasional commentary and satire throughout the war, although public discussion about true contract corruption declined as reforms succeeded.[18] J. Ives Pease's poem "Shoddy"— reprinted in several newspapers—captured the national consensus about

The Dream of the Army Contractor.

Old HUCKLEBURY, the Army Contractor, lay snoozily back in his chair,
After a sumptuous dinner, such as became a millionaire.
Wines were upon the table, gathered from sundry foreign lands,
A vulgar splendor of bottles bearing curious trade-marks and brands.

At first his dream was auriferous : he fancied himself afloat,
Hauling up gold-fish, hand over hand, into a rose-wood boat ;
And as the fishes went flippety-flop among the ebony thwarts,
Their scales in yellow dollars flew off, and he pocketed them by quarts.

But, lo ! a distressing circumstance alloyed the bliss of his dream,
His clothes were turned into army cloth, and they gaped at every seam ;
And the golden dollars fell clinkety-clank from tattered trowsers and coat,
And, where they fell, they burned round holes through the bottom of the boat.

Then, as the old Army Contractor sank, with a shriek, into the deep,
He felt the grasp of a skeleton hand that doubled him into a heap,
And he heard the croak of a skeleton voice—"Look here, old HUCKLEBUR-EE,
You never was born to be drown-ded, so come along with me !

"I am the bones of a soldi-er, as died in the sickly camp,
Reduced by the pizenous food and the clothes that didn't keep out the damp ;
Likeways the sperrits that to us was sarved, worse liquor never I see ;
The thirst was on me—I drank it, and died—and now you must drink with me !"

And then it brandished its bony hands, that skeleton yellow and dry,
Making the vitriolic parts of a deadly cock-tail fly ;
Then came the skeleton voice, again—" Drink, 'tis the cup of Hell !"——
O ! the pallid lips and the glaring eyes, as old H. awoke with a yell !

This poem imagines the immoral army contractor being visited by a skeletal
soldier in his sleep. The poem, authored by Charles Graham Halpine (unattributed), was republished four years later in *Comic Monthly*. The poem
and accompanying image illustrate the early wartime outrage at these cynical war profiteers, who made their riches selling shoddy merchandise to the
Union army. *Vanity Fair*, August 17, 1861, 77. Courtesy of HarpWeek.

SHODDY.

You can't see it?. No wonder you can't,
  With a fifty dollar green back in your eye;
The soldier may starve—the sailor may want,
  What cares Shoddy if even they die?
He's a curse to his kind—his country's worst bane,
  Deserving the noose on the hangman's line;
But, alas, *you* don't get it, and to publish *your* shame,
  Is left alone for this poor Valentine.

N. Y. Union Valentine Co., No. 134 William St., N. Y.

This valentine takes a different approach to the shoddy problem: the cartoonist mocks the government inspectors who had been taking bribes to accept poor meat. Courtesy of the Library Company of Philadelphia.

THE ARMY CONTRACTOR.

For whiskyy os sell bad camphene toddy,
And clothe poor soldiers with flimsy shoddy;
Its not after glory that you *pant,*
Its only the dollars and cents you want.

One of several wartime valentines that mocked the selfish army contractor. The war contractor's long beard and clothing could be intended to portray him as a Jewish merchant turned war profiteer, thus linking wartime attacks on shoddy with antebellum anti-Semitism. Courtesy of the Library Company of Philadelphia.

the true shoddy contractor. In this angry verse Pease seems to have borrowed his scene from "The Dream of the Army Contractor." We see "Old Shoddy" sitting comfortably "in his easy-chair," indifferent to "the shivering soldier's prayer" or the "widows' and orphans wail." As Pease sees it, the "greedy ghoul of the shoddy-mill," who let men suffer in the cold in shoddy uniforms and under cheap blankets, is the worst "'traitor' the nation knows." It surely seems significant that Pease's contractor, unlike Halpine's "Hucklebury" of a year earlier, was undisturbed by the impact of his misdeeds. But even as the public outrage seemed particularly bitter, one journal prefaced the poem with a note that although shoddy was no longer much in evidence, "he still lives—especially in memory and poetry."[19]

Before long, the critics began to draw explicit links between the selling of shoddy and immoral war profiteering more broadly.[20] In so doing, they expanded their critique to include contractors who were not necessarily selling true "shoddy" merchandise. In October 1861 the editor of the *Cincinnati Gazette* surveyed the subscription lists for a new government loan and remarked sarcastically, "We were a good deal surprised at not finding among the subscribers any of the heavy government contractors." The *Chicago Tribune* concluded that these contractors were more interested in "fleec[ing]" the National Treasury, rather than assisting it.[21] In the satirical poem "The Contractor's Plaint," the pitiful contractor, reminiscent of Charles Holt, explains that

> I bought, just for a flyer,
> When merchants were in sorry straits,
> And, wishing to rate higher,
> I sold at higher rates.

But thanks to the recent reforms this contractor was forced to admit that "my golden reign is over, / I've had, like other dogs my day."[22]

Some other dogs, however, seemed to keep doing just fine. The July 1862 poem "Plundermongering" railed at the continuing scenes of the sick and wounded lying in "sultry sheds" while those "thieves count each morning in luxurious beds / Their tens of thousands, won where Avarice treads."[23] Well into the war's second year, those "cruel vipers" still slithered across the northern home front. In September 1862 the *Continental Monthly* published a harsh poem, "On War Contractors," portraying these businessmen as "dead to every gain but gold, / Deaf to every human sigh."[24] The following February the popular monthly issued a caution to the war's entrepreneurs under the heading "Mottoes for Contractors": "When you agree to clothe the body, / Expand your soul and flee from shoddy," the journal warned. And, further, "'Tis wise to feed the soldier well; / For reason *why*—see Dante's 'Hell.'"[25]

In 1864 Putnam P. Bishop published a long poem titled *Liberty's Ordeal*. In 128 pages of occasionally tortured verse, Bishop sought to promote continued patriotic loyalty despite years of hardship. Bishop devoted much of his attention to reminding his readers of the Union army's battlefield heroics and sacrifices, but he also had strong words for northern Copperheads and cowards and especially those war profiteers who had leapt forward when profits were to be made: "A greedy multitude sprang to their feet, / With rotten shoddy, and with tainted meat." But then, Putnam recalled, those same selfish entrepreneurs called for "Peace at Any Cost"

when talk turned to taxation. In 1864 the memories of these greedy contractors remained vivid, but Putnam's retrospective poem seemed to indicate that that particular part of the nation's ordeal was in the past.[26]

ADVENT OF THE SHODDY ARISTOCRACY

The published government investigations and subsequent editorials, cartoons, poems, and other commentary had combined to define two sorts of
evildoers in wartime society, both harking back to antebellum warnings
about duplicity and corruption. The first, and worst, were the sorts of war
contractors portrayed in J. Ives Pease's poem "Shoddy." These were the men
who made their riches by literally selling shoddy uniforms and materials,
and the government officials who were complicit in their misdeeds. But
before long that critique expanded to include men like Morford's Charles
Holt, who cynically profited from the war with seeming indifference to
the Union cause. By expanding the conversation beyond those contractors
guilty of criminal misconduct, the critics and satirists had implicitly raised
a complicated ethical question. What exactly was inappropriate when it
came to war contracting? The Union army depended on a combined system of government arsenals and private contractors. Some contractors
were small businessmen who competed for the occasional government
contract. Others were firms formed specifically to meet a particular war
need. Still others were very large enterprises with substantial government
contracts. Once the War Department and the Quartermaster's Department had corrected the worst abuses in the contracting system and ensured open and competitive bidding for government contracts, the war
effort had every interest in encouraging the production of war goods by
private firms.[27] What, then, was the proper measure of a war contractor
who claimed to be a patriotic citizen?

In November 1861 the *New York Herald* launched a series of satirical
essays that seemed to signal a shift in this developing public conversation.
In the first editorial, the *Herald* described a "social revolution" in the "advent of the shoddy aristocracy." The first months of the war, the New York
paper reported, had produced a change in the city's wealthiest classes.
Even while the secession crisis had robbed some cotton merchants of their
great wealth, the war had brought to the fore a new class of economic
elites, noteworthy for the "largeness of their gloves, the loudness of their
voices, their insane efforts to look through the wrong end of their opera
glasses, and their peculiarity of frequently and rapturously applauding at
the wrong times." Who were these people? the editorial asked. "They were

the government contractors and their families, who had made such heaps of money . . . by operations in shoddy, that they could afford to be great people." In the same way that the war had produced "our shoddy politicians and our shoddy generals . . . these are our shoddy aristocracy."[28]

With this editorial the *Herald* had coined a new term—"shoddy aristocracy"—while also painting a portrait of a social type who could be the proper target of the nation's wrath. In this first iteration, the shoddy aristocrats were still portrayed as people who had profited from their ill-gotten gains, but the markers that defined these social pariahs were based not on how they got their money, but how they *spent* it. The members of the shoddy aristocracy, or "shoddyaristocracy" (it soon evolved into a single word), revealed themselves because they had wealth without the knowledge and taste that is supposed to accompany those riches. They crammed their workingman's hands into gloves designed for the elites. They bought expensive tickets to the opera, but did not know how to behave there.

A few weeks later, the *Herald* continued its discussion of this new "social revolution," mocking the shoddy aristocrats who spend fortunes in expensive hotels, ride around Central Park displaying their new horses, and rent massive mansions vacated by the fallen members of the "Codfish and Cotton Cliques." Now, the *Herald* reported, members of the shoddy aristocracy were busily decorating their new homes with expensive and tacky furniture and art, while throwing grand parties lacking any sense of real style. Like real shoddy, the *Herald* predicted, these people would not last long.[29]

In 1862, the *Herald*'s Kinahan Cornwallis, a transplant to New York from London, published a long novel called *Pilgrims of Fashion*. Cornwallis's sprawling tale followed a wealthy family over many generations, ending in the first year of the Civil War. None of his characters had anything to do with war contracting, but Cornwallis (who was likely the author of the *Herald*'s essays on the "shoddyocracy") devoted much of the novel's preface to an extended treatise on the moral impact of war on society. Wars, he argued, can be "great purifiers," especially for young countries like the United States. Moreover, the adversity of war can lead to useful "social leveling," countering a natural tendency to destructive "extravagance and effeminacy." All these positive results of war, Cornwallis insisted, would eventually come to the United States, but in the war's first year or so the northern states had instead suffered from the deleterious effects of the rise of shoddy. In this version of shoddy, the culprits are not presented as completely corrupt, but they have won excess profits at the expense of the government's well-being and with complete disregard for patriotic concerns. These newly wealthy northerners were wise enough to recognize that in society elites are "judged by their feathers," so they had been buying up homes, carriages, clothing, and all the other trappings of status. Of course, these efforts at grandeur merely make them look "ludicrous." Cornwallis's preface is essentially an academic treatise that runs parallel to the satirical commentary on the North's shoddy aristocracy, but with two key distinctions. Cornwallis adopts a global perspective, arguing that the North's shoddy contractors are comparable to European war contractors, except that America's shoddy contractors are particularly anxious to join the aristocracy. He is also confident that the North's reign of shoddy will be short-lived, soon to be followed by an elevation of society as a whole.[30]

This notion—as articulated by the *Herald* and Cornwallis—that the shoddy aristocracy constituted a social type, and not merely individual selfish rogues, suggested a new way to think about the war profiteer. The problem was not that they were crooked, but that they were newly wealthy interlopers with inappropriate social aspirations. The antagonism, it seems, was as much about economic class as personal behavior. After Cornwallis defined the terms, it would be quite some time before the printed media returned to this new portrait of the undeserving rich. In fact, after late 1862, newspaper talk about shoddy war contractors temporarily declined, as editors and satirists turned their attention to draft evaders, bounty jumpers, and others dodging military service.[31]

In October 1863 the *Dover (NH) Gazette* published a peculiar editorial on "shoddy." Relying heavily on a recent story in the Democratic *New York World*, the *Gazette* declared that the shoddy problem had "suddenly sprung up" again, with contractors selling "flimsy work" while thousands of men in the field suffered. The New Hampshire paper went on to quote extensively from the *World*, portraying the members of the new shoddy aristocracy much as the *Herald* had done two years earlier, as hopelessly uncouth pretenders who spent their newfound wealth on jewels and mansions while only managing to "make opulence shameful."[32] In the next few months northern satirists returned their attention to the shoddy aristocracy, prompting one journal to publish a poem titled "John Shoddy, Esq." beginning with the line "John Shoddy now is all the rage."[33] Columbus, Ohio's *Crisis* took on the women of the shoddy aristocracy in the satirical poem "Who Says 'Fine Feathers Make Fine Birds!'":

Look yonder! Women, stand aside!
Here comes a female swell;
Bow to the greasy, jeweled head,
Of this year's shoddy belle.

Following the lead of the *Herald*, the poem ridiculed the foolish new rich, with their coaches and horses, their diamonds, their silk and lace, their "fancy canes, gay rings and fans." And, as expected, the poet concluded that the true "king birds of the race" "need not the aid of gaudy dress / Their real worth to show." The focus was no longer on the shoddy materials sold to the army, but entirely on how these new members of the economic elite spent their riches. The "female swell" of late 1863, unlike the male swell of two years earlier, has no wealthy pedigree to demonstrate her "real worth" in the face of criticism.[34]

In her July 1863 column, "Gossip from Gotham," written for San Francisco's *Golden Era*, New Yorker Mary Kyle Dallas briefed her western audience on the whole shoddy aristocracy phenomenon, which had destabilized social relations both in the city and in all the neighboring resorts. Dallas went on to note that cartoonists, novelists, musicians, and editors had all taken note of these new shoddy families, providing much mirth for those who did not have to live with them. Even if the rise of the shoddy aristocracy was largely a concern of the eastern elites, their caricatured actions and the discomfort of the nation's true blue bloods attracted attention from coast to coast.[35]

WHO A SHORT TIME AGO WAS PLAIN BRIDGET

In December 1863, *Frank Leslie's Budget of Fun* published a poem, "How Are You, Shoddy?," that built on these emerging stereotypes while introducing a crucial new wrinkle: the Irish contractor. This satirical verse begins: "Oh! a wonderful man is a shoddy contractor." This false patriot, the poet explains, ignores the soldier bleeding on the battlefield while he is busily "aiding the cause of the Union by trying / His pockets, by contracts for shoddy, to fill." These first lines cover familiar terrain, indicting the evil contractor by contrasting his ill-gotten wealth with the suffering of the soldier. But like the poem in *The Crisis* the previous month, "How are you, Shoddy?" shifts its attention to the contractor's wife, adding a new gender component as well as a broader social commentary:

> His wife, who a short time ago was plain Bridget,
> As Mrs. Fitz-Shoddy she now feels her oats;
> She can ride, she can dress, she can primp and can fidget
> For her husband is able to pay all her notes.

The name "Bridget" is crucial here. It suggested a working-class Irish woman who has now been transformed into a wealthy matron with a new,

WASPier-sounding name: "Mrs. Fitz-Shoddy."[36] In the process, the hostility to war contractors became fully yoked to the powerful antebellum strands of nativism and anti-Catholicism.[37] The new war culture presented a fine opportunity for repackaging popular hostility to Irish immigrants in a new patriotic form.

While the fictional Bridget Fitz-Shoddy made the Irish identity of the shoddy aristocracy clear, satirical cartoons had already begun to make the same point. In "One of the Effects of the War," a *Harper's Weekly* cartoon showed a homely—and perhaps Irish—"Army Contractor's Wife" in a gaudy dress shopping at a fashionable store. As she finishes up her purchases, she adds, almost as an afterthought, "Young Man, put me up a Diamond Necklace and a couple of Gold Watches *along of them other things.*"[38] In "Some of the Shoddy Aristocracy," *Harper's New Monthly Magazine* contrasted society in 1860 with the changed world of 1863 in three pairs of cartoons. In 1860 a peddler tries to sell a man a "nice pair of pantaloons" for "only tree dollars," while three years later the same man is fatter, better dressed, and ordering his associate to prepare "twenty-five toosan' pantaloons" for the army. In the second pair, a grocer sells a woman "tree pound and a half of flour" in 1860; in 1863 the wealthy merchant tells a buyer there is a "hunder barls" of flour in the corner. In the final pair, an Irish washerwoman complains that "me back is brock" from bending over her washtub in 1860, and in 1863 she is at a party wearing a flashy ball gown whining that "my neck and arms ache wid the weight of the jewelry."[39] These images from 1863 divorced the notion of "shoddy" from either substandard uniforms or the familiar image of a cynical old war contractor dozing off in his easy chair. The newly defined members of the shoddy aristocracy were not even clearly war profiteers, if that meant something other than contractors who won lucrative contracts. The trait that set them off from accepted society was that they had once been poor and now, thanks to war contracting, they had become wealthy. The mockery, as illustrated in their broken English, was no longer about patriotism; instead it was about undeserving poor immigrants in places where they did not belong.

In early 1864 the *Old Guard*, a monthly journal devoted largely to conservative Democratic political commentary, took repeated shots at the shoddy aristocracy, further illustrating the bipartisan nature of the public outrage. In a satirical report titled "The Shoddyocratic Society of Washington," the journal reported that children in the capital city were being left alone in the hands of "contrabands" (ex-slaves) while their wealthy mothers "frolic night and day."[40] In its next issue, the *Old Guard*'s "Edi-

ONE OF THE EFFECTS OF THE WAR.

ARMY CONTRACTOR'S WIFE. "And say, Young Man, put me up a Diamond Necklass and a couple of Gold Watches *along of them other things!*"

This cartoon features an overdressed wealthy woman spending money indiscriminately. Her language reveals that she is from humble origins, and thus presumably not worthy of her riches. *Harper's Weekly*, February 7, 1863. Courtesy of HarpWeek.

tor's Table" included a mock advertisement from "Dr. Didymus Shoddy," a purveyor of patent medicines, offering a series of potions designed to disguise that the wealthy patient was really from "the lower ranks of society." These medicines, the advertisement promised, would reduce the size of excessively large feet, hands, and ears, the telltale signs of humble origins. The doctor's services were particularly valuable for "ladies, especially the wives of contractors, who find it impossible to get diamond rings over the joints of their fingers."[41] A few months later the journal's "Editor's Table" introduced a new term: "the Shoddyocracy." These war contractors, the *Old Guard* argued, had descended on New York from all over the country, bringing their "elevated vulgarity into the hotels and streets of this favored city." Once again focusing on the unusually large ears and diamonds of these new rich, the *Old Guard* concluded that the city had been "conquered by hordes of newly civilized barbarians."[42]

Boston's *Dollar Monthly Magazine* captured this class-based morality in a series of twelve cartoons mocking "Mr. Shoddy" at an "Evening Party." Mr. Shoddy prepares for the party by donning a ridiculously extravagant outfit. When he arrives, he thinks he is making a great impression, but he drinks too much, dances badly, knocks over a vase, demonstrates terrible table manners, and eventually grows so drunk that he is kicked out of the party into the street. In the final scene Mr. Shoddy is in court, receiving the "usual fine" of three dollars plus court costs. The conclusion to be drawn from these twelve cartoons is clear: even substantial wealth does not make a man one of the nation's elites.[43]

Journalist Robert Tomes surveyed "the fortunes of war" in a long and detailed essay for *Harper's New Monthly Magazine* in July 1864. Tomes recalled the heyday of scandalous contracts and shoddy materials in the war's early months, but noted that governmental reforms had dealt with the worst excesses, leaving a prospering economy where many on the home front *"don't feel the war."* Meanwhile, Tomes argued, excessive profits from war contracting and investments had produced a class of newly wealthy northerners who had fallen prey to "extravagance and wantonness" and were liable to end up poorly. Tomes's account was free of the satire and ethnic hostility of many other contemporary writings, but his detailed discussion seemed to confirm the widespread notion that the North—and particularly New York City—was the breeding ground of economic excess. National readers who had suffered little economic discomfort themselves were particularly happy to take umbrage at the economic excesses of these urban elites, although in truth the comic Bridgets and their spouses bore little resemblance to the war's true economic winners.[44]

In October 1864, the *Ladies' Repository*, a national journal of literature and religion published in Cincinnati, weighed in on the behavior of these excessively "extravagant" women. Perhaps directly inspired by Tomes's essay, the article noted that savvy investments as well as war contracting had produced new wealth in the North. The author appealed to her northern sisters to reject the excesses of their suddenly wealthy husbands. "Your diamonds may flash gayly, but there's blood on them," she explained. "Your silks may glisten royally—your laces float ethereally; but they smell—they smell of treason!" This powerful essay endorsed the notion that some northerners were enjoying undeserved wealth; it also suggested that some women—including the author—believed they had some right to claim a position of authority over these crassly overdecorated rich poseurs. In this short passage, the *Ladies' Repository* combined new prescriptions defined by both gender and class, as recast in a war culture.[45]

Before long, humorists had taken to constructing an entire social world inhabited by the interloping Irish "Shoddy" families, with their excessive wealth and poor taste. One short story presented Mr. and Mrs. Shoddy and their daughters, Almira and Amanda, in a series of three chapters mocking their awkward transition from humble origins to sudden wealth. Throughout this tale the author returns to familiar scenes to illustrate the foibles of the new shoddy aristocracy. The story opens in Central Park, with the sisters on horseback but without the riding skills appropriate to the task. Both Almira and Amanda end up losing control of their steeds, creating chaos for all those around them. In the second scene the Shoddys are throwing a grand "soiree" for fellow war contractors and politicians. One of their guests, from similarly humble roots, brings a goat that ends up starting a fire, destroying the neighbor's house. In the final scene, the family goes to the opera. Outside the theater, Mr. Shoddy gets in a shouting match with a wealthy Irish shoemaker of a similar working-class background. As the two grow agitated, their language becomes rougher and rougher, eventually revealing strong Irish working-class accents. Once inside, the Shoddys demonstrate their collective ignorance. They complain loudly about all the singing in some unrecognizable language, and Mr. Shoddy demands, "When is the opry goin' to begin?" Eventually Mr. Shoddy gets very drunk and the family is shown the door.

"The Shoddy Family" is mostly written in a comic voice, with the author touching on nearly all of the economic and ethnic stereotypes that came to define the shoddy aristocracy. But a more pointed—and poignant—thread also runs through the narrative, in the person of a poor volunteer's wife. This poor native-born woman had worked for the Shoddys and continually reappears, seeking her pay. They have the money but repeatedly push the woman aside, refusing to interrupt their entertainment with such petty matters. In the final scene the girls discover the volunteer's wife dead on the street, holding her baby in her arms. At this, Amanda Shoddy swoons into her sister's arms. This tragic scene—in the midst of a comic essay—calls to mind the stark juxtaposition of wounded soldiers and foolish swells in the harsher cartoons about the war's hypocrites and fools. But here the author adds a powerful female component as the mindless Amanda is confronted with the true womanhood of the patriotic volunteer's wife.[46]

Mr. Shoddy having made much Money through Contracts, is invited to an Evening Party.

Dressing. Kicks the servant out of the room for suggesting subdued colors are most fashionable.

Dressed. Is admired by mother and sisters.

Shoddy is introduced to his hostess. The result of a low bow.

Shoddy is a little awkward while polking.

Shoddy is independent. He breaks a vase, and offers to pay for the same.

The supper table. Shoddy is at home, for he has both hands full.

This series of twelve cartoons shows "Mr. Shoddy" stumbling his way through a social gathering. Although he can afford the finest clothes, as soon as he arrives at the party he reveals that he lacks the refinement to be a true member of society. *Ballou's Dollar Monthly Magazine* (March 1864). Courtesy of American Antiquarian Society.

As the liquor is free, Shoddy is determined to obtain his share.

Under the influence of champagne, Shoddy exhibits to the company some of his lucrative contracts.

And for impertinence and drunkenness, is kicked out of doors.

Shoddy clinging to a lamp-post, instead of hanging to it, as he deserves.

Shoddy insensible to contracts or evening parties.

Shoddy in disgrace. The usual fine, $3 and costs, for being drunk.

The portrait of the laughably oblivious Shoddy family crashing the opera, throwing crass parties, and bumbling through life among the upper crust recurred time and again in the northern press. In "At Mrs. Shoddy's"—an essay in *Harper's Weekly*—the author describes her visit to a formal reception in a Fifth Avenue mansion. "Mrs. Shoddy" and her family display all the excesses of ostentatious wealth, unrefined by good taste. Soon after their arrival, the author is greeted by their "amiable hostess" decked out in "costly laces" and "glittering bracelets." "You look kind o' lonesome, Mrs. Davis. 'fraid you ain't enjoyin' yourself," she exclaims. Soon they are off on a tour of the massive home. Mrs. Shoddy takes particular joy in showing off her art, pointing out details that merely serve to illustrate her complete lack of taste. Eventually it dawns on the exuberant host that she had left guests in the "parler." "What will folks think of me?" she wails, running out of the room. Later that night the author wrestles with this question about shoddy society: "What will folks think of her?"[47]

Some authors expanded their cast of imagined characters to include the Petroleum Family, who had made their undeserved riches through the discovery and sale of oil.[48] Following close on the path established by "At Mrs. Shoddy's," *Frank Leslie's Budget of Fun* published "Petroleum's Ball," describing a party thrown by Mrs. Amanda Petroleum. Mr. Petroleum had been a humble clerk at the Custom House before striking oil. Now, as part of the "new aristocracy," they are set on demonstrating that the "old-fashioned ideas, that refinement and education are necessary to good society, [had] evaporated." As an added benefit, Amanda hopes to "make Rosy Shoddy so mad!" "Petroleum's Ball" is not quite the slapstick farce of some of the earlier tales of the Shoddys, but the author is left unsure about the future of polite society in the face of these strange transitions.[49]

Other humorists took to portraying the laughable experiences that resulted when the Shoddys vacationed. In a March 1864 essay in *Godey's Lady's Magazine*, Mary W. Janvrin imagined a lengthy letter from a Mrs. Ward describing her recent visit to Saratoga, New York, including an extended encounter with the Shoddy family she met there. Mrs. Ward was none too impressed with these shoddy interlopers, but the reader of *Godey's* would have been hard pressed to differentiate between the two pretenders to elite company. "Miss Shoddy," she explained late in the letter, "was dredful good and perlite, and invited me to take a ride in her kerridge, and told me all about her great house on Fifth Avynew in New York, and showed me all her jewelry." The reader might reasonably conclude that neither of these women was quite who she thought she was.[50]

Clearly the meaning of "shoddy" evolved and expanded throughout the war. In the first months of the war, the term described contractors who sold actual shoddy cloth, but it almost immediately expanded to include all faulty uniforms and equipment. By the war's second year many critiques had attached the term to the unethical contractor, not merely the shoddy merchandise, and some satirists had begun detaching the notion of "shoddy" from war contracting at all. That is, the "shoddy aristocracy"— and later the "shoddyocracy"—described people who were enjoying new wealth, regardless of its actual source. By the end of the war "shoddy" seemed to signify both a villainous character and an object of ridicule. And as the term grew divorced from its original meaning, it increasingly became a pejorative term associated with transgressors—largely Irish immigrants—who had violated the accepted rules of class, ethnicity, and gender.[51]

As "shoddy" became an accepted term of derision, it was only natural that the term would find its way into the rough-and-tumble of political debate. In some cases politicians used the term against opponents who had been caught up in real shoddy controversies. In other cases the term seemed to be little more than a way of suggesting falseness. In the fall of 1863, as crucial elections loomed, both the Republican *New York Tribune* and the *Chicago Tribune* claimed that Democrats—even antiwar Copperheads—had been winning the majority of lucrative war contracts. In this formulation, "shoddy" no longer referred to poor merchandise or even excessive war profiteering, but to war contracts won through corrupt means.[52] In "The Shoddy Correspondence," *Frank Leslie's Budget of Fun* portrayed Democratic mayor George Opdyke—who had been caught up in scandal—as "Mayor Shoddy" in a series of satirical letters with Republican Thurlow Weed. Here the term had some basis in fact but was also used for partisan political gain.[53] Partisans across the political spectrum agreed that "shoddy" was an affront to the national cause, and thus the term became useful in political discourse.

The members of the imagined "shoddy aristocracy" seemed to be almost universally understood to be in New York City—living in brownstones on Fifth Avenue, shopping on Broadway, terrorizing Central Park, and scandalizing folks at the Opera House—even though fraud touched all regions of the North, and in fact some of the most strenuous investigations concentrated on General John Frémont's Western Department.[54] This was largely because so many of the widely read journals and newspapers were published in New York. But perhaps there was more to it than that. Published reports of contract fraud did appear throughout the northern states, but the cultural particularities of the shoddy aristocracy seemed to be reserved for the posh streets of New York, even in the pages of newspapers across the country.

The comical image of misbehaving New Yorkers disrupting polite society seemed to enjoy a wide national appeal. Consider one widely reported episode in January 1865. According to one account, "a great sensation was created at the Opera House" by an overdressed couple who were "the very incarnation . . . of shoddy and petroleum." The woman wore a headdress, "ablaze" with forty thousand dollars' worth of diamonds. The man wore a "white satin vest" with diamonds for buttons. The pair sat so close to the stage that—according to the report—some of the orchestra members seemed distracted. The shoddy pair attracted even more attention when they left early, after the fourth act. This story was presented as a factual account, although the descriptions of the shoddy couple matched the physical excesses of their satirized counterparts. The difference, of course, is that in this story no amusing calamity followed their entrance into polite society. The full extent of the story was that two overdressed rich people went to the Opera House. Yet both the *Philadelphia Inquirer* and Philadelphia's *Daily Evening Bulletin* saw fit to publish the story; Washington's *Daily National Intelligencer* ran an abbreviated version; and the *Milwaukee Daily Sentinel* published the entire account under the headline "Shoddy and Diamonds."[55]

This newspaper story was meant to entertain, mocking the false elites who could afford obscene numbers of diamonds yet remained the object of ridicule. Perhaps the editors from other cities recognized that their readers would enjoy a story poking fun at the excesses of wealthy but crude New Yorkers enraging the city's very proper upper crust. Or perhaps they saw these stories about the shoddy aristocracy in New York as the pinnacle of a phenomenon that appeared elsewhere in a muted form. Not long after the war, a Massachusetts paper ran a story about members of the "shoddy aristocracy"—almost certainly from New York City—vacationing at Saratoga. Like the visitors to the Opera House, this family had made their riches in petroleum. The father, an "unfortunate dunce of oleaginous development," would change his outfit "fifteen times before supper on Tuesday" before settling on the right clothing. The daughter, clearly unused to polite company, "'astonished the crowd,' by exclaiming, 'Lor! Mar; I've dropped my diament into the gravy!'" This author, precisely like those who wrote about goings-on in New York City, mocked the Saratoga tourists for their uncouth actions and their uneducated accents.[56] Once again, the Civil War had provided a convenient outlet for broad-based class and ethnic hostilities.

In *The Coward*, his third home front novel, Henry Morford returned to his indictment of shoddy, particularly of the shoddy aristocracy. Published in late 1863, *The Coward*—like Morford's other wartime offerings—includes many characters, a complexity of scenes and events, and a variety of un-disguised moral lessons.[57] Following the tradition of portraying characters on vacation, midway through the novel Morford brings an assortment of men and women together in the White Mountains. Although it was only a few weeks after the bloody Battle of Gettysburg, the sardonic Morford notes that northern society seemed peculiarly able to enjoy vacations and overall prosperity despite the carnage. Places like Saratoga, Niagara Falls, the Catskills, and the White Mountains became gathering places for all sorts of tourists in search of a respite from the city's summer heat. Those vacationers included both "shoddy, grown suddenly rich while remaining incurably ignorant and vulgar" and "officers on furlough, who had fought enough for the time or had no intention to fight at all" and welcomed a chance for "displaying jaunty uniform and decorated shoulder to the ad-miring eyes of that sex." In short, both the North's shoulder straps and its shoddyocracy congregated at such vacation spots, alongside the nation's respectable citizenry.[58]

On the train to the White Mountains, Morford introduces Mr. Brooks Cunninghame, his wife, Julia Brooks Cunninghame, and their two chil-dren, Miss Marianna Brooks Cunninghame and Master Brooks Brooks Cunninghame. Although their names and clothing suggest that the Brooks Cunninghames are of the upper crust, Morford describes the quartet in painstaking detail, noting large hands, bad teeth, reddish hair, and an overall impression that the family are of poor Irish immigrant roots and distinctly uncomfortable in their fashionable outfits. We learn that be-fore the war "Brooks" Cunninghame had been "Patrick" Cunningham, a petty contractor who had made his living with a shovel and a one-horse cart, digging out cellars, laying pipe, and doing other forms of manual excavation. Cunningham had gotten involved in ward politics and man-aged—through a combination of corruption and hard work—to grow his business into a fleet of horse-drawn dirt-carts. With the outbreak of war, he rapidly made his fortune selling overpriced horses to the army, while deftly manipulating local Democrats and Republicans through ties with both Tammany Hall and the Loyal League. In sum, through a combina-tion of cynicism and corruption, the Irish Cunningham had managed to join the shoddy aristocracy.

None of this history is apparent to the other riders on the train, who at first accept the Brooks Cunninghames as proper members of their elite society. Marianna, the well-dressed daughter, soon catches the eye of one of the bachelors on the train, prompting proper blushing and hopes for the future. Things change when the train stops abruptly, bouncing the passengers around in their seats. In response to the unexpected jolt, Julia Brooks Cunninghame cries out and throws herself to the floor of the coach; Marianna yells, "Oh Mammy!"; and an agitated Brooks Cunninghame shouts, "Is it kilt ye are, Bridget?" In just a few seconds the family had revealed their true identity, as working-class Irish rather than true elites.[59]

The Brooks Cunninghames do their best to cover up their errors, joking that "Bridget" is simply Brooks's pet name for Julia, but in the days to come the rest of the guests see through their charade. In one scene, a man cruelly engages Mrs. Brooks Cunninghame in a conversation about her claimed travels in Europe, while the guests around them silently mock her ignorance and dishonesty. Over the next several chapters the family are responsible for several more mishaps and embarrassments, providing the novel with comic interludes. By the time they are ready to head home Mr. and Mrs. Brooks Cunninghame have thoroughly lost track of their adopted identities and are arguing loudly in thick Irish brogues, until an irate Bridget finally declares: "Pat Cunningham, ye'r a coarse, miserable brute, a low Irishman, and money can't make any thing else out of ye!" The reader agrees.[60]

■ By the end of the Civil War the public discussions of war contracting and shoddy had followed a variety of different themes, while the consensus had constructed a few recognizable characters. Like the different sorts of shoulder straps who emerged in the war's first few months, these caricatures gave ordinary civilians unambiguous types to identify and abhor. The first group were those crooked war contractors whose illegal behavior became the subject of published investigations and later court cases. They had been caught red-handed selling shoddy merchandise and in so doing had undermined the war effort. These shady characters evolved into the fictionalized Old Shoddy, whom poets and cartoonists imagined sitting at home in his easy chair, surrounded by ill-gotten wealth. Some imagined Old Shoddy wracked with guilt and getting his just deserts, while others portrayed a raw cynicism untouched by the shame of a proper citizen.

With the passage of time, this public conversation expanded to include the unpatriotic war profiteer. But it was not always obvious who should be excoriated for war profits. After all, the Union war effort relied on independent contractors and entrepreneurial initiative. Morford solved that riddle in a fictional context by making Charles Holt not merely a war profiteer but also a sexual predator. Thus one set of immoral traits reinforced the other, leaving the reader to conclude that the man who would buy up cheap cloth in the first month of the war was just the sort of fellow who would try to seduce his clerk's wife.

A January 1863 editorial called "Making It Pay" offered one approach to the ethical dilemma. The author described a Boston acquaintance who had grown rich manufacturing a substitute for pitch, effectively replacing a naval product that had previously come from North Carolina. The wealthy war contractor recognized that the profits would decline when the war ended, but he was confident that he had made "the war pay" so handsomely that he would survive the peace. The author concluded that there were "a good many people" profiting from the war, "some honestly enough, and some not so honestly." But even the honest ones were living off a conflict that was bringing pain and misery to many Americans, and these war profiteers were "escaping the duty of bearing arms, and the burdens of the war" while lining their own pockets. The ethical answer, the essay concluded, was to judge those who had acquired great wealth by how much they used those riches "to alleviate the misery caused by the war." Those who would "neglect that duty" proved themselves "unworthy of their privileges." The author voiced no objections to entrepreneurs profiting from the war, so long as they recognized the moral obligations that accompanied that wealth. "Duty" was defined not by avoiding wartime riches, but by spending the money wisely and patriotically.[61]

By the middle of the war northern society had settled on a more easily recognizable answer to this ethical dilemma: the shoddy aristocracy. These people were not merely war contractors who made money on the war; they were peddlers, shopkeepers, and small-scale traders who had managed to go from relative poverty to extreme wealth during the war. The markers identifying these men and their families as outside of acceptable behavior was not how they got their money, but the fact that they had made so much so quickly. The press defined the shoddy aristocracy by their humble economic origins and often by their Irish ethnicity. Time and again these fictional trespassers into elite society revealed those origins through unseemly traits that money could not hide. Many still had the weathered faces of the working classes, and a surprising number had the distinctly large hands of the manual laborer. Satirists seemed never to tire of describing shoddy women who could not drag their flashy diamond rings over fat, stubby fingers, or their uncouth husbands who strained to pull on their expensive gloves. The repeated patterns in the stories are striking. The shoddy families threw ludicrous parties, bought ugly art, and made fools of themselves at the opera. And when agitated they reverted to an uneducated-sounding Irish brogue. Even if they had managed to acquire possessions, the dominant culture would not reward them with the coveted mantle of respectability.

The Shoddy family, like Old Shoddy in his easy chair, was a wartime caricature that fit with both the Union's larger approach to the war, and the North's enduring antebellum sensibilities. Both were excessive types, created for satire out of some shreds of reality. In each case the greatest sin was hypocrisy and duplicity. The original shoddy contractors, like the officers in swank hotels who pretended to be active soldiers, sinned by presenting their goods as something other than what they really were. The various Shoddys who purchased homes on Fifth Avenue were objectionable not because of their working-class roots or Irish heritage, but because they were false pretenders. The new nativism in the wartime culture defined Irish interlopers as suspect citizens. This indictment provided a convenient cover for all of those home front citizens—including the very wealthy—who were enjoying general wartime prosperity, nights at the opera, carriage rides in Central Park, visits to posh tourist sites, and expensive soirees. Nothing in the portrait of the shoddy aristocracy suggested that there was anything wrong with these activities in the midst of a bloody civil war, so long as the participants seemed to belong in those settings.

CODA: THE RUSSIAN BALL

On November 5, 1863, less than four months after draft riots had turned the city into a raging inferno, New York City's high society threw a party that seemed almost designed to underscore the absurd excesses of the northern home front. The occasion was the arrival of the Russian fleet in the city. To celebrate the occasion, New Yorkers held a gala ball and banquet at the Academy of Music in honor of the visiting Russian officers. By the end of the evening, they had consumed 12,000 oysters, 250 turkeys, and 3,500 bottles of wine, yet published accounts report that they ran out of food. It was, according to *Frank Leslie's Illustrated Newspaper*, "one of the most distinguished entertainments ever given in the city."

New York's press gave the Russian Ball the extensive coverage befitting such an important social and diplomatic event. The *Times*, the *Herald*, and the *Tribune* each ran long descriptions of the ball, including meticulous discussions of the clothing, the food, the dancing, and the crowds gathered outside the Academy of Music. The national press also took note of the grand evening. The *New Haven Daily Palladium* declared, "The great Russian ball at New York on Thursday night is described as the most magnificent thing of the kind ever achieved in this country." Boston's *Daily Advertiser* ran a very long story, quoting from the New York newspapers. The *San Francisco Daily Evening Bulletin* seemed pleased with the whole affair, as did the *Philadelphia Press*. Some reports read like accounts from a high-society page, while others adopted a more light-hearted tone, but nearly all appeared undisturbed by the sheer opulence of a social event staged in the middle of a horrific war.[62]

Perhaps the most emphatic endorsement of the Russian Ball as a grand—and appropriate—event came from none other than Winslow Homer. Homer, who had already begun to build a reputation as a visual chronicler of battlefield and camp scenes, produced an elaborate engraving titled "The Great Russian Ball at the Academy of Music" for the November 21 issue of *Harper's Weekly*. Rather than portraying Union soldiers on picket duty or men in the midst of heavy combat, Homer filled his image with a sea of fashionable women in swirling dresses, dancing with uniformed Russian officers and handsome northern men.[63]

Although leading newspapers seemed to embrace the Russian Ball, there were some dissenters, or at least those who took the opportunity to take a few shots at the wealthy attendees. The *Dover* (NH) *Gazette* began its account of the ball by announcing that "Shoddy made a wonderful show in New York."[64] The *New York Journal of Commerce* thought the event was impressive, but concluded that the affair was marred by the presence of too many Shoddys, thus placing the evening below the recent reception in honor of the Prince of Wales as a grand social success.[65] These accounts seemed to have no trouble with the event itself, only with some of the guests. Lavish parties, like trips to the White Mountains, were properly reserved for the deserving few.

One commentator did issue a strong critique arguing against this celebratory consensus. In *The Russian Ball: Or the Adventures of Clementina Shoddy*, an anonymous New York journalist took on the excesses of the shoddy aristocracy while also questioning the wisdom of holding such a grand event in wartime. This twenty-four-page poem, published as a small pamphlet shortly after the ball, begins much like many other wartime poems about Shoddy families, with Clementina Shoddy preparing for the upcoming Russian Ball. Her father, who has made millions on war contracts, agrees to pay for the tickets, and Clementina rushes downtown

HARPER'S WEEKLY.

A JOURNAL OF CIVILIZATION

Vol. VII.—No. 360.] NEW YORK, SATURDAY, NOVEMBER 21, 1863. [SINGLE COPIES SIX CENTS. $3.00 PER YEAR IN ADVANCE.

Entered according to Act of Congress, in the Year 1863, by Harper & Brothers, in the Clerk's Office of the District Court for the Southern District of New York.

THE RUSSIAN BALL—IN THE SUPPER-ROOM.—[SEE PAGE 755.]

Artist Winslow Homer is well known for his wonderful portrayals of ordinary people and particularly for his drawings of Civil War camp life. But in this issue of *Harper's Weekly*, Homer captured the finery of the Russian Ball in New York. Unlike the North's "shoddy aristocrats," who received all sorts of ridicule, these partygoers are presented as in their appropriate world. *Harper's Weekly*, November 21, 1863, 737. Courtesy of HarpWeek.

to buy a dress and rent diamonds from Tiffany's. "Although *in private* a slattern," Clementine looks lovely in her new gown and heads off with her family to the Academy of Music. Following familiar patterns, the anonymous poet mocks awkward Shoddy dancers and gluttonous Shottyites crowding buffet tables. The next morning Clementina arises unsatisfied by the experience, while her parents are profoundly hung over.

For much of *The Russian Ball*, the reader is on familiar terrain, although the pamphlet itself probably did not circulate widely. But in the poem's final few verses the narrative takes a harsher turn. Echoing the message in "The Shoddy Family," published by *Frank Leslie's Budget of Fun* at almost precisely the same time, *The Russian Ball* reminds readers of the larger world of want outside the Academy of Music. After contemplating the vast wealth devoted to one night's celebration, the poet notes that "thousands of widows have lived in good cheer / On less than this sum for more than a year." With this in mind, the author argues:

> Oh, Shoddy, if truly you loved your dear land,
> You'd open your heart if you could, and your hand.
> And give of your gold to *their* children and wives
> Who, while you are dancing, are risking their lives.

Rather than buying that dress and those diamonds, the poem asked, why not devote those funds to the families of volunteers in your midst? While the Union soldier lies dying on a southern battlefield, Shoddy is home enjoying his wine. As the wife of a volunteer risks starvation in New York, a girl like Clementina Shoddy—who is not worth a fraction of one of those other women—is enjoying her father's riches. In short, the poem concludes, "And seasons like this when so many hearts call / To God in their woe *is not time for a Ball*." Perhaps northerners remained undisturbed by fancy balls in the midst of wartime, so long as the participants wore their finery as if they deserved it, but the anonymous author of *The Russian Ball* challenged readers to do more—and less—in the midst of war.[66]

■ The multiple versions of the Russian Ball—the event, the extensive newspaper coverage, Homer's illustrations, and the anonymous critical poem—are a useful place to bring part 1 to a close and turn to part 2. Part 1 has considered how northern popular culture created extreme stereotypes of unacceptable wartime behavior as a way of marking out for ordinary civilians where they should not stray from their essential wartime duties, while also offering advice on who should be scorned. That discussion depended on exaggerated satirical types, although often with a foot in reality. But the Russian Ball was a real event, noteworthy in its lavish excess, which prompted only limited objection. It is likely that none of the real participants came from Clementina Shoddy's modest background, and most of the journalist observers seemed unbothered by the wealth of those who attended or the massive expenditures in the midst of war.

The poem *The Russian Ball* raised large questions about war and society. But few wartime northerners seemed drawn to those large issues, and almost no wartime writings called on readers to wrestle with the broader meaning of war in society. On the other hand, patriotic northerners did struggle with questions about individual duty and personal responsibility in wartime. We will turn to those individual questions in part 2. In the broadest sense, part 1 has asked how wartime civilians—and their popular culture—adjusted antebellum warnings about dangerous and dishonest behavior to meet the national challenges and demands of a war for Union. Part 2 shifts that conversation inward, considering how northern civilians came to judge their own behavior, and that of those around them, in the midst of a civil war that posed myriad difficult and unfamiliar choices.

On Fools, Hypocrites, and Scoundrels

PART TWO

On Duty,

Cowardice,

and

Citizenship

CHAPTER FOUR

Our Duty

Sacrifice and Citizenship

In the fall of 1863 an Illinois lawyer penned a fascinating memo on conscription and the Constitution. He devoted most of his energies to considering the legalities of the federal draft law, arguing that conscription was perfectly constitutional and those who objected to the law were largely proposing "false arguments" as an excuse for their own feeling that the whole matter was "disagreeable" to people who opposed the war or did not wish to serve. After two long years, the necessities of war finally required new measures. "At the beginning of the war," the author explained, "and ever since, a variety of motives pressing, some in one direction and some in the other, would be presented to the mind of each man physically fit for a soldier, upon the combined effect of which motives, he would, or would not, voluntarily enter the service. Among these motives would be patriotism, political bias, ambition, personal courage, love of adventure, want of employment, and convenience, or the opposites of some of these. We already have, and have had in the service, as appears substantially all that can be obtained upon this voluntary weighing of motives. And yet we must somehow obtain more, or relinquish the original object of the contest." In sum, those northern men particularly inclined to enlist were already in uniform, and the Union required more recruits.

Although intended as a constitutional interpretation of conscription, this passage offers some valuable thoughts on motivations for enlistment and perhaps on the individual citizen's obligations in that regard. The author was in some senses a usefully disinterested party. As a fifty-four-year-old man, he was not a likely recruit or a candidate for conscription. He did have a twenty-year-old son who would express some inclinations to serve, but it was reasonable to assume that the new law—constitutional or not— would never compel that son into uniform. Of course, as commander and chief of the United States, the author—Abraham Lincoln—was hardly a disinterested party. He needed more men.

Lincoln's memo offered some broad thoughts on individual decision making, patriotism, and—by extension—the responsibilities of citizens in wartime. Able-bodied men, he surmised, might have volunteered from some combination of "patriotism . . . ambition, personal courage, love of adventure, want of employment, and convenience." They presumably weighed the personal and the ideological and came to an appropriate decision. Meanwhile, others contemplated "the opposite of some of these" or the weight of "political bias" and chose not to volunteer. Presumably, a good job, personal inconvenience, or some absence of patriotism, courage, or love of adventure, might have led a reasonable man to stay at home.

The language Lincoln chose seemed designed to avoid any sort of personal judgment of those who had not enlisted. He did not speak of cowardice, selfishness, or a failure of patriotism, although such personal failures were implicitly included in his catalog of motivations. Later in this unpublished memo, Lincoln was even more explicit. "I do not say that all who would avoid serving in the war, are unpatriotic," he insisted, "but I do think every patriot should willingly take his chance under a law made with great care in order to secure entire fairness." Those who had stayed at home through more than two years of bloody fighting were not necessarily unpatriotic. They had simply chosen to stay at home. Under the rules of conscription, such a man—if a proper patriot—would take his chances alongside all the rest.[1]

This memo was essentially a brief for conscription as a just and necessary course. There was little to be gained by attacking the characters of those men who would be now subject to the draft, so perhaps the president intentionally chose circumspect language. Still, Lincoln had previously demonstrated a willingness to question the patriotism of his opponents. A few months earlier, in a widely circulated response to a petition signed by New York Democrat Erastus Corning and a group of his Democratic colleagues, Lincoln had offered a vigorous defense of his approach to civil liberties while taking to task those critics who clung to partisan labels and differences in time of war. In a particularly bold passage, Lincoln declared, "The man who stands by and says nothing, when the peril of his government is discussed, can not be misunderstood. If not hindered, he is sure to help the enemy. Much more, if he talks ambiguously—talks for his country with 'buts' and 'ifs' and 'ands.'" In political debate the man who failed to speak for the cause in unambiguous language was nearly as bad as the traitorous Copperhead Clement Vallandigham, whose recent arrest had prompted the New Yorkers' petition.[2] When circumstances required it, Lincoln did not shun tough talk.

Taken together, Lincoln's unpublished memo on conscription and his published letter on civil liberties provide a valuable window into the president's thinking on constitutional powers in wartime, but they also offer a provocative portrait of the nature of patriotism and the expectations on citizenship in the midst of civil war. On the one hand, Lincoln had no time for those who claimed to represent a loyal opposition while casting themselves as "Democrats" in presenting their partisan critiques. Cavils about important administrative actions, or even ambiguous silence, were outside the bounds of patriotic citizenship. On the other hand, Lincoln seemed willing to be quite generous when it came to the actions—or inactions—of citizens when it came to enlistment. This chapter and the one to follow will consider how the broader wartime public discourse wrestled with the expectations of citizenship both for the North's military-aged men and for the broader citizenry, and also how this conversation shifted once conscription became part of the conversation.[3]

Thus far much of our focus has been on the public discussion in the North about the Civil War's scoundrels, blowhards, and hypocrites, who attracted public scorn, particularly in the first half of the war. Public writings in the northern states defined appropriate wartime behaviors by caricaturing the Union's silly swells, shoulder straps, and shoddy aristocracy. These men and women were condemned for their actions. This chapter shifts to the cultural messages directed toward those who faced more complex wartime decisions. Duty required the patriotic citizen to think hard about complicated choices, but those notions of duty only rarely mandated specific responses.

COURAGEOUS AND OF GOOD CHEER

During the Civil War, northerners recognized and celebrated all sorts of heroism and sacrifice. Men who died gallantly on the battlefield won admiration and praise. Popular fiction and poetry offered endless portraits of heroic young men who went off to war as humble privates, only to return home wearing the uniform of the officer, often with one empty sleeve pinned up as eloquent testimony to bravery and sacrifice. These characters melted hearts, won the girls, and sent a clear message to readers that these were the men society should admire.[4] This discourse did not stint on praising the self-sacrificing women. Those angels of mercy who volunteered to work in hospitals became a staple in the popular journals.[5] Within a year of the war's end several hefty volumes appeared in the North praising the Union's "Noble Women" who had run refreshment saloons, sanitary fairs, and other voluntary activities at home and in the field.[6] Northern readers of magazines, newspapers, and novels had ample portraits of the people who were deserving of their admiration as ideal citizen-patriots.

But most northerners were not those sorts of people. Many lived their daily lives through four years of war with surprisingly modest adjustment to the carnage that raged on the battlefield. They read detailed accounts of the latest battles. Perhaps they attended a political meeting or donated to a voluntary society or bounty fund. In his short story "Wounded," Timothy Shay Arthur describes a husband and wife reading the latest list of wounded from the battlefield. The story builds to the core point that every wounded soldier on the battlefield produced many "wounded" civilians at home. But Arthur also noted "how little those who are not brought into the actual presence of death and disaster on the battlefield realize their appalling nature." "We talk of our losses as indifferently as if men were crates and bales," without fully contemplating the war's costs until the name on the list is a loved one.[7]

Many northern civilians—and women in particular—donated occasional time to a ladies' aid society, sewing group, local "sanitary," or hospital. But they also raised children, went to work, tended crops, attended the theater or variety shows, enjoyed picnics and other outings, visited drinking establishments, attended church, read sappy romances, and went about their daily lives. True, the war was very real to these people even while their own pursuits might have seemed untouched by the conflict. By the end of the war's first year nearly everyone had friends or relatives away at the front. Thousands of letters from military camps flowed back home, where they were passed from hand to eager hand, bringing news of the war to those people insulated from the battlefield.[8] And although the majority of volunteers were unmarried young men, large numbers of families suffered from the lost labor and economic support when their menfolk—husbands, sons, or fathers—marched off to war. Often the folks at home did not know what they were supposed to *do* to demonstrate their patriotism. Idealized patriotic behavior might have been easily recognized, but the expectations born of duty remained surprisingly ambiguous.

The popular discourse offered an eclectic assortment of printed messages to northerners about the proper behavior of citizens in wartime. Novels, short stories, poems, political cartoons, and privately published pamphlets provided readers with a template for how to go about life in wartime. Some of these portraits were stock patriotic characters sacrificing their lives to the war effort. But as we have seen, many of the more familiar recurring caricatures showed the loyal citizen how *not* to behave.

Thus the war's shoulder straps, swells, and shoddy aristocrats became stereotypes, illustrating how some northerners who claimed they were loyal citizens were really outside the bounds of proper wartime behavior for true patriotic citizens.[9] In wartime, the Union cause demanded a balancing of individual goals and circumstances with national priorities. As Lincoln's memo suggested, the crisis allowed for individual choice, but those choices were constrained by law and cultural expectations.

A glance through the hundreds of wartime recruiting posters suggests a range of messages aimed at the prospective volunteer. As we have seen, at the outset of the war, many posters spoke to masculine impulses and presented enlistments as a great opportunity for both glory and revenge. Others appealed directly to citizenship: "Citizens of the Upper End of Bucks [County]," one poster proclaimed, "your country claims your services."[10] But the early war posters appealed to the manhood of possible recruits, not their sense of citizenship. One called for a company of "Eighty Good Men and True." Another promised that "Picked Men" could join the Mounted Rifle Rangers. It is certainly true that these posters included calls for patriotism and displays of flags as well as masculine rhetoric, but the appeal was almost never actually cast in terms of the particular reciprocal obligations of citizenship. Enlistment in those first few months was presented as an opportunity that would no doubt appeal to just the "picked men" the Union needed. "No skedaddlers," one poster warned. Going to war was an opportunity reserved for the few, not an obligation for all.

Before long, the recruiting appeals to patriotism, excitement, and manhood began to be accompanied by pragmatic straight talk. The new messages were designed to lure men who had heretofore not been swayed by the simpler calls, and to compete for those prospective volunteers so that they would fill local quotas and not move on to the next town. Rising bounties became the vital coin of this new realm, but some recruiting posters also promised the best officers, the most exciting duty, and the most reliable equipment. Better to appeal directly to self-interest than to an abstract obligation that perhaps came with citizenship.

Some recruiting speeches and editorials praised those men who chose to volunteer, and urged others to follow suit. But rarely did the argument turn on the duties of the citizen to his nation. "What Ho! Bone and Sinew," a spirited poem in *Vanity Fair*, did make that case. In calling on "ye brawny, stalwart men" and "broad-shouldered chaps" to step forward, the poet urged them to eschew cowardly strategies to dodge the draft by "playing sick" or running off. No, "your country needeth all the raft / Of sinewy Christians" in this time of need, the poem implored. When "the Union's props and girders quake; / On to the rescue ere they break." Here appeals to manhood and good character are intertwined with explicit talk of a nation in need. But even this poem addresses the brawnier workers of the North and stops short of suggesting that enlistment was an obligation—and surely not a universal one—so much as a proper response for those fittest to answer the call.[11]

The humor magazine *Punch* invoked the obligations of citizenship in a satirical poem playing on the popular song "We Are Coming Father Abraham." While the original song was a celebration of recruits answering the president's call, this version asks, "Don't you think you're coming it yourself a little strong? . . . We've nearly sent you white enough, why don't you take the nigger?" The author critiques the Union's military strategy and disappointments on the battlefield before adding,

> But as the matter stands, Old Abe, we've this opinion, some
> If you say Come, as citizens of course we're bound to come,
> But then we want to win, you see; if Strategy prevents
> We wish you'd use the nigger for these experiments.

On the one hand, the author is unusually explicit in declaring that a call for the president is an obligation the citizen is "bound to" answer. But in the next breath he suggests that that obligation is contingent on the citizen's assessment of the quality of military leadership and the fairness of the call itself.[12]

Various northern authors addressed the duties and responsibilities of the patriotic citizen. In November 1861, *Arthur's Home Magazine* tackled the question head-on in the essay "Our Duty." Editor Timothy Shay Arthur argued that no true patriot "can, in this crisis, stand aloof from the conflict." But Arthur's fundamental point was not that ordinary citizens should undertake great sacrifices or personal risks, but that all who care for the cause must "speak out boldly for the right" rather than sitting passively. Moreover, true patriots should "trust the government" and "not grow impatient" in the months to come. This advice would be echoed by other authors in the years to come. The duty of the true patriot was to support the war and the government, and not grow restive about slow progress.[13]

Men and women in the North were flooded with pamphlets discussing the issues of the day. The themes were clear and often explicitly political. Some emphasized that all Copperheads were traitors and should be denounced by patriotic citizens. As months of conflict turned into years, more and more pamphlets seemed aimed at a weary citizenry. Charles Janeway Stillé's *How a Free People Conduct a Long War* echoed Arthur's earlier words in exhorting his readers to endure a long war with patience and equanimity, insisting that such was the price of freedom. The lengthy pamphlet challenged readers to continue to support the war effort and resist destructive divisions, but it made no call for individual sacrifice in the name of that cause.[14] In January 1863, columnist Virginia F. Townsend repeated the same sentiments, calling on readers to "let not our hearts fail us for fear!" while suggesting nothing by way of personal sacrifice beyond being "courageous and of good cheer!"[15]

Sometimes appeals to patriotism took on a directly gendered aspect. Rev. John F. W. Ware concluded that the North faced a fundamental lack of "manhood," in responding to ongoing trials. But the minister remained confident: "I believe the crisis will give us men," he declared. "It is *men* we want,—a broader, freer, surer, more self-relying manhood."[16] In another of the war's particularly famous pamphlets, Caroline Kirkland, writing anonymously, offered "a few words in behalf of the loyal women of the United States." The essence of this fascinating pamphlet was that southern women were earning more praise than northern women because the Confederate cause had demanded great sacrifice of its citizens, whereas patriotic northerners experience "moments when we feel ashamed, almost, of living comfortably; of reading fresh and pleasant books or enjoying social gatherings; of giving our children and young people the indulgences common to their age; of letting our thoughts wander to a happy future, unmindful of what sorrow and suffering may lie between us and that perhaps distant time." Kirkland reassured her middle-class female readers that they should feel proud of their patriotism even though the war was not necessarily forcing them to sacrifice.[17]

In 1864, essayist Mary Abigail Dodge—writing as Gail Hamilton—took her northern audience to task for complaining of high prices and mild inconveniences when in the South human beings were still enslaved and in the field Union soldiers fought on without complaint. "May every man who has added one iota to his country's perplexity that he might fill his own pockets, find his gains to be as rottenness in his bones," she declared. But for the rest, the simple answer was to forgo certain luxuries, take modest measures to be economical about some goods, and simply stop complaining about minor annoyances. The war was, in short, a national test that would "show what manner of people we are." "We can be weak" or "we can be hopeful, cheerful, trustful, patient" during this national trial, she urged. Hamilton's essential message was that the successful war effort would require some material inconveniences for those on the home front, but rather like Stillé, she really only called for quiet endurance rather than active labors in support of the Union.[18]

Oliver Optic, a popular and prolific children's author, made a very similar case to his young readers in *The Student and Schoolmate*. In February 1863 Optic acknowledged that these were "days that try men's souls," although, in truth, "we have been called upon to endure but little positive suffering." Echoing the sentiments in "A Few Words in Behalf of Loyal Women," Optic acknowledged that the North had yet to suffer like those in the Confederacy, but he warned that "we may be called upon to endure more, to make great sacrifices of comfort and plenty." And he urged his subscribers, "Let us show our devotion to the great cause by suffering without a murmur."[19]

The fact that so many northerners seemed to be living life in the midst of Civil War while making no real sacrifices did not escape the notice of the satirists. In June 1862 an essay in *Vanity Fair* commented on the peculiar state of "The Northern Mind." Having adjusted to the realities of war, northerners no longer felt compelled to pour into the streets at the latest "'barbaric yawp' of the newsboy" with news from the front. "Elasticity, not apathy," the author explained, "is a leading characteristic of the Northern Mind." But in practice that elasticity allowed northerners to ignore new stories of carnage. Women sported bonnets and mantillas that were just as lovely as in the antebellum years, while outstripping the fashions of Rebel women in the South. At some level northern society seemed happily untouched.[20]

THE DUTY OF THE HOUR

Quite a few northern religious leaders spoke and wrote on the political issues of the day, publishing dozens of sermons on "patriotism" and "duty" and similar themes. The message in these prowar pamphlets was almost universal. First, they insisted that there was no conflict between being a good Christian and supporting a just war. Second, they generally concluded that this was indeed a just war and the good Christian was morally compelled to support the government. Some ministers couched the argument in terms of abolitionism, but others simply argued that the preservation of the Union was itself a cause that the Christian should support. Although the cause was just, these ministers never spelled out any particular actions or sacrifices that they expected of their flock, beyond a general support of the government and the war effort. The published sermons concluded that the proper Christian path was to support the war despite the horrific bloodshed, but these spiritual leaders did not use their pulpits to urge parishioners to action.[21]

Consider, for example, the June 1861 sermon of J. Romeyn Berry, delivered in Albany, New York. "Let no man think that the duty of Christian patriotism is fulfilled by the mere experience or profession of a love of country," Berry intoned. "That love, like all others, is essentially active, and demands a cheerful and ready loyalty when the cause of public righteousness and order is involved." Berry seemed to be telling his flock that it was not enough to declare themselves patriotic; they must also be "cheerful" in their loyalty. Later in this pamphlet, Berry is more specific in asking, "[What are] the demands of this patriotism?" But his answer is still surprisingly modest. A proper patriot should evince a "cordial co-operation with the General Government, in overthrowing the conspiracy which is now warring against us." "Cordial co-operation" is hardly the rallying cry for supreme patriotic self-sacrifice.[22]

In his February 1863 sermon "The Duty of the Hour," Brooklyn minister Samuel Spear followed precisely the path set out by Stillé in arguing that the present crisis called for patriotic civilians to support the government and avoid partisan conflicts that might undermine the war effort.[23] A few months later, Amos S. Chesebrough of Glastonbury, Connecticut, applauded his flock for supporting the war in keeping with the "principles of Christianity." "You have submitted without a murmur to your new burdens," he applauded. "You have manfully sustained the Government in its requisitions. Many of you have done the highest deed of patriotism possible." Here Chesebrough—using the gendered language of masculinity— credits those men who had enlisted, as well as those who had supported the war in other ways. But he falls well short of equating patriotic sacrifice with civic obligation.[24]

In 1864 Boston's Rev. F. D. Huntington spoke of the "personal humiliation demanded by the national danger." Huntington stressed that "doubtless every citizen must do everything in his ability, according to the obvious rules and common-sense conditions of success, to render this impending movement physically powerful. As a true patriot, and a true Christian,— and it cannot be too often repeated that he can never be a true Christian without being a true patriot,—he will uphold and help the forces that represent the faith that is in him and the cause he holds right and dear, by his gifts, by his daily speech, by his public spirit and attention to the public interest, by all cheerful, patient, prompt, untiring sacrifices." Again, one is struck by how modest the expectations are. The good Christian patriot must support the war within the "common-sense conditions of success." This apparently involved demonstrating appropriate enthusiasm through his speech, his "public spirit," and his overall cheerfulness.[25]

The prowar northern press echoed these themes. Time and again, good citizenship seemed to be measured in enthusiastic support for the war despite setbacks, rather than in any active personal sacrifice. In early 1863, Captain Samuel W. Fiske of the Fourteenth Connecticut Volunteers, writing to the *Springfield Republican* under the name "Dunn Browne," addressed "the spirit of the nation." Fiske acknowledged that events on the battlefield were "trying the spirit of the nation" with "disappointment, discouragement and reverses on all hands." He admitted that soldiers commonly grumble and that he and his comrades "have good reason to grumble," but he said it was discouraging to "find that the people of the North are usurping our (supposedly exclusive) privilege." Soldiers had a right to grumble, but civilians had earned no such privilege.[26]

Only days after the disastrous Battle of Chancellorsville, the *Chicago Tribune* ran an editorial calling on its readers not to despair or succumb to talk of peace and compromise. "Who so falters now, is not only a traitor, but a coward," the paper declared. Apparently cowardice was defined not by the failure to act, but by the failure to believe.[27] Six months later an editorial in a San Francisco newspaper echoed the themes in Stillé's pamphlet, but with a twist. Like Stillé, the author urged readers to have patience in the face of a long war, but the editorial suggested that folks who could not be patient should enlist rather than complaining.[28]

In July 1863, San Francisco's *Golden Era* published a particularly sophisticated analysis of the notion of "love of country." The author argued that although we commonly think of "patriotism" as synonymous with "love of country," the latter may be little more than "a purely instinctive feeling" with no accompanying notion of an obligation "to sacrifice anything in the way of personal welfare or convenience." That is, the essay explained, the man who loves his country because it provides him with comforts and benefits is not necessarily a patriot. Coming as it did in the midst of the Confederate invasion of Pennsylvania and the imposition of a federal draft, this editorial appeared to be easing toward a call for individual sacrifice—and enlistment—in the name of patriotism. But the author moved in a very different direction, using this introduction as the basis for an extended critique of those southerners who claimed to love their country but acted selfishly in dividing it. Thus, in effect true patriotism was illustrated by national unity, not by individual sacrifice.[29]

Each of these commentators had a different approach to the question of "duty" during wartime, but all shared a conclusion that duty was not really synonymous with sacrifice.

WHY NOT ENLIST?

Certainly in the war's first eighteen months the public conversation among prowar northerners urged young men to enlist, but the discussions almost exclusively cast the issue as an individual decision that allowed for multiple legitimate responses, much as Abraham Lincoln would later articulate those choices in his memo on conscription. In one of the more pointed commentaries, the poem "Why Not Enlist" imagines the able-bodied man with his farm and house "and cattle and sheep" who worries too much about personal gain rather than the nation's needs. This shameful man finds excuses not to enlist by looking at his neighbors, who have their own reasons to stay home, including a "pretty young wife, with a sweet little babe in her arms," or a mother who is "widowed and old" and about to lose her farm. The poet criticizes the men who use their families and farms as an excuse to stay home, while at the same time he presents other perfectly acceptable reasons to make that decision. In the end, the decision remained with the individual, although society reserved the right to judge decisions as selfish or cowardly.[30]

Immediately after the war, Mary S. Robinson wrote a trilogy about the Civil War home front. In the first volume, *The Brother Soldiers: A Household Story of the American Conflict*, Robinson traced the lives of a New England family in the first year of the war. Shortly after the surrender of Fort Sumter, the family's middle son, Daniel, writes from college seeking permission to enlist and postpone his final year in school. Daniel is torn about abandoning his studies, but he feels that "I ought to serve my country in her need" and that "I'm young and strong, just the one that ought to go; one who could give the least excuse for not going." The author's word choices here are instructive: the young man concludes that he "ought" to go, given his circumstances, rather than that he feels morally or ethically compelled to do so.[31] Later in the novel, with Daniel away at war, the conversation turns to Horace, the family's oldest son, who lives in St. Louis and works in an uncle's store. His inquisitive younger sister asks whether Horace will join Daniel in the army, to which her mother replies, "He'd hardly want to go, I think. He's older than Daniel, and settled in business, so he couldn't leave very well; and if he could, we couldn't spare both sons."[32] Here again the decision to volunteer is seen as a careful weighing of personal considerations.

At first, Horace shares his mother's assessment. As time passes, he has second thoughts, but still remains at home. "I've sometimes thought if I wasn't so deep in business, that I might go," he writes, "but it's impossible at present." In August, Horace sends home a letter summarizing the political and military situation in St. Louis and around Missouri and announces that he has finally decided to enlist. "I thought my duty would be done by giving money to the war," he explained, "but it was a mistake, I've enlisted in Company A."[33] Horace's decision to enlist is a highly personal choice, prompted by his own assessment of the turmoil he was witnessing in St. Louis and his growing hatred for the Confederacy. Horace's manly duty required him to consult his conscience and weigh the situation carefully and honestly. Duty did not dictate a particular decision, so long as he followed his inner guide. Horace's parents are not pleased, both because he has gone to war without coming east to see them and because he is curtailing his budding career in commerce. Robinson presents Horace's enlistment as a typical "family sacrifice to the country" and as the natural consequence of war, but the parents do not swell with patriotic pride so much as they accept their sons' individual decisions as unavoidable.

The Brother Soldiers is in some senses a straightforward novel of military adventures. Both sons send long letters from the front, describing their experiences and the progress of the war. But the moments when the two brothers each enlist suggest a more complex story. Both brothers feel a sense of duty to country, but they seem to be motivated by particular events rather than pure martial enthusiasm or ideological abstractions. Moreover, each young man weighs his options with care, giving due consideration to the perfectly good and honorable reasons to stay at home. Daniel wants to continue his studies; Horace has a budding career to consider. As presented, these are legitimate considerations and not excuses to mask cowardice or hypocrisy. In Horace's case, the impression is that he would not have been moved to enlist had he been living in a community more insulated from the war, and that decision would have been perfectly reasonable. Both brothers' decisions were unaffected by obligations to wives, children, lovers, or even employees, and neither faced any particular community pressure to act. They made their decisions from among acceptable options. Their clear duty was to take the decision seriously and draw conclusions that were not selfish.

The moment when a young man contemplates enlistment recurs over and over again in wartime short stories and novels. It was, after all, a moment full of dramatic possibilities. Various authors imagined different sorts of scenes, often dependent on the particular character tensions they were attempting to produce, but the fundamental similarities in these scenes are striking, underscoring the conclusion that this was indeed a highly individual decision. Many, although not all, of these male characters speak of their duty to country; very few mention any particular hostility to the South, and comments about slavery and emancipation are quite rare.

In almost every case the man presents enlistment as a personal desire that requires the approval of the central woman in his life. And regardless of whether that conversation is with a mother, wife, or sweetheart, the woman must approve the decision. In Louise Chandler Moulton's "One of Many," Nelson goes to his fiancé Margery and asks, "Shall I go?" Margery tells him to return the following day so that she can think about it. The next day she gives her permission.[34] As we shall see in chapter 6, this crucial scene is often presented as a test of the woman's own patriotism and acceptance of her feminine duty, but the other side of this coin is that in many cases men conclude that they cannot enlist because a female loved one refuses to consent. Moreover, these conversations are commonly presented as a serious discussion about competing obligations, clearly wrapped in the language of personal gender obligations as well as patriotic duty to nation. In "The Cool Captain," Charley would love to enlist, but he must remain home and support his widowed mother.[35] The main figure in "John Morgan's Substitute" does not enlist because he has a wife and five children.[36] Burt Haviland realizes that he cannot volunteer while he is responsible for a wife and child at home. The collective message is that good men (and good women) sometimes surveyed their own circumstances and concluded that they should not enlist.

The poem "The Emigrant Volunteer's Wife" suggests a different approach to the notion of citizenship and duty. Written in the voice of a soldier's wife, with two small children at home, the poem describes how the young couple had "cross'd the old ocean" to come to "the land of the free." Ten months earlier, when Lincoln called for troops, her "noble husband" had explained to her that he had no right to share in the "benignant blessings" of their adopted land if he shrank from his duty. In this short poem, Mrs. S. K. Furman, a regular contributor to the *Ladies' Repository*, imagined an idea of duty that explicitly weighed the benefits of national citizenship against obligations to country. It is significant that this distinctive notion of a reciprocal relationship between nation and citizen is presented in the voice of a recent immigrant rather than that of a native-born American. Perhaps immigrants who came to American shores owed their adopted homeland particular sacrifices. But of course those recent immigrants were less likely to have been reading poetry in the *Ladies' Repository*, leaving open the possibility that the message was intended to suggest what "other people" should be doing.[37]

Other plots suggested an interesting counternarrative to this idea that enlistment was essentially a collective decision, with the loved one measuring patriotic goals against personal obligations. In wartime fiction, angry or disappointed lovers often enlisted in fits of pique. In "Strategy," Leo suspects that Clara really loves his brother, so he abandons the field by enlisting.[38] Dick Temple, another hapless character, volunteers after his beloved follows her father's instructions and rejects him in favor of a wealthy man.[39] On multiple occasions, disappointed love or some unfortunate misunderstanding drives a young man to enlist without consultation or the approval of his loved ones. It is significant that in these impulsive choices the man is motivated by some combination of love, anger, or honor, but he never appears to be particularly concerned about duty or patriotism.

Virginia F. Townsend's "Enlisted! Enlisted!"—published in August 1862—opens with eighteen-year-old orphan Margaret Lowe furious with her brother Theodore, three years her senior, who has gotten drunk at a party and made a fool of himself. Margaret declares that she wants no more to do with him, and he storms out of the house. Theodore decides that he can erase his embarrassment and get a measure of vengeance on his angry sister by enlisting in the Massachusetts Volunteers. When she learns Theodore's news, Margaret begs him to reconsider, and Theodore— no longer intent on wounding his younger sister—says all the appropriate things about how he must respond to his duty or appear to be a coward. Townsend ended her story with Theodore away at the front and Margaret at home, miserably regretting her harsh words and begging God's forgiveness. The reader could have absorbed conflicting messages from this story. On the one hand, a night of drunkenness and his sister's harsh words had prompted Theodore to behave like a man, making the decision to serve his country. On the other hand, Townsend seemed to be suggesting that Margaret drove her brother into uniform and lived to regret it.[40] The following year Townsend turned to very similar themes in a story in the *Ladies' Repository*. In this case, Mary and Paul are unhappily married. Mary, a social climber, whines to Paul because her friend's husband makes more money. Paul, apparently sick of things at home, turns around and enlists, leaving Mary alone with their young child. Like Theodore in the previous story, Paul insists that he enlisted for good and appropriate reasons, but Townsend's message to her female readers in both stories appeared to be very similar: watch how you treat your man, or he might be "driven to the war." In both stories the woman is distraught. It was apparently one thing to support the decision to enlist, but quite another to feel responsible for a rash act.[41]

AVOID THE DRAFT

The terms of discussion and the nature of individual decision making shifted in late 1862, when the Union turned to a state militia draft to fill the ranks. Now the Union (like the Confederacy before it) was acting on the belief that all eligible men of military age should be liable for military service or at least some level of risk. In practice, any man selected on draft day had a wide range of paths for avoiding service. He could demonstrate any of a long list of medical disabilities. He could avoid service by working in a protected occupation deemed necessary for the war effort, or by claiming to be a conscientious objector. He could petition that he was the sole support for a widowed mother. Or he could simply insist that he was too young or too old to be eligible for the draft. If all of these strategies failed, the man "called to service" could elect to pay a three-hundred-dollar commutation fee or hire a substitute to send in his stead. (Later in the war the Union limited the option of the commutation fee to conscientious objectors.)[42]

The new conscription rules obviously put demands on draft-aged men, but they also shifted the obligations on communities. The crucial community goal now was to meet local quotas in order to avoid the draft. In July 1862 "A Young Man" wrote to the *Boston Daily Advertiser*, putting this point directly to local merchants. These men, as employers, could act "speedily and effectually, not by shouldering the musket, or paying bounties" but by guaranteeing the young men in their employ that their jobs would be safe when they returned from the war. Such promises, the author insisted, would immediately yield a regiment ready to march to the front. "Do you feel the importance of the crisis?" he asked. If merchant-citizens answered yes, then they would promise protected jobs to recruits.[43]

The new draft rules pressured communities to raise bounties in order to meet local quotas. In late 1862, and even more so in 1863 and 1864, printed broadsides called for citizens to "avoid the draft" by contributing to bounty fund drives, suggesting a new form of patriotic voluntarism. Increasingly bounty fund drives were cast in terms of informed self-interest. Successful fund-raising could protect a community from the sacrifices and disruptions of draft day.[44] Here again the popular commentary encouraged contributions to bounty funds. In the short story "More Precious

Than Gold," a wealthy man brags continuously about his generous donations to various wartime causes, including the local bounty fund, implying
that his actions indicate he is unusually patriotic. Finally, a local woman
humiliates the braggart by telling him that her husband, who had been
killed in battle, was the true patriot and his sacrifice had been "more precious than gold." In one sense this story draws a contrast between the
contributions of home front patriots and the much more poignant sacrifices of the soldiers and their families. The key point, however, is not that
the braggart's efforts were inconsequential, but that his excessive boasting
was inappropriate. Like the criticisms of the shoddy aristocracy, this sort
of story served to make ordinary northerners who were safe at home feel
that their own actions were above reproach so long as they did not engage
in silly boasting.[45] Good citizens contributed to bounty funds but did not
brag about it.

The Unionist press seemed largely pleased with the militia draft. After
all, the draft promised to spread the war's burdens more broadly across
the entire population. In late 1862, when the Union announced a state
militia draft to raise six hundred thousand men, the prowar *Chicago Tribune* was thrilled: "It brings home to every member of society, and most
sharply suggests to the individual that he has a personal share in the safety
and ruin of the nation." Moreover, this new plan "lays the burden of the
war equally upon all who have shared the benefits of our institutions."[46] A
correspondent to the *Milwaukee Daily Sentinel* agreed, declaring that the
nation could not afford to wait for volunteers to come forward. The author added the peculiar note that "thousands of loyal men of strong arms
and brave hearts, who would be drafted with pleasure, are now waiting to
see if enough will not volunteer." Rather than perceiving conscription as
a stigma, this writer apparently saw responding to the draft as a worthy
obligation of citizenship, whereas voluntary enlistment constituted an op-
tional form of service.[47]

In early August 1862, the *Bangor Daily Whig and Courier* ran a particularly thoughtful editorial approving of the new draft legislation. "No
nation in the world ever conducted a war with so few personal sacrifices,"
the editorial argued. Other than the absence of soldiers and the actual
losses on the battlefield, "there is nothing to tell us that the country is
carrying on a war greater in magnitude than the world has seen in years."
In this situation, with nearly a million volunteers in uniform, there is "no
disgrace upon the patriotism of the people" to turn to a draft. Moreover,
the editorial stressed, this draft was only for nine months and would not
be a true hardship for most people, and "should it happen that a person

finds it difficult to go from any cause," there should be no trouble finding a willing substitute. In short, "very few will be obliged to serve unless perfectly willing," and this was a good thing.[48]

Frank Leslie's Illustrated Newspaper took the economic argument to its logical conclusion, suggesting that the real answer to the manpower crisis was to only draft wealthy people. On the one hand, these men did not have to worry about supporting their families at home, since they would leave behind ample resources. On the other hand, if they did not feel like going to war, they could easily hire a substitute. Although the piece began as a commentary on economic justice, the author adopted the language of practical patriotism to expand his point. The money that the wealthy draftee paid to avoid service would enable "some more patriotic poor man" to go to war while providing for his family. Meanwhile, "our property-holder can feel that he has served his country, through the patriotic medium of the pocket." The latter point had a cynical edge, as the author noted that the wealthy conscript could enjoy the "feeling" of patriotism even if "the man fitted-out by his gold may at that moment be bleaching his bones on a distant-battlefield."[49]

There seemed to be little stigma attached to those men who responded to the lure of bounties, so long as they were serious recruits and not potential bounty jumpers. One Milwaukee paper surveyed the situation in July 1862 and urged young men to step forward and claim their bounties because the war was likely to end soon. "Those who enlist now will have all the bounties provided by the State and Government, and in all probability will be back to their homes and businesses in six months," the paper advised. A Maine newspaper made almost precisely the same point, noting that recruits to new regiments would make $140 immediately and an additional $75 and 160 acres of land after the war. "Let the patriotic young men now rally to the flag! The cause needs men NOW!" the Bangor paper declared. "Fill up the quota of Bangor before next Saturday night!" In this case the newspaper spoke about the nation's "needs," but it appears that the true need was to fill the local draft quota.[50]

The patriotic poem "March Up!" made the point quite clear:

March up and claim the bounty, boys,
Fight of your own free will . . .
Before Conscription's arm of steel
Shall make its stern arrests.

Here the argument is framed not in terms of economic self-interest or the obligations of citizenship, but as an opportunity to exercise "free will" and enlist "like freemen" rather than serving as conscripts. The author is not necessarily criticizing those men who wait to be drafted, but he does indicate that the enlistee has the better of the bargain.[51] A prospective recruit who played the bounty game with too much cynicism, though, was subject to criticism even if he did not break the rules. In "The Song of the Eleventh-Hour Patriot," the poet mocks the able-bodied man who is content to see others suffering while announcing that he will only enlist "when the Bounty is high enough."[52] As with the line between the honest war contractor and the corrupt war profiteer, it was one thing to accept a bounty and another thing to appear too clever about it.

"Kate's Soldier" brought together many of these themes about individual decision making and collective responsibility. The story begins with wealthy Kate Barclay declaring, "If I were only a man!" much to the amusement of her older cousin, a major in the Union army. The bellicose Kate has particularly harsh words for any "cowardly soul" who would only go to war for money, but the major insists that he has a friend, Mr. Keene, who would happily enlist except that he has a younger sister who requires his financial support. In a provocative piece of gender inversion, Kate hires Keene as her personal "substitute" and promises to take in his fifteen-year-old sister should he fall in battle. Kate quickly bonds with the brother and sister, to the point that she feels some remorse that she is responsible for sending Keene off to war. But he is happy to have the chance to serve, and his sister seems surprisingly understanding, even when the two women learn that Keene has been killed in action. As is so often the case in Civil War fiction, the reports of Keene's death were in error. He was actually captured and eventually returns home as a paroled prisoner. In the story's final passages, Kate and Keene are engaged to be married before he returns to the front. "Kate's Soldier" endorsed the fundamental point that men of honor and courage might choose to stay at home because of personal obligations, or they might be able to fight only if the price is right. It also illustrated how the patriotic citizen—in this case a wealthy young woman—can support the war effort with generous donations.[53]

Many northerners objected to the draft on ideological or constitutional grounds, producing a vigorous debate in elite circles and threats of political violence in numerous communities.[54] Others questioned the premise that all eligible men should be called on to serve. As one correspondent to *The Liberator* put it, "universal conscription" was the wrong path for the country because many men who were subject to the draft might have quite legitimate personal, familial, or religious reasons to not serve. This critique accepted the general notion that patriotic citizens might have good personal reasons to stay at home.[55] San Francisco's *Golden Era* hoped a federal draft would not prove necessary, arguing that "the impressed soldier can rarely be depended upon" and that a nation that relies on force to fill the ranks undermines its own cause.[56] On balance, most northerners appeared to be content with a system that shared the risk, as long as it also protected the selected.

COME IN OUT OF THE DRAFT

Much like the satirical commentary on shoulder straps, the shoddy aristocracy, and the swells, the published material surrounding the draft concentrated on belittling those weak-kneed, cowardly, despicable types who came up with ridiculous schemes to avoid the draft. Cartoonists had a field day with these fellows. Magazine readers chuckled at images of men using makeup to disguise their age, conscripts hiring elderly women to play the part of widowed mothers, and devious scoundrels faking strange medical ailments. When later legislation protected older married men from the draft, the wags joked about how this was a boon to homely spinsters.

But like the discussions of the shoddy aristocracy or shoulder straps, these early reactions to the wartime draft evaders generally concentrated on the absurd or pathetically dramatic efforts to avoid military service by cheating the new system. "The Draft in Monkeytown," a humorous poem first published by the *Salem Register*, lampooned the cowardly men who were running from the draft "like rats from a sinking craft." Other verses mocked the physical ailments claimed by men who would otherwise have happily stepped forward:

> One would go right off and enlist,
> But he had twelve corns as big as his fist,
> And a great carbuncle on his wrist,
> That gave him a terrible twist.

And once they had received their exemptions for "fifty ulcers inside his head" or "a back crooked like the figure 9," or a spleen "mortified black as sin," these draft evaders rushed home to "show with great glee their Exemption Papers." Throughout "The Draft in Monkeytown," the poet maintains a light tone as he portrays these hapless cowards, assuring readers, "I know you'd have laughed / To see 'em so tickled when clear of the draft." The lengthy doggerel verse satirized the absurd, but with little sense of true outrage, perhaps because the draft evaders were still seen as terrible potential soldiers.[57]

The song "Come In out of the Draft," published in Philadelphia, portrayed a pathetic conscript's efforts to avoid service. First, he tries to convince a young female friend to marry him, but she loves another. Next, he attempts to hire a substitute for two hundred dollars, but the man robs him instead. Then he brings his sad tale to the mayor, who laughs in his face. The song ends with his friends all singing, "Come in out of the draft."[58] The complex cartoon "Offering a Substitute. A Scene in the Office of the Provost Marshall" captured the experiences of several draftees who hoped to avoid service. Despite their protests, the fat man, the thin man, and the physically worn out man all fail to get past the inspecting surgeon, who concludes that each will be improved by a few miles of hard marching.[59]

Vanity Fair pounded away mercilessly at those young men of high society who were avoiding the 1862 militia draft. In "Volunteers, or Drafts," the journal mockingly compared draft evaders and their fathers to the wealthy citizens of ancient Rome.[60] The following week *Vanity Fair* ran a long essay joking about all sorts of draft evaders who had adopted a wide range of subterfuges to avoid military service.[61] A week later the journal described a curious disease, "weak knees," that only seemed to affect men of draft age.[62] In November, *Vanity Fair* ran an entire column on the bizarre—and perhaps imagined—excesses of "the substitute market," including one Cincinnati man who reportedly paid $450 for a dead pig, dressed in a hat and coat, as his substitute. "Such conduct is considered reprehensible at Cincinnati," the journal reported, "as tending to cast disparagement on the pig."[63]

In "The Song of the Draft," a long satirical poem, the monthly journal took on a long list of the war's hypocrites and cowards, including "the amateur braves" who had once donned "buttons and lace" to impress the ladies but now found "their brains going daft, as they read in the papers the news of the draft!"; those who "rushed to the steamers" to pursue newly realized passions for "the Rhine or the Alps"; and "the newspaper warriors" who suddenly discovered physical ailments that kept them from serving but vowed that "they'd continue to *write* in defense of the draft." The final verse of "The Song of the Draft" praises "the jolly brave fellow who never knew fear" and who said:

> . . . "When my land wants me, I mean to be here;
> I'm stout in my lungs, and I'm stout in each limb;
> My ear isn't dull, and my eyes isn't dim."
> So at Doctors' Certificate loudly he laughed
> And awaited, in peace, the results of the Draft.

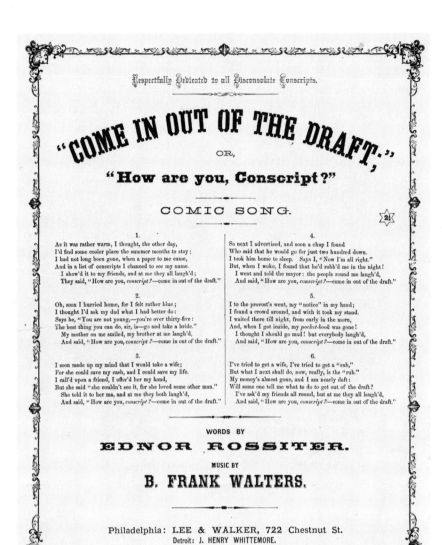

Throughout the war years, satirists often turned to song, producing scores of published song sheets commenting on the war's most hapless or dishonest citizens. This song skewers the conscript who is desperate to find some way to avoid service. Walters, "Come In out of the Draft." Courtesy of the Library Company of Philadelphia.

OFFERING A SUBSTITUTE. A SCENE IN

This complex lithograph mocks the diverse assortment of men who turned up at the Provost Marshal's Office in hopes of being excused from duty. Courtesy of the Library Company of Philadelphia.

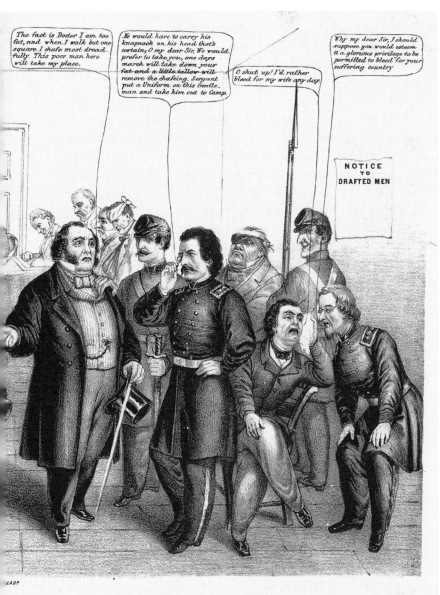

OFFICE OF THE PROVOST MARSHALL.

147

The poem, then, mocks the North's cowards, frauds, hypocrites, and fools. But who is praised? Not the man who enlisted in 1861, or even the recruit who stepped forward when the government called for conscription. In this telling the hero is the "brave fellow" who simply followed the rules and agreed to accept the results, whatever they might be.[64]

In Charles Farrar Browne's imagined town of Baldinsville, Indiana, Artemus Ward was proud to announce that he had assiduously signed up for the draft in every community he had visited. But as he walked the town's streets, he encountered a citizenry intent on avoiding conscription. Much like Ward's earlier commentary on "war meetings," this piece presents an assortment of hypocrites and fools. Ward sees sixteen citizens ride by on horseback, each carrying a letter declaring that he is a draft-exempt postal employee. He then encounters one of the town's leading citizens, who is suddenly claiming to be a habitual drunkard and thus excused from service. The town resolves to hold a meeting to discuss the issue, and the local professor rises to quote Virgil, only to be thoroughly misunderstood. The newspaper editor announces that he could not go because he was needed at home to report on the "VIGOROUS MEASURES TO PUT DOWN THE REBELLION!" After much incoherent blathering about the war, the citizens of Baldinsville dispersed with the conviction that they would have no draft.[65]

Throughout the fall of 1862, humorous stories of bizarre draft evasion schemes cropped up all over the northern states. A New Bedford paper reported that "persons heretofore supposed to be men" had "attempted to evade the draft by leaving that place in women's dress." A Boston paper picked up the story without comment. Meanwhile, the *Boston Daily Advertiser* announced that the post office had taken measures to keep draft evaders from finding jobs as postmaster's assistants to avoid conscription.[66] One story that made the rounds described a clever entrepreneur who advertised that he would sell an "infallible" method for avoiding the draft, for just one dollar. The story claimed that he received dollars from over four hundred men, all of whom learned the same secret: "Enlist."[67]

Many of the cartoons, poems, and songs targeted those able-bodied men who discovered some strange illness when the provost marshal came calling. The poem "Much Sickness from 'Exposure to a Draft'" played with the notion that strange illnesses had suddenly struck all sorts of healthy people:

One is halt and one is blind, a third is deaf as any post
A forth [*sic*] is gone in consumption, and can hardly walk, almost;

A fifth is dying daily from a weakness of the spine,
And sixth is fading slowly in a general decline.[68]

An Ohio paper reported that a local man claimed that he deserved a medical exemption as an "idiot" because he had voted for James Buchanan.[69] In November, *Yankee Notions* ran a story on the strange exemption certificates signed by various doctors. One certified that "A.B." had nearly contracted cholera in 1849. A second affirmed that "C.D." had suffered from colic in 1852. "E.F." had suffered several serious nosebleeds that might recur if he were drafted. Another had a tendency to fall off horses. The final man merited exemption because a lady had recently boxed his ears, causing debilitating humiliation.[70]

Petroleum Nasby, as portrayed by humorist David Locke, was similarly foolish and selfish when faced with the specter of a draft. He offered ten reasons that "Shows Why He Should Not Be Drafted." He claimed exemptions for a variety of maladies, including baldness, dandruff, blindness in one eye, unsound teeth, a "holler" chest, "kronic diarrear," "verrykoss vanes," "bunyons on both feet," and a variety of "rupcherds" requiring him to be "entirely enveloped with trusses."[71] The popular "Song of the Exempts" followed similar themes, imagining a chorus of exempt men celebrating their fake status as "o'e forty-five" or suffering from physical "troubles as many as Job." In the final verse the singer declares, "You call me a sneak—I heed not your twaddle; I'm exempt, I'm exempt; I mean to skedaddle!"[72]

Sometimes the familiar story was turned on its head. In one newspaper squib, a conscript who happily stepped forward to be inspected, confident that the inspecting physicians would excuse him for a "physical infirmity," finds that he has been approved for military service and will have to find a substitute.[73] Another story described a man who sought exemption for "weak knees," only to have the surgeon certify that he "is weak in the knees, a great coward who shrinks from defending his country," and should be held to service.[74]

In late 1862, the northern press—particularly in the Midwest—hammered away at stories of draft evaders running off to Canada. In August the *Chicago Tribune* ran almost daily stories about prospective draftees heading for Canada with their pockets full of cash, creating an expatriate community of cowards in Windsor.[75] In a cover illustration for *Yankee Notions*, cartoonist Howard Del pictured a wealthy New Yorker facing the "horns of a dilemma" in the form of a charging bull with horns labeled "bounty" and "draft." The disheveled man's response is to contem-

Song of the Exempts.

TUNE—"*I'm Afloat.*"

I'm exempt, I'm exempt. I vow and declare ;
I'm exempt, I'm exempt from the " draft," I will swear ;
What though the rebels our soil may invade,
And *wipe out* each general of pick-axe and spade ?
Oh ! what do I care though a million are slain,
And our starry-gemm'd banner is tramped on the plain ?
Oh ! what do I care who may fall or may thrive ?
I'm exempt, I'm exempt, I'm o'er forty-five !

I'm exempt, I'm exempt, I vow and declare ;
I'm exempt, I'm exempt from the " draft," I will swear ;
Oh ! what do I care what my neighbors may say,
That I've jumped o'er ten years in less than a day ?
Oh ! what do I care for my nation and laws?
I heed not her shame, I seek not applause ;
But still for the *Almighty Dollar* I'll drive ;
I'm exempt, I'm exempt, I'm o'er forty-five !

I'm exempt, I'm exempt, I vow and declare ;
I'm exempt, I'm exempt from the " draft," I will swear ;
I always was healthy from heel unto nobe,
But now I have troubles as many as Job ;
You may wink and may sneer, and say " it's all gas,"
That such a lame " ho'se" with the doctors won't pass :
But I'm pains, I'm aches, from head to the toe ;
I'm exempt, I'm exempt from the " draft," you must
      know !

I'm exempt, I'm exempt, I vow and declare ;
I'm exempt, I'm exempt from the " draft," I will swear ;
I'm free to confess that I find greater charms
In a trip to the country than taking up arms ;
I'm off, I'm off, with the very first train,
And when the war's over I'll come back again ;
You call me a sneak—I heed not your twaddle ;
I'm exempt, I'm exempt ; I mean to skedaddle !

Nick Nax, a popular comic magazine, ran this satirical song in November 1862. A jubilant coward declares, "I'm exempt, I'm exempt; I'm o'er forty-five!" In the next verse he admits that he has aged "o'er ten years in less than a day." But, he asks, "what do I care for my nation and laws?" The critique is not of the draftee who claimed a legitimate exemption, but of the man who mocks the Union's laws. "Song of the Exempts," *Nick Nax*, November 11, 1862, 213. Courtesy of HarpWeek.

plate a quick excursion to either Canada or Europe.[76] The humorous card titled "The Frightened Conscript" portrayed a well-dressed toad, having been conscripted, contemplating a run for Canada.[77]

In the short story "A Romance—The Conscript," Artemus Ward told the tale of Philander Reed, a dry goods clerk in upstate New York, who is drafted, passes his medical fitness test, and cannot come up with the three-hundred-dollar commutation fee. Philander chooses to skedaddle to Canada, much to the disgust of his sweetheart, Mabel. Ward builds the entire story around patriotic songs of the day, presenting a clever inversion of popular airs such as "Do They Think of Me at Home?"[78] Nasby adopted a similar course when draft day neared. Two weeks after offering his case for why he should not be drafted, the fictional Ohioan reports from Canada, where he and a handful of fellow conscripts have sought sanctuary.[79] Two months later the resourceful Copperhead returns home, believing that he

The satirists loved to poke fun at wealthy conscripts who fled the country ahead of the provost marshal. Here cartoonist Howard Del mocks a draftee who when faced with the "horns of a very horrible dilemma" contemplates whether to flee to Europe or Canada. *Yankee Notions* 10 (October 1862): cover. Courtesy of HarpWeek.

Wartime cartoonists periodically produced humorous cards featuring wartime characters as animals. In this small (2½-by-4-inch) chromolithograph, the artist portrays a "frightened conscript" as a hefty toad heading for Canada. Courtesy of the Library Company of Philadelphia.

THE FRIGHTENED CONSCRIPT.

has successfully eluded the draft, only to be captured by a "soljer" as soon as he arrives in Toledo. A disappointed Nasby is "allowd to volunteer to fite against my convickshens," and so his military career begins.[80]

Particular tales of cowardly self-mutilations reappeared time and again in the press, suggesting that they touched a popular nerve. In response to the state militia draft of 1862 the *Danbury (CT) Times* reported that four draftees in nearby Fairfield chopped off their trigger fingers to avoid military service. The *Milwaukee Daily Sentinel* picked up the story in August, reprinting it along with another report about a Connecticut man who bled to death when he "so mutilated his right hand by a bush-scythe, to get rid of the draft." The *Chicago Tribune* ran the same story, although identifying the men as from Danbury and adding an amusing wrinkle: apparently one of the four men got confused and used his right hand to cut off his left forefinger. The *Newark (OH) Advocate* also reprinted the Danbury story,

On Duty, Cowardice, and Citizenship

upping the ante a bit by reporting that in fact five Fairfield men had cut off their trigger fingers. The *Advocate* added a similar report about a drafted New York farmer who claimed that he had accidentally cut off his toe with an axe, only to get caught in his lie when he could not produce the boot he had been wearing. By September the story of the Connecticut cowards had made its way to the West Coast. San Francisco's *Daily Evening Bulletin* reprinted the story without elaboration. Portland's *Morning Oregonian* indicated that with this story, Danbury "has exceeded all others, so far, in its production of these cravens." The *Oregonian* added reports of a Missouri soldier who had cut off his own right hand to get out of further service and an Iowa woman who grew so enraged with her husband for enlisting that she cut off one of his fingers in his sleep! The Portland paper expanded on the point by reprinting a tale of an underage Ohio boy who—"in decided contrast with these cravens"—decided to hang himself when he was rejected for military service. *Frank Leslie's Illustrated Newspaper* reproduced this suicide story, originally published in the *Elyria (OH) Democrat*.[81]

The North's cartoonists had great fun with the early draft evaders. In "Beauties of the Draft," cartoonist A. A. Turner produced a series of *carte de visite*–sized images, mocking a variety of cowardly traits. One portrayed a conscript at the examining surgeon's office, claiming, "I'm weak in the back." In fact, he carries a stack of bills strapped to his back, as a generous bribe to the doctor. A contrasting image shows a soldier kissing his wife good-bye, with the caption "No Substitutes Wanted."[82] One drawing in *Vanity Fair* showed a large fellow with a thick working-class accent, dressed in clerical garb, trying to convince the draft board that he was in fact a minister.[83] The following month the same cartoonist drew a man at the draft board claiming an exemption because he was "an idiot." The examiner looked him over and accepted the claim.[84] In November 1862 *Harper's Weekly* ran a cartoon showing dozens of men hanging from a hot air balloon heading out of town, having exhausted all other options for avoiding the draft.[85] A cartoon in *Frank Leslie's Budget of Fun* portrayed a young urban swell at the draft office insisting that he is "exactly sixty-three" and thus too old for the draft.[86] Although many editorials indicated that hiring a substitute was a perfectly appropriate act for conscripts with good reasons to avoid service, the cartoonists still had a few chuckles at their expense. In July 1862, Howard Del drew a foppish-looking fellow with a rolled-up umbrella approaching a hulking laborer as a possible substitute, only to be told that he should try the "big monkey at Barnum's" instead.[87]

These small humorous cards, placed on *carte de visite* mounts, commented on various traits that appeared during the draft. In the first a man bribes a doctor to exempt him for a bad back; the second shows a wife swigging from a bottle as her husband prepares to leave; the third mocks the notion of enlisting for "honor and glory." Turner, "Beauties of the Draft." Courtesy of the Library Company of Philadelphia.

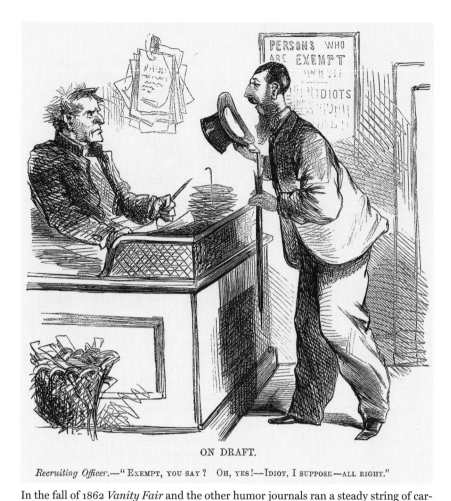

ON DRAFT.

Recruiting Officer.—"Exempt, you say? Oh, yes!—Idiot, I suppose—all right."

In the fall of 1862 *Vanity Fair* and the other humor journals ran a steady string of cartoons making fun of every sort of dishonest draft evader (while also poking fun at all the possible routes to exemption). In this case the conscript is happily claiming to be an "idiot" to avoid service. A few weeks earlier the same artist drew a huge, scowling man who claimed to be a minister. *Vanity Fair*, September 20, 1862, 143. Courtesy of HarpWeek.

■ The message to the ordinary citizen who was liable to the 1862 militia draft seemed clear: those who run or dissemble or cheat are worthy of the nation's scorn. Any man who was willing to disfigure or cripple himself deserved to be mocked from coast to coast. *Vanity Fair*, always good for an innovative idea, suggested that the nation should "contrive false fingers to match the false hearts of fellows who would thus render themselves unserviceable to their country in her hour of danger."[88] And as with the public

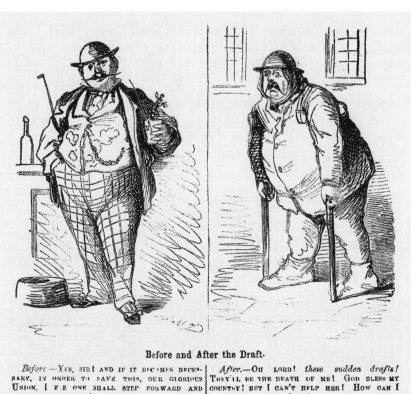

Before and After the Draft.

Before.—YES, SIR! AND IF IT BECOMES NECESSARY, IN ORDER TO SAVE THIS, OUR GLORIOUS UNION, I FOR ONE SHALL STEP FORWARD AND SHOULDER A MUSKET!

After.—OH LORD! *these sudden drafts!* THEY'LL BE THE DEATH OF ME! GOD BLESS MY COUNTRY! BUT I CAN'T HELP HER! HOW CAN I SHOULDER A MUSKET! EH!

Comic artists often targeted the strange and amusing transitions that the war produced among the home front citizenry. As we have seen, many of these paired images ridiculed the transitions enjoyed by members of the shoddy aristocracy. Here we have the other side of that coin. In the first image we see a well-dressed and very healthy-seeming fellow, declaring to all who will listen that he will gladly shoulder a musket when he is needed. In the "After" image the same man has been drafted, but he has transformed himself into a frail man who needs canes to walk and could never be expected to serve in uniform. It is not so much the exemption as the hypocrisy that deserves ridicule. *Yankee Notions* 11 (October 1862): 309. Courtesy of HarpWeek.

scorn aimed at the North's "shoulder straps," the true hypocrites came in for the greatest criticism. In "Before and after the Draft," the first of a pair of cartoons showed a husky, well-dressed man first declaring his willingness to "shoulder a musket" for "our glorious union" while the second portrayed the same man—after the draft had been announced—stooped over and supporting himself with two canes, clearly unable to go to war.[89] The humor magazine *Nick Nax* published a similar cartoon, featuring three images of Mr. Jones. In the first, our wealthy hero is mulling over whether to enlist "to wage war against Secesh" or hire a substitute. In the second, Mr. Jones is in a panic when he discovers that his houseboy has handed his name and details over to the draft enrollers. In the final frame, Mr. Jones has discovered a debilitating illness that requires him to rush overseas and out of harm's way.[90]

By contrast, the good citizen played by the rules. The man who cooperated with the enrolling officers and waited patiently to see if his name had been called was a truly patriotic citizen. Once he was called to service, it was perfectly acceptable for him to take advantage of all legal avenues to avoid service, including the purchase of a reasonable substitute (as opposed to a dead pig). The *Chicago Tribune* had been an outspoken advocate of a draft since early on the war, making the argument that such a plan would properly distribute the burdens of war to all citizens. "It brings home to every man his personal responsibility as a member of society, and most sharply suggests to the individual that he has a personal share in the safety and ruin of the nation," the paper proclaimed. When men faced the draft, "the mask falls, the traitor stands exposed, or he takes his place in the ranks to do citizen's duty." The militia draft promised to not only fill the ranks, but also expose the cowards and traitors.[91]

But even in this first round of state militia drafting, northerners distinguished between a shared risk and actual military service. In a November 1862 summary of recent draft activities, the *Milwaukee Sentinel* was generally pleased with the results but noted, "The married men who were drafted were among those least able to go." One man in particular had seven children at home and a bedridden wife; another had nine children and was the sole source of support for his elderly parents; a third had six children and a sickly wife. These cases of "peculiar hardship," the editorial noted, called for the assistance of the "really benevolent [and] goodhearted" in the city.[92] The newspaper seemed to be following the logic of Lincoln's conscription memo in concluding that honorable and patriotic men might have perfectly valid reasons to remain at home. As 1862 came to a close, even those who welcomed the state militia draft did not see patriotic duty as equated with absolute—or even substantial—personal sacrifice. Patriotic citizenship merely required that men examine their own circumstances and consciences and contemplate volunteering in a forthright manner. By early 1863 the terms of this national discussion, and these personal decisions, had begun to shift.[93]

CHAPTER FIVE

No Man of Honor Shall Shrink from Running His Chance

Federal Conscription and Individual Obligations

One of the great challenges in understanding the Civil War is to come to terms with forty-eight months of warfare as a single event, and also as a narrative thick with patterns of change and broad developments. In his magisterial multivolume history of the Civil War era, the historian Allen Nevins described the conflict up until 1863 as "the improvised war" and the years from 1863 to Appomattox as "the organized war."[1] Nevins's framework focuses largely on the institutions required to wage war and support the armies in the field. Both the Union and the Confederacy found themselves engaged in a massive conflict long before they had constructed the institutional apparatus to fight such a war. The transition from improvisation to organization was indeed critical, and one might argue that the North's successful mobilization of its superior manpower and material capacity proved critical to its ultimate success.

By early 1863, several things were clear to northern observers. From a military standpoint, there was no reason to believe that a Union victory was around the corner. Politically, the Republican Party and the Lincoln administration had suffered serious losses in the off-year elections, leaving open the possibility that the president might not survive a reelection campaign. By January, the Union army was a war for liberation, thanks to the controversial Emancipation Proclamation. Two months later Congress passed the Enrollment Act of 1863, laying the groundwork for the first federal draft in US history.[2]

The wartime discussions in the northern print press did not go through abrupt transitions in the winter of 1862–63, but clear transitions did emerge. The Emancipation Proclamation changed the political terrain and had an enormous impact on public conversations within the African American community, although abolitionism rarely cropped up in the

158

home front fiction. The new federal conscription legislation, expanding on the earlier state militia draft and signaling a much more dramatic shift in the Union's approach to filling the ranks, quickly became a subject of intense commentary in newspapers and journals. As we have seen, when the second year of the war came to a close and hopes for a short conflict became a distant memory, the home front satire directed toward the North's disreputable types grew harsher. And with the costs of war mounting, civilians—both men and women—wrestled with new discussions of the meaning of citizenship and participation.[3]

THE COWARD

The pressures surrounding conscription drove much of this evolving wartime discussion, but hovering just beneath the surface was a more fundamental set of questions about bravery, cowardice, and citizenship. In his third home front novel, *The Coward*, Henry Morford offered his own perspective on the broader question of individual character. Like Morford's previous two novels, *The Coward* is long and complex and includes various sections where the novelist offers his thoughts on wartime events, unfiltered by plotlines. And like his previous efforts, Morford's final wartime novel attracted substantial attention in the periodical literature.[4]

The Coward begins in West Philadelphia in June 1863, as the state is bracing for Robert E. Lee's invasion and Governor Andrew Curtin has called for emergency troops. Carlton Brand is a healthy young man with a military commission awaiting him as soon as he reports for duty, but more than two years into the war, business obligations have persistently kept Carlton from donning a uniform. Brand's fiancé is the aggressively patriotic Margaret Haley, who welcomes Lee's invasion for providing the "means of rousing the sluggish pulse of men who would otherwise have stagnated in trade and pleasure." Although Carlton has stayed at home, twenty-two-year-old Margaret is confident that he will "do his duty," and she tells his younger sister she would prefer that he face "a thousand deaths" than that he prompt "the least suspicion of a want of true manhood."[5] Alas, Margaret's confidence in Carlton unravels when she overhears him admitting to his sister, "I dare not go. I am a coward!" Margaret is disgusted and promptly cuts off all contact. But Carlton's explanation to his sister muddies the water a bit. His problem, he explains, is that he knows that he is a coward, and if he found himself facing enemy fire he would run in fear, thus failing to do his duty and bringing disgrace on his war-hero father. The Pennsylvanian accepts personal humiliation rather than putting himself in a situation in which, he is convinced, he will fail and others will pay the price. This leaves the reader with a thorny problem: is it cowardly to avoid military service if one is convinced that serving would be disastrous?

Things get worse for poor Carlton. When the word gets out that he has failed to report for duty, Carlton's invalid father learns that Carlton is a fraud and a coward. As Lee's army marches into Pennsylvania, Carlton takes a train for New York City, where he buys a ticket to Liverpool.

Several chapters later the plot shifts to the White Mountains, where an assortment of familiar names (including Margaret), and new characters[6] come together for swimming, hiking, and horseback riding. One of this group is the mysterious Horace Townsend, who quickly finds himself at odds with a Captain Cole over Margaret's attentions. The reader figures out that the captain is a disreputable shoulder straps, while Horace is someone to admire even though he is not a soldier. Cole conspires to make Townsend look like a coward, but the reader knows better. In a crucial scene, young Master Brooks Cunningham falls in a swimming hole and is close to drowning. As several other men, including Captain Cole, look on without acting, Horace arrives and promptly leaps into the cold water to save the boy. And in case the point was insufficiently clear, several chapters later Horace gallantly saves a climber who has fallen off a cliff, again upstaging Captain Cole.[7]

The novel eventually shifts to a Virginia battlefield in April 1864. Townsend is now in the Union army and is still squabbling with Cole. As the regiment prepares to charge, Townsend challenges Cole to a peculiar duel: they will charge together, and whoever gets the farthest is the winner. The two men set off, surrounded by Union soldiers who are intent on victory. The two rivals care nothing about the battle, only about their own conflict. Both men fight valiantly until Cole finally breaks and runs and is killed by a shell fragment. Townsend wins their private duel and is then wounded himself.

Margaret visits Townsend in the hospital and finally recognizes that the wounded soldier is in fact her old fiancé, Carlton Brand (he had worn a beard while in the White Mountains, which was apparently sufficient to fool her). Carlton comes clean, explaining that he had a history of fainting at the sight of blood, which had convinced him that he was a coward when in fact he had some sort of neurological condition. This fits with what the reader has seen over the previous year. Repeatedly, when circumstances had forced Carlton to act, he had behaved valiantly, although he periodically passed out after the fact. But when events gave him a chance to reflect, Carlton had steered clear of dangerous situations and avoided military service. Of course, this all changed near the end of the novel, when a distraught Brand/Townsend—who thought he had lost Margaret for good—essentially engages in an almost suicidal duel against his hated adversary.

We are left to wonder what Morford expected the reader to learn from the life of "the coward." Carlton Brand ends up with Margaret, suggesting that he must have made good choices along the way. Their crucial conversation in the hospital seemed to validate his previous decision to avoid military service. He was not a coward, just someone who fainted at the sight of blood. Finally, Carlton ends up in the Union army, charging valiantly against Confederate forces, receiving heavy wounds while his adversary is killed. With that fateful charge he seemed to throw off the taint of cowardice, but at what cost? After all, his motivations had nothing to do with patriotism: he charged to defeat Captain Cole. Who are we to admire, the man who declined to serve because of his own sense of self-knowledge, or the almost suicidal love-sick soldier who bravely charged the enemy lines with no larger purpose in mind? Morford offers us a clue in his brief preface, where he explains, "The aim of the writer, eschewing all such tempting personalities, and quite as carefully avoiding all dry didactic discussion of the theme of courage and its opposite, has principally been to illustrate the tendency of many men to misunderstand their own characters in certain particulars, and the inevitable consequence of their being misunderstood by the world, in one direction or the other."[8] Morford's point was that Carlton Brand illustrated how individuals do not always recognize their own strengths and weaknesses. Carlton thought he was a coward and acted honestly and with integrity given those convictions, even though they led others to judge him harshly. When he adopted a new (bearded) persona, other characters no longer considered Carlton a coward, although his private ambivalence continued.[9] Events call into question Carlton's self-knowledge (he was not really a coward), but they also illustrate the limitations of hostile public perceptions. Even his fiancé did not see his true nature.

Morford was not alone in questioning the meaning of cowardice. Authors of wartime stories commonly presented characters and situations that were not quite as they seemed. In "Tried and True," Anna W. Shirley tells Ellen and Charles's complicated tale. The couple had been deeply involved until Ellen heard that her beloved had declined a challenge from his college classmate, Paul. Charles's version of things was that he was a man of God, and Paul had been drunk, thus he refused to fight a duel over a misunderstanding. Ellen sees it differently and turns her back on the man she felt was a coward. As the plot unfolds, Paul gets engaged to Ellen, and Charles and Paul end up as captains in the same regiment. Charles—who had already demonstrated his bravery in previous battles—risks his life to save Paul's, thus ensuring Ellen's future happiness. He dies asking that Ellen be told "I was not a coward."[10] A few months later, Mary E. Dodge's "Netty's Touchstone" raised the specter of cowardice and confusion yet again. George Holmes tells the lovely Netty that he has taken measures to avoid being drafted, and Netty assumes that this shows he is a coward and beneath contempt. In fact, George has enlisted.[11] These two stories, like Morford's novel, turned on an honorable man being falsely accused of cowardice, and an unthinkingly patriotic woman misjudging him. In each case the female character is an honest observer, representing popular perceptions much as Ward's Baldinsville women assessed the behavior of their men. Wise readers would conclude that perhaps true cowardice is impossible to judge without knowing what is in a man's heart.

IF A MAN IS ADVERSE TO SERVING FROM ANY CAUSE

While Henry Morford wrestled with the complicated nuances surrounding cowardice and bravery, other northerners framed their analysis around the particular issues surrounding the Enrollment Act of 1863.[12] In 1863, when the state militia draft gave way to the more expansive federal draft, northern newspaper editors pushed hard to get the new system under way. "When so many noble volunteers have joyfully gone before them," the *Chicago Tribune* asked, "what right has any laggard at home, born of the same country . . . if now, in her extreme need and peril, he is called upon at this late and momentous hour, to take his chance of being conscripted, that he also may have the privilege of dying for her."[13] Here we have a clear statement of the obligations of citizenship in wartime. The good citizen was expected to "take his chance" along with everyone else.

A month after draft riots swept through New York City in July 1863, the *Tribune* was still celebrating conscription as "the most democratic leveler and equalizer of all extant institutions," ensuring equal sacrifice in time of war. Only the "coward or sneak" would refuse to take his chances in a fair draft lottery. While rioters and political dissenters continued to criticize the inequities built into the draft laws, the Republican paper praised the system of exemptions as the ideal way to ensure that those men who felt unable to serve had options available to them within the law and within the bounds of proper citizenship. "Although each citizen is a soldier, and liable to a regular militia duty," the paper explained, "and although we have a nominal United States army, we are free from the military exactions which nearly every European government imposed upon its subjects . . . in times of peace." Even when conscription is "forced upon the Government by a military necessity," the individual's needs remain protected. Thus, the editorial argued, men whose labor "supply the sinews of war" must be exempted. Moreover, those who feel that "the demands of families are absolute" can pay the three-hundred-dollar commutation fee. So long as just provisions remain in place to protect those who feel that they cannot serve, "no one can grumble."[14]

William Lloyd Garrison's *Liberator* was similarly enthusiastic about the new conscription legislation as the best way to fill the ranks while distributing the sacrifices across the entire population. The new law, the abolitionist paper argued, improved on the state militia laws by providing greater protection for the poor sons of widowed mothers and other needy young men. The editorial noted with approval that the federal laws allowed for the hiring of substitutes and the payment of a three-hundred-dollar commutation fee. Thus Garrison's paper—like other prowar journals—explicitly praised the Conscription Act's provisions that accommodated those conscripts who preferred to avoid service.[15] A month later *The Liberator* quoted extensively from a speech by abolitionist Gerrit Smith making the same points. Smith applauded the conscription legislation as the appropriate solution to the challenges facing the Union, yet he had no particular concerns about the law's provisions that seemed to favor men of means. After all, the rich men who procured substitutes would stay at home providing continued employment for the North's less wealthy laborers.[16]

In August, a Washington correspondent to the *Tribune* went a step further, applauding the three-hundred-dollar commutation fees as providing loyal citizens with an affirmative opportunity to support the war when drafted, even if they were unable to serve themselves: "For if a man is adverse to serving from any cause,—whether from dread of the fatigues of this service, from the inconvenience of leaving his business, or from hostility, or aversion to the war, he can at any rate save himself from the hardship, the inconvenience, or the wickedness, if he so regards it, of participating in the war, by the payment of three hundred dollars." The author presented military service—even for the draftee—as little more than a choice among an array of equally valid options.[17]

Massachusetts's *Newburyport Herald* adopted a somewhat different stance. Noting that several of New England's more prominent citizens had recently been drafted, the newspaper called on them to follow their own "writing and preaching" and "come forward cheerfully to perform the duties of soldiers" as an example to other citizens. But even here the editorial made allowances for personal considerations, noting that these civic leaders should not "attempt to obtain exemptions, unless the case for that exemption is good, and will be apparent to others." The author hoped that the drafted leaders would serve if exemptions were not in order, rather than hire a substitute, but the argument targeted civic leaders who could be an important beacon to working-class draftees. Moreover, the editorial specifically addressed those vocal patriots who had been calling on others to enlist. These men faced charges of hypocrisy, not simply poor citizenship, if they failed to go to war. And since they had claimed a public identity, their reasons for avoiding conscription ought to be apparent to others. Even that charge of hypocrisy only applied to men who were drafted and elected not to serve, not to able-bodied men who had called on others to enlist without volunteering themselves.[18]

Although in this study we are concerned primarily with public discussions on the home front, soldiers in the field embraced a similar perspective regarding conscription. On the one hand, men who were already in uniform welcomed conscription and questioned the behavior of those who avoided service. On the other hand, these same men seemed happy to accept appropriate exceptions, especially where family or friends were concerned. As the historian Reid Mitchell explains, "While most soldiers were eager that shirkers be drafted, they were also reluctant that their brothers, sons, or fathers be exposed to the hardships of military life." Thus some veterans—even while celebrating the abstract idea of conscription—wrote home urging young men to avoid enlisting, lie about their ages if necessary, and take advantage of any opportunities to avoid service.[19]

In the months after the federal draft became law, a Connecticut volunteer, Captain Samuel W. Fiske, writing to the *Springfield Republican* as "Mr. Dunn Browne," penned a series of sardonic commentaries on the state of enlistment and conscription. Perhaps not surprisingly, he was particularly critical of able-bodied men who hired substitutes to serve in their place, but his chief objection was that the hired substitute or man who enlisted merely to earn huge bounties was a worthless comrade. And much like the home front commentary, Fiske aimed his harshest language at the North's hypocrites, who spewed patriotic rhetoric but refused to serve, or those dishonest types who broke the rules to avoid service.

Fiske disliked false soldiers and corrupt cowards, but he devoted much of his energy to urging those patriotic men whose names had been

On Duty, Cowardice, and Citizenship

selected to step forward and serve. Fiske repeatedly used the language of engaged patriotism rather than invoking the language of citizenship. "Come on then, my brave friends who have hitherto been kept at home by the presence of other important avocations," he wrote on July 27, 1863. A month later he insisted that "some of the best class of our citizens . . . who find it very inconvenient indeed to leave their homes and businesses, some who have excellent reasons for not coming" must step forward and serve, "or else the draft is a failure." In sum, "let the draft be the occasion of a noble and manly volunteering," he urged. Speaking to these potential patriots, Fiske repeatedly argued that the war would soon be over and that these last-minute volunteers would be crucial to sealing the Union victory. Those conscripts who stepped forward when called, he promised, would be "honored as true patriots and worthy comrades" by the men already in the field, and they would be able to share in the Union victory. In November Fiske explained that things had changed. "When I came the question was, 'Can you afford to go to war?'" But with the latest call for men "the question is, 'Can you afford to stay at home?'" As Fiske explained, the man who stays home will risk having no role in a glorious victory or, worse, will face the chance of having failed to help avert a terrible failure.

In this series of public letters, Fiske consistently sought to convince the patriotic men at home that serving in the military was a choice in their best interest. He recognized, much as Abraham Lincoln had done in his memo on conscription, that they had thus far decided to remain at home for compelling personal reasons, but the variables they had weighed had shifted. The experience would make them better men, he insisted, and for the rest of their lives they could claim some role in a glorious cause. Those who chose to stay home and tend their farms and businesses and be with their wives and children would be denied the "proud privilege" of being honored veterans.[20] Even the soldier in the field who hoped for reinforcements framed the issue as one of personal deliberation rather than in terms of the absolute obligations of national citizenship.

Wilbur Fisk, a private from Vermont, wrote a similar series of letters home to the *Green Mountain Freeman*. Like Samuel Fiske, Wilbur Fisk seemed especially unhappy with those draftees who were trying to avoid doing their part. In April 1863 he wrote, "It would seem as if the conscription act had made cowards of many and they were afraid their own precious blood would be spilled. It isn't fair play." The draft, he argued, is simply a matter of "drawing cuts to see who shall go to war, and no man of honor shall shrink from running his chance." Months later, Fisk returned to the same theme while on furlough in Poughkeepsie, New York. He was pleased to see able-bodied men picked for the draft, and outraged by those men who faked injuries or in other ways conspired to avoid serving.

But even as he was chastising the North's unmanly cowards, Fisk's comments made clear that there were draftees at home who had obligations that should rightly keep them at home, whereas other men really were not physically fit to serve. Unlike Samuel Fiske, Fisk seemed happy to accept conscripts and bounty men as comrades, assuming that they were healthy and prepared to undergo rigorous training. But in perhaps his angriest letter on the subject, Fisk told his readers about a recruit who had arrived with his pockets bursting with bounty money but who was physically unable to withstand the rigors of war. The poor fellow fell into rapid decline, eventually dying alone and friendless, of some camp ailment. Fisk wanted soldiers who would serve, but also could serve well.

Despite his talk of the draft as a moment when each man should take his chance, Wilbur Fisk really concluded that soldiering was best reserved for those men who were ready and able to stand the tests. "Unless a man has patriotism of the most exalted kind . . . and believes that we are fighting for God and humanity," he wrote, the conscript cannot be a good soldier. "Standing target for the rebel minies, is one of the most uncomfortable positions a man was ever placed in . . . and we do not worry that some men pray to be excused when the country calls for such work." The soldiers in the field, he continued, recognize "the man who has resolutely made up his mind to do his duty, like a worthy American citizen, who scorns to pay his $300 or plead disability, [and] all honor to him." For the rest, "we need not wonder that he resists when called. . . . It is the most natural thing in the world that he should do so, and we shall have all charity possible for him." Fisk used the language of both manhood and citizenship, and against those standards he judged harshly those who declined to serve. Yet he stopped short of declaring that every man should serve. In fact, the man who privately concluded that he would make a poor soldier could easily read Fisk's words as encouragement to avoid service. And while both soldiers recognized that by 1863 the Union needed more men, neither Fisk nor Fiske seemed displeased with the able-bodied conscript who had declined to volunteer in the first two years of the war, so long as he obeyed the law when his name was called.[21]

When nineteen-year-old Rhode Islander Elisha Hunt Rhodes chose to enlist in the first weeks of the war he wrote, "I, in common with the other young men, feel that it is my duty to serve in the field." But in order to do so he had to overcome the resistance of his widowed mother, who finally concluded, "'If you feel that it is your duty to enlist, I will give my

On Duty, Cowardice, and Citizenship

consent.'" The following August, as the Union ranks had begun to thin, Rhodes wrote that the regiment was having a hard time finding new recruits, and he concluded that "if men are not patriotic enough to volunteer to save the country I hope a draft will be ordered." Nearly a year later he celebrated that the Union "will now enforce the draft and we shall be all right."[22] A dedicated soldier for the entire four years of war, Rhodes saw the draft as a proper and necessary tool to save the Union, and he felt that it was required only because of a failure of patriotism back home. But his decision to enlist, and his mother's approval, turned on a personal sense of his own duty rather than an abstract sense that all men—even young unmarried men—should share that feeling.

New Jersey's General Robert McAllister considered conscription from the perspective of a commanding officer and came to quite similar conclusions. In July 1864 he wrote to his wife, Ellen, expressing frustration with the "young and able-bodied men" who had failed to step forward and "show their courage in a trying time like this." Two months later he was pleased with the latest draft call and the new recruits it promised. When these men began to arrive, the general told Ellen that he did not want bounty men. Instead, "the drafting is the only true way to keep up an army and get good men."[23]

Like the use of "shoddy" in political debate, critical commentary about draft evasion often found its way into partisan political discourse. In October, New York conservative Republican Thurlow Weed took on the war's powerful hypocrites in a letter in his Albany newspaper, the *Evening Journal*. Weed pointed to New York mayor George Opdyke, whose son had been drafted, and Theodore Tilton, the abolitionist editor of the New York *Independent*, who had been drafted himself, noting that both had been outspoken abolitionists and strong advocates of the war effort, yet when the draft came Opdyke's son and Tilton both "skulked" rather than serving. Weed, no fan of the "boisterous abolitionists" in his party, was not so much outraged that these powerful men had taken advantage of the substitute laws to avoid service; rather, he deplored the hypocrisy and "false pretenses" that their actions revealed.[24] In the cartoon "Look Sharp!" a wounded Union soldier sits at a bar, confronting an abolitionist Republican whose able-bodied son cowers behind him. The soldier declares that in 1860 he had supported Lincoln, but with the election of 1864 approaching he was going to throw his support behind McClellan rather than joining forces with the hypocritical "cowards" who support the war but then buy their sons' safety.[25]

In August 1863 the editor of the *Portland Transcript* noted that some

LOOK SHARP!
THE ELECTION.
AN ACTUAL INCIDENT.

REPUBLICAN DEACON.--There is no end of the matter, but the Extermination of Slavery, or the White Race.

SOLDIER.--D - - n you: why don't you and your coward Son, whom you bought off when he was Drafted, go to the War.

I VOTED FOR LINCOLN!
When he called, I went to defend the Constitution and the Union.

NOW I VOTE FOR McCLELLAN!!
Vote for LINCOLN and you vote yourself an Abolition Conscript within Four Years.

This large lithograph produced during the 1864 campaign, "Look Sharp!," shows a wounded soldier attacking a hypocritical Republican who supports the war but protected his son from military service. At one level, this is a partisan political statement, warning voters about supporting a war to end slavery, but the artist has framed his argument as an attack on hypocrisy. Courtesy of the Henry E. Huntington Library, San Marino, California.

of the younger men who worked for the paper had been drafted, adding—with a touch of wit—that the editorial staff's older and married members, who had been excused from the draft, stood ready to subdue the Rebels when the war reached its final stages. If lawmakers had chosen to treat married men over the age of thirty-five as a separate draft category, the dictates of citizenship held them to no higher standard. They would proudly follow the law, which conveniently excused them from service.[26]

In one unusual variant on the larger question of citizenship and service, in early 1863 reports circulated about immigrant factory workers in Jersey City, New Jersey, who had refused to become naturalized citizens for fear of being drafted. In response, irate native workers had forced their immigrant coworkers out of the factory until they had received their citizenship papers and were thus liable to the risk of conscription. Here again the assumption seemed to be that the right to work should be accompanied by the shared risks of citizenship. The workers should not have to enlist, but they should have to take their chances on draft day like everyone else.[27]

Even more so than the state militia drafts of 1862, the newspaper discussions following announcements of four federal drafts in 1863 and 1864 seemed to connect citizenship with recruiting, rather than enlisting. In May 1863 Colorado's *Tri-Weekly Miner's Register* published an editorial on the draft. The western paper encouraged its military-aged readers to enlist, thus avoiding the humiliation that could accompany being called in a draft. But the real goal of the editorial was for readers to devote themselves to recruiting in order to meet the quota and avoid the latest draft. "Every citizen should do everything in his power to encourage enlistments," the paper urged. Thus we have a surprising paradox: able-bodied men should enlist out of a sense of self-interest (to avoid humiliation), but one following the path of good citizenship would promote volunteering for the public good, rather than necessarily enlist oneself.[28] Other local newspapers did not bother with the niceties of citizenship at all. The approach of draft day provoked editorials calling on donations to bounty funds simply to spare the community the "disgrace" of a draft.[29] In response to the federal call for half a million more men in early 1864, the *Round Table* urged renewed attention to recruitment, declaring that "each citizen should consider himself as responsible" for securing one recruit. The responsibilities of citizenship required northerners to recruit suitable volunteers; apparently it did not require northern citizens themselves to serve.[30]

In August 1864, a young reader wrote to the *Boston Daily Advertiser* asking why he should enlist in the Union army. In an extended—and quite extraordinary—editorial, the *Advertiser* argued that the correspondent had a "patriotic duty" to serve the cause. But even in making this strong call for volunteering, the newspaper stopped short of suggesting that mere citizenship—as opposed to active patriotism—required this sacrifice of eligible men. "The question," the editor explained, "is one for each of us to answer in his own conscience, while, fortunately, we have to find also an answer to our neighbors and to the law. If we have escaped a draft; if our families, and friends, and acquaintances, think that we are of more use with the cane than the musket; if we have persuaded ourselves of the same thing, and are doing our duty with personal exertion, and pecuniary aid in other ways, to fill the ranks of our armies and swell the treasury coffers; then we may lay our heads upon our pillows with a good conscience."

This editorial essentially leaves the decision up to each individual, in consultation with his own conscience, friends, and family. The obligation is to think carefully about the decision. The appropriate choice is more complicated than mere personal inclination. Later in the same editorial, the author considers the "'benefit'" that each man might accrue from enlisting or from "helping others to enlist" and concludes that such a benefit ought "to be measured by the stake he has in that country." This introduced more hard questions, because "each man must tell for himself how far his interest is bound up with the existence, the integrity, the prosperity of his country. Each one must judge how far he is responsible for sustaining all of these, and how far he can excuse himself from the calls made in their behalf." The editorial seemed to be moving toward the idea that citizenship does involve reciprocal obligations between the citizen and his nation, but those obligations are highly individual and contingent and not absolute. Thus each man is left to judge for himself whether he is really obligated to enlist, based at least partially on how much he feels he owes his country.[31]

I AM SICK, DON'T DRAFT ME

The federal drafts in 1863 and 1864 produced new rounds of satirical commentary about draft evaders and other hypocrites. Humorist Artemus Ward wrote perhaps the most widely circulated critique of the whole affair in his "Circular No. 78." Presented in a style that mocked the flood of officious government documents flowing from Washington, Ward's circular presented six propositions intended to clarify recent government decisions:

1. A young man who is drafted and inadvertently goes to Canada, where he becomes embroiled with a robust English party, who knocks him around so as to disable him for life, the same occurring in a licensed bar-room on British soil, such young man cannot receive a pension on account of said injuries from the United States Government, nor can his heirs or creditors.

2. No drafted man . . . will be permitted to go round by way of Canada on account of the roads being better that way. . . .

3. Any gentleman living in Ireland, who was never in this country, is not liable to the draft, nor are our forefathers. This latter statement is made for the benefit of those enrolling officers who have acted on the supposition that the able-bodied male population of a place included dead gentlemen in the cemeteries.

4. The term of enlistment is for three years, but any man who has been drafted in two places has a right to go for six years. . . .

5. The only sons of a poor widow, whose husband is in California, are not exempt, but the man who owns stock in the Vermont Central Railroad is. So also are incessant lunatics, habitual lecturers, persons who were born with wooden legs or false teeth. Blind men—unless they will acknowledge that they "can't see it"—and people who deliberately voted for John Tyler.

6. No drafted man can claim exemption on the ground that he has several children whom he supports and who do not bear his name, or live in the same house with him, and who have never been introduced to his wife, but who, on the contrary, are endowed with various mothers, and "live round."

In this clever short piece Ward managed to lampoon devious draft evaders, bumbling enrolling officers, incompetent bureaucrats, and the sometimes absurd complexity of Washington's wartime regulations.[32]

The poem "The Sick Brigade," published in *Yankee Notions* in March 1863, mocked the men who claimed medical exemptions, in an extended parody of "The Charge of the Light Brigade." "Although they had no reason why, Theirs but to push and try," the poet intoned. And as "the ten hundred" reached the doctor's office they found "Skulkers in front of it, Skulkers in rear of it, Skulkers surrounded it."[33] Numerous northern song sheets played on similar themes. "I Am Sick, Don't Draft Me" was to be sung to the tune of "The Girl I Left Behind."[34] "I Am Not Sick, I'm Over Forty-Five" was perhaps written in response, mocking another popular route to exemption.[35] Henry Work's "Grafted into the Army" takes a some-what different approach. Written in the voice of a worried mother, the song describes how "Our Jimmy" has been drafted by the army despite her protests. Although the tone seems light, Work's humor is pretty dark. The final verse reads:

> He looks kinder sickish—begins to cry–
> A big volunteer standing right in his eye
> Oh what if the ducky should up and die
> Now they've grafted him into the army.

In this case the draftee who tried to avoid service and failed received little sympathy.[36]

The process of examination and medical scrutiny at the offices of the provost marshals attracted substantial public attention as each new draft day approached. One long story in the Philadelphia *North American* offered an insider's look into both the legitimate and the fraudulent. For some, the goal was to convince the examining surgeons that they suffered from various debilitating ailments. But for the men who were seeking to become paid substitutes, the goal was reversed, as the infirmed sought to demonstrate that they were physically sound. The reporter provided a de-tailed factual description, but he could not resist sharing a few humorous stories, including one long account of a man who claimed to have a bad leg. The savvy surgeon had the man put under with ether, and when he came to he was informed that the doctor had cured his bad leg and he was fit for service. Another man arrived with recently pulled teeth, making him ineligible for the infantry, so the provost marshal simply assigned him to the cavalry.[37] Yet another showed up wearing a large truss, though there was no physical evidence of any rupture. The physician ordered him to sit, stark naked, waiting for the rupture to manifest itself.[38] An inspect-ing physician in Kennebec, Maine, fooled a man who claimed to be deaf by saying that the man's bad knee was "sufficient to exempt any man." When the draftee corrected him, the doctor caught him in his lie.[39] But despite many humorous stories of fake medical claims, the press generally sup-ported a high medical standard for soldiers, and thus medical exemptions for fairly minor ailments.[40]

Conscription rules giving advantages to married men and those with widowed mothers produced all manner of commentary.[41] The very popular "A Bachelor's Soliloquy on the Conscript Act" imagined a young bachelor's contemplations, along the lines of Hamlet's "To be or not to be" speech, as he weighed the benefits of marriage and military service.[42] A cartoon in

On Duty, Cowardice, and Citizenship

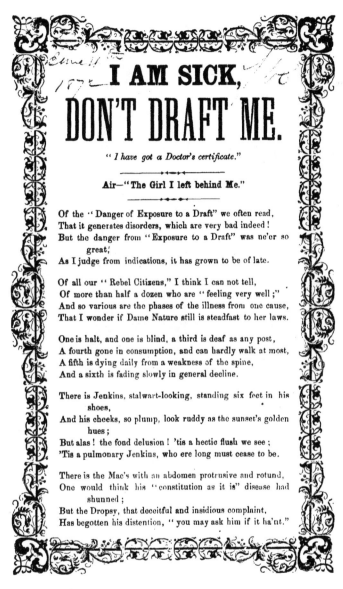

Frank Leslie's Budget of Fun portrayed the devious "Mr. Fitz Muzzle," who had hired his washerwoman and her twin infants to play the role of his dependent family.[43] Another confused and comical conscript claimed an exemption because he was entirely dependent on his widowed mother for support.[44] A Howard Del cartoon showed a poor widow offering to pretend to be a young man's widowed mother to protect him from service.[45] In an amusing inversion of roles, "Cool" pictured Charlie and Kate chat-

A LIBERAL OFFER.

ROAST CHESTNUTS—" *Young man, if you want to adopt a venerable mother, to escape the Conscription, I'm a lone widdy, and it'll do us both good.*"

As northern men faced federal conscription, cartoonists produced scores of new cartoons mocking their strategies for avoiding service. Here Howard Del shows a woman in the park hawking roasted chestnuts suggesting to a young dandy that she would gladly play the role of his widowed mother to help him escape conscription. "I'm a lone widdy, and it'll do us both good," she promises. *Frank Leslie's Budget of Fun* (June 1863): 16. Courtesy of HarpWeek.

ting in a drawing room. She is pointing out to him that if they got married he would be insulated from the draft; he—like "the Bachelor"—is decidedly cool on the idea.[46]

Often the favorite targets were those wealthy northerners who found ways to skirt active service. In "Advice to Tom Tidler" *Vanity Fair* mocked those men who claimed to be heading to the shore "for their health" just as draft day loomed.[47] As in 1862, when the draft dodgers were also hypocrites the ire grew particularly fierce. "Precept and Practice" made the

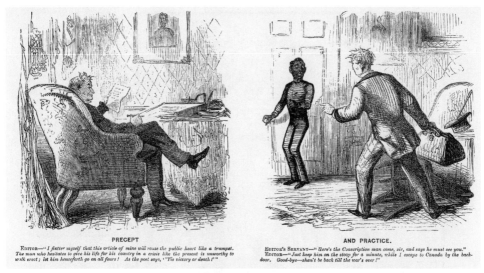

PRECEPT

EDITOR—"*I flatter myself that this article of mine will rouse the public heart like a trumpet. The man who hesitates to give his life for his country in a crisis like the present is unworthy to walk erect; let him henceforth go on all fours! As the poet says, '"Tis victory or death!'"*

AND PRACTICE.

EDITOR'S SERVANT—"*Here's the Conscription man come, sir, and says he must see you.*" EDITOR—"*Just keep him on the stoop for a minute, while I escape to Canada by the back-door. Good-bye—shan't be back till the war's over!*"

This clever pair of cartoons turns on several familiar themes. In the first scene, the newspaper editor is congratulating himself on his latest patriotic offering, urging his readers to greater sacrifice. In the second, the same man is rushing out the door on his way to Canada, one step ahead of the "Conscription man." Note that the editor has an African American servant, perhaps an additional dig at his hypocrisy. *Frank Leslie's Budget of Fun* (June 1863): 8. Courtesy of HarpWeek.

point in two frames. In "Precept" we see a self-satisfied newspaper editor, congratulating himself for his latest patriotic editorial; in "Practice" the same man learns that the "conscription man" is at his door, and the hypocritical coward instructs his butler to create a diversion as he heads off for Canada.[48] The theme of the approaching conscription agent recurred often in northern satire in 1863. A cartoon in *Yankee Notions* mocked a terrified boardinghouse resident trying to avoid the bearer of bad news by having the maid claim that the house only accepted female lodgers.[49] Another showed a famous actor offering a "fine impersonation of 'manifest insanity'" in an attempt to fool the enrolling officer at the door.[50]

With each new draft day, the press sought out the especially peculiar—and humorous—stories about avoiding service. A New Haven paper reported a convoluted tale in which a man showed up in his son's place for the draft inspection, because he would appear too old, but the provost marshal saw through the ruse.[51] *Comic Monthly* described a Philadelphia draftee who hired a substitute, but then grew so worried that the man would run off that he got the fellow drunk and had him arrested for public drunkenness to keep him under wraps.[52] In an image that harked

This cover of *Yankee Notions* features an interesting variation on the wartime critique of hypocrisy and dishonesty. Here we see a provost marshal chatting with a new recruit who had earlier won an exemption from the draft because of his bad back. But now, with government bounties at a newly attractive level, the man's back has magically healed, and he has enlisted and taken his bounty. *Yankee Notions* 12 (December 1863): 353. Courtesy of HarpWeek.

back to the previous year's humor, the cover of the September 1863 issue of *Yankee Notions* featured a lisping swell announcing his plan to have his front teeth pulled out to avoid service.[53] Another portrayed a foolproof plan to avoid the draft: specially designed shoes that would produce a limp.[54] And in perhaps the most emphatic indictment of wartime hypocrisy, a *Yankee Notions* cartoon near the end of 1863 featured a man who had gotten out of the draft with a bad back and then later enlisted to take advantage of rising bounties.[55]

The press took particular joy in reporting ironic cases where cowards received their just deserts. Shortly after the New York City draft riot, a story circulated in northern newspapers about four Connecticut men who ran to New York to escape the draft, only to die in the riots.[56] In June 1864 the *Boston Daily Advertiser* was pleased to report the "coward's fate" of a man had tried to pass an elderly woman off as his poor widowed mother. When this ruse failed, the conscript arranged to have his eight front teeth pulled, recognizing that an infantryman without teeth could not load his rifle. The provost marshal thwarted his plans by assigning the unscrupulous—and now toothless—fellow to the artillery.[57] In an inversion of this theme, a Philadelphia newspaper reported that a local draftee could have taken advantage of an exemption because he had false teeth, but he failed to do so out of embarrassment.[58] As northerners grew agitated about the very real threat of a federal draft, the nation's humorists poked fun at conscripts who failed to take their chances like a man.

THE VOICE OF THE DRAFT

Beyond the world of satire and cartoons, northerners wrestled with the obligations that accompanied conscription. The authors of sentimental fiction used conscription as a way to illuminate character strengths and flaws, often casting the issues along gender lines. "John Morgan's Substitute" turns the whole issue of draft avoidance on its head. When draft day arrives John Morgan, an entirely healthy thirty-five-year-old man, finds that his name has been chosen. He reports the news to his wife, and mother of their five young children, adding, "God knows, it is not for my own sake, Mary! I do not think I am afraid to die. I would go with more than willingness, with joy, if I had not so much to leave." The reader quickly concludes that John should not have to go to war, but he cannot afford a substitute. The dilemma is solved when Ash Thornycroft, the son of the wealthy local mill owner, arrives at their door volunteering to serve as John's substitute. The love of Ash's life has died, leaving him with no impediments to service, and he explains that he had simply been waiting to step forward as a substitute for a worthy drafted man. Thus the proud husband and father who should not fight is spared, and the reader is left to wonder why the healthy and heroic Ash had waited so long to enlist.[59]

Kathie's Soldiers, a children's book written shortly after the war, suggests that young readers learned similar lessons. When Kathie's uncle is drafted, he elects to hire a substitute, concluding that he should remain at home to care for Kathie's widowed mother and her family. Meanwhile, Kathie's cousin wants to enlist as a drummer boy, but he yields to his mother's wishes and agrees to go off to boarding school instead. Both the boy and the man might have been inclined to put on a uniform, but each made the appropriate decision in staying home.[60] The enormously popular children's author Oliver Optic wrote many exciting tales of youths going off to war, but in one of his many didactic moments he told his young readers that "obedience is the first lesson we learn as citizens. We must obey the laws, rather than our own inclinations." The draftee who obeyed the rules, and the boy who obeyed his mother, were both living up to society's expectations.[61]

Although a draftee had options, conscription was often a test of character. In "Netty's Touchstone" the draft illuminates the essence of Henry Kirtland, one of Netty's suitors. The silver-tongued Henry reports that he has been drafted, but he has "already cancelled the obligation" by hiring a man who would be a better soldier than he, so that he can continue being a better businessman than his substitute might have been. Henry has merely availed himself of the rules at his disposal, but his glib comments suggest that his decision reflected a poor character rather than proper deliberation. As we have already seen, Netty mistakenly believes that George—her other suitor—was avoiding the draft out of cowardice. Poor George stood wrongly accused, but it is noteworthy that Netty was upset with George not because she thought he had failed to enlist, only because he had failed to take his chances on draft day.[62]

Draft day provides an even more valuable litmus test for Edith in "The Narrow Escape." Edith's healthy and vigorous twenty-three-year-old beau comes by her home, full of enthusiasm because the draft enroller had visited his boardinghouse and he had managed to sneak out the back undetected. Edith, who had only experienced a conversion to ardent patriotism earlier that day, responds with illuminating indignation:

> I might have looked past a natural shrinking from the hard and dangerous life of a soldier—excused you on the ground of constitutional impediments, if you will call them so—and on this plea accepted your failure to spring to the rescue when your country was assailed—still believing in your honour—still having faith in your will to do right, no matter how stern the demand might be, when it came clear and unmistakable. I can understand that there may be good reasons why one may hold away from the act of volunteering, and I gave you the benefit of this assumption. But when the danger becomes so imminent that an allotment has to be made for defence, only the meanest spirits seek to evade their duty.

In this short speech, Edith summarizes the entire issue. An honorable man might have all sorts of fine reasons for choosing not to enlist, but the man who sneaks away to avoid being enrolled for the draft is—in the words of her uncle—"a coward and a poltroon." The manly "duty" Edith speaks of is not a duty to serve, but a duty to take his chances in the draft lottery along with everyone else.[63]

Some of the most depraved fictional characters are those men who were not drafted at all, but claimed to be. One cartoon featured the front door of "A. Jones," who had run from his creditors by posting a sign announcing that he had been drafted.[64] W. O. Eaton's "Victim of the Draft" told the humorous tale of Abijah Bighead, who saw in the draft an opportunity to exploit. Although not called himself, Abijah forged a stack of draft certificates in various names, and took to the streets seeking donations from sympathetic civilians. Many offered assistance, either to help him purchase a substitute or to support his family in his absence, but one man seemed to articulate the broader consensus when he told Abijah that now that he was drafted, he must serve. "'I've run the risk of going; so have you'; the man explained, 'you've lost; now go in and win!'" Still, the nefarious plan works quite well until Phelim Doody, a seemingly dim-witted cartman, uncovers the scam and wants in on the action. Then, in the story's final twist, Doody is drafted and demands all of their shared plunder or he will reveal Bighead as a fraud. In this fashion Abijah Bighead becomes a "victim of the draft" without being drafted.[65]

In early 1865, only months before the end of the war, cartoonist T. F. G. Miller captured an array of the war's hypocrites and cowards in a series of four drawings for the *Soldier's Casket*. The first man, a clearly scruffy sort, claims to object to the draft because he does not want to have to tent with "low, wulgar, twash!" The second man, a bounty jumper, objects that the draft undercuts his business. The third man had been a hearty supporter of the draft until new laws expanded the age range, making him draft eligible. Now he finds the whole thing "wicked and unconstitutional." The fourth man, a newly elected member of Congress, remains enthusiastic about conscription, with the knowledge that the law exempts him.[66] In each case, the joke turns on some form of hypocrisy, not simply on cowardice. The manly path was to take a chance along with everyone else.

The war and conscription posed particular challenges for northern Quakers. For many, the answer was clear. As committed pacifists they opposed war and refused to cooperate with the military in any form. For others, the fact that the Union army had become an army of emancipation complicated matters, leading some to throw their support to the war effort.[67] For the war's pacifists, conscription also posed particularly challenging questions about the nature of citizenship. In late 1864 the *Friends*

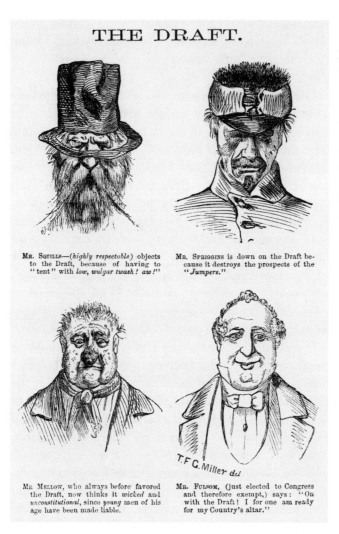

THE DRAFT.

MR. SQUILLS—(*highly respectable*) objects to the Draft, because of having to "tent" with *low, vulgar twash! aw!*"

MR. SPRIGGINS is down on the Draft because it destroys the prospects of the "*Jumpers.*"

MR. MELLOW, who always before favored the Draft, now thinks it *wicked* and *unconstitutional*, since *young* men of his age have been made liable.

MR. FULSOM, (just elected to Congress and therefore exempt,) says: "On with the Draft! I for one am ready for my Country's altar."

T.F.G. Miller del

In this collection of images, cartoonist T. F. G. Miller captures four different types of hypocrites who floated to the surface in response to the draft. *Soldier's Casket* 1 (January 1865): 64. Courtesy of the Henry E. Huntington Library, San Marino, California.

Review affirmed that whereas the Society of Friends objected to all forms of military conflict, they acknowledged that the federal government had a legitimate right to claim a certain level of sacrifice from all citizens in wartime. This opinion opened the door for supporting the assignment of conscripted Quakers to work with freedpeople or wounded soldiers.[68]

The nation's artists and cartoonists periodically poked fun at the North's pacifist Quakers, particularly at those who seemed to have trouble following the Society's teachings. A few months after the fall of Fort Sumter, a *Vanity Fair* cartoonist portrayed a patriotic Quaker donating to a fund for volunteers under the guise of supporting the "government

Magee, 316 Chestnut Street, Phila.

Friend Jane,—I have brought thee a
Stiff and a Hat, which I hope will prove
serviceable in these times.

Several patriotic envelopes played on the theme of Quakers—ostensibly pacifists—supporting the war effort. This envelope, published in Philadelphia, shows "Friend Jane" offering her friend (or husband?) a musket and military kepi to replace his familiar staff and hat. The image also seems to call into question the manhood of the Quaker man, as contrasted with the woman. Courtesy of the Library Company of Philadelphia.

police" (an acceptable act).[69] Several patriotic envelopes pictured patriotic Quaker women pushing guns on recalcitrant Quaker men.[70] In the midst of the 1862 draft, *Yankee Notions* played with the fact that Quakers could claim a draft exemption by portraying two men in a saloon who were pretending to be Quakers but in the end could not resist the lure of the liquid "draughts."[71] Following Robert E. Lee's 1863 invasion of Pennsylvania, some of the state's Quakers were the target of severe criticism. One cartoon in *Frank Leslie's Budget of Fun* showed two members of Pennsylvania's Society of Friends cynically raising their prices during the invasion while letting "the New Yorkers and Jerseymen" do their fighting for them. Here we have another approach to a familiar theme. The cartoonist seemed outraged that Quakers were hypocritically enjoying unusual profits while protected by their status as conscientious objectors.[72]

As we have seen, many of the North's pamphleteers called on northerners to endure a war that was dragging on beyond all expectations. Surprisingly, though, even later in the war it was still rare for published sermons to challenge readers or parishioners to make uncomfortable sacrifices. Instead, the message seemed to be that the good citizen supported the government and followed the rules. Thus New York minister Joseph T. Duryea reminded his flock that their commitment to "civil liberty" did not give them license to pursue "their selfish ends by transgressing law[s]" at their

A PRUDENT PROCEEDING.

EXCITED NEW YORKER—"*Look here!   Your State's invaded—its soil polluted!   What are you going to do?*"

OLD EPHRAIM (to his Son)—"*Son Ephraim, send for the New Yorkers and the Jerseymen, to fight for us, while I and thou mark up the prices.*"

Whereas some patriotic envelopes joked about pacifist Quakers supporting the war effort, other wartime commentary claimed that members of the Society of Friends were avoiding the war's dangers while profiting from the conflict's opportunities. In this cartoon, published two months after the Battle of Gettysburg, "Old Ephraim"—a Pennsylvania Quaker—prepares to profit from the invasion while men from New York and New Jersey do the fighting. Note that in this image, much like the political lithograph "Look Sharp!," we see the hypocritical older man, with his weak son hovering behind him. *Frank Leslie's Budget of Fun* (September 1863): 12. Courtesy of HarpWeek.

whim.[73] Philadelphia Presbyterian William Bell Stewart devoted one April 1863 sermon to a harsh discussion of the northern hypocrites who refused to support the war, firing some particular salvoes at those "who would resist the draft." Yet Stewart offered his flock no guidance about volunteering or making sacrifices to support the war, so long as they uttered no disloyal sentiments.[74]

Moses Smith, a Congregational minister in Plainville, Connecticut, had his own distinct perspective on the draft. In September 1863 Smith informed his flock that he had recently been drafted and had resolved to present himself for service. Smith's published sermon recounted his own thinking in great detail. He treated the fact of his selection and the subsequent approval of the examining surgeon as evidence that his becoming a conscript was God's will. Having been selected, the minister concluded that paying the commutation fee would open him up to charges of hypocrisy given his previous patriotic sermons. And to hire a substitute would burden the army with another "wretched creature" where "true men" were required. In sum, Moses Smith did not join the army because any patriotic impulse drove him to it. He joined because the dictates of citizenship had brought him to that conclusion after he was drafted. Like all good citizens, he had taken his chances. Once his name had been called, it would have been hypocritical, unpatriotic, and unmanly to stay home, even though he was a man of the cloth.[75]

Rev. William J. Potter faced the same challenge that Smith had confronted, and he came to a similar conclusion, but the two clergymen followed slightly different logical paths. Potter, a celebrated abolitionist Unitarian minister in New Bedford, Massachusetts, received his draft notice in August 1863. Like Smith, Potter took the opportunity to write an extended commentary—entitled "The Voice of the Draft"—intended both for his own flock and for a wider audience. As a supporter of the Union war effort, Potter urged his readers to encourage enlistment and cooperate with the draft. The virtue of a volunteer army, he explained, was that it gave each man the opportunity to assess whether he was personally well suited to military service. As Potter saw it, the conscript still had ample opportunity to avoid service if he felt unfit for such a duty. As a draftee, Potter weighed the options—hire a substitute or pay a commutation fee—in the light of his own personal circumstances and concluded that he would submit himself for military service as an ordinary private.[76]

One way to understand the decisions made by Smith and Potter is that both men responded to their sense of patriotism and mission, refusing to hide behind the protection of the pulpit. Smith clearly worried that his own failure to act would render his previous patriotic words hypocritical and thus ineffectual. But it is also worth noting that both men were explicit in responding to the call of *conscription*. Either man could have enlisted—as a soldier or as a military clergyman—at any point in the previous two years. The moment each was conscripted posed a new and distinct question, a question calling for serious contemplation. Significantly, neither man treated the draft as a compulsion to service, but it did pose new questions for both, particularly insofar as they saw themselves as providing guidance for others. Once drafted, each man chose to serve. Their message to the loyal citizenry was that military-aged men had no obligation to enlist, but once drafted they were—as citizens—obligated to look into their own souls and decide whether they had the capacity to serve. Even at that point a draftee could avoid serving, but only after examining his conscience.

BREAKING HEARTS

Let us close this discussion with two intriguing stories that illustrate the fundamental ambiguities embedded in home front fiction and the importance of military service. In her serialized 1864 novella *Breaking Hearts*, Mary A. Howe skirts conventional themes in building a complex love story. The story begins in 1863 with the wealthy John Althrop reading in the paper that he has been drafted. When the war began, the patriotic Mr. Althrop had joined a rifle club and contemplated volunteering, but he had eventually talked himself out of the idea. Now conscription had put the issue to him once again, and he concluded that although he was a strong abolitionist and every bit as brave and patriotic as the next man, that did not mean he should feel compelled to enlist. Instead, he paid his three-hundred-dollar commutation fee, promising himself that if he were to be called a second time, he would surely go. Meanwhile, John had convinced himself that he would like to have a wife, and he found himself watching his lovely neighbor—Sallie Mosby—as she danced in her yard.

Unfortunately for John, a young officer appears at Sallie's home, flashing his fancy uniform. John, perhaps regretting his own status, takes to calling this intruder "Shoulder Straps," but he also overhears Sallie telling a friend that she had no interest in Mr. Althrop. John is both annoyed and jealous, so he lures his cousin Buckwood Lee into a complex scheme where Buck will woo Sallie and then break her heart, and in exchange for this duplicity John will arrange to get Buck a commission as a major in the army. At this stage in the story, Howe has introduced three central male characters: an apparent soldier/suitor who is presumed to be a fraud; a disreputable fellow who is only willing to enlist if he can wear the uniform of an officer; and a central figure with no redeeming traits whatsoever.

The plot unfolds with predictable complexity. Buck and Sallie fall in love, which enrages John, who is really still smitten with Sallie. He gets annoyed with her and reveals the plot, leaving Sallie furious with both men. Buck, now angry as well, throws up his hands and volunteers as an enlisted man (following a popular fictional pattern). Over the next several months Buck writes from the front, recounting how his battlefield heroics have earned him a promotion. He eventually suffers a minor injury and is hospitalized. Sallie, who has long since forgiven him, sends affectionate but no longer romantic letters. Meanwhile, the captain who had visited Sallie earlier reappears, and we learn that far from being a fraudulent shoulder straps, he is Sallie's uncle, and he had in fact dyed his hair to appear young enough to enlist (inverting another popular trope). Closer to home, John is still in love with Sallie, but each time they seem on the verge of getting together a new fight breaks out and they are furious all over again.

In the next to last episode of this serialized drama, John learns that one of his tenants—the poor wife of a Union soldier—is dying after a difficult childbirth. Finally, John reveals his selfless side by rushing to the poor woman's home, encountering Sallie on the way. Both mother and child die tragically, but in the final scene of *Breaking Hearts* the two lovers walk back to John's house in the rain, and love blossoms.

Breaking Hearts is a home front story thick with war-related messages. Sallie, a symbol of idealized True Womanhood, occasionally sews clothing for men in the local hospital. Sallie's uncle appears periodically as a symbol of martial valor. Buck transforms from a selfish rake to an accomplished soldier, earning his stripes rather than conspiring to get them through deceit. But what is the reader to make of John Althrop? Howe establishes on several occasions that he is a devoted abolitionist, and a generally sympathetic lovesick fellow. But in the story's first pages John talks himself out of enlisting, and he never revisits this stance. His only real act of benevolence comes when he goes to the aid of a poor soldier's wife. (There is no Ebenezer Scrooge–like transformative moment, where he actually vows to do better in the future.) Yet it is the wealthy civilian, and not his cousin Buck, who wins the girl and presumably lives happily ever after.[77]

The following January author Ella Rodman published "'He' and I," another wartime love story with a murky message. As the story begins in late 1863, the narrator is happily engaged to be married, yet wracked by doubts about her beloved. Like John Althrop, the narrator's fiancé is a healthy civilian in the midst of war, but that does not seem to explain her reservations. Into this seemingly happy world comes the dashing Captain Nellwidge, a handsome Union officer home on leave, fresh from helping to capture Vicksburg. She does her best to attract the captain and make her fiancé jealous, but her lover is unmoved, noting that he gives soldiers their "due honor" for serving their country, "but not undue honor."

At this point in the story, the reader might have concluded that the soldier who had enlisted and served honorably was the better catch. But Rodman had a different narrative in mind. As the story evolves, the captain turns out to be a bit of a rogue, making inappropriate advances toward the heroine (who of course had been flirting with him). Meanwhile, her fiancé falls deathly ill and then slowly recovers, without ever realizing that his beloved had been trying to make him jealous all along. In the end, the narrator—who had been distraught at her fiancé's illness—is pleased to report that she will never again toy with her love's affections. She is pleased to have survived her own misdeeds with no ill effects. In this unusual wartime love story, Rodman portrayed the soldier as the bad guy, while the civilian with no interest in serving wins his beloved.[78] Rodman, like Howe, seemed intent on telling a romantic love story with the Civil War as a backdrop, but with no prescriptive messages about patriotism, bravery, or sacrifice.

The stories by Howe and Rodman illustrate a larger truth about the northern home front, both in fact and in fiction. Many of the war's fictional characters, much like the consumers who read their stories, approached wartime decisions with the same cluster of goals and aspirations that would have driven their antebellum narratives, but with the additional personal challenges the war posed. Romantic fiction, like didactic pamphlets and speeches, told these readers that the Civil War posed legal obligations and complex personal choices. In making those decisions, the good citizen weighed both the personal and the national. Devotion to the Union in the midst of Civil War really did change things. Serious prowar men thought hard about enlisting, even though most older than their mid-twenties elected to stay home. The specter of conscription did not eliminate that free choice; it simply shifted the ground on which the good citizen must reconsider decisions. The path of manhood still left ample room for men to weigh all the variables and stay at home (particularly if wartime romance required it).

As we shall see in the next chapter, northern women—who read much of the war's romantic fiction—faced particular obligations and choices, framed by their multiple gender roles in northern society. While northern men were expected to look inward in making personal and familial decisions even while consulting with family and friends, northern women received a different set of messages. The wartime fiction offered women advice on how to respond to the challenges of war, but the greater challenges came when female characters faced those moments when men in their lives wished to enlist or feared conscription.

CHAPTER SIX

The Woman Hides Her Trembling Fear

Good Wives and Selfless Volunteers

Although the military dangers of the Civil War fell largely on northern men, the Union war effort certainly depended on the enthusiastic labors and support of women. When federal, state, and local forces mobilized to recruit, organize, and supply huge armies, their emphasis was largely on military materiel and logistics, leaving room for patriotic-minded volunteers to offer valuable service. Women and men on the home front responded with an intricate web of voluntary societies ranging from small sewing groups or hospital-visiting associations to the two huge national relief organizations: the United States Christian Commission and the United States Sanitary Commission. These societies raised funds, prepared packages, mailed religious tracts, and funded agents who went out into the field. Others cooked meals for soldiers traveling to and from the front. Meanwhile, women volunteered at local hospitals, joined the ranks of the newly established Union nursing corps, or in a few celebrated cases ventured off on their own to distant battlefields.

Other northern women engaged in public political debate. The Women's National Loyal League, founded by Elizabeth Cady Stanton and Susan B. Anthony in 1863, supported the war effort while pushing for a national amendment barring slavery. The following year, a group of elite women in Washington, DC, formed the Ladies' National Covenant, promising to not purchase imported goods. A few orators, including Anna Elizabeth Dickinson, became stump speakers supporting the Republican Party and the Union cause. All of this activity assisted the war effort in material ways, while also enhancing the sense that the Union cause was truly a citizens' war engaging all who chose to support it.

While middle-class white women were prominent in filling the ranks of the North's voluntary societies, other northern women supported the war effort with their labor and material sacrifices. Working-class women took advantage of new opportunities in munitions factories, clothing manufactories, hospitals, and all manner of war-related labor. Women on farms across the northern states had to adjust and expand their labors when male family members or hired laborers joined the military. Families of other volunteers endured the lost wages of loved ones. Some northern communities, most famously Chambersburg and Gettysburg, Pennsylvania, saw Confederate armies on their streets, putting local women in unfamiliar and sometimes terrifying circumstances. For Union families in the border states, such travails were measured not in days, but in months and years.[1]

But voluntarism, material self-sacrifice, and periodic acts of selfless heroism tell only part of the story. The vast majority of northern women stayed at home throughout the war. Whereas large numbers of southern women—white and black—became transplanted refugees because of invading armies, only those northern women along the border generally risked that fate.[2] It is true that families suffered deprivations when breadwinners were in uniform or casualties of war, but the substantial majority of Union soldiers were young, unmarried men. Other northern households probably did not endure great material hardship, and many fared quite well during the wartime economy. Prices rose, but the North did not face the inflation and shortages that ravaged the Confederacy; jobs were plentiful; businesses prospered after the war's first few months; and for large number of families life went on.[3] The greatest test of patriotism for many women came when their fathers, sons, lovers, or husbands began talking about enlistment.[4] For those who had loved ones in uniform, the continuing challenge came when the months dragged on, fears mounted, and men at the front turned to correspondence from home for words of encouragement.[5]

Wartime publications had much to say both to and about northern women. In the antebellum decades, printed popular culture had played a major role in shaping assumptions about gender roles, particularly as they applied to women and men in the middle classes. Much of this prescriptive template—defined in fiction, sermons, editorials, and popular women's magazines—presumed a life cycle where women moved through a series of stages, defined by family roles. Thus the prescribed, although certainly not always lived, narrative expected women to be, in turn, daughters, sweethearts, spouses, and mothers. In each role, women were to meet an array of widely accepted cultural expectations.[6] For the modern reader, nineteenth-century marriages challenge our comprehension. On the one hand, the nation's laws and economic realities meant that marriage was a grossly imbalanced institution, where wives enjoyed very little public autonomy. On the other hand, the same gendered assumptions that presumed inherent distinctions between men and women produced ironic results, where virtues associated with womanhood—including piety, domesticity, and morality—enjoyed cultural esteem even where they lacked legal authority.[7] Moreover, as the century progressed it appears that increasing numbers of married couples—especially in the northern states— embraced the notion that the ideal marriage should be a partnership grounded in love and respect, even when the legal system recognized no such equality.[8]

For our purposes, the crucial point is that northern women of all sorts—both in fact and in fictional portrayals—navigated the war years as individuals who assessed situations, responded to events, formulated opinions, and made decisions. Much as the antebellum literature provided prescriptive advice on how to behave, the wartime print culture offered guidance about proper gendered behavior for both women and men. Here again the wartime conversation shifted from peacetime prescriptions as the mix of women's roles to be contemplated now included the role of the patriotic citizen in a new war culture. The concept of women as active contributors to a wartime cause was not new. American women had played multiple roles in supporting the cause during the American Revolution, and this patriotic legacy remained a part of national memory. Moreover, after the Revolution the new nation came to recognize and celebrate the political importance of "republican mothers" in training future generations of white male citizens.[9] But if antebellum American women understood that they had a vital political role in creating and fostering a successful republic, the immediate challenges of the Civil War were different. Ideologically engaged republican mothers had been recognized as critical in constructing a successful democratic republic. But now that the Union was threatened by war, mothers were not asked to train their sons, but to sacrifice them. Patriotic women felt moved to support the war effort, but the choices they would confront did not always yield obvious answers.[10]

The interplay of individual choice and devotion to the Union is crucial here. The antebellum cultural conversation that had defined True Womanhood suggested that women—and especially young women—had various personal choices but were constrained by gendered expectations and legal statute. Those who strayed too far from prescribed behavior, so the popular fiction suggested, were liable to face disappointment, if not disaster, in their personal lives. With the coming of the Civil War, those individual choices became complicated by a collectively shared commitment to the Union. As individual readers, northern women sought guidance on how to be good patriots in wartime, but the messages they received recognized that the desires of individuals and the needs of their families periodically conflicted with the demands of the nation.

WHO ARE THE BRAVE?

Quite a bit of wartime writing, particularly in the first months of the war, celebrated the patriotic sacrifices of northern women, even while often seeming to circumscribe their roles according to accepted gender norms. That is, patriotic women sacrificed and suffered. In October 1861, Gertrude Karl addressed this matter in her poem "Who Are the Brave?," which concluded, "Oh yes! It is brave to go and die / And tis brave to stay and say good-bye."[11] The following year Oliver Wendell Holmes compared three sorts of northern homes: the home of the traitor, where potential recruits are urged to "STAY!"; the wealthy "halls where Luxury lies at ease," where young men are told to "WAIT!"; and those "peaceful homes, where patriot fires, on love's own altar glow," where the young "Soldier of Freedom" is urged to "GO!" In Holmes's idealized patriotic home, women suffer in silence and mask their feelings:

The woman hides her trembling fear,
The wife, the sister checks a tear,
To breathe the parting word of cheer.

Their patriotism, as Holmes explains it, is in *not* saying what they are feeling.[12]

In much of the early war poetry and song, the northern woman was portrayed as the grieving mother whose son was suffering on some distant battlefield.[13] Historian Alice Fahs argues that with the passage of time, northern popular culture created a "feminized war," which celebrated women's wartime sacrifice and suffering as a central patriotic narrative of the war. These patriotic women were presented as enduring hardship, but—in contrast to the women in Holmes's verse—they were not merely passive vessels of the nation's pain. The patriotic women in these celebratory narratives actively gave over their men—sons, husbands, lovers— to the war. The popular wartime discourse constructed and praised this idealized gender role, while also recognizing that many good women would struggle with that sacrifice.[14]

Women certainly played other roles in northern society and in the imagined world created by the North's authors and cartoonists. As we have seen, the satirists constructed caricatures exaggerating some of the worst failures of both women and men. Thus in the first months of the war northern readers enjoyed portrayals of breathless women swooning over men in uniform, or oblivious volunteers preparing bizarrely inappropriate packages to send to the front. Later in the war, as northern outrage over the "shoddy aristocracy" exploded into the press, newly wealthy women became targets of ridicule at least as much as their contractor husbands. In this fashion, women shared in the good-natured teasing and the cruel mockery that became a part of this ongoing examination of home front behavior.

Of course the cartoonists (where identified) and the satirists were usually men, often lampooning what they perceived as the gendered behaviors of women, overly concerned with fashion and parties and romance when they should have been thinking about more important matters. Although the war had shifted the satirical messages, and had raised the stakes considerably, many of these comic characterizations of women—much like the cruel mockery of Irish immigrants—reflected antebellum caricatures repackaged in wartime situations.

But such satirical commentary seemed addressed to those northerners who were not guilty of these disreputable traits. Female readers could revel in the conviction that whatever their own shortcomings, they were surely not as absurdly self-absorbed as the women and men in those cartoons. These were amusing portraits of seemingly distant "other people," not prescriptive advice telling female readers how to meet their multiple gender roles in time of war. Other authors spoke directly to women, offering praise as well as encouragement. That was a much more serious public conversation, appearing in editorials, pamphlets, short stories, and home front novels. Female readers of these published texts were given directions about how to be a proper patriotic citizen, mother, wife, or sweetheart in the midst of war.

A CALL TO MY COUNTRYWOMEN

In the August 1862 issue of the *Ladies' Repository*, editor Rev. D. W. Clark published "An Appeal to Christian and Patriotic Women upon Their Duties in Relation to the War." The Cincinnati-based journal—which described itself as "a monthly periodical devoted to literature and religion"—had adopted a strongly prowar and abolitionist stance, and Clark's lengthy essay mapped out a clear path for his female readers in eleven subsections. First, he established that the national cause was just and the enemy evil, and that all women, as mothers and citizens, had a deep interest in the

On Duty, Cowardice, and Citizenship

issues. Although women were not needed on the battlefield, they had a vital role at home as moral agents. In Clark's eyes, these obligations went well beyond showing "courage and good cheer," as suggested by Timothy Arthur a year earlier.[15] Patriotic women should be vigilant in watching their neighbors, ready to "detect and expose the covert traitors" around them, while doing their best to "kindle anew the spirit of patriotism" and push the cause of "antislaveryism" at every opportunity. Clark expected his female readers to not merely endure, but be actively engaged in uncovering dangerous elements. From this extended discussion of the value of gendered moral suasion in wartime, Clark turned his attention to the concrete sacrifices his female readers should consider. Most importantly, patriotic mothers must happily give up their sons to the cause. Meanwhile, all women should find ways to aid the sick and wounded soldiers who were, after all, someone else's sons, and they should also do what they could to assist those families of volunteers who had lost their breadwinner to the war.[16]

Here was a lengthy prescriptive essay that went well beyond calling for passive support for the war effort. The editor of the midwestern *Ladies' Repository* imagined an army of patriotic women, vigilant in denouncing traitors and frauds they encountered, while making modest—but significant—steps to aid the men in the field. A month later, Clark was pleased to report that a reader had written to describe how she had been inspired by his essay to help a volunteer's family pay their rent.[17]

A half year later, popular author Gail Hamilton published "A Call to My Country-Women" in the *Atlantic Monthly*. Hamilton had had her fill of women's magazines bemoaning the fact that women were merely the weaker sex, unfit for much more than raising children and pious prayer. True, she noted, some women could write, or nurse, or sew for the cause, but in truth the Union had more than enough women doing all of those things. For Hamilton, what the cause needed from women was "the soul of fire" required "to endure to the end." The important contribution patriotic women could make was to avoid the pitfalls of "faint-heartedness" while "tolerat[ing] no coward's voice or pen or eye." Hamilton shared Clark's view that women should be on the forefront of the North's ideological battles, even though she demonstrated less interest in encouraging active voluntarism.[18]

The following month, Caroline Kirkland responded to Hamilton in an unsigned pamphlet titled "A Few Words in Behalf of the Loyal Women of the United States by One of Themselves." Kirkland began by noting an awkward truth: the "soul of fire" that Hamilton celebrated sounded much more like the Rebel woman than the more comfortable, almost pampered, loyal woman of the North. But "why should we simulate a 'white heat' if we did not feel it, or see any occasion for it?" Kirkland asked. After all, she reasoned, her treasonous sisters to the South were sacrificing because circumstances of their own making had forced sacrifice upon them. By contrast, Kirkland's pamphlet acknowledged, there "are moments when we feel ashamed, almost, of living comfortably; of reading fresh and pleasant books or enjoying social gatherings; of giving our children and young people the indulgences common to their age; of letting our thoughts wander to a happy future, unmindful of what sorrow and suffering may lie between us and that perhaps distant time." In fact, there was no reason for shame. If the war required more of northern women, they would rise to the occasion.[19]

In this public exchange these two powerful women seemed a bit at odds over whether northern women — or at least the middle-class white women who were presumably their audience — had to manifest "fire" simply because the nation was at war. But consider their curious common ground. Neither woman seemed unhappy with their legions of sisters who were engaged in all sorts of voluntarism, but nor were they interested in spurring others to similar sacrifices. Far from it. The message to female readers seemed to be that there were plenty of women in the North who were anxious to nurse, and sew, and hold fund-raisers, so those women at home who did not feel compelled to make such personal sacrifices should still feel good about themselves so long as they evinced a proper patriotic spirit. In a very direct sense, these words mirrored the popular conclusions about military-aged northern men. Those men who chose to enlist deserved their country's praise, but those who declined to make major personal sacrifices to support the war were not necessarily the object of criticism so long as they demonstrated a proper interest in, and enthusiasm for, the cause.

WHAT WOMEN CAN DO

Northern women who read the Hamilton and Kirkland essays might have felt freed from the cultural pressures to join organizations and throw themselves into the fundamental busy-ness that some of their neighbors had made their lives' work. But short of exuding a fiery patriotism, it was still unclear how they were to act on a daily basis. Where was the line between the passive patriot and the woman of unacceptable character? The broader printed conversation offered further guidance on how to proceed

On Duty, Cowardice, and Citizenship

as a patriotic woman in wartime, and even more examples of the sorts of women who deserved the nation's scorn.

Both Hamilton and Kirkland—more so than Clark—gave northern women a sort of political permission to go about their daily lives with little attention to patriotic voluntarism, but the northern press did heap praise on those women at home who gave their time to the cause.[20] Shortly after these two essays wrestled with the larger significance of women's roles in wartime, Clara J. Lee offered her own thoughts to the readers of *Arthur's Home Magazine* in "What Women Can Do." Lee's optimistic piece called on women to be cheerful in the midst of the war's carnage, while doing their own modest work within a woman's sphere. In sum, Lee counseled, "she can work, and hope, and pray."[21] M. E. Rockwell made a similar point in the short story "Mrs. Gray's Sympathy." Mrs. Gray was almost paralyzed with perpetual worries about the war, yet she failed to lift a finger to support the Union war effort until her friend Mrs. Bowman gave her a stern lecture about how truly patriotic women should be both cheerful and active in volunteering.[22] But the following year *Arthur's Home Magazine*'s Virginia Townsend seemed to echo the earlier authors in reassuring her readers that there was actually no reason for women to venture to the front as nurses and volunteers, where they would really just be in the way.[23] Even as both Lee and Rockwell had urged readers to turn to war work, their counsel seemed as much aimed at giving northern women a sense of purpose as at encouraging women to take on necessary war work. Aunt Hattie's "Letter to the Girls" used knitting for soldiers as an example of a valuable skill that young girls could learn, but the short essay seemed far more focused on the importance of learning valuable skills as a youth than on the benefits that might follow such labors.[24]

Louisa May Alcott's largely autobiographical *Hospital Sketches* was one of the relatively few works of home front fiction that put woman's voluntarism center stage. Published originally as short essays in Boston's *Commonwealth* magazine, *Hospital Sketches* tells the story of Tribulation Periwinkle, a young New Englander who volunteers in a Washington, DC, military hospital during the summer of 1862. In the novel's opening line, Tribulation declares, "I want something to do," which prompts a spirited family conversation about possible careers or distractions for a young woman, until her brother suggests that she "go nurse the soldiers." By the end of the second page, Tribulation has "enlisted," cut her hair, and set off for Washington. *Hospital Sketches* is a superb piece of fiction, combining sentimental literary traditions, occasional moments of clever humor, and realistic commentary on life in a military hospital. Although Tribulation's own motivations seem unrelated to larger notions of patriotic duty, the impulse to "do something" in the midst of war likely struck a chord among female readers of both the novel and the earlier essays.

In a "postcript" to *Hospital Sketches*, Alcott addressed queries she received about the original sketches, offering an unusual window into the reader responses to her story. Most of Alcott's answers concerned the lives and spiritual health of the soldiers, as well as her own emotional reactions to her hospital experiences. One answer, perhaps in response to a question from a prospective nurse, explained that nurses were not "obliged to witness amputations" and similar operations, but she did note that she knew at least one volunteer nurse who abandoned her position because she could not handle either the blood or the fatigue. Alcott's tone was not didactic, and she did not describe nursing as a patriotic duty or calling, but no doubt her sketches inspired other young women to pursue similar adventures.[25]

The notion of female volunteers inspiring others to action figures in the story "The Narrow Escape." As the story begins, Edith is riding a Philadelphia streetcar and overhears two hospital volunteers discussing how the patients needed more "carpet slippers." Edith had been on her way to do some personal shopping, but she abandons her plans and instead spends all her money on materials at the dry goods store to sew slippers for the soldiers. This surge in patriotism eventually leads her to break up with her boyfriend, who was trying to avoid military service.[26] "These Are My Sons" described a St. Louis woman who devoted herself to nursing while neglecting her friends and any social life. Finally her secret is revealed when her husband—a Rebel soldier—turns up in her hospital and promptly dies. Three days later, after the shortest possible period of mourning, the patriotic nurse returns to her post. Here the lesson seemed to be that selfless voluntarism could somehow offset the sins of a traitorous husband. Presumably the properly loyal wife of an appropriately patriotic husband need feel no such compulsion.[27]

Readers of *Peterson's Magazine*, one of the nation's popular women's magazines, could conclude that patriotic voluntarism was a good thing, but hardly a duty. Such messages might have been welcomed by northern women of relative leisure, but they also reached other readers, such as Iowa's Mrs. Paschal and the members of her *Peterson's Magazine* reading club, who perhaps found that their farming obligations left little room for patriotic voluntarism. When it came to women's roles, the obligations of domesticity—and the demands of farm labor—prevailed.[28]

Many popular short stories concerned women who turned to nursing when their own loved ones had been wounded or killed. As soon as Louise Chandler Moulton's "Kitten" learns that her love has died at the first Battle of Bull Run, she abandons all of life's pleasures except working with soldiers.[29] Moulton used a similar plot device a few months later, when her character Margery Dane heads to Baltimore to nurse her dying fiancé and ends up finding her true calling nursing the wounded.[30] In "One of Three," Maud journeys to Washington to care for her sister's wounded beau and soon throws herself into hospital work.[31] In each of these stories, and many more, nursing the wounded is presented as noble work for women, but the motivation is invariably highly personal, triggered by a loved one falling in battle.[32]

Sophie May's "Begging for the Soldiers" describes young Louisa's frustrating day traveling around her small village in search of donations of money or yarn for her soldiers' sewing circle. At each stop she is met with silly excuses, suggesting a community unwilling to make even the slightest sacrifice for the war. We learn that Louisa is personally driven by the fact that her brother is in uniform and her fiancé is about to leave for the seat of war. The women left at home, she declares, must match the courage of their men with "fortitude and faith" of their own, even while those around them are indifferent. Here the author was not simply praising the noble volunteer, but taking to task those civilians who failed to help; however, the expectations on the ordinary citizen untouched by the war still amounted to no more than the sacrifice of a pair of socks.[33]

Discussions of voluntarism took on a slightly different form in the war's final eighteen months, as cities and towns across the nation staged large fairs to help fund the activities of the United States Sanitary Commission. In Chicago, two local women—Mary Livermore and Jane Hoge—orchestrated the entire event. In other major cities, especially New York, Philadelphia, and Boston, male volunteers sat at the top of elaborate committee structures, but women did the lion's share of the planning and implementation as well as the volunteering on the ground.[34] These sanitary fairs attracted huge amounts of public attention, dominating the local press both before and during the events. Newspapers published endless pieces praising the contributions of benevolent women.[35] But other commentators went against the grain, arguing that the fairs were unnecessary, the donors were often cynical self-promoters, and the events exploited women by putting them on display in unseemly situations that violated proper gender roles.[36] On balance, the public discourse celebrated the contributions of the thousands of fair women, and no doubt in many circles there was substantial cultural pressure to get involved with a committee or do a stint working at a fair table. But these activities were short-lived, and the volunteers were hardly being encouraged to make substantial or long-running personal sacrifices.[37]

As we have seen, northern satirists took great pleasure in mocking the "shoddy aristocrats," particularly those newly wealthy "Mrs. Shoddys" who paraded around in their new jewels and finery. For those women who wore their wealth with more familiar ease, or at least less obscene exuberance, the cultural messages were more mixed. The ongoing attack on the (largely imaginary) Shoddys provided substantial cover for northern women who merely continued to live a comfortable life in the midst of war. But other commentators targeted women for their extravagances, suggesting that such behavior was unpatriotic. The *New York Herald*, for instance, returned to this theme periodically throughout the war, noting in 1864 that northern women continued to enjoy their "silks and satins" long after their Rebel adversaries had forgone such luxuries.[38]

In an extraordinary sermon published in 1864, Michigan minister William Nutting laid out a seemingly tough set of expectations for the North's women:

> Let the women, too, of our land,—the mothers, sisters, daughters, and sweet-hearts of our brave army, look to it if they are entirely without sin in this matter. While so many of them have nobly gone to stand by the couch of the wounded, sick, and dying, while so many more at home are plying busy feet and fingers to supply the suffering soldier's wants, how many, even among these last, are still the gay votaries of pleasure and costly fashion! How many even, have embarked in extravagances never known before, the fruits of the sufferings and blood of their brave defenders! Cannot, ought not, every daughter of America to sacrifice every selfish pleasure, extravagance, at least, to that costly, glorious object for which their sons and brothers so freely sacrifice their lives? Where is the earnest, unselfish spirit of the women patriots of the Revolution? Surely, every woman's earnest sympathy and love, and courage are due to this sacred cause, such sympathy, and love, and courage as shown themselves by real, unshrinking sacrifice!

While some observers seemed to feel that women on the home front could behave as they wished, by 1864 Nutting had lost patience for those women who failed to sacrifice at least their "selfish pleasures" for the cause, while others were giving up so much.[39]

Even while the popular press praised the heroines on the home front, as we saw in chapter 1, satirists found ample targets among women who exhibited more energy than common sense. Cartoonists belittled women on the home front who seemed unaware of the war's harsh realities. Authors of fiction occasionally portrayed characters with a similar inability to grasp the true magnitude of the situation. One story in *Peterson's Magazine* concerned a small-town woman who rushes to the train station with her friend Faith to see off the departing troops. The narrator's own story is a complex one of love found, and lost, and then found again at the train station. But while this woman is weighed down with the magnitude of events around her, the immature Faith is swept up in the excitement of the occasion, cheeks flushing as she waves with enthusiasm to the handsome men marching to the train, seemingly unconscious of their uncertain futures. The young female reader could sympathize with the heroine's complex love story while recognizing that Faith's silly enthusiasm, unfiltered by an understanding of the significance of the occasion, was decidedly inappropriate.[40]

In January 1863 a cartoonist in *Frank Leslie's Budget of Fun* portrayed Mrs. Major Wiggles chatting with her husband, home on furlough, commenting on how fortunate Mrs. Colonel Waggles was that her husband had fallen in battle, since "black does so become her."[41] Neither wife seemed to grasp what her husband had signed up for, or the terrible stakes involved. Other humorists found legitimate patriotism nicely coinciding with stylish couture. In "The Patriotic Young Lady," a young woman stands before the offices of the local Sanitary Commission wearing a daring skirt revealing her ankles. "Never mind your ankles, Jeannie," her friend declares, "we had better go with short skirts than our brave soldiers without bandages."[42] Both cartoonists drew on the same reservoir of gendered stereotypes, portraying silly wartime women as unbothered by the true horrors of war. But whereas Mrs. Wiggles was still blissfully unaware nearly two years into the war, the younger Sanitary Commission volunteers seem to have figured out how to make the Union cause coincide with their fashion goals. Both images stand in contrast to the harsh portrayals of the Irish Mrs. Shoddy and her daughters, flashing undeserved finery in the midst of war.

In one particularly pointed story, "Red, White and Black," we meet Caroline, a vivacious coquette who impulsively agrees to accept the romantic overtures of Jerome, who has just enlisted. But when it is time for Jerome to leave a few days later, Carrie is irate, apparently having assumed that his devotion to her should negate any perceived duty to country: "To your country! Wait till you are needed more imperatively. Thousands are ready to go, are going; thousands abler than you. Why should

RATHER SUGGESTIVE.

Mrs. Major Wiggles (to her husband, who is at home on a short furlough)—"*My dear Charley, isn't it nice?*—*Mrs. Colonel Waggles has just heard that the Colonel was killed in the last battle, and black does so become her, you know*—*her complexion is just like mine!*" [The Major don't see it.]

This cartoon returns to an early war theme: the young wife who does not quite grasp the significance of the war. Here Mrs. Major Wiggles is commenting to her husband, home on leave, how fortunate it is that Mrs. Colonel Waggles gets to wear mourning, since "black does so become her." *Frank Leslie's Budget of Fun*, January 1, 1863, 3. Courtesy of HarpWeek.

you rush, thus hastily forward? It is a madness; a piece of folly! You are excited with the occasion. Because others are going, you go; and you call it patriotism, courage. It is neither; you are a coward, because you dare not stay behind. And more than that, you love your own glory better than you love me!" Poor Jerome tries to change her feelings, but when he leaves for the front, his true love continues to stew at home. The author did not mince words: "She, nursing an insane sense of wrong, born of her defective education as a woman—of her ignorance; alone, too, in the inaction of domestic life, had hung out the pale colours of distress." Fortunately, over time Carrie matures and comes to understand Jerome's duty to his country, declaring, "Life has wider meanings to me now. This war has been my education." Here, in completely unambiguous terms, the reader received a clear example of the worst sort of female behavior and learned that such

On Duty, Cowardice, and Citizenship

PATRIOTIC YOUNG LADY—" *Never mind your ankles, Jennie; we had better go with short skirts than our brave soldiers want bandages.*"

In this cartoon the "patriotic young lady" stands before a Sanitary Commission head-quarters, handing over clothing that can be turned into bandages. She is sporting un-usually short skirts that reveal her ankles. This sort of sexualizing of women's wartime voluntarism became a popular theme in comic satire, particularly during the explosion of Sanitary Fairs. The young lady has found a way to be both patriotic and attractive, while perhaps pushing the cultural standards a bit in the name of the Union. *Frank Leslie's Illustrated Newspaper*, July 9, 1864, 259. Courtesy of HarpWeek.

flaws were less the product of a failed character than of "defective educa-tion as a woman."[43]

Virginia Townsend, coeditor of *Arthur's Home Magazine*, periodically grew short with women or men who failed to comprehend and properly respond to the war's challenges. In November 1861, barely six months into the conflict, Townsend's "Home Pictures of the Times" portrayed an array of wartime characters. The first is the daughter of a wealthy New York merchant who complains bitterly about how the national crisis has disturbed her annual trip to Saratoga Springs. "'I meant to create a sensation, and now the miserable war must start up and spoil it all,'" she whines. Townsend's second sketch features a young couple facing the debate over enlistment. At first Charlotte balks at Walter's patriotic plans, but finally she relents and agrees to support him as he supports the Union. The last sketch portrays the widowed Mrs. Johnson, who "swallowed down her sobs" and supported her son as he enlisted. In the final scene Mrs. Johnson learns that her son has fallen on the battlefield, leading Townsend to pen an unapologetically didactic conclusion addressed to her "dear reader": "Let us, who mourn no beloved dead on battle fields, be humble, be pitiful, and grateful to God that no blow has fallen upon our homes."[44] The following year Townsend wrote a similarly moralizing story titled "Hospital Nurse." In this tale Constance volunteers as a nurse despite her best friend's insistence that such efforts are really unnecessary. Constance finds the whole experience very rewarding, as she ends up nursing a dying soldier in his final hours. Meanwhile, her cynical friend suffers no ill effects for her continuing indifference. The author seemed to be encouraging women to find fulfillment in voluntary activity, but only if the spirit truly moved them.[45]

RATHER DIE A WIDOWED MAID THAN
LIVE A COWARD'S BRIDE

In the popular literature, perhaps the most important role for the patriotic woman was to encourage men to enlist. Here the roles of mother, sweetheart, and wife became intertwined with the republican gender role, as revised in time of war to emphasize the responsibility of women to help preserve the Union. Rather than merely raising and marrying good republican men, they were now expected to urge them into battle. Barely a week after the firing on Fort Sumter, the *New York Post* asked the simple question "What Can Woman Do?" The first response was simply that "she can give her husband, son, or brother, cheerfully to the holy cause of liberty and Union." By being personally brave, women could encourage men to serve rather than stay home. "If they are brave, men dare not be cowards," the author insisted. Cartoonists made this point repeatedly. Mary, a parlor maid, is labeled "the best kind of recruiting sergeant" when she refuses to kiss the cook until he volunteers. In "Good for Charley" we see an irate "Little Popkins"—who "thought the war barbarous"—sitting by himself while his friend Charley, in uniform, enjoys the attentions of the

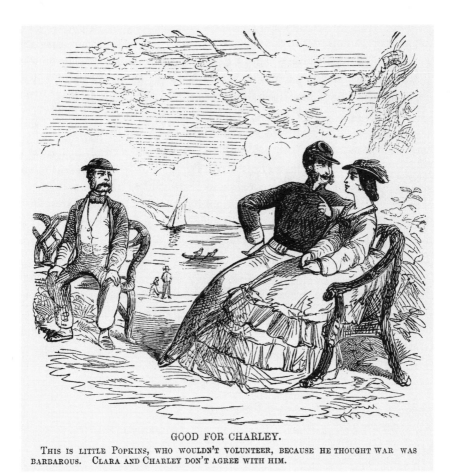

GOOD FOR CHARLEY.

THIS IS LITTLE POPKINS, WHO WOULDN'T VOLUNTEER, BECAUSE HE THOUGHT WAR WAS BARBAROUS. CLARA AND CHARLEY DON'T AGREE WITH HIM.

This cartoon from early in the war is quite unambiguous. Men who sit at home complaining that war is "barbarous" will not win the pretty girl. This cartoon from *Vanity Fair* provides advice for men but also guidance for young women. *Vanity Fair*, June 15, 1861, 77. Courtesy of HarpWeek.

attractive Clara. The message to young men was clear: the man in uniform would win the girl. Young women readers absorbed a similar lesson about the ideal mate.[46]

Popular composers published songs playing on the notion of bellicose women shoving their men into uniform. "The Female Recruiting Sergeant" describes a woman urging men to enlist, promising that the ladies at home can take on their roles as merchants, ministers, politicians, and policemen. In the popular song "The Northern Girl's Song," the heroine declares that she would "rather die a widowed maid than live a coward's bride." A more humorous tune, Henry Clay Work's "We'll Go Down Our-

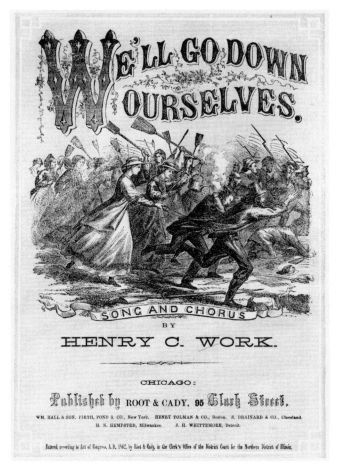

Henry Clay Work's popular song, with its dramatic cover art, commented on how the North's women were prepared to take up the fight if their men provided cowardly. Work, "We'll Go Down Ourselves." Courtesy of Library of Congress, Music Department.

selves," asks a group of patriotic women what they will do if the North runs out of male recruits. "We'll go down ourselves / And teach the rebels something new," the bellicose women declare. The illustrated cover of this widely circulated song sheet showed an army of women, armed with brooms and teakettles filled with boiling water.[47]

Comparable themes dominated much of the early war fiction, although generally without the ironic tone. Mary W. Janvrin's "The Red, White and Blue" is the story of wealthy Bostonian Norman Wendell, who is gradually tempted to enlist by the sight of patriotic flags and brave young soldiers, despite the sarcastic antiwar comments from his equally wealthy, and "far from manly," friend Augustus Deland. For a time Wendell resists the call of service because he is so smitten with the "young and beautiful" Rose, but when Rose barely acknowledges him at a volunteer event, Wendell concludes that he might as well follow his patriotic urges and enlist. When Rose learns that Wendell is about to leave for the seat of war, she reveals her true affections, and he marches off with the memories of her good-bye kiss on his lips, while the cowardly Deland is left alone at home.[48] In "The Loyal Lover," the lovely Ella weighs marriage proposals from two equally suitable gentlemen. Neither man is a soldier or even wrestling with enlistment, but Mr. Andrews is uncompromisingly—almost blindly—patriotic and prowar, whereas Mr. Floyd insists on assessing each issue from all sides. In this wartime morality tale, the unreflective suitor wins the patriotic Ella's heart.[49]

In each of these two stories the more patriotic man wins the beautiful girl, although in neither case does the young woman put pressure on the men to rise to the occasion. Kate Sutherland's "The Laggard Recruit" made the point more emphatically. In this short story Flora James and her best friend openly mock her suitor Frank Howard because he has not volunteered. Frank feels that he is simply not well suited for soldiering and calls Flora and her friend "bloodthirsty" in their patriotism. "Men who stay home, court our smiles in vain," she replies. Finally Frank relents and joins the Union army, then goes to see Flora to claim his reward. But the "laggard recruit" learns that he is too late: Flora has given her heart to Thornton Harvey, who had enlisted on the story's first page.[50]

Harriet Babb's "Jennie Jewitt: The Young Recruiting Officer" raised the ante a year later. As soon as the war begins, Jennie Jewitt becomes an ardent patriot, cajoling relatives and friends into enlistment through a combination of enthusiasm and harsh shaming tactics. Mr. H. is not inclined to enlist, but he does wish to win Jennie's heart. Finally he signs up, and (like Frank) goes to Jennie to seek his romantic trophy. The ardent young recruiter sends him packing, declaring, "If . . . you have no higher motive in serving your country than pleasing me, you will not accomplish much" either as a soldier or lover. Babb closed her story by urging all young women to embrace their love of country and "tolerate no rival lovers."[51] These unambiguous stories and cartoons made it clear to young women that they should only accept suitors who are willing to enlist, yet the message to young men was a bit murkier. Military enlistment seemed likely to improve one's romantic fortunes, but only if the timing was right and the motives pure.

Bostonian Louise Chandler Moulton tackled the issue of a mother's sacrifice in the sentimental "Captain Charley." Charley, a strong and patriotic young man, wants to enlist, but his widowed mother does not wish to give up her only son. Charley, underscoring the notion that each man must make his own choice, reminds his mother that "if you were poor" he would gladly stay home to care for her, but in fact she did not need his material support. His mother silently weighs the same issues: "Had she any right to deny the good cause the blows that stout arm could strike?" Both mother and son seemed to balance the personal needs of family against the benefits to the nation, and each concluded that Charley must go. In this case, Charley's mother demonstrates the patriotic maturity that the young—and frivolous—Carrie (in "Red, White and Black") had lacked.

When Charley's regiment leaves for the front, the idealized patriotic mother swells with pride, giving in to tears only after the troops are out of sight. As the story unfolds, Charley is badly wounded and loses his arm, ensuring that he will return home safely. Charley concludes, "Perhaps God thought you were the one, mother, after all, who needed me the most."[52] In having poor Charley lose his arm, Moulton, who apparently could never resist a useful cliché, allowed her main characters to remain safe and happy, free from further concerns about patriotic duty. In wartime fiction, the amputated arm proved a popular way for authors to bring menfolk back to the home fires without any loss of honor.[53]

Home front novels routinely included scenes of young men considering enlistment. The reader often gets a good measure of the female characters based on how they respond. In the first pages of Henry Morford's *Days of Shoddy*, Kate Haviland declares, "I wish I were a man" so that she could enlist. A few chapters later, when a leading male character enlists with his wife's blessing, Morford injects an extended critique of northern women who fail to put enough pressure on men to serve while their southern counterparts are earning reputations as Rebel patriots.[54] In *The Coward*, Morford uses the novel's heroine—Margaret Hayley—to give voice to Carlton Brand's own fears about himself. Carlton, the reader will recall, had refused a military commission, claiming that business responsibilities kept him at home. Margaret, his fiancée, tells a close friend that she would rather he face danger, "to a thousand deaths, if necessary, rather than towards the least suspicion of a want of true manhood." When she learns that Carlton is afraid to serve, Margaret breaks off their engagement. Meanwhile, Carlton's nemesis, Dick Compton, enlists, provoking a huge quarrel with his own girlfriend, Kitty, who wants him to stay at home. In the end both couples are reconciled when Carlton demonstrates that he is in fact not a coward and Kitty embraces her wounded lover's heroism.[55]

In August 1862, as manpower shortages became more critical, cartoon-

A HINT FOR THE HOUR AND THE MAN.

Patriotic Wife.—"Now, you go and enlist, there's a dear, and I'll take your place be-hind the counter."

The "patriotic wife" tells her shopkeeper husband that she can take his place behind the counter while he enlists. Cartoonist Howard Del is offering guidance to patriotic women about how to get their husbands to enlist, while also suggesting that the man who stays home because of a family obligation should inspect his motivations with care. *Vanity Fair*, August 2, 1862, 136. Courtesy of HarpWeek.

ist Howard Del drew the "Patriotic Wife" of the foppish shopkeeper, assuring her husband that she can take his place behind the counter while he is off at war.[56] That same month a Milwaukee paper ran a humorous piece about a New Yorker who said that he would enlist only if his wife approved it, to which she replied that if he did not go, she would enlist herself.[57] Throughout the conflict, members of the Society of Friends debated the propriety of supporting a just war, while satirists occasionally mocked the Pennsylvania pacifists. One patriotic envelope pictured a Quaker woman urging her husband to exchange his staff for a gun; another showed a patriotic Quaker wife cheering her husband on as he marched off to war.[58]

Some of the harshest literary criticism was reserved for women who refused to support their loved ones who wished to enlist.[59] Jane G. Austin, a noted children's author, wrote an unusual variation on this theme in "The Captain's Cousin." In this story, originally published in *Dollar Monthly Magazine*, a young bride is devoted to her much older husband, but her handsome and charming cousin is equally devoted to her. While the wealthy husband is away each day accumulating riches, the lovesick cousin spends many a pleasant afternoon with the bride, secretly hoping to woo her away from her elderly spouse. The suspicious husband overhears a conversation between the young pair and discovers that his wife has insisted that her cousin stay out of the army so that he is available to entertain her with picnics and horseback rides. (The wife, it seems, does not fully understand her cousin's more romantic design.) With this information in hand, the husband contacts the girl's aunt, who sweeps into town and explains to the young girl that patriotic women should encourage their men to enlist. Properly instructed in the ways of patriotism, the young girl releases her cousin from his promise, and he promptly enlists, thus protecting the young woman from dangerous temptations. In this peculiar story, Austin seems to be saying that the silly bride was being unacceptably selfish in keeping her cousin out of uniform, yet her inappropriate relationship with that cousin remains oddly unexamined. In the end, by acting the role of the patriotic True Woman with her cousin, the young bride is also protecting her marriage, even if she does not fully understand that.[60]

In Mary A. Lowell's "The Soldier's Bride" we meet Ora, who pleads with Russell, her fiancé, to stay at home. When Russell enlists against her wishes, the irate Ora breaks off the engagement and marries a lesser man who has refused to serve. A distraught Russell is badly wounded and loses two limbs. He ends up falling in love with a homely hospital nurse with a heart of gold, and the pair wed. In an odd twist, the story ends with Russell and Ora each happily married to suitable matches.[61] A similar story features Nellie and Lu, two attractive sisters. Nellie is involved with Nelson Britt until the devious Lu steals his heart away. Nelson enlists with Lu as his sweetheart, but then he is wounded and loses an arm. Lu—who has already established that she lacks a moral center—promptly dumps Nelson in favor of a foppish man who had not volunteered. At this point Nellie steps in and reclaims the one-armed Nelson, and the two end up in married bliss. But, as in the "Soldier's Bride," the unsavory couple—in this case Lu and her cowardly partner—close the story with similar happiness.[62] The suggestion in both stories is that like-minded men and women can find happiness together, regardless of their patriotic commitments, so long as they are true to their own values when they made decisions.

Joanna H. Mathews's home front novel, *Guy Hamilton*, examines the relationship between Guy Hamilton—a border-state man who enlists in the Confederacy—and his Unionist sister Anna. Guy returns to town in disguise to visit his sister, but he is discovered by Walker Stuart, a Union officer and Anna's suitor. Anna begs Walker to release her brother, but the federal soldier refuses to go against his own sense of duty. Furious, Anna turns her back on Walker and accepts the overtures of another man. Months later, after a predictable series of events involving false reports that Walker has been mortally wounded followed by the happy discovery that he had been mistakenly identified, Anna and Walker reconcile.[63] This strange story ends with Anna agreeing to defer to Walker "as to what was duty." "I will never dispute your decision," she promises. Thus the novel's strong heroine finds happiness when she no longer stands between her man and his sense of duty. In this case the duty concerned arresting her brother—as opposed to enlisting—but the message is very similar: properly patriotic women should accept the decisions of their men.[64]

"One Year Ago," published in September 1862, offered a similar message to young women. A woman recalls how she had objected when her husband had wanted to enlist. "I did not think of duty," she admitted. "'t was an idle sound to me." In fact, when James went off to war, she secretly wished that a cannon ball would tear off his right hand so that he would come home to her, wounded but safe. But eventually word of his valor in real battles made her "heart beat proud," and she regretted her previous fears. Now, a year later, James is home with some undisclosed injury and itching to get back into the fight, and she—like a true patriot—declares, "I'd gladly give you back to war. I know that you were right." Once again, the wife is happiest when she comes to accept that her husband is correct.[65]

A half year later, the *Ladies' Repository* ran a poem that seemingly had a similar message. In this case "The Soldier's Wife" is home alone on a farm with her infant child, while her husband is off at war, "guarding the land that was dearer than all." "Though he wears not a bar on his shoulder, / Nor glittering star on his breast," she proudly declares him "the noblest, the bravest, the best." It almost seems as if this young wife, too, is happy to make any sacrifice to the cause. But the author—Oberlin graduate Emily Huntington Miller—ends the poem with a harsh twist:

But now, though the land in her glory
Stand crowned from the sea to the sea
I shall feel, if he come not to share it
Her triumph is little to me.

It was one thing for fate to take her husband from her baby and her home to fight for a noble cause, but that cause will mean little to her without her husband's safe return.[66]

AN ABSENT, SOLDIER HUSBAND

For those women with men already in uniform, the call to sacrifice continued. Letters from soldiers and newspaper editorials reminded women that their patriotic support encouraged men to do their duty, while unhappy letters from home only encouraged unrest and desertion. In the worst cases, the press accused women at home of promoting desertion. Shortly after Abraham Lincoln issued the Emancipation Proclamation, one colonel in the Sixty-Second Illinois Infantry claimed that several deserters had received letters from women at home, attacking emancipation and criticizing the war.[67] Patriotic women were expected to send their husbands cheerful letters, encouraging them to stay in uniform even when things at home were going poorly.[68]

Nowhere were these points made more clearly than in the story "Absent without Leave." The tale opens with a jubilant John Howland returning home to New Hampshire to see his fiancée, Annie. The reunion immediately sours when Annie learns that her beloved has left his regiment without permission. She wants nothing to do with a cowardly deserter and tells the hapless John that even his own mother would rather learn that he had died on the battlefield than know that he had deserted. The only answer, Annie insists, is for John to return to his regiment, even if that means facing a firing squad. As a contrite John rushes off to find his comrades, Annie—who had masked the "weak woman" within throughout the conversation—dissolves in tears: "all the woman's nature broke forth." John finds his regiment in the heat of battle, with several officers captured and the men about to be routed. He grabs a rifle and rallies the troops in heroic fashion, freeing his captured colonel in the process. Several days later John meets with the colonel, expecting to lose his sergeant's stripes and fearing that he will still face execution. But in the meantime Annie has sent the commander a letter, pleading John's case. Thanks to her intervention, John receives a promotion and a thirty-day furlough. Even if the plot

On Duty, Cowardice, and Citizenship

PENFIELD-BROSS.

AFTER THE WAR.

Naval Officer.—" You'll have to make the port fin do now, Mary :—I left the starboard one at New Orleans."
Trump of a Wife.—" If you had stayed at home to save both of them, you never should have picked up this armful."

Wartime artists and authors reserved special praise for those women who embraced men who returned from battle with missing limbs. In this drawing, by one of the war's more popular illustrators, we see a naval officer commenting that he only had his "port fin" to hold her, since he "left the starboard one at New Orleans." She comments that had he stayed at home, he would never "have picked up this armful." *Vanity Fair*, June 20, 1863, 7. Courtesy of HarpWeek.

strained credulity, the prescriptive message was clear. The good woman brings out the better nature in her man, even if she must mask her own nature to do so. And when she does, good things follow.[69]

The wartime literature commonly reserved the greatest honor for women who embraced the war's victims, such as the kindly nurse who falls in love with the disfigured soldier in "The Soldier's Bride." One particularly poignant cartoon in *Frank Leslie's Budget of Fun* showed "Julia" walking down a country rode with her beau, who was home from the war with both arms missing. Given the situation, she took the "bold" step and put her arm around his waist, since he could not do the same to her.[70] Artist Penfield-Bross adopted a similar theme, portraying a veteran who had lost an arm at New Orleans cuddling with his lover, who assures him that had he not lost his one arm to the war, "he never should have picked up this armful."[71] Stories commonly described soldiers with missing limbs or other debilitating wounds as particularly attractive mates. In the familiar pattern, the wounded soldier would return home worrying that his missing arm would make him seem like less of a man, only to be embraced by the patriotic heroine who assures him that his empty sleeve is evidence of his true manliness.

In an interesting reversal of these themes, Ella Rodman's "Angel of Mercy" portrayed a passionate but terribly homely woman who devotes all of her energies to nursing Union soldiers. One of her patients falls in love with the noble nurse even though she is older and physically unattractive. After he declares his love, the nurse reappears at the hospital as a lovely younger woman. She had, we learn, adopted a disguise so that she could concentrate on her duties without unnecessary distractions. Instead of the woman embracing the damaged man, we have a man falling in love with a physically unappealing but highly patriotic woman, only to discover that she is in fact a great beauty.[72]

Young women in this imagined world commonly bonded with their mothers-in-law, suggesting how the dislocations of war forced shifts in family roles. In "The Dead Soldier's Ring," a Union soldier dies in a distant hospital and sends his ring home to his true love. In an act of supreme patriotic sacrifice, the young woman moves in with her lover's mother and devotes her days to caring for the aging widow.[73] The wealthy hero in "The Opal" answers the Union's call, although his best friend urges him to stay home and let poorer men do the fighting. Both his mother and his betrothed—Alice—support his decision, despite their unvoiced fears. When Edward is mortally wounded at the Battle of Fair Oaks, Alice (who had secretly followed the army) scours the battlefield until she finds him. A military clergyman marries the couple before Edward expires. In the final scene, mother-in-law and widow mourn together.[74] Caroline Orne's "The Two Young Soldiers" concerns two brothers—one married and one single—who enlist together. Their mother and the one son's wife join the cause as military nurses. In the story's triumphant climax, the two women arrive at a distant hospital just in time to witness the tragic death of the married son.[75] Like numerous other wartime stories and poems, a proper death is understood as the height of patriotic sacrifice for all concerned. And as in "The Opal" and many other romanticized wartime tales, the loved one is present at the deathbed even if it is hundreds of miles from home.[76]

Other authors embraced the valiant sacrifices made by northern women in their own deaths. Ohioan Almena C. S. Allard's poem "The Soldier's Dying Wife" presented a young bride's final message to her husband, who was off at war:

Tell him how I longed to see him,
But was happier, the bride
Of an absent, *soldier husband,*
Than with a *coward* by my side.[77]

Emilie Mozart's maudlin story "Sacrifices for Country" praises the young bride who encourages her new husband to enlist and then dies of grief when she learns of her husband's death in the field.[78] The January 1865 story "Annie Lann: The Soldier's Bride" blended several familiar melodramatic themes. At the outset, Annie Lann refuses to release her lover to enlist, until finally—very much like in "The Captain's Cousin"—the young girl's aunt comes to town to explain to her how a patriotic lady must behave. A chastened Annie agrees to let her beau enlist. The story then skips ahead a year, where we find Annie dying of some unknown disease while, unbeknownst to her, her lover is dying in a far-off hospital. The reader is left to celebrate these simultaneous deaths as the supreme act of patriotism and love.[79]

The North's popular journals, largely aimed at white middle-class readers, only occasionally acknowledged the particular challenges faced by poor and working-class women (and almost never put a human face on the lives of African Americans). One notable exception was Carry Stanley's "The Volunteer's Wife," published in *Peterson's Magazine* in October 1861. The protagonist is Margaret Campbell, whose husband George fell out of work during the secession winter, when the economy tumbled in the face of national uncertainty. Anxious to support his family, George enlists in the Union army against Margaret's wishes. For a time Margaret prospers, as local grocers happily accept the credit of a Union volunteer until George's first paycheck arrives. But everything collapses in July when Margaret sees George's name among those listed as killed at Bull Run. Now a widow, Margaret finds herself with no means to support herself and her child. For weeks she struggles along, piecing together a feeble income but with no prospects for the future and no assistance from the local government. Finally, Stanley writes her heroine out of this impossible situation by revealing that George had not died at Bull Run, but had only been wounded and captured. As was so often the case in the wartime fiction, George managed to escape and find his way home, where he surprised his desperate wife. "The Volunteer's Wife" is a distinctive tale in that it stresses the emotional and material strains of war on northern women, while the characters make no reference at all to patriotism or the Union cause. It is a story of the war as a source of economic despair as well as a possible route to material well-being. But in true sentimentalized fashion, the author skirts the material challenges of widowhood by allowing the "deceased" husband to return.[80]

In other popular stories, a young woman's poverty is an important plot device that the war manages to erase. "Helen Christian" is a poor orphan, financially dependent on Paul's family. She loves Paul, who is off at war, but rejects his proposal because she despises his wealthy mother and sister. In the end, Helen marries Paul, thus winning both happiness and wealth.[81] In "The Tuberose," Edward is in love with Jessie but somehow does not realize that she is desperately poor. When Edward goes off to war, Jessie takes to selling flowers on the street. When he returns home (having been wounded and imprisoned), Edward realizes her financial plight and quickly marries her.[82] In Elizabeth S. Phelps's somewhat more sophisticated "A Sacrifice Consumed," we meet Ruth, a poor seamstress, and her beau, John, a humble clerk. When John tells her that he wants to enlist, Ruth at first resists, but he convinces her that it is the right path. Ruth, as Phelps explains, had "a brave heart, although it was a woman's." In this sad tale, Paul dies at Antietam, but Ruth endures in the knowledge that she had done God's will for "her country."[83] In the first two of these stories, love and patriotism erased poverty; in the third, poverty brought the two lovers together. None of the three forces the reader to consider the true burdens of separation and loss on the nation's poor.

The return of furloughed soldiers provoked a whole series of new gender dramas between young men and women, often portrayed in fiction and occasionally mocked by cartoonists and satirists. A *Vanity Fair* cartoon called "Tales out of School" featured two young girls trying to convince a pair of boys to play colonels home on furlough visiting their Cousin Susan and Aunt Lucy, a scenario that would no doubt include stolen kisses.[84] The romantic short story "The Last Cold Snap" concerns a northern man who enlists as an infantryman and returns on furlough as a decorated major with a badly injured leg. After some flamboyant heroics on a sleigh ride, the hero wins the affections of a charming young woman.[85] On other occasions those home front kisses were at the expense of the men in camp. In the humorous story "How Private Jake Fay Got Leave of Absence," we learn that when Jake enlisted he left behind an attractive girlfriend who promptly took up with a local fellow. On discovering this betrayal, Jake arranged for a leave of absence long enough to go home, beat up the interloper, and then hand the beaten coward over to his unfaithful girl before returning to the front.[86]

Sarah A. Southworth's unrelentingly melancholy story "Marcia Grant's

Love" introduces the reader to Marcia and Allen, who are engaged to be married. Allen has just returned home on leave, and he promptly falls in love with the young and lovely Rose and proposes marriage. Marcia overhears the proposal and breaks off all contact with her ex-fiancé. After Allen returns to the war, Marcia learns that Allen has been horribly wounded. She informs Rose, feeling that her hated adversary is the one who should respond to the news. But Rose is unmoved, leaving Marcia to rush to the front to find her beloved on his deathbed. Allen, disappointing to the end, dies while whispering Rose's name to the distraught Marcia. Marcia Grant is true to her love and supportive of the patriotic wounded soldier, yet she receives no reward in the story's final moments.[87]

"John Gant, Coachman" offered a similarly heartbreaking message, but with a class twist. Sullen John Gant spends his days mooning over Alice, his employer's lovely daughter, and his evenings reading the novels of Dickens, Bronte, and Hawthorne, all the while ignoring Sally, the charming maid. When Alice marries a handsome and wealthy colonel, John, in despair, enlists. In battle, he saves his hated rival but receives a bad wound in the process. Sally nurses the dying John, who—much like Marcia Grant's great love—continues to whisper Alice's name. Alice is happily and obliviously off with her (now one-armed) colonel. The author's message seems to be that John's real mistake was reading too many novels while neglecting the lovely maid of his own station.[88] Both of these stories used the war as a backdrop for a tragic tale of unrequited love and loss; neither author seemed particularly interested in patriotic messages.

Home front mothers were the subject of all manner of romanticized poetry and fiction. Many authors concentrated on the patriotic suffering of these women, but others took a more explicitly didactic tone, urging the mothers of soldiers and potential recruits to do the right thing. In March 1862, the *Boston Daily Advertiser* ran a poem called "The Recruit," in which an enlistee addresses his worried mother, declaring, "Mother, be the wish but spoken, Mother dear—and I shall *desert*!" The patriotic response is "A deserter? never, never! As to me, God's will be done."[89] In one of the dozens of "strange twists of fate" stories that fill the wartime literature, Harriet E. Francis described a Mrs. Shelden, whose son is off at war. His letters are not getting through, and she has become distressed. A philanthropic friend encourages the morose woman to get involved in the war effort, donating clothing to a local woman's sewing group. The story then shifts to a hospital ward, where the wounded son is opening a pair of slippers made by Ohio ladies, only to discover that his gift was made out of his mother's donated coat. Thus Francis underscored the notion that any aid sent to an anonymous soldier might actually end up comforting one's own son.[90]

Several home front novels reinforced the same cluster of messages about proper women's roles found in the short fiction. Hannah Bradbury Goodwin's short novel *Roger Deane's Work*, written for distribution at the Boston Sanitary Fair in 1863, seemed intent on guiding young women through the war's challenges. Shortly after the Baltimore riots, Roger Deane—a young farmer—resolves to enlist in the Union army. First he seeks the approval of his widowed mother and his sweetheart, Alice. Both support Roger's decision in proper patriotic fashion, dissolving in tears as soon as he leaves the room. With Roger off at war, Alice and her future mother-in-law bond, while devoting their energies to the war effort at home. In keeping with the book's intended audience at the Sanitary Fair, Goodwin includes lengthy passages praising female volunteers who make numerous sacrifices for the war effort, while taking to task the "giddy young girls" who do nothing and who will no doubt skip over any paragraphs celebrating voluntarism. Instead, these "silly women [rivaled] each other in the giving of parties and wearing of jewels, and flirted with shoulder-straps and gilt-buttons." Meanwhile, Roger is wounded in the foot and returns home on crutches. His crippled condition opens up another moment for moralizing, as Roger worries that Alice will only be with him out of pity, and her father declares that she would be "unworthy of any man's love" if she turned her back on a wounded soldier. Of course the patriotic and true Alice had no such intention. The two marry, start a business, and devote their spare time to voluntarism.[91]

DUTY: I HATE THAT WORD

Bostonian Maria D. Weston's complex novel *Bessie and Raymond* included a wealth of characters wrestling with the intertwined dictates of patriotism, Christianity, and gender. In an unusual variation on many such novels, the Bessie in the book's title is a perpetually annoying and disappointing character. In the first chapter we meet Frederick Sedgwick, who has decided to enlist with the full support of his wife, Julia, and his worried mother. Julia and her children move in with Mrs. Sedgwick, and they quickly form a deep intergenerational bond. Meanwhile, Bessie Jenkins is furious with her beau, Raymond, who is also contemplating enlisting. Bessie appalls Julia and Mrs. Sedgwick when she shares her worry that Raymond might come back badly wounded—that she might be stuck with a man with one leg or some other unsightly deformity. When another character tries to explain to Bessie that Raymond is following his sense of "duty," she responds, "Duty: I hate that word." And for a time she keeps Raymond at home.

These early chapters establish character traits that will persist throughout the novel. Soon Kate Sisson joins the Sedgwick household, where she attracts the romantic attention of Arthur Bryant. But Arthur falls in her estimation when he refuses to enlist, and he loses all hopes when he declares his goal of profiting off the war. Meanwhile, Kate and Julia take up sewing for the troops, while Bessie declares that she will not work for strangers. When they receive news that Kate's brother has fallen in battle, Bessie brags that she had successfully kept Raymond from enlisting, thus protecting him from such a fate. In an ironic twist, the civilian Raymond is injured by a runaway horse, leaving an ugly gash on his face. Bessie worries that he might be scarred.

The long novel proceeds in this vein through many complex twists and turns, featuring male and female characters who both embrace and reject their gender-prescribed roles. Raymond finally overcomes Bessie's objections and enlists, doing his duty as he sees it. He is wounded at Chancellorsville but recovers enough to return to his regiment in time to be wounded and captured at Gettysburg a few months later. Bessie, still furious that he has abandoned her, finally agrees to send him a supportive letter in prison, coming rather late to some semblance of the ideals of True Womanhood. The other female characters continue behaving as proper patriotic women in wartime. When Frederick is wounded, Julia and Kate volunteer at a local hospital. All of them do their best to direct Bessie to the life of a Christian patriot. As the North braces for a draft in 1863, one of the central characters points out that "it does not speak well for the patriotism of some of our able-bodied men" that such a measure was needed. But another minor character proclaims that she would happily pay a commutation fee to keep her son out of uniform. This unpatriotic woman gets her just deserts: her undrafted son is killed when he is thrown from a runaway carriage. Once again, when women keep their men out of the army, they end up putting them in harm's way at home.[92]

■ The bulk of wartime writings—including satire, editorials, and domestic fiction—portrayed women responding to the routine challenges of life in wartime. Many of these women were of the middling classes, presumably reflecting the intended audience; a few were wealthy; and a few were from more modest means. For the authors of short stories and novels, the intention seemed to be to portray women and men whose experiences and personal crises would be familiar to readers. Consumers of this fiction, particularly young women, read about—and presumably discussed—the challenges and tragedies encountered by wartime women in similar circumstances. Thus it is no surprise that so many of these female characters struggled with how to deal with love and marriage in the midst of war.

It would not be accurate to say that this home front fiction simply amounted to familiar antebellum love stories recast in a wartime setting. These female characters, very much like those in the popular and often highly prescriptive antebellum fiction, wrestled with gender rules and the ultimate goals of finding love and domestic bliss. And often the narratives amounted to the weighing of life choices, as measured against the dictates of True Womanhood. But the Civil War added a new layer to these highly personal choices, driven by the idealized goal of preserving the Union. For these middle-class women, the Civil War produced even greater constraints on how they should approach life's decisions. Most importantly, when characters debated enlistment, women were expected to weigh their responses based on their roles as wives and mothers, but also on their roles as patriotic citizens committed to the Union. Their devotion to the Union also came into play as women assessed potential partners. The dictates of manhood urged young men to examine their consciences when they considered volunteering, but they also knew that their decisions would be judged by the larger community of men and women. The choices men made about enlistment shaped what women were expected to think of them. And properly patriotic women would stay with, or even gravitate to, men who had been disfigured while fighting for the Union. In these ways, familiar gendered dramas took on a republican shape when the fate of the Union was on the line.

MIRIAM RIVERS, THE LADY SOLDIER

A few of the wartime novels, and particularly the popular short dime novels, imagined women in more unfamiliar and sometimes quite fanciful roles, providing readers with an escapist experience as opposed to presenting them with models of the sorts of choices they might encounter in their normal lives. Two of the more sensational examples will illustrate some of the key themes.[93]

One 1862 novella, *The Lady Lieutenant*, tells the ostensibly true tale of Kentuckian Madeline Moore. Madeline's lover, Frank, enlists against her wishes, so she disguises herself as a man to enlist and be with him. In camp, Madeline gets Frank—who fails to recognize her—to tell her

On Duty, Cowardice, and Citizenship

all about his love for his girlfriend back home. In the months to come Madeline gets wounded and captured and manages to escape, leading to various new military adventures. Finally, Frank is wounded and Madeline reveals herself to him and nurses him back to health.[94]

The short novel *Miriam Rivers, the Lady Soldier*, is a remarkable exploration of gender roles in wartime, including a dizzying array of gender transgressions. Miriam and her sister live with their widowed mother in an unnamed western state. When the war breaks out, their mother regrets that she has no sons to send to fight the Confederacy. The sisters organize a company of nurses, but the government refuses to let women travel with the local regiment. An annoyed Miriam cuts her hair, poses as a man, and enlists to serve under Ulysses S. Grant. Prior to Grant's attack on Fort Donelson, Miriam in her male disguise is assigned as a spy to learn about the fort's defenses. She manages to obtain a crucial password by posing as a Confederate officer and flirting with Estella, a prosouthern woman. Later Miriam is wounded, captured, and sent to Richmond's Libby Prison, where she befriends Sutherland, a Union soldier. Miriam turns to her old friend Estella for help. Giving up half her earlier disguise, Miriam admits to Estella she is a Union officer, but does not let on that she is really a woman. Estella, still in love, gets the prisoners transferred to the nearby Belle Isle prison in anticipation of an escape. At the island prison Sutherland tells Miriam (still posing as a man) that he wishes he could meet a woman with such beautiful eyes. Readers who were willing to accept this turn of events were presumably not surprised when Miriam reveals her identity and the two immediately start kissing. At this point Estella arrives, now disguised as a man, and helps lead the Union officers to safety. By the end of the action-packed book, Miriam and Sutherland are married, and she is serving as a (female) nurse. Estella falls in love with another escaped prisoner, and they also marry.[95]

Neither of these books, or the other sensational novels that featured the adventures of heroic cross-dressing women, provided much in the way of practical direction for northern women who were attempting to navigate their own roles on the northern home front. Certainly these exciting stories provided readers—both women and men—with examples of how patriotic women could conceivably throw off the shackles of gender convention and achieve great things (particularly if they were masters of disguise), but no doubt many readers saw these as escapist fiction and distinct from the familiar domestic wartime fiction. Nonetheless, young readers probably did not miss the fact that in each of these stories the heroine found romance and complete happiness only after she had abandoned male garb and adopted the nurturing role of the patriotic northern woman.

■ Similar to the northern writings on swells, cowards, and shoulder straps, the satirical commentary on wartime women mapped out an array of extreme behaviors that society deemed unacceptable, or at least embarrassing. And like the portrayals of those male transgressors, the humor about women who foolishly failed to grasp the war's true meaning implicitly confirmed to female readers that their own behavior was probably not so bad, even while the cartoonists reinforced belittling gender stereotypes about women.

Both the wartime satire and the prescriptive editorials urged women to be informed citizens, aware of what the war meant for the fate of the nation, but they rarely demanded more from wartime women. Beyond some joking about the excesses of home front voluntarism, the cartoons, editorials, and fiction had surprisingly little to say about women's volunteer work. The historian can find ample evidence of newspapers covering—and generally praising—the activities of voluntary societies, sewing circles, fair committees, and similar patriotic organizations. But women at home who were not inclined to devote themselves to voluntarism received multiple messages that such efforts were really not necessary. In wartime fiction, those women who turned to some form of war work usually did so in response to a personal challenge or tragedy, and the message seemed to be that such work could serve a valuable therapeutic purpose. Rarely did they act out of a larger sense of duty because the nation needed their efforts. (Recall that Alcott's Tribulation Periwinkle took up nursing for "something to do.") Moreover, the handful of women who expressly declined to join voluntary organizations did not face any "punishment" in the fictional plots. Like those men who declined to enlist, the women who failed to offer their services might have robbed themselves of psychic or spiritual gains, but they were not treated as poor citizens deserving of negative consequences. They were, instead, making personal choices that only rarely provoked scorn.[96]

Northern women who read widely in the wartime literature would have come away with one very clear lesson about female gender expectations: patriotic women were to cooperate with enlistment and conscription while accepting any sacrifice and suffering that might come their way. Here the popular discourse left the prowar woman with little choice. Young women considering offers from competing suitors should prefer men who enlisted, or men who were at least unambiguously patriotic. Women who had fiancés, husbands, or sons who spoke of enlistment should swallow their fears and support their men. Tears should be shed only after the volunteer marched off to war. If the men in their lives balked at volunteering or conspired to dodge the draft, it was appropriate to shove the recalcitrant men toward the military or to spurn their romantic advances. These were clear cultural expectations, although the home front literature included so many examples of women—especially young women—who struggled with these wartime demands that readers could easily have concluded that not every reasonable woman could really meet those challenges. That is, the cultural message told women how they should behave in such circumstances, but it also suggested that not all good women were strong enough to rise to the occasion.

The recurring fictional discussions of enlistment reveal the importance of companionate marriage in midcentury America. Time and again we learn that women did have the power to keep their men at home, and men of honor had some obligation to submit to their partners' wishes. In fact, in multiple story lines the desires of a female loved one explicitly trumped the patriotic urges of potential volunteers. Good men, it seemed, really would listen to the concerns of spouses or lovers who wanted them to stay home. But the man or boy who remained at home to satisfy a woman's demands routinely suffered some sort of debilitating accident, suggesting that informed self-interest would lead one to enlist rather than accept the risks of remaining at home. And in quite a few stories and poems those women who initially kept men at home learned a stern lesson about the importance of patriotic sacrifice, often cast as the need to defer to the desires of their men. As a final clear message, men who served and came home with missing limbs or otherwise disfigured deserved—and received—the love and admiration of patriotic women. Many plots suggested that the truly lucky couples were the ones where the man bravely went off to war and eventually returned to his sweetheart, nearly in one piece but with one empty sleeve.

These messages were more challenging than the cultural messages aimed at northern men. Men who were not inclined to enlist could find ample support for their position, so long as they thought hard about their choice, cooperated with enrolling officers, and did not break the law to avoid service. But in domestic fiction aimed at female readers, the man who chose to support the war effort from the comfort of home would not win the girl of his dreams, and the married man who avoided service risked ridicule from his patriotic wife. Nonetheless, the messages aimed at women and at men were not entirely at odds. While the man who did not see himself as a soldier in uniform was not a good match for the more aggressively patriotic heroine, in several stories the male character who was reluctant to serve found some perfectly fitting match. More than one plotline included men who remained at home settling down with women who preferred it that way.

On the eve of the Civil War, northern women navigated a dense thicket of choices and constraints, largely defined by their gender (as refracted by both race and class). Despite substantial legal and cultural barriers, white women in the expanding middling classes had long been engaged in public discourse, as authors, poets, reformers, orators, artists, and engaged political observers. Meanwhile, women routinely made personal and family choices about spouses, children, households, and occupations. Here again law and culture often intervened, but a broad consensus agreed that women brought particular domestic expertise to their many personal and familial roles, and thus a sort of gendered deference to female moral authority coexisted alongside structural barriers limiting their absolute powers.

The Civil War destabilized many aspects of life, even for those fortunate enough to be far removed from the seat of war. Communities that rarely contemplated national matters were called on to provide men and materials to support the war. Familial obligations and affections conflicted with the demands of the Union cause. The war forced individual households, as economic units, into adjustments both large and small. And northern women, accustomed to a level of primacy within their own domestic worlds, faced decisions that brought their traditional roles and values into sharp conflict with notions of patriotic citizenry. As they had in the antebellum decades, these women engaged in—and consumed—a lively printed discourse about the obligations and decisions they faced. That public conversation yielded a fairly clear consensus about what the ideal patriotic woman should and should not do when faced with the war's toughest choices, but it also left ample room for the good woman to fall short of those ideals, so long as her heart was in the right place.

Will They Fight? Should They Fight?

African Americans and Citizenship in Wartime

African Americans had a very distinctive place in the North's wartime public conversation. The very nature of the conflict elevated race in the national consciousness, but that discussion concentrated on slaves in the Confederate states as opposed to free northern blacks. Early in the war, southern slaves became the subject of political and military discussions, but they were rarely discussed as individual actors making personal decisions or struggling with ethical dilemmas. When enslaved people fled to Union lines, their actions prompted responses by military and governmental authorities, eventually producing the inelegant term "contrabands" to explain how it was that the Union army—not yet dedicated to the grander goal of emancipation—could be complicit in freeing the property of Confederate sympathizers. Today many scholars will point to the agency of these escaped slaves who effectively forced white officers and officials to respond to their actions, but at the time published reports treated them as objects of discussion rather than as individual actors.

Modern readers would perhaps be surprised at how invisible free blacks were in wartime literature set in the northern states. Harriet Beecher Stowe's *Uncle Tom's Cabin*—published in book form in 1852—was certainly a tremendously popular antebellum novel, and her poignant portrayal of enslaved blacks and fugitive slaves found a huge and enthusiastic audience among northern readers. Several personal narratives by escaped slaves—including Frederick Douglass, William and Ellen Craft, Harriet Jacobs, and Solomon Northrup—found appreciative readers in the North. But this popular fascination with the plight of the antebellum slave apparently did not translate into a similar interest in the everyday lives of free northern blacks. The dozens of novels and short stories set in the northern states during the war years include almost no African American characters, even in subordinate or incidental roles. The reader who subscribed to the popular literary journals or enjoyed the latest home front novels read about a northern world that occasionally included class and ethnic divisions, but almost no racial diversity.[1]

This is not surprising when we recall that in 1860 African Americans represented less than 2 percent of the total population in the Union states.[2] The vast majority of white northern readers—whether or not they were interested in the lives of enslaved southern blacks—had little personal contact with African Americans in their personal worlds, and there is little reason to believe that these white readers gave much thought to the personal worlds, or the legal and economic status, of those few free blacks in their communities. Wartime authors seemed to act on similar assumptions, creating characters and plots that paid little attention to blacks on the home front.

These observations raise complex interpretive issues about prescriptive literature during the Civil War. It is entirely possible that elite northern African Americans in the northern states read the popular novels and short stories written by white authors for white audiences. Perhaps some middle-class black readers even internalized particular cultural messages about gender and class behavior. But it is very difficult to imagine that African American readers could find much of prescriptive value concerning proper behavior in wartime when the circumstances that black northerners faced bore so little resemblance to those encountered by the white characters populating wartime novels, short stories, and poems. This was particularly true for the first year and a half of the war, when the United States explicitly excluded northern blacks from the Union army. Surely poems about heroic volunteers and selfless mothers and wives did not resonate with those black northerners who were denied the option of sacrificing for the Union.

Later in the war, the Union agreed to accept black volunteers, and before long energetic recruiting drives—staged by both white and black recruiters—targeted northern free blacks (as well as freed southern slaves). Once the Union began putting blue uniforms on black recruits, the terms of discussion within the black community shifted, and the individual decisions faced by black northerners moved closer to those that had occupied the thoughts of white citizens: Who should be expected to enlist? What is the proper role of the patriotic wife or mother? But even though the recruiting rhetoric directed toward African Americans sometimes sounded like the recruiting speeches and posters directed at white men, the legal— and ethical—issues were different. African Americans were asked to support a nation at war even though they suffered inequalities at home and in the military. Meanwhile, many commentators addressing black audiences favored a commitment to the war as a war for emancipation rather than as a war for Union. In short, African American citizens in the North navigated a distinct set of questions and challenges during the Civil War, both before and after Abraham Lincoln issued the Emancipation Proclamation.[3]

Although the mainstream journals and novels rarely spoke directly to African American readers, a substantial assortment of black newspapers and abolitionist journals aimed at a mixed audience helped fill that void.[4] A close reading of these papers, in combination with the speeches and other public pronouncements by members of the black community, provides a portrait of the ongoing discussion of how African Americans—both individually and collectively—should respond to the Civil War. Like the mainstream Unionist press, one is struck by the extent to which the African American and abolitionist press were engaged in a shared national conversation. Newspapers routinely reprinted stories from other African American weeklies, keeping readers across the nation abreast of events and debates within the black community in other cities.

This discussion among African Americans was obviously different from the wartime debates that occurred within the northern white community. It merits discussion in this final chapter, despite the small size of the North's black population, because that conversation was so different and because the issues raised during the war would have such an enduring impact on the decades to come. But this final chapter also plays another role in this larger story. By examining the black debate we gain a new perspective on what whites did and did not talk about. Two themes in particular will emerge from this discussion.

First, the conversation in the black community was consistently about collective obligations and aspirations, whereas much of the popular prescription in white publications concerned the personal decisions of individuals. The white satirists created exaggerated stereotypes illustrating personal behaviors outside cultural expectations. The literary portrayal of enlistment and voluntarism concentrated on the significance of individual decision making, by both men and women, as part of a national cause. White men and women had freedom of choice, but the consensus was that they should have appropriate reasons for placing individual concerns over national interests. By contrast, the discussions in the black press debated collective responses to changing events, rather than individual choices. White men and women may have been searching for highly personal answers to questions about how patriotic individuals should support the Union, but black readers absorbed a different sort of public debate about what they should do as a group, and also as individual members of that group.

Second, the African American debate often turned on questions about citizenship and reciprocity that rarely appeared in white discourse. Black northerners regularly asked how much they should sacrifice to support a nation that refused to treat them as equals. That conversation allowed for the possibility of different individuals coming to different conclusions, but they regularly framed the entire question around the collective responsibility of free blacks to the Union cause. Why should we fight for their war? they asked. As we have seen, during the four years of Civil War white men and women routinely spoke of "duty" as an important abstraction, but it was unusual for citizens to weigh the benefits of citizenship against its obligations. People did not speak in terms of debts owed to the Union that must be repaid in times of crisis. As we consider the debates within the African American community, it is useful to remain attuned to how white and black northerners observed the same events and issues from very different perspectives.

NO RIGHTS WHICH THE WHITE MAN
WAS BOUND TO RESPECT

In the months from before the election of 1860 until the outbreak of the Civil War, African Americans in the North watched events with interest but also with skepticism. As Dr. John Rock explained to a Massachusetts audience in January 1860, the Republicans embraced a worthy goal in limiting the expansion of slavery, "but they do not carry it far enough. . . . They go against slavery only so far as slavery goes against their interests."[5] Frederick Douglass, perhaps the North's most distinguished black leader, was personally impressed with Lincoln but warned that the Republicans were not likely to seek the end of slavery. Although he initially seemed inclined to support Lincoln, in the end Douglass and several of the North's other leading black abolitionists supported the candidacy of Gerrit Smith and his radical abolitionist party. Still, African American leaders generally embraced Lincoln's victory as a positive thing. The subsequent secession of the Confederate states and the outbreak of Civil War did not guarantee a happy future, but most saw it as a step in the right direction.[6] As Douglass wrote shortly after the firing on Fort Sumter, "He who faithfully works to put down a rebellion undertaken and carried on for the extension and perpetuity of slavery, performs antislavery work."[7]

But beyond expressing enthusiasm for the Union war effort, it was unclear what free blacks in the North were expected to do. In the first weeks of the war several groups of black men organized and volunteered their services to the Union cause, but neither the individual states nor the federal government was ready to accept their offers.[8] Only a few weeks after the fall of Fort Sumter, a group of leading black Philadelphians issued a statement "recommend[ing] that the colored citizens stand prepared, so that when officially solicited by the Government we may render such service as only men can render, who know how precious *Liberty* is." At least one black Philadelphian had his doubts. William Cropper, who described himself as a Captain in a local militia company, declared that "I, as the Captain, in behalf of the Company, am resolved never to offer or give service, except it be on equality with all other men."[9]

In the first months of the war other African American editors and individuals weighed in on both sides of the issue, disagreeing about whether free blacks ought to offer their services in a war that was not yet about slavery, and to a government that declined to treat them as equals.[10] The debate was a lively one, leaving ample room for young black men to adopt various positions. The *Christian Recorder*, the Philadelphia-based organ of the African Methodist Episcopal (AME) Church, did not mince words: "To offer ourselves for military service now, is to *abandon self-respect and invite insult*."[11] And even those who would have been happy to volunteer knew that they likely faced rejection.

When a correspondent called for raising a black regiment, Frederick Douglass sounded a cautionary note. The notion "meets our entire approval," he wrote, but "for the present we are between two fires." Although black men were willing and able to fight, "we want to fight for freedom," and in those early days of the war the Union was not pursuing emancipation. Still, the prescient Douglass noted, African Americans should arm themselves and prepare for that day "when a few black regiments will be absolutely necessary." New York minister J. W. C. Pennington added, "To say we will sit back in the shade and take *no* part [in the war] is unpolitical, unphilosophical, unmanly, and . . . almost . . . traitorous to our own cause."[12] The following month New York's *Anglo-African* put the issue succinctly: "In aiding the Federal government in whatever way we can, we are aiding to secure our own liberty, for this war can only end in the subjugation of the North or the South."[13]

For the first year of the war, much of the public conversation in the North about African Americans concerned policies directed at southern slaves. Several Union officers in the field acted in advance of federal policy, freeing runaway slaves who found their way to Union military lines and in other ways exceeding the Lincoln administration's official stance on slavery. Lincoln, alert to the political implications, pushed back against his more aggressive generals. Eventually the Union settled on a policy that approved the freeing of southern slaves who could be deemed "contraband of war," on the grounds that their forced labors had been supporting the Confederate war effort. The black press followed these developments with interest, recognizing that the Union army was gradually becoming an agent of emancipation.[14]

The mainstream white press followed the evolution of northern policies toward enslaved southerners, processing the developments through the multiple lenses of politics, military strategy, and abolitionism. In these early months only a few satirists seemed to contemplate the relationship between events in the South and the status of free blacks in the North. In the cartoon "Something of a Change," several white northern boys mocked a free black man, sneering that "it was all wery well when yer was a 'crisis,' but now yer ain't nothin' but 'counterband,' and niggers ain't better than any one else." The following year, as white men faced conscription and the Union army was still refusing the services of black soldiers, Bobbett-Hooper Stephans's cartoon "Drafts" showed a well-dressed black man enjoying a draft beer as a group of uniformed white draftees marched by. Here the terms of the mockery had become inverted, as the black man called to them: "Yah! Yah! Darkey hab de best ob it now. Dar's de white man's draft, and here's de niggar's!" Both cartoons presented African Americans as somehow responsible for the conflict, but not (yet) fully engaged in the war effort.[15]

When the Civil War broke out, the relationship of African Americans to their governments—local, state, and federal—was unclear and inconsistent. In 1857, in *Dred Scott v. Sanford*, the Supreme Court had declared that blacks were not citizens of the United States. Chief Justice Roger Taney's infamous opinion surveyed the status of blacks in America since the Constitution and concluded that African Americans "had for more than a century before been regarded as beings of an inferior order, and altogether unfit to associate with the white race, either in social or political relations, and so far unfit that they had no rights which the white man was bound to respect."[16] This decision came as particularly startling news to the North's free blacks, who had not experienced political or economic equality in their own states, but who had—in many communities—claimed some citizenship rights. As African Americans considered their wartime roles, their legal relationship to the nation would remain a source of debate. If they were not citizens of the United States, did they have

SOMETHING OF A CHANGE.

"No sir-ee, yer don't come no more of yer airs 'round here; it was all wery well when yer was a 'crisis,' but now yer ain't nothin' but a 'counterband,' and niggers ain't better than any one else."

The wartime cartoonists rarely portrayed northern African American civilians in their cartoons. In this interesting exception, several young white men—sporting military caps—are telling a young black man that it was one thing when he "was a 'crisis'" but "now yer ain't nothin' but a 'contraband.'" Note how in the name of satire the artist shows these white characters seeing the free black man as symbolic of the "crisis" that led to war, and now of those slaves who had become "contrabands" of war. The cartoon is really commenting on slavery, although the African American in the drawing appears to be a young free black man. *Vanity Fair*, August 10, 1861, 4. Courtesy of HarpWeek.

an obligation to support their nation at war? The issue was particularly thorny because in practice absolutes did not apply. The *Dred Scott* ruling spoke to federal citizenship, but seemingly left the citizenship rights of free blacks in their own states undisturbed.[17]

One newspaper story hinted at the potential legal implications of the conflict. In August 1861 the *Chicago Tribune* reported on a "Practical Joke of a Chicago Fire Zouave" while on duty in Alexandria, Virginia. According to the story, a Virginia gentleman approached a Union checkpoint in the company of his personal servant. The haughty Virginian had a pass permitting him free passage through Union lines. He instructed his slave to climb down from the carriage to show the pass to the Zouave on duty. The

DRAFTS.

Gentleman of Color.—"YAH! YAH! DARKEY HAB DE BEST OB IT NOW. DAR'S DE WHITE MAN'S DRAFF, AND HERE'S DE NIGGAH'S!"

This cartoon, published in *Vanity Fair* nearly a year after "Something of a Change," comments on different ironic transformations created by the war. Here we see a very well-dressed African American man enjoying a cool "draft" while a column of white draftees march by. At this point in the war, black soldiers were not allowed in the Union army, but this man seems perfectly happy to be ineligible for the "white man's draft." *Vanity Fair*, July 26, 1862, 6. Courtesy of HarpWeek.

Union soldier cleverly noted that the document instructed him to "pass the bearer," so he let the slave—who technically bore the note—cross the lines, but he refused to pass the white Virginian, who now had no pass in his hand. When the Virginian realized that he had been fooled and called for this slave to return to the carriage, the Zouave barred his way, noting that the pass only permitted him to go through the checkpoint in one direction. Thus the black man was essentially forced into freedom by the letter of the law. The abolitionist *Liberator* and other northern newspapers quickly picked up this story.[18] The tale no doubt delighted northern readers because it showed a member of Virginia's slaveocracy being made a fool of at the hands of a Union soldier. But the story also suggested something potentially significant about race and legal identity. The simple legal document referred to the "bearer" with no reference to race, servitude, or citizenship. In the eyes of the Virginian (and no doubt in the eyes of the officer who signed the pass), the intent of the pass was unambiguous. But when the figure in power chose to read the document unfiltered by the assumptions that Justice Taney had articulated a few years earlier, the results were very different.[19]

A few weeks later, Secretary of State William Seward took a small, but symbolically weighty, step toward enhanced black citizenship when he signed a passport for noted African American abolitionist Henry H. Garnet. The short official document described Garnet as "a citizen of the United States" deserving of "all lawful aid and protection" in his international travels. *The Independent* praised Seward's action, declaring that "by one stroke of the pen [Secretary Seward] has reversed the infamous doctrine of Judge Taney." Other abolitionist newspapers, including *Douglass' Monthly*, promptly reprinted the short story. In this case the black "bearer" would carry a pass in his own name, signed by the secretary of state.[20]

Another humorous story that made the rounds of the northern press suggested the other side of the coin when it came to black citizenship and military participation. In "A Philosophic Negro," first published in the *Cincinnati Gazette*, a correspondent recounted a conversation he had had with an elderly black man who served as a cook for the Ninth Illinois volunteers. In a widely reprinted version, the cook acknowledged that he had had "a little taste" of the fighting at Fort Donelson but that he had run at the first opportunity, and would have run sooner had he seen the fight coming. When pressed, the black man insisted that cooking, not courage, was his chosen profession. And although he valued the lives of others, he valued his own life more, and he felt that "patriotism and honor" were no more than "vanities" for others to embrace. This story presented the African American man as perfectly sensible, but thoroughly uninterested in any of the talk of courage, duty, or patriotism that might have been driving white soldiers in his regiment into battle. As was commonly the case with reprinted newspaper stories, editors took liberties with the material they borrowed. *The Liberator*'s version of the story added more dialogue, including a series of telling lines quoting the cook as saying, "De guberment don't know me; I hab no rights; may be sold like old hoss any day." And when asked if he felt the white soldiers would miss him if he were killed, the elderly man replied, "A dead white man ain't much to dese sogers, let alone a dead nigga." This pointed statement called into question why any black man would risk his life for the Union cause.[21]

In the summer and fall of 1862 free blacks in the North and their white abolitionist allies continued to observe events and debate the appropriate role for African Americans in this war. Various threads intertwined in this public conversation. Late in the year the *New York Tribune*'s Samuel Wilkeson recounted a conversation with an "Intelligent Negro" he had encountered in Virginia. The man, whom he knew only as Tom, explained that when the war first began, southern slaves had been prepared to cast their lot with the Union army at the first opportunity. But now, having been disappointed by the treatment they had received at the hands of Yankee soldiers, Tom—according to Wilkeson—announced that southern black men would fight for whichever side offered them emancipation in exchange for their services, and until then he would feel no particular loyalty to either side.[22] This provocative story came on the heels of various published reports critiquing the treatment of freedmen by the Union army.[23] Meanwhile, other stories argued that some slaves remained loyal to the South, seemingly calling into question any northern presumption that freedmen would blindly fight for the Union.[24]

Closer to home, northern readers received regular reminders that free blacks in the Union did not enjoy equal treatment, or even physical safety. In September 1862 *Douglass' Monthly* ran two stories about violent attacks on northern blacks.[25] In Ohio, local black men offered their services as guards at Columbus's Camp Chase, only to be rejected once again. The *Chicago Tribune* published an extended metaphor on "the white man's war," comparing the war effort to a major fire, where white citizens preferred to have their property destroyed rather than accept the aid of black volunteers to douse the flames. The poem "The Negro on the Fence" made the same point, describing a white man whose wagon had become stuck in a ditch. A "brawny negro" who passed by offered his services, but the arrogant white man refused the black man's aid, even when his bigotry threatened to starve his wife and children. The poem ends with the wagoner still stuck in the mud, while "the negro sat upon the fence" nearby, his assistance refused.[26] In the cartoon "A Consistent Negrophobist," *Harper's Weekly* adopted similar imagery. The cartoon shows a foolish "Drowning Gentleman" refusing to accept a rope from a black savior, declaring, "What decent White Man, do you suppose, is going to allow himself to be saved by a confounded Nig——" before sinking to his death.[27] Even as the North was turning to state militia drafts to fill the ranks, the northern press seemed to be asking why free blacks should feel loyalty to the Union cause.

From the Evening Post.

THE NEGRO ON THE FENCE.

Hearken to what I now relate,
And on its moral meditate.

A wagoner, with grist for mill,
Was stalled at bottom of a hill.
A brawny negro passed that way,
So stout he might a lion slay.
" I 'll put my shoulder to the wheels,
If you 'll bestir your horse's heels ! "
So said the African, and made
As if to render timely aid.
" No," cried the wagoner, " Stand back !
I 'll take no aid from one that's black ; "
And, to the negro's great surprise,
Flourished his whip before his eyes.
Our " darkey " quick " skedaddled " thence,
And sat upon the wayside fence.
Then went the wagoner to work,
And lashed his horses to a jerk ;
But all his efforts were in vain
With shout, and oath, and whip, and rein.
The wheels budged not a single inch,
And tighter grew the wagoner's pinch.
Directly there came by a child,
With toiling step and vision wild.
" Father," said she, with hunger dread,
" We famish for the want of bread."
Then spake the negro : " If you will,
I 'll help your horses to the mill."
The wagoner, in grievous plight,
Now swore and raved with all his might,
Because the negro wasn't white ;
And plainly ordered him to go
To a certain place that's down below.
Then rushing came the wagoner's wife,
To save her own and infant's life ;
By robbers was their homstead sacked,
And smoke and blood their pillage tracked.
    Here stops our tale.   When last observed,
The wagoner was still "conserved "
In mud at bottom of the hill,
But bent on getting to the mill :
And hard by, not a rod from thence,
The negro sat upon the fence.

This poem appeared in various northern publications in the months before the Emancipation Proclamation. An allegory about the use of black troops, the poem describes a stubborn wagoner who refuses to accept the help of a black passerby, preferring instead to have his whole world destroyed while "the negro sat upon the fence" and waited. *Liberator*, September 19, 1862, 32. Courtesy of the Library Company of Philadelphia.

WHY SHOULD THE NEGRO FIGHT?

As tales of mistreatment at the hands of whites circulated in the black press, other reports described white northerners who were trying to keep refugee freedpeople out of their communities.[28] These accumulated outrages and humiliations prompted one northern editor to ask, "Why Should the Negro Fight?" Even as the momentum seemed to be increasing to open the ranks of the Union army to black volunteers, the author suggested that conservatives who opposed such a measure really had little to fear. After all, why would black men choose to fight for the Union when they were treated so poorly by the United States?[29] David Locke, in the voice of irascible Copperhead Petroleum Nasby, satirized the point in his essay "On Negro Emigration." Nasby, recognizing that fifteen black refugees have found their way to his imaginary Ohio community of Wingert's Corners, decides to take action before these southern newcomers overcome the town. He proposes a series of resolutions that deftly mock northern resistance to an interracial society, including exaggerated fears of lost jobs, concerns about political revolution, and the disturbing specter of racial intermarriage. If this "negro emigration" persists, he warns, "our kentry will be no fit plais for men uv edjucashen and refinement." The only answer was to drive all African Americans from the town before matters got worse. Nasby concludes with the resolution "That the Ablishnists who oppose these Resolushens all want to marry a nigger." Locke's point was clear: for many white northerners, racial differences were more acceptable from a safe distance; and black northerners had to navigate a world of ignorance and bigotry.[30]

By late 1862 the discussions about African American support of the Union war effort had shifted as the Lincoln administration gradually moved toward twin policy reforms: embracing emancipation as a war aim and accepting the possibility of arming black men to fight that war. In July 1862 Congress had passed the Second Confiscation Act and the Militia Act, effectively opening the door for the use of black labors in the struggle against the Confederacy. Lincoln's Preliminary Emancipation Proclamation in September made things more explicit, declaring that as of January 1, 1863, all slaves held in areas of the Confederacy still in rebellion would be free, and establishing that the Union army could begin accepting black recruits. Lincoln's announcement did not automatically free any slaves, nor did it touch the institution of slavery in Union states and occupied territories, but the impact was still huge. Suddenly the Union army was an army of emancipation, and black men were invited to take a hand. By the time the Emancipation Proclamation took effect on January 1, 1863, plans for raising regiments of black soldiers were well under way. In the meantime, the federal government had begun to take further steps to overturn the notorious *Dred Scott* decision. In November, Attorney General Edwin Bates ruled that free-born African Americans were indeed citizens.[31]

With the opportunity to fight on the horizon, the discussion among northern blacks became more concrete. In February, the *Christian Recorder* ran an editorial headlined "Colored Soldiers," which addressed the two central questions: "Will They Fight? Should They Fight?" On the first question, the AME paper was unambiguous: the history of black Americans made it clear that they had never "failed to show their courage when the hour and place has come." But though there was no doubt that the black men would fight valiantly in the field, the *Recorder* sounded a cautionary note about the second question. Before rushing to volunteer their services, they "should know whether they are to have all the rights and privileges of other citizens in every state of the Union, and receive as much compensation for their services as any other soldier according to their rank in the army."[32] Frederick Douglass had no such reservations. On February 6 the proud orator delivered an address in New York, declaring, "We are ready, and only ask to be called into service."[33]

The African American press followed these new military developments with care, reporting regularly on recruiting meetings, the exploits of black soldiers in the field, and—eventually—the unequal treatment that those new soldiers were receiving. In the first months of 1863 the enthusiasm for enlistment in the northern black community seemed almost comparable to the surge of patriotism among white volunteers in the weeks after Fort Sumter. Those black men who had been anxious to fight finally had their opportunity, and they responded with energy. But even in these heady days, black recruits were not blind to their subordinate status. Orators at a recruiting rally in Boston openly acknowledged that they were asking young black men to join an army that would refuse to commission black officers, to fight for a nation where they did not enjoy full equality, but the speakers made the case for fighting rather than sitting out the conflict. "If you want commissions, go earn and get them," one speaker challenged. Another reminded the audience that the attorney general had essentially overturned *Dred Scott*, meaning that blacks enjoyed equal citizenship. Another argued that free blacks—at least in Boston—already enjoyed near equality in many areas of public life. But the important message was that if black men stepped forward, win or lose, their sacrifices would be a valuable step toward equality.[34]

In March, African Americans and white abolitionists gathered in Brooklyn to discuss the "citizenship of colored persons" and the implications of Bates's decision. Several speakers underscored the fundamental reciprocity of national citizenship, arguing that the citizen enjoys rights but also must accept responsibilities. This line of argument quickly turned to military service, with members of the gathering making the explicit argument—rarely seen in white recruiting discussions—that rights of citizenship implied an expectation of service and individual sacrifice.[35] At a recruiting rally in New Bedford, Massachusetts, Boston minister L. A. Grimes echoed many of the same points, insisting that it was the "duty" of African American men to answer Governor John Andrew's call for black troops.[36]

Since the outbreak of the war, Frederick Douglass had been a leading African American voice pushing the Lincoln administration on emancipation, while insisting that the North should arm black men in the Union cause. In March, Douglass issued "A Call to the Negroes to Arm," urging his fellow black New Yorkers to journey to Massachusetts and join the regiments forming there. In this widely read pronouncement, Douglass acknowledged that the administration had been disappointingly slow to act, but he insisted that there would be ample time to criticize after the war was over. Now, he insisted, was time to act. In making his case, Douglass—who would have two sons serve in the Union army—had particularly strong words for those black men who dismissed the conflict as a "'white man's war,'" labeling such skeptics as mere "cowards" afraid of risking their lives for the cause of liberty. "This is our golden opportunity," Douglass concluded. "Win for ourselves the gratitude of our country—and the best of our prosperity through all time." Douglass's famous call—which he also published under the title "Men of Color to Arms!"—is a noteworthy benchmark in what would be an extended public discussion among northern blacks. "I will not argue" with those who disagree, he announced, because to argue "implies hesitation," and this was no time for doubts.[37]

During this enthusiasm for black military participation, the *Boston Transcript* and *The Liberator* both published a powerful poem by abolitionist Mary A. Denison. "The Negro's Vision" describes two grand armies meeting for bloody battle. One side seemingly stood with the "angels," while the other fought for the "legions of the lost." But time and again the army fighting on the side of good suffered defeat on the battlefield, while the angels looked down from above without lending a hand. "Oh! Why . . . does hell prevail?" they cried. An angel explained that they had failed because they had refused to let black men fight and "we fight not for unholy prejudice." Victory, the angel promised, would come when the forces of good finally chose to "arm the millions chained and drooping there."[38] By March 1863 it seemed as if the time for victory had arrived. A few months later, a private in the famed Fifty-Fourth Massachusetts volunteers penned "A Negro Volunteer's Song," recalling that for many months African Americans had called on the Union to "give us a flag." Now, the poet-soldier declared, their time had come:

So rally, boys, let us never mind the past;
We had a hard road to travel, but our day is coming fast,
For God is for the right, and we have not need to fear, —
The Union must be saved by the colored volunteer.[39]

On Duty, Cowardice, and Citizenship

A SKETCH WITH COLOR IN IT.

Boy.—" Come, darky, hurry up them fish-balls! Yer forgettin' yer station in society, maybe, since the Proclamation set in !"

This cartoon comments on the impact of national events on northern African Americans. The white customers—clearly boys of the working classes—are criticizing the black man for putting on airs since the Emancipation Proclamation. Meanwhile, the reality is that his position in northern society appears unchanged. *Vanity Fair*, February 1863, 7. Courtesy of HarpWeek.

In those heady months after the Emancipation Proclamation, the North's abolitionist and black press concentrated on the dramatic policy changes and on the new opportunities facing the African American community. The mainstream white press paid careful attention to the political and military implications of these new policies but had less to say about the importance of the changes for free blacks. The often racist *Vanity Fair* satirized the changed status of African Americans in February 1863 with "A Sketch with Color in It." This cartoon shows a black waiter serving two white boys at a restaurant. One rude boy turns to the older black man to complain about the slow service and says, "Yer forgettin' yer station in society, maybe, since the Proclamation set in!" Once again, *Vanity Fair*'s joke is about how national developments affecting slavery might have inadvertently destabilized racial hierarchies in the North.[40]

The image of white customers chatting with black waiters seemed a particularly popular device, perhaps illustrating how infrequently many white northerners interacted with free blacks. *Frank Leslie's Illustrated Newspaper*, one of the North's most widely circulated publications, captured one popular black perspective for its white readers in a short squib. A hotel guest asks his black waiter, Jim, why he has not enlisted to go and fight the slaveholders. Jim asks, "Did you ebber see two dogs fightin' ober a bone?" The puzzled patron admits that he has, and Jim explains that in those conflicts the bone never takes a hand in the fighting. "De Norf an de Souf are de two dogs fightin'," he explains; "we nigs are de bone."[41] The waiter, rather like the southern "Philosophic Negro," is presented to white readers in demeaning caricature, but his words reflect a sensible perspective on the nation's conflict.

Two months after the Emancipation Proclamation, Frederick Douglass had instructed his followers that the cause of patriotism would brook no debate and that any African American man who declined to join the fight was acting out of cowardice and not conviction. It did not take long to discover the limits of Douglass's influence and of his optimism. Barely a week after Douglass's original call to "men of color," African American John W. Menard penned a rebuttal from Washington, DC. Menard prefaced his remarks by observing that even the fact that individuals share a common race is hardly evidence that "we must float on the same tide of public opinion." As Menard understood events, the Civil War was about the restoration of the Union and "the perpetuity of a *white nationality*," and an "inherent principle of the *white majority* of this nation is to refuse FOR-EVER republican equalty to the black minority." The only answer for black Americans was "a separation from the white race," rather than taking up arms to fight a white war. Douglass responded to Menard's challenging letter with a short comment, arguing that the future of the black man was not in racial separation in Africa, but in building an interracial world in the United States. In so doing, Douglass stayed with his core principles, but he abandoned the notion that he could win the day without argument. And he certainly did not hint that he felt that John Menard's views presented him as a coward.[42]

Meanwhile, in Michigan the State Central Committee of Colored Men issued a statement declaring that all citizens had an obligation to serve their country in times of crisis but that "we cannot feel willing to serve a State while it concedes all that is due to others and denies much, if not the most, that is due to us." With this declaration these potential Michigan recruits articulated an understanding of citizenship that suggested reciprocal obligations. If the state was not living up to its end of the bargain, these men were not willing to step forward even in a time of need.[43]

Despite these dissenting voices, by April Douglass had completely cast his lot with the Union war effort, taking on a position as a recruiter for the Fifty-Fourth Massachusetts Colored Volunteers. That month he published "Another Word to Colored Men" in *Douglass' Monthly*. Here again Douglass argued that the only course for the black man was military service. Such sacrifices, he insisted, would "give his countrymen a higher and better revelation of his character." Douglass acknowledged that Congress had placed limits on the capacity of the black soldier to rise through the ranks as an officer, but the optimistic orator was still confident that if black men served valiantly on the battlefield, it would be impossible to deny them the stripes of the commissioned officer. Douglass also argued that the free blacks of the North had to step forward rather than letting freedmen from the South represent their race on the battlefield. Otherwise critics would argue that the heroism of the black soldier should be "set to the credit of slavery," not regarded as evidence of the strengths of the race. Douglass continued to present black military participation as a lever that could move white opinion.[44]

Even as Douglass established himself as the leading spokesman for black enlistment, dissident voices continued to emerge, underscoring the crucial point that individual black men claimed room to make their own decisions. Rev. Samuel Johnson, of Lynn, Massachusetts, made such a case in "A Sermon for the Present Hour," a strongly worded statement that support for the Union should be conditioned on that Union's commitment to racial equality. "Hatred of the negro in the North is more cruel than slavery in the South," Johnson declared. If citizenship implied an obligation to serve the country, black citizens had every right to offer a conditional loyalty predicated on treatment as political and social equals.[45] At a recruiting meeting in New York on April 20, black leader Henry Highland Garnet adopted a similar position, arguing that black men should not enlist because the military denied them opportunities for promotion and true honor.[46]

In May, the recalcitrant AME Church finally endorsed black enlistment. On May 23, the *Christian Recorder* published a set of resolutions just passed at the church's annual meetings in Philadelphia. The members of the conference acknowledged the heroism that black soldiers had already demonstrated on the battlefield and resolved that "the great political interests of the colored people of these United States are at last thrown into the balances of military equity." The time had come for black men to fight.[47]

Through the spring and summer of 1863 the news in the black community was substantial; the messages were mixed. On the battlefield, regiments of the United States Colored Troops (USCT) performed valiantly when given the opportunity, and their white comrades occasionally acknowledged that these new recruits honored their uniform.[48] In May, two regiments of black soldiers took part in a bloody charge at Port Hudson on the Lower Mississippi. Although the charge went badly, the men of the USCT earned public praise. A few weeks later, two regiments of recently freed slaves successfully fought off a rebel attack at Milliken's Bend on the Mississippi River, above the strategically crucial city of Vicksburg.[49] Black northerners watched these developments with enthusiasm. Surely these military successes would yield larger benefits.

But reports from the military provided ample support for northern naysayers as well. Confederate officials made it clear that they felt no obligation to recognize African Americans soldiers as legitimate enemy combatants. In May the Confederate Congress passed provisions allowing for the enslavement of captured black Union soldiers and the execution of their white officers. Even if the individual Confederate states declined to enforce these harsh provisions, reports soon began to trickle north of Rebel troops executing black troops on the battlefield rather than taking prisoners.[50] As Gerrit Smith put it, the fact that the Union had finally agreed to recruit black men was hardly evidence that "our nation is not ruined" when "the Government has not the manliness to promise to see to it that captured blacks shall, instead of being murdered or sold into slavery as the rebels threaten, be treated as prisoners of war."[51] Meanwhile, the Union did little to entice the more reluctant black recruits: the federal government refused to offer members of the USCT equal pay, and military officials routinely gave black regiments unappealing assignments as manual laborers rather than letting them prove themselves in combat.

Closer to home, the African American press regularly printed accounts of violent attacks on free black citizens. In Washington, DC, white rioters who objected to arming black men attacked USCT recruits and threatened further violence.[52] In June, *Douglass' Monthly* reported that striking Irish longshoremen in New York had assaulted black laborers who had taken their jobs.⁵³ A few weeks later these individual episodes of racial violence were dwarfed by the draft riots in New York City. The riots, which began on July 13, started as a violent response to the draft itself, but before long angry rioters began targeting black victims throughout the city. The vicious assaults seemed to reflect a hostility to emancipation, antagonism toward black labor competition, and raw racism. In one infamous scene, a mob of several hundred hung a black man from a tree and then proceeded to set the corpse on fire. Another mob set the Colored Orphan Asylum ablaze. By the time a combination of local police and Union troops managed to subdue the rioters, New York City had suffered about $2.5 million in damages, and somewhere between 120 and 150 had died. Powerful accounts of tragic scenes filled newspapers across the nation, often illustrated with drawings of black victims hanging from lampposts or the Colored Orphan Asylum in flames.⁵⁴

These events at home and on the battlefield became intertwined in the public discussions among the North's African Americans. Increasingly, the rhetoric surrounding recruiting took on the form of a complicated debate among equally defensible positions. On April 30, speaking at a "meeting of colored Loyalists" in Rochester, Douglass acknowledged Jefferson Davis's recent threats to execute black Union troops, and he—like Gerrit Smith—took the Union to task for failing to ensure the safety of its black troops. Whereas the previous month Douglass had rejected black concerns about military service as "cowardice," now he acknowledged that it was "manly on the part of the young men to hesitate before entering service under such degrading circumstances." Douglass also had harsh words for the United States for failing to offer black soldiers equal pay or access to military commissions, and he recognized that "the whole mass of colored citizens could not enlist," but he still hoped that "those boys who wanted to go into the service of their country" would receive the full support of the community.⁵⁵ A letter to *The Liberator* in June urged that the white officers chosen to command the new Fifty-Fifth Massachusetts Colored Volunteers be able to reassure potential black recruits about "all apprehension that the strictness of military rule is aggravated by an unfriendly disposition toward their race."⁵⁶ The *New York Evening Post* reported on a gathering of Louisiana freedmen who expressed a willingness to fight for the Union despite being informed of "the dangers that would be peculiar to them because they were negroes."⁵⁷ In sum, military recruiters and those who were particularly enthusiastic about black recruiting had come to recognize that the arguments for enlistment had to be made in the context of the rational and reasonable arguments against fighting for the Union. And these arguments required attention to individual considerations and also the collective interests of the free black community.

MANHOOD, EQUAL RIGHTS, AND ELEVATION

The complexity in the debate over black enlistment was illustrated in early July 1863, when African Americans in Philadelphia gathered for a mass rally. The impulse for the meeting came from Pennsylvania's Supervisory Committee on Enlistments for Colored Regiments, which had received permission to raise three regiments of African American volunteers. The Supervisory Committee's ultimate goals were clear: there was no place for "unreasoning prejudice" when "every colored recruit acts as an unpurchased substitute for a white man," they announced. By the end of June, roughly four hundred black men from Pennsylvania had already traveled to Massachusetts to enlist, where they counted against the Bay State's enlistment quotas. This new effort would ensure that African American volunteers from Pennsylvania would be credited to their home state.[58]

Prior to the National Hall rally, fifty-five prominent members of the African American community issued a proclamation directed to local "men of color." This extraordinary document appeared as a published broadside and in local newspapers, but it became best known as an eight-foot banner that hung from the window of the Supervisory Committee's offices on Chestnut Street. As we have seen, the early recruiting broadsides aimed at white men usually featured martial images and rhetoric appealing to patriotism and manly valor. Later in the war the texts shifted to appeals to self-interest: avoid the draft, earn a bounty, select your own regiment. In stark contrast, this lengthy appeal to black recruits used no visual imagery and nearly seven hundred words of text. Whereas other recruiting broadsides spoke directly to the individual, this proclamation addressed African American men collectively. The authors stressed that the war presented an excellent opportunity to demonstrate their manhood, particularly when compared with immigrants or freedmen. "Are freemen less brave than slaves[?]" it asked. This emphasis on the manhood of the readers (words such as "manly" and "manhood" appear no less than twenty times in the text) intersected with a broad appeal to liberty and the promise of equality: "A nation or a people that cannot fight may be pitied, but cannot be respected." Nothing in the proclamation appealed to the interests of the individual as opposed to the broader goals of the black community. Rather, the words "our," "we," and "us" appear over fifty times.[59]

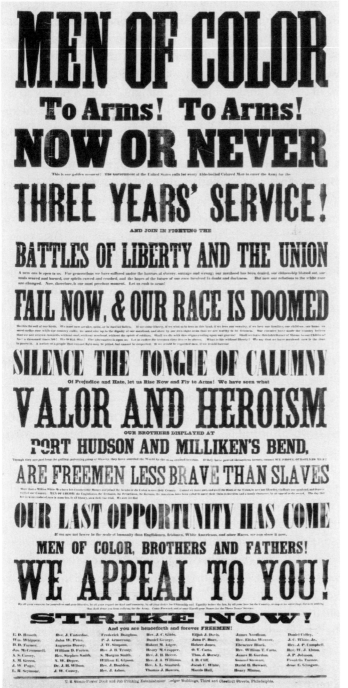

This recruiting broadside first appeared as an eight-foot banner hanging outside the offices of the Supervisory Committee on Enlistments for Colored Regiments, in Chestnut Street, Philadelphia. Unlike recruiting posters directed toward young white men, this broadside aimed at black readers called on potential recruits to think of the collective goals of their race. Courtesy of Library Company of Philadelphia.

The crowd of black Philadelphians heard speeches by three of the great stars of northern abolitionism: local Republican leader Judge William Kelley, charismatic orator Anna Dickinson, and the great Frederick Douglass. Whereas the "Men of Color" proclamation sought to inspire men to fight for a cause and for the collective good of African Americans, while saying nothing of the counterarguments that might "deter" a potential recruit, the messages from each of these speakers sought to convince the reluctant recruit by grappling with all of the elephants in the room. Kelley, the ex-congressman from Philadelphia, challenged the manhood of the black men in the audience, urging fathers to "disinherit and denounce" sons who "prove cowards" and imploring mothers and sweethearts to spur those who refused to serve. Then Kelley spoke directly to the issues of pay imbalances and unequal treatment. He offered no promises for the future, but instead challenged the white men and women in the audience to use their influence to redress those wrongs.

Anna Dickinson, the fiery young Quaker, spoke frankly about the insults that had been leveled on patriotic blacks who had been denied the opportunity to serve until recently, and she acknowledged the grim truths about unequal pay and bounties and admitted that she had "no answer to that." Rather than joining a white man's fight, she argued, why not take up this cause to end slavery and further the rights of black Americans? "The black man will be a citizen only by stamping his right to it in his blood," Dickinson declared, to a chorus of thundering cheers.

Finally, Frederick Douglass mounted the platform and promised the audience that his words would be "plain and practical." As he saw it, African Americans could take two views on the matter. The "narrow view" would be that black soldiers deserved equal pay and treatment and should accept nothing less. But Douglass reiterated his long-held "broad view" that the best way to achieve "manhood, equal rights and elevation, is that we enter the service." Or, to put it another way, even if a black observer had good reason to quarrel with northern society and the federal government, it was clear that in a choice between the Union and the Confederacy, the Union cause was the most just. "Young men of Philadelphia," he concluded, "you are without excuse. The hour has arrived, and your place is in the Union army."[60]

The speeches by Douglass, Dickinson, and Kelly were reprinted in pamphlet form as well as in *The Liberator* and other northern publications.[61] Taken together they provide a valuable articulation of the thoughts and concerns of some portion of the northern black community. Clearly it was not enough for recruiters to offer a chance to strike a blow against slavery, nor was the potential recruit likely to be moved solely by the opportunity to prove his manhood, either as an individual or as a member of a mistreated race. These considerations continued to figure in the thoughts of many audience members, but the men who were persuaded by these arguments were probably among those Pennsylvanians who had already enlisted in Massachusetts. By July 1863 the recruiting of black men had become like the efforts to recruit white volunteers: a matter of balancing carrots and sticks. But for the potential black recruit the variables were different.[62]

Two years into the war, potential white volunteers were weighing the benefits of bounties and other inducements, against the rising threat of conscription. Many no doubt also contemplated the larger ideological issues. The Emancipation Proclamation prompted some to enlist, while the prospect of a war against slavery alienated other potential volunteers. Black northerners also had to consider the prospects of a soldier's paycheck (and eventually bounties) as well as the chance of conscription, and nearly all supported the goals of the Emancipation Proclamation, even though many were disappointed that it did not go far enough. But Douglass, Dickinson, and Kelly underscored the point that the reluctant black recruit had to be convinced that this was really his fight. And that decision, in contrast to the decisions facing white men, combined collective considerations with individual concerns. The reasonable black man asked why he should accept inferior pay, limited opportunities for advancement, and the prospect of poor assignments to fight for a nation that refused to treat black Americans as equals. None of the speakers could really cast the argument in absolute terms. Their ultimate conclusion was that black men should sign up for the USCT because that was the best option available for the entire race, and an opportunity for shaping the future that ought not be squandered.[63]

I CANNOT ENTER THE FIELD TILL I ENTER AS A MAN

In the months following Philadelphia's July recruiting rally, the public conversation about recruiting and black citizenship continued. In his poem "Men of Color," J. C. Hagen echoed familiar themes, urging men of color to "prove your manhood, prove your power" and, in so doing, "free your race!"[64] But increasingly the equation of military service with racial advancement ran up against inconvenient realities. African American leader John Mercer Langston put the central question to Secretary of State Seward: what precisely was "the duty of colored men in view of the fact that the wages offered to them as soldiers are less than those offered to whites"? Seward's terse reply, published in the *New York Times* on August 2, was that "the duty of the colored man to defend his country whenever and wherever and in whatever form, is the same with that of the white man," regardless of "what the country pays us." Seward went on to admonish Langston that "the true way to secure her rewards and win her confidence is not to stipulate for them, but to deserve them." "It is no time," he concluded, "for any American to be hesitating about pay or place."[65] Frederick Douglass was not pleased with the secretary's glib comments. "We have in our simplicity always supposed that the relation of the citizen, to the State is one of reciprocal rights and duties," he wrote, whereas Mr. Seward seemed to have an understanding of citizenship more akin to that of a "subject" and not a true citizen.[66] The secretary of state may have been willing to endorse Henry Garnet's citizenship, but he was not buying the argument that the nation owed the black Union volunteer equal treatment.

In November, responding to a new call for troops, a correspondent to *The Liberator* penned some "brief words on present interests." This letter, by L. Holmes of Massachusetts, argued that "men can be had, if they can be assured that they may be led and treated as a republican army, fighting for liberty, should be." But so long as members of the USCT suffered under poor leadership, inferior supplies, and insulting treatment, black men should not be expected to join the cause.[67] Meanwhile, satirist Charles Graham Halpine—using the voice of his popular Irish character Miles O'Reilly—mocked those northerners who still resisted black enlistment, proclaiming, "I'll let Sambo be murdered in place of myself on every day in the year!"[68] Such sentiments from the white community were hardly likely to lure new black recruits into uniform.

The pay issue would dominate the public discussion of black soldiers for nearly a year, as members of the USCT staged various protests and the men of the Fifty-Fourth Massachusetts famously refused all pay until they were granted equal treatment.[69] Douglass himself, who had been so deeply committed to black enlistment that he had become a paid recruiter, eventually threw up his hands in disgust and stopped supporting black recruiting for a time.[70] Major George L. Stearns, who had been a crucial architect of the Union's efforts to recruit men into the USCT, announced that he had resigned his post in response to the continuing mistreatment of black soldiers.[71] In April 1864 the chaplain for the Fifty-Fourth Massachusetts resigned over the pay disparity, explaining, "I cannot enter the field till I enter as a man."[72] While soldiers in the field chafed at the persistent insult, African Americans at home had more reason to question whether they should enlist. When Congress finally relented and voted to provide members of the USCT with equal compensation and bounties, the black press reported the news with satisfaction but with no sense of celebration. *The Liberator* quoted the new bill and then went on to publish the names of the forty-nine congressmen who had voted nay.[73]

The dueling perspectives on black military participation persisted into the war's final year. In late June 1864 a Union soldier stationed near Petersburg sent two long letters to the *Boston Journal*, commenting on the heroism of members of the USCT as well as their mistreatment at the hands of both the Confederate troops and the Federal army. As the author, "Carleton," saw it, "our government and the nation are not ready to be just or generous to the colored race." *The Liberator* reprinted Carleton's letters, but added that his tone "is greatly exaggerated." Although black Americans did not yet enjoy "full justice," one could not conclude that they "had no motive to engage in the struggle." Once again, readers of the abolitionist *Liberator* had fodder to support contradictory opinions on black military service.[74]

The lines between battlefield and home front, and between soldier and civilian, blurred when men in uniform began appearing on the streets of northern cities and towns. In the black community, the intersection of these two worlds further illuminated their society's larger realities. Here again the news was mixed. As the recruiters had promised, stories of black military heroism earned white praise. In March 1864, when the men of the Twentieth USCT marched through the streets of New York, they "received a grand ovation at the hands of the wealthiest ladies and gentlemen of New York" barely seven months after African Americans had fled angry white mobs on those same streets. The contrast was not lost on the *New York Times*, which noted that these new volunteers probably saved a thousand white men from conscription. It is "a noble vengeance," the paper noted, to "do good to them that persecute you."[75]

Members of the black community had at least some reason to believe that black military participation was producing positive results at home. In July 1864, Philadelphia's *Christian Recorder* was pleased to report that in the previous eighteen months "we find a great improvement in the morals of our scattered and down-trodden people." The AME paper concluded that these developments were largely owing to the war. Local black soldiers had passed their wages and bounties on to their families, producing improvements in the appearance of African American women and children on the city's streets. Moreover, young boys were earning healthy sums "blacking colored soldier's boots," and other small businesses had expanded to serve the broader community. Thus the *Recorder* argued that black men in the Union army had produced broader benefits to northern blacks.[76]

But these sorts of positive developments did not magically signal the erasure of racism and segregation in the wartime North, nor were African Americans given much evidence that larger changes were around the corner. Some of the vibrant public debates during the war years concerned the access of black men and women to urban streetcars. Most cities had some system of horse-drawn streetcars, generally pulled along fixed tracks. Approaches to racial segregation varied from community to community, reflecting a combination of local law and the policies of the individual streetcar companies. Many cities enforced racial segregation: black riders were forced to stand on a platform in the open air next to the driver while white passengers could sit in the segregated car. Such policies provoked angry responses from the black community along class and gender lines, in addition to their objection to racial segregation itself. Members of the urban black elite found it insulting to be forced to ride standing alongside lower-class whites; black women refused to ride in a masculine physical space that offered no gender protection.[77]

During the Civil War these battles over streetcar segregation became interwoven with public debates about the status of returning African American soldiers and their larger place in northern society. They questioned what members of the black community should make of a society that refused to let black soldiers who were home on furlough, or recuperating from battlefield wounds, ride in the city's cars.[78] Moreover, they wondered why northern blacks should support a war for Union when the wives and mothers of USCT troops could not ride the cars to visit them in camps or hospitals. The issue came to a head in a series of highly publicized court cases and protest campaigns across the country, from San Francisco to Cincinnati to Philadelphia.[79] And, significantly, campaigns in one city received ample coverage in the African American press across the country. Thus, for instance, San Francisco's *Pacific Appeal* and *Elevator* covered William Still's 1862 campaign to end segregation in Philadelphia, and when San Francisco's Charlotte Brown turned to the courts to challenge that city's segregation policies, Philadelphia's *Christian Recorder* kept its readers apprised of the developments.[80]

Philadelphia's streetcar battle began to heat up in the final year and a half of the Civil War, provoking extended discussions about race, gender, and northern society.[81] In December 1863 William Still wrote a long letter to the Republican *Philadelphia Press*, recounting the humiliations he had faced on a local streetcar, bound for Camp William Penn. This letter struck a nerve in the North and was widely reprinted, reaching sympathetic audiences as far away as the *London Times*.[82] The following July the African American rector of St. Thomas's Episcopal Church wrote a poignant letter describing how the conductor on the Lombard and South Street cars refused to let him board the cars with his desperately ill son.[83] In December, a group of leading African American citizens petitioned the city railroads to end the segregation on their cars and in so doing join the majority of the streetcar lines in other northern cities in removing racial segregation. The petition took particular notice of the members of the USCT who had trained at Camp William Penn, or who had returned home to the city's hospitals, only to be denied visits from their loved ones who were not permitted to ride the cars.[84]

In January 1865, Charlotte Brown won her lawsuit in San Francisco, ending segregation in that city's cars. One local white newspaper responded with a mocking cartoon titled "The Effect of Judge Pratt's Decision," which portrayed the unseemly chaos the cartoonist imagined following the entry of the "colored heathen" onto newly integrated cars. In June 1865, with the battle still raging in Philadelphia, local black leader and Union veteran Octavius V. Catto—who had signed the famous "Men of Color" broadside two years earlier—called on a large audience at the Union League to "vindicate your manhood" by demanding that black women and children be protected from assaults at the hands of racist drivers.[85] One wonders if the irony was lost on him.

■ Three years after the war had ended, Anna Dickinson—the young white orator who had spoken so passionately at Philadelphia's National Hall five years earlier—published a controversial novel entitled *What Answer?*[86] Writing in the midst of political battles over southern Reconstruction and the future of freedmen, Dickinson turned her sharp analytic gaze toward racism closer to home. Set in the middle of the Civil War, *What Answer?* has at its center an interracial marriage between a white Union soldier and a woman of mixed race. This tragic couple faces unrelenting racism from both white and black communities; the pair end up dying in the midst of the New York City draft riot. Although contemporary reviewers focused on Dickinson's portrayal of miscegenation, the novel has much to say about the heroism of black soldiers and their treatment when they return home. One entire chapter is set in a Philadelphia streetcar in 1863. In this dramatic scene a USCT veteran who has lost a leg in the war is about to be forced off the car when the novel's white hero, Willie Surrey, steps forward and saves the day. Dickinson's message in that scene seemed to be that white men of goodwill could turn events in a positive direction.[87] But though the streetcar scene offered a glimmer of light, the novel ends on a dark note. In the final pages the war has just ended and Robert, a USCT veteran who lost an arm at the charge on Fort Wagner, goes with a white comrade to vote in New York City. But when the uniformed black man attempts to exercise his franchise, he is turned away by angry racial epithets. A despairing Robert turns to his friend and asks the question that gives the novel its title: "1860 or 1865? Is the war ended?"[88] Dickinson, the radical abolitionist who had implored Philadelphia's blacks to join the cause in 1863, seemed less confident about the future five years later. If the decision to go to war had been made by black Americans on the understanding that their sacrifices constituted a down payment on future citizenship rights, the North's African Americans in 1868 had reason to feel shortchanged.

We Are Coming Father Abraham

Patriotism and Choice

Antebellum Americans in the free states lived in a world of personal choices constrained by all of those things that infringe on any individual's pure freedom of movement: economic limitations, family concerns, cultural restraints. White women, and particularly married women, faced additional legal limitations, restricting their political, economic, and legal choices. African Americans—even free blacks in the northern states—endured far greater restrictions on their freedoms of movement and action. Immigrants, whether naturalized citizens or recent arrivals, faced cultural and legal barriers, shaped by both ethnicity and class. Aspiring members of the middle class sought economic security, but also cultural respectability. Various constraints limited what individuals could do, but very few regulations indicated what people *must* do. And those regulations that did exist almost never came from the federal government. The booming market economy and the democratic political system depended on individuals making informed choices.[1]

The Union war effort largely functioned within this context. At all levels of wartime life, public officials relied on familiar market forces to shape individual decisions. Certainly the patriotic citizenry were anxious to support the national cause, and thousands gave voluntarily to help win the war, but in multiple ways the Union depended on the same sort of market forces that had driven growth and expansion in the antebellum years. Military and economic policies depended on northern citizens weighing options and making choices.

Consider the routes the Union took to outfit its armies. Although federal arsenals played an important role in producing military goods, a large portion of wartime production was funneled through competitive war contracting. Unlike in the Confederacy, there was relatively little government seizure of goods, with or without compensation. (The exceptions were armies on the march, but they were commonly in the South, appropriating goods from enemy noncombatants.) Independent contractors competed for valuable contracts to produce much of what the army required. And although late in the war the federal government passed a modest income tax, a sizable portion of the cost of the war was paid for through the voluntary purchase of war bonds. Essentially the government gambled on citizens investing in the war effort.[2]

The Union filled its military ranks through a combination of patriotic rhetoric, appeals to manhood, and carefully manipulated market incentives. Men who considered enlisting had a choice to make, with personal costs and benefits to weigh. By the end of 1862 those recruiting strategies were no longer producing enough men, so both sides turned to conscription. Today we think of the draft as the ultimate imposition of national military needs in opposition to individual choice, but during the Civil War conscription was largely the application of market forces in different forms. The fundamental purpose of the federal Enrollment Act was not to assemble regiments full of unwilling conscripts, but to spur communities to more aggressive recruiting. Thus well in advance of draft day each congressional district would be given a quota that must be filled, by either recruits or conscripts or hired substitutes.

These draft quotas pressured towns and urban wards to raise bounty funds to attract willing recruits. The federal legislation shaped local behavior. Those communities used market forces—in the form of bounties or other inducements—to find volunteers. But even if that ominous draft day came, the power of choice did not disappear. Many of those selected could claim some sort of exemption and avoid service. And of those draftees who were personally "called to service," the majority turned to the market to hire a replacement. In the end, roughly 8 percent of the Union army was composed of draftees or substitutes, while huge numbers of volunteers had stepped forward in response to the bounty fund drives.[3]

In each of these examples—war contracting, bond sales, enlistment drives, and conscription—the Union relied on individual citizens to make informed decisions. To a remarkable degree, the Union war effort depended on the choices civilians made.[4]

■ This book has argued that those individual choices did not occur in a vacuum. Prowar northerners—in fact and in fiction—thought hard about what they should do and how they should support the Union war effort. They weighed their nation's needs against their honest assessments of their personal and familial obligations. And they applied a similar standard in measuring the behavior of both friends and strangers in their communities. Much as middle-class northerners had grown accustomed to turning to advice manuals, travel guides, sermons, political pamphlets, and all sorts of prescriptive literature in navigating the many challenges of an antebellum world in flux, these wartime citizens found guidance and solace in printed materials. They constructed a new wartime cultural world out of a combination of very familiar literary forms, often recast to meet the demands of war, and a variety of new forms of wartime writing (recruiting broadsides, patriotic envelopes, satirized caricatures) that spoke directly to the nation's new challenges.

This collective conversation almost never turned on an explicit calculation about the obligations of citizenship. Union League pamphlets and patriotic sermons pounded away at the idea that a nation at war required unbending loyalty, but that uncompromising loyalty could be expressed without sacrifice. Whereas African Americans routinely discussed their relationship to the United States in terms of reciprocal rights and obligations (an analysis that commonly found the nation lacking), the wartime discourse among white northerners was only rarely couched in terms of individual citizens owing a debt to their nation. The preceding chapters have argued that this diverse array of published materials, produced by hundreds of authors, artists, and orators from across the political spectrum, did produce some remarkably consistent rules to guide attitudes and decisions. In fact, those shared concerns—articulated by both passionate Republicans and strong-willed War Democrats—helped solidify a war culture that prospered outside the world of partisan politics.[5]

First, the Civil War required that citizens demonstrate a certain level of attention and knowledge (in addition to loyalty), even if the reader sat safely at home a thousand miles from the seat of battle. Male swells and female socialites could enjoy their daily lives, but they really should understand that there was a war on. Second, wartime citizens—even more so than antebellum readers imbued with republican values—would not tolerate dishonest cheats, especially if that dishonesty led them to profit from the war. Men who paraded around wearing shoulder stripes they had not earned, or war contractors who grew fat selling shoddy merchandise, deserved loud national ridicule. This was a close cousin to the third major rule: northern society hated hypocrites. Whereas the popular fiction seemed surprisingly tolerant of able-bodied men who remained safely at home, wartime satirists and cartoonists continually targeted the editor or politician who blustered about supporting the war until the provost marshal came calling. And in the world of romantic fiction, perhaps the most despised character was the young woman who loved to see her man in uniform, but rejected him when he came home disfigured by the war.

This cluster of rules, summarized in part 1, defined a range of wartime caricatures often presented in extreme satire. I have argued that these stereotypes defined the sorts of selfish decisions that only the worst northern citizens would make, leaving ordinary readers happily content that they had chosen acceptable paths. The war contractor who only made a tidy profit, or the military-aged civilian who sat in the local bar but wore no fake shoulder straps, could rest assured that he was not one of these terrible citizens.

The popular satire also had a culturally conservative message, reinforcing antebellum prejudices. Thus wartime hostility to real shoddy contractors transformed into mockery of poor Irish immigrant men and women, in the guise of satirical attacks on the fictional Shoddy family of Irish-accented pretenders. In this satirical world, the war provided a handy excuse for reinforcing nativism and class antagonism in the name of patriotism. Perhaps the fortunate or the clever could grow wealthy in wartime, but newfound wealth did not guarantee social respectability or entrance into the middle class. Meanwhile, the massive scale of the conflict provided enormous opportunities for brave and ambitious men to earn advanced military ranks, but the home front culture sought to ensure that the men who claimed the respect of the shoulder straps had earned that privilege. Finally, although the Civil War offered ample opportunity to celebrate the pathbreaking public contributions of northern women, the popular home front fiction generally presented women in very familiar gender roles, and the cartoonists turned to belittling gender stereotypes in presenting wartime women. In each of these ways, the war culture pushed back against the wartime forces that threatened to destabilize home front society.

The discussions of the complex decisions surrounding enlistment and conscription—the focus of much of part 2—begin with the same rules. Men talking about volunteering must not be hypocritical when it came to their actions. Draftees must not lie to avoid service. The discussions of decision making and sacrifice in wartime fiction had many wrinkles, but two rules were at the core. The first of these was simply that a good citizen followed the laws. Once the federal government had established a set of regulations surrounding conscription, the duty of the good citizen was to follow those rules and take his chances along with everyone else. Men who ran to Canada, or maimed themselves to avoid service, or attempted some form of deception, deserved contempt. Women who urged men in their lives to break the rules earned the same hostility. The second fundamental rule, which was at the heart of all discussions, was that northern men and women should think hard about their decisions, looking deep into their own consciences. A man could choose to remain at home so long as he could convince himself and those around him that this was the proper decision. And if that same man had his name called on draft day, he was expected to revisit his decision in the light of this new information, looking within himself anew. The guidance provided by the Civil War literature did not demand that civilians—even strong patriots—make any specific sacrifice as their duty to the nation. They only had to obey the laws and then look to their own consciences for guidance.

■ In the twentieth century, things would be very different. A half century after the Civil War, as Americans mobilized for what would become known as World War I, that national mobilization became symbolized by posters of a bearded "Uncle Sam," wearing a jaunty top hat and a patriotic blue coat, pointing out at Americans and declaring, "I Want You." A version of this ubiquitous image first appeared in England early in World War I; it was first introduced in the United States in 1917, and reappeared throughout both World War I and World War II. The message seemed clear: in a time of war, the nation—embodied by "Uncle Sam"—expected men to enlist and, more broadly, all good citizens were expected to sacrifice for the cause. That image and message suggest an understanding of the obligations of citizenship. By accepting membership in a nation, the citizen agrees to make contributions to the larger good when Uncle Sam calls. These obligations were partially encoded in laws, but citizenship also implied mutual expectations that were not defined by statute, thus "Uncle Sam Wants You," as opposed to "Uncle Sam *Requires* You," to step forward.

In 1917, not long after the Uncle Sam image reached American shores, President Woodrow Wilson issued his "Proclamation Establishing Conscription," in which he explained that the new national conscription law "is in no sense a conscription of the unwilling; it is, rather, selection from a nation which has volunteered in mass. It is no more a choosing of those who shall march with the colors than it is a selection of those who shall serve an equally necessary and devoted purpose in the industries that lie behind the battle line."[6] Wilson saw the draft for national service, both military and economic, as no more than selecting individuals from a nation that had volunteered en masse to serve their country. Surely not all Americans shared the president's vision of national conscription, but there is no doubting that he worked within a framework defined by an expectation of universal voluntarism. Two generations later, when newly elected president John F. Kennedy declared that "the torch had been passed to a new generation of Americans," the new chief executive called on his listeners to "ask not what your country can do for you, ask what you can do for your country."[7] Even in peacetime, patriotic Americans were to contemplate the debt they owed their nation, and how best to meet those obligations.

Abraham Lincoln navigated a very different political culture as a wartime president. Lincoln, one of the greatest writers and orators to occupy the office, had ample opportunity to offer his thoughts on how loyal Americans should behave, and must behave, during the American Civil War. As we saw in chapter 4, in his unpublished memo on conscription Lincoln made a strong case for the constitutional right to conscript soldiers, but he also acknowledged that patriotic Americans might have had good reasons to decline the opportunity to volunteer. This is the crucial distinction. The president embraced the importance of individual choice, though he also defended the government's right to pass legislation that would shape those choices, putting pressure on the recalcitrant.

Throughout his four years in office, Lincoln penned hundreds of messages intended to praise, congratulate, endorse, and console northern citizens. A close reading of his published personal papers yields a remarkable list of such small notes and short speeches.[8] Many answered requests from friends seeking a position or favor; other comments addressed volunteer groups or regiments of returning soldiers. Some, like the famous Bixby Letter, were poignant notes to relatives of fallen soldiers. Taken together, these messages from Lincoln—some of which were published at the time, but many of which were no more than a few scrawled sentences—offer a window into the president's thinking about the obligations and duties of citizens in wartime.

Certain patterns are striking. When asked to endorse someone seeking a position, Lincoln spoke of his personal connections to the applicant, and often to the individual's virtues and skills. He almost never spoke of the applicant's patriotism or service to the Union.[9] In speaking to home front volunteers or regiments of soldiers, Lincoln offered his personal thanks for their sacrifices, but he never used the language of duty or obligation. The president took every opportunity to thank people for making personal choices to support the war effort, while never suggesting that they had been under any constitutional or ethical obligation to do so.

In fact, the entire body of Lincoln's writings offers very few words about what constituted good citizenship.[10] His most direct comment on civic duty came in a letter written to a 105-year-old Connecticut pastor, on learning that the elderly man had traveled two miles to cast a vote for the president's reelection. "I take the liberty of writing to you to express my personal gratitude for the compliment paid me by the suffrage of a citizen so venerable," he wrote. "The example of such devotion to civic duties in one whose days have already extended an average life time beyond the Psalmist's limit, cannot but be valuable and fruitful. It is not for myself only, but for the country which you have in your sphere served so long and so well, that I thank you." Here, in a very rare reference to citizenship and duty, the president singled out political participation as the greatest civic obligation. In a letter to twelve-year-old Willie Smith, Lincoln praised the young lad for his support and expressed particular satisfaction that someone his age "already take[s] so lively an interest in what just now so deeply concerns us." A good citizen, it seemed, stayed informed. The obligation of the engaged citizen was to participate in the public debate, not necessarily to embark on any particular action. Actions followed informed choices, not government dictates.[11]

Whereas volunteers during World War I and World War II had responded to the expectations of a rather stern-faced "Uncle Sam" telling the viewer that he "wanted them," during the Civil War one of the North's popular songs was "We Are Coming Father Abraham, 300,000 More."[12] The lyrics celebrated those young men who had volunteered to serve the Union army at the behest of their "father Abraham."[13] Here again the distinction is crucial. Uncle Sam told American viewers that they were called, in keeping with Wilson's notion of "conscription in mass." Father Abraham had requested volunteers, and the song celebrated those who voluntarily chose to respond.

■ In this world of choices, the more difficult issues surrounded the true nature of patriotic duty. Antebellum Americans had little sense of national citizenship as an identity that encompassed both rights and responsibilities, framed as an explicit reciprocal relationship between the individual and the state. Northern elites, in the guise of the Union Leagues and dozens of pamphlets, pushed for enhanced wartime nationalism and unconditional loyalty, but generally without the expectation of concomitant sacrifice. Philip Nolan's greatest sin was not his youthful treason, but his subsequent rejection of his country. But Civil War northerners did believe that commitment to the Union included some responsibilities that each person must honestly contemplate. At the very least, they were expected to remain loyal and endure without complaint. White men who honestly assessed their situations and concluded that they really could become soldiers felt some duty to act. White women had a culturally scripted role to play in supporting those decisions, even while that patriotic role often clashed with long-held domestic ideals. But sometimes good women simply could not meet that expectation. And, to muddy the waters further still, good men were expected to defer to the wishes of the women in their lives if they insisted that he stay at home.

This popular conversation rarely defined those duties as based on the obligations of citizenship, or as the price of membership in the Union. Soldiers who had already enlisted spoke of their duty to the flag, and sometimes they applied that same language of duty to civilians who had failed to step forward, but in their personal writings they tended to reserve their ire for Copperheads who failed to support the war effort rather than pro-war civilians who declined to enlist.[14] Men and women at home recognized a duty to take the decision—and the war—seriously, but not a duty to sacrifice. The conversation within the African American community offers an illuminating contrast. While white northerners in this cultural discourse did not articulate an explicit relationship between the freedoms and privileges they enjoyed as citizens, and the responsibilities they now faced, free black men and women noted the irony in being asked to sacrifice for a nation that denied them those rights. Some found the absence of equality to be a powerful obstacle to service; others hoped that wartime sacrifice would yield the benefits of full citizenship.

■ Historians of the Civil War era often point to the Thirteenth, Fourteenth, and Fifteenth Amendments as crucial legacies of four years of violent conflict. The Thirteenth Amendment ended slavery in the United States. The Fourteenth Amendment defined federal citizenship, overturning the Supreme Court's *Dred Scott* decision, which declared that African Americans were not citizens. The Fifteenth Amendment expanded voting rights to black adult male citizens. Together these amendments broke new ground both in expanding definitions and by explicitly excluding women from the rights to suffrage that had been commonly associated with citizenship. These amendments, and the scores of court opinions that followed, defined and refined the meaning of citizenship, with a focus on the particular rights and privileges that citizens—both black and white—could reasonably expect from the federal government and from their individual states. Thus the terms of discussion focused on membership, legal rights, and constitutional protections.[15]

It is striking how distinct those postwar constitutional developments were from the conversations that preceded them. Although wartime writers addressed the plight of the slave and the fate of the contraband, their fictional white characters on the imagined northern home front only rarely spoke of slavery and emancipation. And while much postwar debate centered on the rights and obligations of citizenship, such concerns were largely absent in the wartime cultural conversation. These observations merely reflect how quickly the terrain had shifted in a short period of time, in ways that would have been unpredictable a few years earlier. The presence of a conquered South populated by—among others—newly freed black men and women and unrepentant southern whites produced new political and legal debates that had little to do with the North's wartime world.[16]

Nearly two years into the Civil War, Charles Stillé turned to history for clues about how a free people could win that long war. He urged his readers to endure in times of despair. In the end, northerners endured long enough to win the People's Contest. They did so not because some great national power forced them into action, but because hundreds of thousands of citizens made individual decisions supporting the Union cause. The decisions they made, and the published materials that informed their decisions, are a window into a historic moment when individualism, nationalism, and personal choice converged.

Notes

1. Stillé, *How a Free People Conduct a Long War*. The LPS edition was reprinted from a pamphlet by the same name distributed by the Union League of Philadelphia. Stillé published a preliminary version of this pamphlet in *Harper's Weekly*, March 7, 1863, 150–51.

2. For an excellent short analysis of the complex events at the end of 1862, see McPherson, *Crossroads of Freedom*. Of course the party in power commonly loses some ground in the off-year election, but the political campaigns surrounding these first wartime elections illustrated rising discomfort among the northern citizenry.

3. Friedel, "The Loyal Publication Society."

4. "Patriot" is a word open to multiple interpretations and understandings, and it is not my intention to interrogate the term very carefully. Here I am setting the bar rather low. My patriots are people who essentially remained loyal to the Union cause, even if they were not always happy about the actions of Abraham Lincoln, his administration, or his military leaders. It remains to be seen what they felt that loyalty required of them.

5. The scholarship on northern dissent is substantial, although not exhaustive. See Gray, *The Hidden Civil War*; Klement, *The Copperheads in the Middle West*; Shankman, *The Pennsylvania Antiwar Movement*; Weber, *Copperheads*; Sandow, *Deserter Country*. For the northern political spectrum during the Civil War, see White, *Emancipation, the Union Army, and the Reelection of Abraham Lincoln*, 13–15. On efforts to identify and suppress treason, see Blair, *With Malice toward Some*.

6. My contention here is that "we"—people who read about the Civil War and historians who write about it—tend to think very little about these ideas in these terms. Certainly specialists do understand that there was a vast middle between the rabid Copperhead and the ardent patriot. My goal is to focus the lens toward these northerners in the middle.

7. On American combat deaths in major wars see Fischer, "American War and Military Operations Casualties." The estimate of military deaths in conflicts with Native Americans and pirates comes from Wikipedia, assembled from multiple sources. http://en.wikipedia.org/wiki/United_States_military_casualties_of_war (last modified September 10, 2014).

8. I have argued elsewhere that northerners were able to turn to antebellum institutions and traditions in adjusting to the peculiar challenges posed by the Civil War. Gallman, *Mastering Wartime*; Gallman, *The North Fights the Civil War*.

9. Births minus deaths.

10. http://www.census.gov/geo/reference/centersofpop.html. Note that these figures include the southern states.

11. For important broad surveys of these decades see Wilentz, *The Rise of American Democracy*, and Howe, *What Hath God Wrought*.

12. Blumin, *The Emergence of the Middle Class*; Blumin, "The Hypothesis of Middle-Class Formation in Nineteenth-Century America"; Ryan, *Cradle of the Middle Class*.

13. Welter, "The Cult of True Womanhood"; Richard, *Busy Hands*, 13–39. For the economic changes undergirding this shifting gender landscape, see Cott, *The Bonds of Womanhood*. It is important to note that Welter's study examined cultural prescriptions aimed at a particular audience. It did not intend to capture actual behavior. For women's political behavior and public discourse in the Early Republic see Zagarri, *Revolutionary Backlash*.

14. In her best-selling 1797 novel, *The Coquette*, Hannah Webster Foster told the sad tale of Eliza Wharton, a young New England woman who resisted a sensible suitor in favor of a charming and unscrupulous rake. As contemporary readers might have predicted, poor Eliza ends up dying alone, unmarried and pregnant. Foster, *The Coquette*. Foster's novel remained a best seller throughout the antebellum decades. Susanna Rowson's *Charlotte Temple*, first published in England in 1791, offered similar didactic messages for young female readers throughout the early nineteenth century. Rowson, *Charlotte Temple*. For another popular antebellum best seller rich with prescriptive messages for young women, see Wetherell, *The Wide, Wide World*.

15. Halttunen, *Confidence Men and Painted Women*, 1–55.

16. Gallman, *Receiving Erin's Children*, 37–54.

17. Hemphill, *Bowing to Necessities*. For further discussion of etiquette manuals as an expanding form of prescription see Halttunen, *Confidence Men and Painted Women*, and Levine, *Highbrow/Lowbrow*.

18. Henkin, *City Reading*. For a study of how newcomers learned to read the nineteenth-century city, see Barth, *City People*.

19. On publication and consumption patterns and reading habits see Zboray, *A Fictive People*; Sizer, *The Political Work of Northern Women Writers*, 29–30; Cullen, *The Art of Democracy*, 36–46; Anne C. Rose, *Victorian America and the Civil War*, 123–24; Zboray and Zboray, "Books, Reading, and the World of Goods"; Kelley, *Private Woman, Public Stage*, esp. 10–13; Henkin, *City Reading*, 32. For circulation figures see Bureau of the Census, *Statistics of the United States in 1860*, 321–22. According to Frank Mott, roughly a third of the nation's periodicals in 1860 were published in New York State. Mott, *A History of American Magazines, 1850-1865*, 103.

20. For the expansion of the postal service see Henkin, *The Postal Age*. For communication and culture in antebellum America see Hochfelder, "The Communications Revolution and Popular Culture"; Brown, *The Strength of a People*; Blumin, "The Social Implications of U.S. Economic Development."

21. Mott, *A History of American Magazines, 1850-1865*, 383, 416–18, 452–93, 520–29. Mott makes the point that the 1850s saw the start of a new era in American publishing, not only because new journals emerged but because of the emergence of new editors and—in some cases—an increased focus toward writing for a national audience. See esp. 3–4.

22. Of course, for nearly two years the North's able-bodied black men were refused the opportunity to serve.

23. The scholarship on northern conscription is substantial. See Geary, *We Need Men*; Murdock, *Patriotism Limited.*

24. Many scholars have offered slightly different versions of these numbers, generally relying on raw data from the US census and Gould, *Investigations in the Military and Anthropological Statistics of American Soldiers*. Unless otherwise noted, I am relying on the statistics assembled by Fogel, "New Sources and New Techniques." Fogel's analysis is particularly useful because he considers young men who turned eighteen after the war began. For a somewhat different but quite useful analysis, see Hattaway, "The Civil War Armies." Hattaway estimates that one hundred thousand men in southern states remained loyal to the Union (175) and should be added to the Union ledger sheet, but he seems to neglect those men who turned eighteen during the war. As far as I can tell, neither Fogel nor Hattaway considers the roughly eight hundred thousand immigrants who arrived in the Union during the war. The men among these newcomers were not immediately subject to conscription, and they enlisted in smaller proportions than native-born northerners, but a sizable number ended up in the Union ranks, contributing to the 2.1 million total. That 2.1 million figure also includes some boys who were under eighteen and some men who were over forty-five when they enlisted. Given these variables, the 40 percent figure noted in the text seems quite conservative. A small portion of Union volunteers were under eighteen (under 2 percent) or over forty-five (about .5 percent) at the time of their enlistment. For a discussion of this data see Wiley, *The Life of Billy Yank*, 298–302. For a valuable study of immigrants and conscription, see Anbinder, "Which Poor Man's Fight?"

25. The data for the Confederacy are much weaker than the data for the Union. For a valuable overview of the evidence, see Hattaway, "The Civil War Armies," 174–79.

26. McPherson, *Ordeal by Fire*, 386–88.

27. Fogel, "New Sources and New Techniques," 22–24. Fogel's study was largely interested in evaluating the health of Union soldiers. A large percentage of young men who faced medical examination were rejected, but that percentage rose steadily with older cohorts.

28. Hacker, "Economic, Demographic, and Anthropometric Correlates of First Marriage," 318. The mean age of marriage for men was 26.9.

29. Russell Frank Weigley, *A Great Civil War*, xvi. My thanks to Liz Varon for directing me to this quote. On the economic composition of the Union army see McPherson, *Ordeal by Fire*, 386–88, and Gould, *Investigations in the Military and Anthropological Statistics of American Soldiers*. Note that scholars often associate the rise of the middle class with urbanization and a shift toward nonmanual labor, as well as with a broader set of cultural, ideological, and economic changes (see Blumin, *The Emergence of the Middle Class*). The data assembled by Gould and McPherson make it clear that a very large percentage of the Union army, like the nation as a whole, came from agricultural communities. As Weigley implies, by the Civil War the sensibilities that shaped the new middle class had expanded beyond the nation's cities.

30. See Bailyn, *Pamphlets of the American Revolution.*

31. Friedel, "The Loyal Publication Society"; Friedel, introduction to *Union Pamphlets of the Civil War*; Paludan, "'The Better Angels of Our Nation,'" 362–64. For a

valuable discussion of these pamphlets as an underexamined source, see Neely, *Lincoln and the Triumph of the Nation*, esp. 17–26.

32. Edward Everett Hale, "The Man without a Country," *Atlantic Monthly* 12 (December 1863): 665–80. For commentary on Hale's essay see Lawson, "'A Profound National Devotion'"; Lawson, *Patriotic Fires*, 122–28; Thomas, *Civic Myths*; Duquette, *Loyal Subjects*.

33. Bellows, *Unconditional Loyalty*. Like Hale's essay, this sermon and the larger issue of unconditional loyalty has received substantial scholarly attention. See Nagler, "Loyalty and Dissent"; Lawson, *Patriotic Fires*, 124; Rable, *God's Almost Chosen Peoples*, 230–32; Blair, *With Malice toward Some*, 203–4; Duquette, *Loyal Subjects*.

34. The key point here is that I am differentiating between those writings that are aimed at affecting public policy, military decisions, or individual voting and those intended to affect the behavior of the patriotic reader. My goal is to consider the publications that are addressed to individual decision making and the nature of civic obligation in wartime.

35. Although his interests are different, William A. Blair makes similar observations about the importance of wartime community discourse and printed publications in defining treason and disloyalty. See Blair, *With Malice toward Some*, esp. 60.

36. I am not going to present myself as an expert on the literature on parody and satire, but among the titles I found interesting and valuable in framing this analysis are Hutcheson, *A Theory of Parody*; Margaret A. Rose, *Parody*; and Denith, *Parody*.

37. The classic studies of Civil War literature are Edmund Wilson, *Patriotic Gore*, and Aaron, *The Unwritten War*. For a study of Civil War popular culture, see Fahs, *The Imagined Civil War*. On women writers and the war years, see Sizer, *The Political Work of Northern Women Writers*, and Young, *Disarming the Nation*. On constitutional issues and literature see Diffley, *Where My Heart Is Turning Ever*. On wartime poetry, see Marius, *The Columbia Book of Civil War Poetry*. On patriotic envelopes see Boyd, *Patriotic Envelopes of the Civil War*.

38. Locke, Browne, Newell, and fellow satirist Samuel Clemens (Mark Twain) were all born between 1833 and 1836, illustrating the fundamental newness of this particular satirical form.

39. For useful overviews of wartime humor, see Nickels, *Civil War Humor*; Fahs, *The Imagined Civil War*, esp. 195–224; Grinspan, "'Sorrowfully Amusing'"; and "Civil War Humor," special issue, *Civil War History* 2 (September 1956).

40. Secretary of the Navy Gideon Welles commented on Lincoln's humorous readings in his diary. See Bray, *Reading with Lincoln*, 207–8. Secretary of War Edwin M. Stanton reported that Lincoln read an essay by Artemus Ward to the cabinet on September 22, 1862, before sharing the Preliminary Emancipation Proclamation. Seitz, *Artemus Ward*. See also Fahs, *The Imagined Civil War*, 195–96. A few months after Lincoln's election a "NY correspondent" to San Francisco's *Daily Evening Bulletin* described James Buchanan chuckling at a cartoon in *Vanity Fair*. *Daily Evening Bulletin*, January 11, 1861.

41. I have not spent much time with the children's magazines in this project, both because my chief concerns are for the thoughts and decisions of adults and because that work has already been done so thoroughly. See Marten, "For the Good, the True, and

the Beautiful"; Marten, *The Children's Civil War*; Marten, *Children and Youth during the Civil War Era*; and Marten, *Lessons of War*.

42. On parenting advice, see Casey, "The Mightiest Influence on Earth."

43. For the North's wartime commitment to Union, see Gallagher, *The Union War*. For the ongoing wartime construction of nationalism in the North see Lawson, *Patriotic Fires*. For a valuable discussion of northern values see Hess, *Liberty, Virtue, and Progress*. In very different contexts, Hess makes a similar argument about the links between personal values of individualism and the national cause.

44. The literature on republican ideology is vast. For an excellent point of entry, see Shalhope, "Toward a Republican Synthesis." The transition from republicanism to liberalism is another large and contested topic. For a collection of essays by one of the major figures in this debate see Appleby, *Liberalism and Republicanism*. For an analysis of fears of wartime corruption, tied to these antebellum republican concerns, see Michael Thomas Smith, *The Enemy Within*.

45. My reading of these various prescriptive texts as statements about cultural expectations of masculinity draws on the texts themselves, as informed by extensive readings on nineteenth-century masculinity. For some of the foundational texts on nineteenth-century masculinity see Rotundo, *American Manhood*; Bederman, *Manliness and Civilization*; Greenberg, *Manifest Manhood*; Hoganson, *Fighting for American Manhood*; Stephen W. Berry II, *All That Makes a Man*.

46. See Scholnick, "'An Unusually Active Market for Calamus'"; Seitz, *Artemus Ward*, 79–80; Nardin, "Civil War Humor."

47. West, "Frank Leslie's Budget of Fun."

48. Morford, *Shoulder Straps*; Morford, *The Days of Shoddy*; Morford, *The Coward*.

49. Tammany Society, *Celebration at Tammany Hall, on Friday, July 4th, 1862*; Tammany Society, *Celebration at Tammany Hall, on Saturday, July 4, 1863*; Morford, *Rhymes of Twenty Years*.

50. Morford, *Over-Sea*.

51. When I first stumbled upon Henry Morford, his novels were completely absent from scholarly discussions. Edmund Wilson, Daniel Aaron, and Alice Fahs made no mention of his fiction. More recently, some of Morford's writings have attracted limited attention. See, for instance, the mentions in Neely, *The Union Divided*, and Michael Thomas Smith, *The Enemy Within*.

52. *Dover (NH) Gazette*, November 20, 1863.

53. *Urban Union* (Ohio), September 16, 1863.

54. *Philadelphia Press*, August 12, 1863.

55. *Philadelphia Press*, November 20, December 9, 12, 1863, January 8, 1864. The *Press* published three entirely separate reviews of the novel, all critical but generally positive.

56. *Cleveland Morning Leader*, July 25, 1864.

57. *Daily Evening Bulletin*, July 22, 1864. This quotation was from a long advertisement, although the hasty reader could easily have missed that point.

58. *Frank Leslie's Illustrated Newspaper*, December 8, 1866.

59. *Harper's New Monthly Magazine* 27 (November 1863): 850; *Evening Star* (Washington, DC), August 13, 1864.

60. In addition to the publications cited above, various Internet searches identified a long list of journals and newspapers that reviewed a Morford novel or mentioned some other writing. Many mentioned the author quite frequently. National journals reviewing or citing Morford: *Atlantic Monthly, Continental Monthly, Frank Leslie's Illustrated Newspaper, Harper's New Monthly Magazine, Living Age*. Selected newspapers (organized alphabetically by state of publication): *Golden Era* (San Francisco, CA), *Hartford Courant, Daily National Intelligencer* (Washington, DC), *Evening Star* (Washington, DC), *Chicago Tribune, Bangor Daily Whig and Courier, Cass County (MI) Republican, Dover (NH) Gazette, New York Herald, New York Daily Tribune, New York Times, Penny Press* (Cincinnati, OH), *Dayton Daily Empire, Cincinnati Daily Press, Daily Cleveland Herald, Cleveland Morning Leader, Daily Ohio Statesman* (Columbus), *Western Reserve Chronicle* (Warren, OH), *Urban Union* (Ohio), *Columbia (PA) Spy, Pennsylvania Daily Telegraph* (Harrisburg), *Reading Gazette and Democrat, Lancaster (PA) Intelligencer, Evening Telegraph* (Philadelphia, PA), *Philadelphia Press, Philadelphia Inquirer, Daily Evening Bulletin* (Philadelphia, PA), *Pittsburg Daily Gazette and Advertiser, Burlington (VT) Free Press, Vermont Watchman and State Journal, Milwaukee Daily Sentinel*. This list only suggests the range of publications reviewing Morford's novels.

61. For a discussion of circulation rates and the dominance of eastern publishing houses see Fahs, *The Imagined Civil War*, 42–43. On circulations more broadly, see Mott, *A History of American Magazines, 1850–1865*.

62. Levine, *Highbrow/Lowbrow*.

63. See Ray, *The Lyceum and Public Culture*; Gallman, *America's Joan of Arc*.

64. The fact that American publishing houses were almost exclusively in the Northeast supports the observation that Americans who read novels were consuming books from the same market.

65. Mott, *A History of American Magazines, 1850–1865*, 102.

66. Oliver Wendell Holmes Sr., "Bread and the Newspaper," *Atlantic Monthly* 8 (September 1861): 346–52. On the diversity of wartime voices as well as the emergence of certain cultural patterns, see Sizer, *The Political Work of Northern Women Writers*, 6–13. On the increased importance of newspapers in wartime reading patterns see Zboray and Zboray, "Cannonballs and Books," 251–52.

67. See chaps. 3 and 4.

68. Mott, *A History of American Magazines, 1850–1865*, 116–18. The *Golden Era* regularly quoted from four New York papers—the *Ledger, Courier, Herald*, and *Mercury*—and periodically reprinted stories from other eastern and midwestern papers. Quite a few of the war-related poems and short stories published in the newspaper were set in the East. Certainly readers had exposure to material from across the northern states.

69. *Golden Era*, November 8, 1862. For an example of an entire column devoted to essays from the *Atlantic Monthly*, see August 2, 1863.

70. Gale Publications, *19th Century United States Newspapers*, digital collection, accessed April 2014, http://gdc.gale.com/products/19th-century-u.s.-newspapers/ (behind paywall). Each of the following newspapers (arranged alphabetically by state) reprinted material from *Vanity Fair* between 1861 and 1863: *Daily Evening Bulletin* (San Francisco, CA); *Tri-weekly Miner's Register* (Central City, CO); *New Haven Daily Pal-*

ladium; *Daily National Intelligencer* (Washington, DC); *Freedom's Champion* (Atchison, KS); *Rocky Mountain News* (Cherry Creek, KS); *Bangor (ME) Daily Whig and Courier*; *The Liberator* (Boston, MA); *Lowell (MA) Daily Citizen and News*; *Boston Daily Advertiser*; *Boston Investigator*; *New Hampshire Statesman*; *New York Herald*; *Frank Leslie's Illustrated Newspaper* (New York, NY); *Daily Cleveland Herald*; *Scioto (OH) Gazette*; *Ripley* (OH) *Bee*; *Newark (OH) Advocate*; *Morning Oregonian* (Portland, OR); *North American and United States Gazette* (Philadelphia, PA); *Weekly Dakotian* (Yankton, SD); *Vermont Chronicle*; *Wisconsin State Register*; *Milwaukee Daily Sentinel*. My argument here is not that these twenty-four newspapers are representative of the major American newspapers but, rather, that this digital collection has assembled a wonderfully odd array of newspapers from all over the country, yet *Vanity Fair* crops up in nearly every one. Tests of the reach of the two major illustrated weeklies—*Frank Leslie's* and *Harper's*—would of course yield even greater national penetration. The lesser New York humor magazines are also mentioned with surprising regularity in these newspapers. Note that this analysis excludes newspapers published in Confederate states, although many of these also reprinted pieces from *Vanity Fair*.

71. The research design for this book does not include any systematic review of the personal papers of either civilians or soldiers. What follows are just a few examples to suggest larger patterns.

72. Mohr, *Cormany Diaries*, 526, 501 (Rachel Cormany's diary entries for March 26, 1865, and January 16, 1865).

73. Elder, *Love amid the Turmoil* (quote from 265, November 30, 1863).

74. Smith and Cooper, *A Union Woman in Civil War Kentucky*.

75. Newspapers commonly paid particular attention to the exploits of local regiments, while also keeping their editors abreast of national military developments. For one town's experience with war reporting see Gallman and Baker, "Gettysburg's Gettysburg." I have argued elsewhere that the events surrounding both secession and war made northern civilians increasingly attuned to national news reporting. See Gallman, *Mastering Wartime*.

76. Quoted in Matthews, *The Golden State in the Civil War*, 150.

77. *Civil War Letters of General Robert McAllister*, esp. 464. The essay McAllister spoke of was presumably Robert Tomes, "The Fortunes of War," *Harper's New Monthly Magazine* 29 (July 1864): 327–32.

78. Rosenblatt and Rosenblatt, *Hard Marching Every Day*.

79. It is striking how often soldiers' letters suggest that they are getting two flows of information: from various newspapers sent from home (and passed from hand to hand), and from other newspapers published near where they are based. For more on soldiers' reading see Wiley, *The Life of Billy Yank*, 154; Robertson, *Soldiers Blue and Gray*, 82–83.

80. For a fascinating novel about the lives of the urban working class during the Civil War see Anonymous, *Six Hundred Dollars a Year*. Essayist Fanny Fern (Sara Willis Parton) did write about the hardships of working-class women during the war, although her essays were directed at middle-class readers. Virginia Townsend also published several stories featuring working-class women as central characters. See Sizer, *The Political Work of Northern Women Writers*, 134–35.

81. My point here is that the prescriptive literature that addressed citizenship and proper wartime behavior was not directed to the working classes. There was certainly a tremendous amount of partisan political commentary, including pamphlets and editorials, which attempted to shape the political behavior of poor voters, along with recruiting posters and rhetoric aimed at different ethnic groups. And there was substantial commentary about ethnic soldiers and about the misdeeds of Irish draft rioters. Prowar northerners generally wanted immigrant workers to support the war, enlist in the army, and not riot in the streets. Some writers did comment on how the war brought economic hardship to working-class northerners, particularly to poor women. But the sources under investigation rarely offered guidance on citizenship aimed at either the working classes or ethnic groups.

82. While it was true that this literary world did not reach all corners of northern society, I do not wish to suggest a narrow understanding of "middle class" here, particularly if the term calls to mind urbanizing Americans. The home front stories and novels include many rural and small-town settings, with characters who are a part of the larger cultural world.

83. This is not a surprising discovery. African Americans made up less than 2 percent of the total population in the northern states, and they were—on average—less literate and less wealthy than whites. Most white readers in the Union states had little personal contact with African Americans, and presumably were not expecting to find black characters in the home front fiction. Several scholars have noted the prevalence of racial themes in the northern weeklies, but the examples generally focus on slaves and contrabands. See Fahs, *The Imagined Civil War*, 2–3, 150–94. In his extensive reading in wartime children's literature, historian James Marten finds similar patterns. Some children's magazines became increasingly political and patriotic during the war, and in that context they featured stories embracing abolitionism and describing the plight of the contraband. But only rarely did this children's literature focus on free blacks in the North. See Marten, *Lessons of War*, 8–9; Marten, *The Children's Civil War*, 43–45.

84. Abraham Lincoln, "Message to Congress in Special Session," July 4, 1861, in Basler, *The Collected Works of Abraham Lincoln*, 4:438–39. The historian Phillip S. Paludan took this as the title of his study of the northern home front. Paludan, *A People's Contest*.

85. A case could be made that Abraham Lincoln, the great orator, was a deft propagandist. See Paludan, "'The Better Angels of Our Nation.'"

CHAPTER ONE

1. This militaristic outcry was not unanimous, nor was it identical in every community, but in those key weeks the North's pro-Union civilians rallied around the flag with enthusiasm. For one city's response to Fort Sumter, see Gallman, *Mastering Wartime*. For the patriotic poetry and song that characterized the war's first year, see Fahs, *The Imagined Civil War*, 61–92.

2. "The Flag Mania," *Vanity Fair*, May 11, 1861.

3. See Gallman, *Mastering Wartime*.

4. Gail Hamilton [Mary Abigail Dodge], "Mob Patriotism," in Hamilton, *Skirmishes and Sketches*, chap. 12. This essay was originally published early in the war.

5. "Hurrah for the War!," *Vanity Fair*, May 18, 1861.

6. "The War Fever," *Arthur's Home Magazine* 18 (October 1861): 201.

7. Woolf, *Off to the War!*

8. Seitz, *Artemus Ward*; John Q. Reed, "Civil War Humor: Artemus Ward"; Melville D. Landon, "Artemus Ward," biographical sketch in Ward [Charles Farrar Browne], *The Complete Works of Artemus Ward*, 11–24. The *Complete Works* originally appeared in four volumes. The 1875 edition combined all volumes into a single book, with consecutive pagination. Each of the essays cited here also appeared in many wartime newspapers and journals.

9. Ward, "War Fever in Baldinsville," *The Complete Works of Artemus Ward*, 119–22.

10. Ward, "A War Meeting," *The Complete Works of Artemus Ward*, 123–26 (originally published in *Vanity Fair*, October 4, 1862). We will return to some of the satirical power of women taking up weapons in place of men in chap. 6.

11. Holmes, *Rose Mather*, 9–19.

12. Durden, "Not Just a Leg Show." Note that Durden's research focuses on the decades shortly after the Civil War.

13. Scholnick, "'An Unusually Active Market for Calamus,'" 150.

14. For an excellent, illustrated commentary on the "swell" see Lubin Lavendaw Kiddes, "Letter from a Destitute Swell," *Vanity Fair*, April 5, 1862. Although this humorous essay appeared a year into the Civil War, it makes no reference to the conflict.

15. HLC, "Humors of the War," *Vanity Fair*, June 29, 1861.

16. "Rejected National Hymns," *Vanity Fair*, June 29, 1861. Alice Fahs discusses the competition to name a national song in *The Imagined Civil War*, 72–75.

17. "Scene in a Fashionable Hotel," *Vanity Fair*, July 20, 1861; WF, "Airy," *Vanity Fair*, October 12, 1861. As we shall see, as the war progressed a potential recruit's insistence on a fine commission was often a literary device used to mark a character as unsavory or self-absorbed.

18. "The Swell's Soliloquy on the War," *Vanity Fair*, September 7, 1861. Also see *Boston Daily Advertiser*, September 6, 1861; *Frank Leslie's Budget of Fun*, October 1861.

19. *Vanity Fair*, October 26, 1861; *Vanity Fair*, November 23, 1861; TMJ, *Vanity Fair*, December 14, 1861. Fashion inspired by the military also found its way into women's magazines. See, for instance, "Bag, or Pouch, for Zouave Jackets," *Godey's Lady's Book and Magazine* 63 (September 1861): 244; "New Style Zouave Jackets," *Godey's Lady's Book and Magazine* 64 (February 1862): 120.

20. *Frank Leslie's Budget of Fun* (October 1861); "By Jove, Too Bad," *Yankee Notions* 10 (November 1861): 332; "Prepared to Dye for His Country," *Yankee Notions* 10 (July 1861): 213; "Cruel," *Comic Monthly* (July 1861): 13.

21. *Yankee Notions* 10 (July 1861): 206; "The Sweet Little Man," *Living Age* (Boston), October 12, 1861. The poem was originally published in the *Transcript* (Boston). It was later reprinted in various places, including the *Golden Era*, January 4, 1863.

22. "An Appetizer," *Yankee Notions* 11 (November 1862): 343; *Comic Monthly*, September 1863, 10.

23. "Opinion of an Overworked Man," *Vanity Fair*, July 26, 1862; Howard Del, "Illustration 1," *Vanity Fair*, August 9, 1862; "The New 'Social Evil,'" *Vanity Fair*, September 6, 1862; "Dodging the Draft—A Swell's Strategem," *Frank Leslie's Illustrated Newspaper*, September 19, 1863; WF, "Dangers of the Park," *Vanity Fair*, October 4, 1862.

24. "True for Once," *Frank Leslie's Illustrated Newspaper*, July 16, 1864, reprinted in *Frank Leslie's Budget of Fun* (October 1864): 12.

25. "Sympathy," *Yankee Notions* 14 (January 1865): 15.

26. *Frank Leslie's Budget of Fun* (October 1861): 16.

27. "Sketches of the War," *Ballou's Dollar Monthly Magazine,* January 1862.

28. "The Luxury of Giving," *Vanity Fair*, June 29, 1861. Although the tenor of this article seems humorous, the letters home from Union soldiers suggest that the concerns were real. One of my personal favorites was the letter from Philadelphian Hanna Smith offering to send her soldier son a pet cat. He replied that the poor cat would likely end up on a dinner plate. See Gallman, *Mastering Wartime*, 72.

29. "Humors of the War," *Vanity Fair*, August 17, 1861; "Why Shouldn't He?," *Vanity Fair*, August 17, 1861; "The Ladies—Bless Them!" *Vanity Fair*, September 20, 1862; "Lemon Aid for the Army," *Vanity Fair*, June 13, 1863.

30. "The Knitting of the Socks," *Vanity Fair*, November 23, 1861; "The Army of the Knitters," *Arthur's Home Magazine* 19 (January 1862): 61, quoting a poem in the *Boston Transcript*. While these two poems had a light flavor, "The Dream of the Knitter" [*Ballou's Dollar Monthly Magazine* (March 1862)] adopted a much more reverential tone in imagining a patriotic woman's thoughts as she knitted for the army.

31. *Frank Leslie's Illustrated Newspaper*, November 22, 1862.

32. Ward, "The Draft in Baldinsville," *The Complete Works of Artemus Ward*, 127–32. See also "Tangled and Raveled," *The American Mail-Bag, or Tales from the War* (London: War and Lock, 1863), 271–89. Story by an unknown author, reprinted from an American source.

33. Orpheus C. Kerr [Robert Henry Newell], "From Washington," *Yankee Notions* 10 (November 1861): 374. The story says it is quoting from the *Philadelphia Sunday Transcript*. Havelocks were military headgear that featured a flap that fell down the back to protect the soldier from extreme sun. These were really more appropriate for desert warfare, but at the beginning of the war home front sewing groups were producing havelocks to ship to the front.

34. WS, "Technicalities Nowhere," *Vanity Fair*, July 19, 1862; *Vanity Fair*, October 5, 1861; "A Soldier's Wife Objecting to an Exchange," *Chicago Tribune*, July 22, 1862.

35. "A Fashionable War Epistle," *Frank Leslie's Budget of Fun* (September 1861); "Nothing like Military for Catching the Girls," *Nick Nax* (May 1862): 7; "Ruling Passions, andc.," *Nick Nax* (May 1862), 7; "Awful Possibility," *Vanity Fair*, March 29, 1862; Howard Del, "A Ray of Hope," *Vanity Fair*, August 23, 1862. See also "The Matrimonial Market," *Vanity Fair*, May 30, 1863.

36. Allie Allyn, "Generalship," *Godey's Lady's Book* 68 (February 1864): 180.

37. *Vanity Fair*, October 5, 1861.

38. "Polly Snoofles after Seeing the Soldiers Off," *Yankee Notions* 10 (September 1861): 264; "A Thoughtful Wife," *Frank Leslie's Budget of Fun* (September 1861); "An

Object of Interest," *Vanity Fair*, August 9, 1862; Penfield-Bross, "Humors of the Draft," *Vanity Fair*, June 6, 1863. We are left to wonder whether her point is really that any man who waits to be drafted is a man who can easily be replaced.

39. "Women Are All Alike," *Yankee Notions* 10 (August 1861): 252; *Yankee Notions* 10 (July 1861): 253.

40. "Patriotic Mother," *Frank Leslie's Budget of Fun* (September 1861): 13.

41. *Yankee Notions* 10 (November 1861): 325.

42. "Had Him There," *Yankee Notions* 10 (December 1861): 357.

43. "A True Patriot," *Yankee Notions* 11 (February 1862): 40.

44. Here again I am indebted to the work of James Marten, including Marten, *Lessons of War*.

CHAPTER TWO

1. Morford, *The Days of Shoddy*, 31–42.

2. For soldiers' motivations, see McPherson, *For Cause and Comrades*.

3. Author's personal collection.

4. On wartime photography see Gallman, "Snapshots." On wartime images see Neely and Holzer, *The Union Image*. On patriotic envelopes see Gallagher, *The Union War*; Boyd, *Patriotic Envelopes of the Civil War*.

5. Fanny Fern, "Street Thoughts," *Golden Era*, August 17, 1862. Fanny Fern (Sara Willis) was a popular columnist who wrote for the *New York Ledger*, where this column presumably originated.

6. "A Peaceable Man" [Nathaniel Hawthorne], "Chiefly about War-Matters," *Atlantic Monthly* 10 (July 1862): 43–61. For a discussion of this important essay from a different perspective, see Duquette, *Loyal Subjects*, 25–29.

7. Blondheim, *Copperhead Gore*, chap. 17. This is a reprint of the original novel with an excellent introduction. The novel was originally published by Wood with the title *Fort Lafayette*.

8. "Home Guards," *Vanity Fair*, May 25, 1861.

9. "Not Used to It," *Vanity Fair*, June 1, 1861; "Humors of the War," *Vanity Fair*, July 7, 1861.

10. "The Song of the Home Guard," *Vanity Fair*, August 3, 1861.

11. "A Member of the Seventh Regiment Dining," *Vanity Fair*, May 25, 1861; "The Defenders of Fort Delmonico," *Vanity Fair*, November 23, 1861. See also "The War," *Vanity Fair*, June 22, 1861.

12. Ward, "Touching Letter from a Gory Member of the Home Guard," *The Complete Works of Artemus Ward*, 202.

13. "Jeanette and Jeannot," *Vanity Fair*, November 9, 1861. The original song is about a conscript leaving his lover and going off to war, while she worries that he will find another lover in his travels. Glover et al., "Jeanette and Jeannot."

14. "The First Campaign of the Home Guard," *Frank Leslie's Budget of Fun*, June 1862.

15. *Frank Leslie's Budget of Fun* (September 1861); "Gather Up the Fragments," *Chicago Tribune*, January 31, 1862.

16. "Vanity Fair to a Certain Young Gentleman in Broadway," *Vanity Fair*, October 19, 1861.

17. "Effects of the War on M. De Laine . . . ," *Ballou's Monthly Magazine* 15 (March 1862): 298–99.

18. Review of *New York State Army List*, *Vanity Fair*, April 12, 1862; "Uniform Depravity," *Vanity Fair*, April 19, 1862; "Wrapscandals," *Vanity Fair*, April 26, 1862; "Young Man! Take Off That Uniform!," *Vanity Fair*, May 3, 1862.

19. "A Fancy Soldier."

20. "The Home Guard's Complaint," *Vanity Fair*, June 14, 1862.

21. "The Soldier on Leave," *Vanity Fair*, August 9, 1862.

22. "Self Respect," *Vanity Fair*, February 2, 1862.

23. Morford, *Shoulder Straps*, 41–49.

24. Ibid., 50–62, 115–28. It is quite remarkable how frequently young men in wartime fiction managed to stop runaway carriages.

25. It is not surprising that Morford would create a romantic love interest who is a civilian, but it would have been a simple matter for the author to have constructed some excuse for why Frank was not in uniform had he felt that was required to make his hero appear sympathetic.

26. This was a fictional regiment.

27. Morford, *Shoulder Straps*, 218–31.

28. As we shall see, Charles Holt in Morford's *Days of Shoddy* combines a similar set of immoral traits in both his private life and his public wartime dealings.

29. Morford, *Shoulder Straps*, 446–60.

30. Ibid., 460–82. Egbert goes to his death carrying a sword given to him by Mary, the woman he had hoped to marry before his evil scheme was uncovered. Oddly enough, whereas most of Morford's scoundrels end up getting their just deserts, Egbert reforms his behavior and dies a hero's death.

31. For selected reviews of Morford's *Shoulder Straps* see *Philadelphia Inquirer*, June 3, September 1, 5, October 15, 1863; *New York Herald*, August 19, 31, 1863; *Harper's New Monthly Magazine* 27 (November 1863): 350; *Atlantic Monthly* 13 (February 1864): 264. See also the discussion of Morford in the introduction.

32. The novel also has other characters who symbolize other Morford themes, some of which will be discussed later in this volume.

33. "A Hint to Absentee Officers," *Chicago Tribune*, May 16, 1862.

34. *New York Times*, August 3, 1862.

35. *Wisconsin Daily Patriot*, August 6, 1862.

36. *Chicago Tribune*, July 21, 1862.

37. *Wisconsin Daily Patriot*, July 22, 1862, quoting a Washington paper. See also *New York Times*, August 14, 1862.

38. General Orders No. 19, August 14, 1862, *The War of the Rebellion* (series 1, vol. 12, part 3), 573.

39. "Our Harrisburg Letter," *Philadelphia Inquirer*, August 18, 1862.

40. *Official Records*, 31:569.

41. *Vanity Fair*, November 22, 1862.

42. "The Discarded Lieutenant's Lament," *Vanity Fair*, December 13, 1862.

43. "Strip Off the Uniform," *Chicago Tribune*, November 26, 1862.

44. *Daily Delta* (New Orleans), September 10, 1862.

45. "Letter from Philadelphia," *San Francisco Bulletin*, January 10, 1863.

46. "Hard after Them," *Wisconsin Daily Patriot*, January 26, 1863.

47. "Sauce for the Geese," *Vanity Fair*, March 9, 1862.

48. "Our War Correspondent," *Vanity Fair*, October 25, 1862.

49. Ward, "The War Fever in Baldinsville," *The Complete Works of Artemus Ward*, 119–22.

50. Artemus Ward Jr., "The Flambeau Family," *Yankee Notions* 12 (January 1863): 3.

51. Barber, *War Letters of a Disbanded Volunteer*, 258–60.

52. Ella Rodman, "A Daguerreotype in Battle," *Peterson's Magazine* 44 (September 1863): 187–90.

53. Mary A. Howe, "Breaking Hearts," serialized in the *American Monthly Knicker-bocker* (February, March, April, June 1864). See chap. 5.

CHAPTER THREE

1. Morford, *The Days of Shoddy*.

2. In the children's book *Kathie's Soldiers*, author Amanda Minnie Douglas used a similar device, as young Kathie's nemesis is the mean-spirited daughter of a war contractor. See Marten, *Lessons of War*, 158.

3. See Gallman, *The North Fights the Civil War*, 92–105; Mark R. Wilson, *The Business of Civil War*. For early commentary on contract fraud nationwide see "Shoddy Uniforms, Shoddy Shoes and Contractors," *Chicago Tribune*, April 25, 1861; "Army Supplies—Plundering Contractors," *Chicago Tribune*, June 4, 1861; "What Are the 'Fortunes' of War?," *Vanity Fair*, July 13, 1861.

4. See Gallman, *Mastering Wartime*, 287; *Report of the Commission Appointed to the Governor of Pennsylvania to Investigate Alleged Army Frauds*; Mark R. Wilson, *The Business of Civil War*, 24–26. *Mastering Wartime* cites newspaper reports on fraud in *Philadelphia Inquirer*, May 15, 21, 1861; *Philadelphia Public Ledger*, May 27, 1861; *Christian Recorder*, June 1, 1861.

5. Mark R. Wilson, *The Business of Civil War*, 151–59.

6. Much like the famed British investigations of poverty and disease in Victorian England, these government documents served to define the public's understanding of the issue, framing discussions of reform. For a fascinating cultural analysis of these British reports see Poovey, *Making a Social Body*.

7. See Mark R. Wilson, *The Business of Civil War*; Weigley, *Quartermaster General of the Union Army*.

8. Wevill, engraver, *Before. After.* Although the Library Company of Philadelphia estimates that these images date to 1863, the artist seems to be capturing the spirit of the war's first months.

9. *Vanity Fair*, June 8, 1861.

10. *Vanity Fair*, July 6, 1861. For early reports of the Girard House clothing contract and subsequent scandal, see *Philadelphia Press*, April 20, 23, 25, 30, May 11, 20 1861; *Daily Patriot and Union* (Harrisburg), April 23, 1861. *Lancaster Intelligencer*, May 14,

June 4, 1861; *Huntington Globe*, June 4, 1861. *Weekly Mariettian*, June 8, 1861. *Vanity Fair* ran another cover illustration on the Pennsylvania war contracting scandal on September 21, 1861.

11. Barber, *War Letters of a Disbanded Volunteer*, 40–43, 100–110.

12. "The Dream of the Army Contractor," *Vanity Fair*, August 17, 1861; Miles O'Reilley, "The Shoddy Millionaire's Nightmare," *Comic Monthly* 6 (July 1865): 5. *Vanity Fair* does not identify the author of the poem. *Comic Monthly* credits the poem to Miles O'Reilley, the pseudonym of humorist and Union war veteran Charles Graham Halpine. Note that the two publications gave the poem different titles.

13. "Song of the Shoddy," *Vanity Fair*, September 21, 1861.

14. "Shoddy."

15. "The Army Contractor."

16. "Shoddy—The Way It Is Made," *Scientific American*, October 12, 1861.

17. *New York Herald*, November 27, 1861. See also Mark R. Wilson, *The Business of Civil War*, 150.

18. See, for instance, "Humorous Letter from the Army," *Chicago Tribune*, December 20, 1861; "Death Song of a Government Horse," *The Crisis* (Columbus, OH), April 9, 1862, reprinted from *Vanity Fair*; "Leeches," *The Crisis*, April 9, 1862; "A Kick from a Horse," *Vanity Fair*, August 9, 1862; *Weekly Vincennes (IN) Gazette*, October 3, 1863.

19. J. Ives Pease, "Shoddy," *Continental Monthly* 2 (October 1862): 485–86. For reprints of the same poem see *The Liberator*, October 24, 1862; *Wisconsin Daily Patriot*, March 30, 1863. For another reference to the battle against shoddy as essentially won, see *Continental Monthly* 1 (March 1862): 351.

20. See, for instance, "A Sorrowful Dialogue," *Continental Monthly* 1 (January 1862): 109.

21. "The Patriotism of Government Contractors," *Chicago Tribune*, October 18, 1861. The article quotes the *Cincinnati Gazette*.

22. "The Contractor's Plaint," *Vanity Fair*, February 2, 1862.

23. "Plundermongering," *Vanity Fair*, July 12, 1862.

24. "An Army War Contractor," *Continental Monthly* 2 (September 1862): 365. See also "Who Kills Our Soldiers?" *Chicago Tribune*, January 11, 1862.

25. "Mottoe for Contractors," *Continental Monthly* 3 (February 1863): 232.

26. Bishop, *Liberty's Ordeal*.

27. See Mark R. Wilson, *The Business of Civil War*; Gallman, *Mastering Wartime*; Gallman, "Entrepreneurial Experiences in the Civil War."

28. "Social Revolutions—Advent of the Shoddy Aristocracy," *New York Herald*, November 6, 1861. This article was reprinted in the *New Hampshire Statesman*, November 30, 1861.

29. "Social Revolutions—the Shoddy Aristocracy Begins Housekeeping," *New York Herald*, November 16, 1861. See also "The Shoddy Aristocracy," *New York Herald*, November 24, 1861.

30. Cornwallis, *Pilgrims of Fashion*, vii–xiv.

31. These characters will appear in the next two chapters.

32. "Shoddy," *Dover (NH) Gazette*, October 30, 1863, quoting *New York World*. The

Gazette's story reads as if something is lost in translation from New York to New Hampshire. The quotes from *The World* are about the shoddy aristocracy, while the *Gazette* seems to be portraying an upsurge in the sale of shoddy.

33. "John Shoddy, Esq.," *Frank Leslie's Budget of Fun* (January 1864).

34. "Who Says 'Fine Feathers Make Fine Birds!'" *The Crisis*, November 18, 1863. See also, "Shoddy," *Round Table*, January 2, 1864.

35. Mary Kyle Dallas, "Gossip from Gotham," *Golden Era*, July 12, 1863.

36. "How Are You, Shoddy?," *Frank Leslie's Budget of Fun* (December 1863).

37. See Anbinder, *Nativism and Slavery*; Ignatiev, *How the Irish Became White*.

38. "One of the Effects of the War," *Harper's Weekly*, February 5, 1863.

39. John M'Lenan, "Some of the Shoddy Aristocracy," *Harper's New Monthly Magazine* 27 (September 1863): 574–75.

40. "The Shoddyocratic Society of Washington," *Old Guard* 2 (February 1864): 48.

41. "Editor's Table," *Old Guard* 2 (March 1864): 72.

42. "Editor's Table," *Old Guard* 2 (June 1864): 144. See also *Old Guard* 3 (January 1865): 47.

43. "Mr. Shoddy Having Made Much Money through Contracts . . . ," *Dollar Monthly Magazine* (March 1864): 251.

44. Robert Tomes, "The Fortunes of War," *Harper's New Monthly Magazine* 29 (July 1864): 227–31. This essay was immediately reprinted in the *Continental Monthly* (July 1864): 277–82. See also Mark R. Wilson, *The Business of Civil War*, 181–82; Gallman, "Entrepreneurial Experiences in the Civil War." These accounts spread nationwide. See "Shoddy in New York," *Daily Evening Bulletin* (San Francisco), September 10, 1864.

45. "A Lady on the Extravagance of Her Sex," *Ladies' Repository* (Cincinnati) (October 1864).

46. "The Shoddy Family," *Frank Leslie's Budget of Fun*, December 1, 1863.

47. "At Mrs. Shoddy's," *Harper's Weekly*, July 29, 1865.

48. The "Petroleums" are a convenient image for the modern reader, since both the Petroleums and the Shoddys are almost precisely like the main characters in a popular TV show of the 1960s, *The Beverly Hillbillies*.

49. "Petroleums Ball," *Frank Leslie's Budget of Fun*, March 1, 1865. For another comment about both shoddy and petroleum see Delta, "A Trip in the Streetcars," *Godey's Lady's Book* 70 (June 1865): 509–11. The satirical accounts of the petroleum aristocracy do not portray them as Irish.

50. Mary W. Janvrin, "Mrs. Ward's Visit to Niagara: And Her Acquaintance with the Shoddy Family," *Godey's Lady's Book* 69 (August 1864): 145–56.

51. The *Shoddy Songster*, compendiums of popular songs published in 1864 and 1865, included a diversity of patriotic and humorous songs, although none had anything to do with war contracting or fraud. Apparently in this instance "shoddy" in the title was meant as a self-deprecating joke about the volume itself.

52. "Shoddy," *Chicago Tribune*, October 20, 1863. The article quotes the *New York Tribune*. The partisan *Chicago Tribune* repeated used the shoddy angle against Democrats. See *Chicago Tribune*, July 16, 18, September 3, 1864.

53. "The Shoddy Correspondence," *Frank Leslie's Budget of Fun* (January 1864). For

an example of "shoddy" being used in a political campaign, see *A Black Record!* For an extended discussion of the use of "shoddy" in political discourse, see Michael Thomas Smith, *The Enemy Within*, esp. 32–33.

54. Mark R. Wilson, *The Business of Civil War*, 153–54.

55. *Daily National Intelligencer* (Washington), February 9, 1865; *Milwaukee Daily Sentinel*, February 13, 1865. The *Sentinel* story quotes the "New York correspondent to the *Philadelphia Inquirer*." The *Philadelphia Daily Evening Bulletin* published the same story on February 7, 1865.

56. *Lowell (MA) Daily Citizen and News*, August 12, 1865.

57. Morford, *The Coward*.

58. Ibid., 222.

59. Ibid., 227–32.

60. Ibid., 310.

61. "Making It Pay," *Golden Era*, January 4, 1863. This essay appears in the California paper without attribution, but it seems that the editors reprinted the story from an eastern author.

62. *Frank Leslie's Illustrated Newspaper*, November 21, 1863; *New York Times*, November 6, 1863; *Boston Daily Advertiser*, November 7, 1863 (quoting New York papers), November 9, 1863 (listing food consumed); *New Haven Daily Palladium*, November 7, 1863; *Philadelphia Press*, November 10, 1863; *San Francisco Daily Evening Bulletin*, November 18, 1863.

63. Winslow Homer, "The Great Russian Ball at the Academy of Music, November 5, 1863," *Harper's Weekly*, November 21, 1863. Homer also produced the cover illustration of the same issue, "The Russian Ball—in the Supper Room." On Homer's Civil War see Wood, *Near Andersonville*.

64. *Dover (NH) Gazette*, November 20, 1863.

65. *Boston Daily Advertiser*, November 7, 1863, quoting the *New York Journal of Commerce*.

66. [Reed], *The Russian Ball*. Some archives attribute this pamphlet to Charles J. Stedman. *Frank Leslie's Budget of Fun* published "The Shoddy Family" on December 1, 1863. *The Russian Ball* was probably published about a week earlier. It is unclear how widely read this small pamphlet was. One Milwaukee newspaper quoted the poem's passages about shoddy at length and with approval. *Milwaukee Daily Sentinel*, November 24, 1863.

CHAPTER FOUR

1. Basler, *The Collected Works of Abraham Lincoln*, 6:445–46. Basler dates this document to around September 14, 1863. Nicolay and Hay originally dated it about a month earlier. For a discussion of this document as a constitutional argument, see Neely, *Lincoln and the Triumph of the Nation*, 192.

2. Abraham Lincoln to Erastus Corning and others, [June 12, 1863], Basler, *The Collected Works of Abraham Lincoln*, 6:266–67. See Neely, *Lincoln and the Triumph of the Nation*, 86–87; Neely, *The Fate of Liberty*, 198–99; Thomas, *Civic Myths*, 76–77; Blair, *With Malice toward Some*, 178–80.

3. For a more extended discussion of Lincoln's approach to citizenship and wartime, see Gallman, "The President as Pedagogue."

4. Needless to say, this idealized portrait was of heroic *white* men, especially in the first two years of war.

5. See Sizer, *The Political Work of Northern Women Writers*.

6. Moore, *Women of the War*; Brockett and Vaughan, *Women's Work in the Civil War*.

7. Timothy Shay Arthur, "Wounded," *Arthur's Home Magazine* 22 (September 1863): 21–24. Reprinted in Arthur, *Home-Heroes, Saints and Martyrs*, 134–36.

8. See Mitchell, "The Northern Soldier and His Community."

9. For a broader discussion of how nineteenth-century fiction shaped popular understandings of citizenship, see Thomas, *Civic Myths*.

10. Recruiting poster, April 19, 1861. This discussion of recruiting posters is based on my examination of hundreds of recruiting posters housed in various archives and collections. A large number of these posters are assembled in the *Civil War Treasures* collection at the New-York Historical Society and available through the *American Memory* digital collection at the Library of Congress website.

11. "What Ho! Bone and Sinew," *Vanity Fair*, September 6, 1862.

12. "To Abraham Lincoln, on His Demand for Three Hundred Thousand Men," *Frank Leslie's Illustrated Newspaper*, September 20, 1862, reprinted from *Punch*.

13. "Our Duty," *Arthur's Home Magazine* 18 (November 1861): 62.

14. Stillé, *How a Free People Conduct a Long War*. See also Gallman, "How a Free People Conduct a Long War." For favorable reviews of this pamphlet, see *Chicago Tribune*, February 2, 1863; *The Liberator*, February 27, 1863.

15. Virginia F. Townsend, "Eighteen Hundred Sixty-Three," *Arthur's Home Magazine* 21 (January 1863): 66.

16. Ware, *Manhood*.

17. [Kirkland], *A Few Words in Behalf of the Loyal Women of the United States*. We will return to this pamphlet in chap. 6.

18. Hamilton, "Words for the Way," in *Skirmishes and Sketches*, 233–45, quotes 238, 242. This is a collection of essays. The essay is undated, but in the text Hamilton refers to the war having dragged on for three years.

19. Oliver Optic, "Teacher's Desk," *Student and Schoolmate* 12 (February 1863): 61. Reprinted in Marten, *Lessons of War*, 3–4.

20. "The Northern Mind," *Vanity Fair*, June 21, 1862.

21. In addition to the examples to follow, see Wadsworth, *American Patriotism*; Adams, *Christian Patriotism*; Haskell, *Christian Patriotism*; Boardman, *Civil Government*; Duryea, *Civil Liberty*; Paddock, *God's Presence and Purpose in Our War*; Collier, *Moral Heroism*; Fransioli, *Patriotism*; Bellows, *Unconditional Loyalty*. For wartime religion see Rable, *God's Almost Chosen Peoples*.

22. J. Romeyn Berry, *Christian Patriotism*.

23. Spear, *The Duty of the Hour*.

24. Chesebrough, *Christian Politics*.

25. Huntington, *Personal Humiliation Demanded*.

26. Sears, *Mr. Dunn Browne's Experiences in the Civil War*, 52–55 (entry dated January 17, [1863]).

27. *Chicago Tribune*, May 8, 1863.

28. "Patience or Enlist," *Daily Evening Bulletin* (San Francisco), January 6, 1864.

29. "Love and Duty," *Golden Era*, July 5, 1863.

30. "Why Not Enlist," *Milwaukee Daily Sentinel*, July 29, 1862.

31. Robinson, *The Brother Soldiers*, 10, 22. The first quote is in a letter home; the second is in a conversation with his younger sister when he is at home.

32. Ibid., 46.

33. Ibid., 72, 143.

34. Louise Chandler Moulton, "One of Many," *Harper's New Monthly Magazine* 27 (June 1863): 120–21. Nelson is mortally wounded at Antietam. The examples of similar conversations are too numerous to cite.

35. Louise Chandler Moulton, "The Cool Captain," *Harper's New Monthly Magazine* 28 (May 1864): 774–79.

36. "John Morgan's Substitute," *The American Mail-Bag*, 332–42.

37. Mrs. S. K. Furman, "The Emigrant Volunteer's Wife," *Ladies' Repository* 23 (August 1863): 480.

38. "Strategy," *The American Mail-Bag*, 235–45.

39. "In the Hospital," *The American Mail-Bag*, 246–53. The story "Tangled a Blue" in the same collection has a similar plot device. *The American Mail-Bag*, 271–89.

40. Virginia F. Townsend, "Enlisted! Enlisted!," *Golden Era* (San Francisco), August 10, 1862. Note that although Townsend was a New Englander and this story is set in Massachusetts, it appeared in a San Francisco newspaper, illustrating the national scope of wartime sentimental fiction.

41. Virginia F. Townsend, "Driven to the War," *Ladies' Repository* 23 (April 1863): 209–12.

42. Murdock, *One Million Men*.

43. "Merchants, Will You Recruit?," *Boston Daily Advertiser*, July 31, 1862.

44. For a discussion of home front bounty fund drives see Gallman, *Mastering Wartime*; Murdock, *One Million Men*, 154–68.

45. T. B. Arthur, "More Precious Than Gold," *Peterson's Magazine* 43 (February 1863): 155–56.

46. *Chicago Tribune*, August 7, 1862. For similar comments see "Common Sense to the Rescue!," *Frank Leslie's Illustrated Newspaper*, August 16, 1862.

47. "Let Us Have a Draft!," *Milwaukee Daily Sentinel*, August 7, 1862.

48. "The Draft," *Bangor Daily Whig and Courier*, August 8, 1862.

49. "Let Us Have a Draft," *Frank Leslie's Illustrated Newspaper*, August 2, 1862.

50. "Inducements to Enlist," *Milwaukee Daily Sentinel*, July 24, 1862; "Now Is the Time to Enlist," *Bangor Daily Whig and Courier*, July 21, 1862. The poem "The Bounty" in *Farmer's Cabinet (New Hampshire)*, August 4, 1862, makes a similar point. See also "Recruiting Bounties," *Frank Leslie's Illustrated Newspaper*, August 9, 1862.

51. "March Up!," *Vanity Fair*, August 23, 1862.

52. "The Song of the Eleventh-Hour Patriot," *Vanity Fair*, October 18, 1862.

53. "Kate's Soldier," *Golden Era*, January 4, 1863. This story was reprinted in *The American Mail-Bag*. Neither publication indicates an author or an original place of

publication. The story had some other fascinating gender dynamics, in that the wealthy Kate effectively purchased her own soldier who would go on to be her husband.

54. See Gallman, *The North Fights the Civil War*.

55. "Universal Conscription," *The Liberator*, August 29, 1862.

56. "Will It Necessitate Drafting," *Golden Era*, August 17, 1862.

57. "The Draft in Monkeytown," *New Hampshire Sentinel*, October 30, 1862. The paper notes that the poem was reprinted from the *Salem Register*. It likely appeared in other papers as well.

58. Walters, *Come In out of the Draft*.

59. *Offering a Substitute*.

60. "Volunteer, or Drafts," *Vanity Fair*, August 9, 1862.

61. "The Revelations of Draft," *Vanity Fair*, August 16, 1862.

62. "Weak Knees," *Vanity Fair*, August 23, 1862.

63. "The Substitute Market," *Vanity Fair*, November 1, 1862.

64. "The Song of the Draft," *Vanity Fair*, August 23, 1862.

65. Ward, "The Draft in Baldinsville," *Vanity Fair*, September 20, 1862, reprinted in *The Complete Works of Artemus Ward*. This story will reappear in chap. 6.

66. Both stories from *Boston Daily Advertiser*, August 15, 1862. The first story refers to an unnamed New Bedford paper. The quote is from the *Advertiser*.

67. "Evading the Draft," *Wisconsin State Register*, August 30, 1862. Citing *Forney's War Press*.

68. "Much Sickness from 'Exposure to a Draft,'" *Nick Nax* (November 1862): 216.

69. "Good Ground for Exemption," *Nick Nax* (November 1862): 222, citing the *Ohio State Journal*.

70. "Exempts," *Yankee Notions* 11 (November 1862): 229. For other examples of humorous commentary on draftees seeking medical exemptions, see "Getting Out of the Draft," *Yankee Notions* 12 (January 1863): 18.

71. Nasby, "Shows Why He Should Not Be Drafted," *The Nasby Papers*, 9. The essay is dated August 6, 1862.

72. "Song of the Exempts," *Nick Nax* (November 11, 1862): 213. This song also appeared in other forms across the North, including various songbooks and as a separate song sheet. See Devon, *War Lyrics*, 54–55.

73. *Daily Evening Bulletin* (San Francisco), November 7, 1862.

74. "One of the Exempts," *Nick Nax* (November 1862): 203.

75. See multiple stories on draft evaders in Canada in *Chicago Tribune*, August 5, 6, 7, 8, 9, 11, 13, 1862. For other newspapers making the same point about draft evaders running off to Canada, see *Wisconsin Daily Patriot*, August 28, 1862; *Lowell Daily Citizen and News*, September 9, 1862. The press picked up the same narrative again with the passage of federal conscription laws in 1863. See *New York Herald*, April 3, 1863; *Chicago Tribune*, April 4, 1863; *Boston Daily Advertiser*, July 11, 1863.

76. Howard Del, "Take a Horn," *Yankee Notions* 11 (October 1862): cover.

77. *The Frightened Conscript*.

78. Ward, "A Romance—The Conscript," *The Complete Works of Artemus Ward*, part 3, chap. 4.

79. Nasby, "In Canada," *The Nasby Papers*, 10–11 (essay dated August 30, 1862).

80. Nasby, "Is Finally Drafted," *The Nasby Papers*, 11–13 (essay dated October 17, 1862).

81. *Milwaukee Daily Sentinel*, August 21, 1862; *Chicago Tribune*, August 27, 1862; *Newark (OH) Advocate*, August 29, 1862; *Daily Evening Bulletin* (San Francisco), September 11, 1862; *Morning Oregonian*, September 24, 1862; *Frank Leslie's Illustrated Newspaper*, September 27, 1862.

82. *Beauties of the Draft.*

83. "On Draft," *Vanity Fair*, August 30, 1862.

84. "On Draft," *Vanity Fair*, September 20, 1862. These two cartoons are unsigned but seem to be by the same artist.

85. "The Draft," *Harper's Weekly*, November 8, 1862.

86. "The Draft—Plea for Exemption," *Frank Leslie's Budget of Fun* (December 1862).

87. Howard Del, "Homeopathic," *Vanity Fair*, July 26, 1862. See also WF, "The Substitute Business," *Vanity Fair*, August 23, 1862.

88. "To Parties Concerned," *Vanity Fair*, August 23, 1862.

89. "Before and after the Draft," *Yankee Notions* 11 (October 1862): 305.

90. Untitled, *Nick Nax* (November 1862): 218.

91. *Chicago Tribune*, August 7, 1862.

92. *Milwaukee Sentinel*, November 21, 1862.

93. This discussion has emphasized the decisions men and their families faced about enlisting in the Union army. In a fascinating analysis of the "home guards" in Illinois, Thomas Bahde argues that during the first two years of the war some Illinoisans joined these irregular militias out of a concern for home defense and out of "a vision of republican citizenship that prioritized local interests over obligations to state or federal authority." This understanding of citizenship led these men to stay at home, at least during the first years of the Civil War. Bahde, "'Our Cause Is a Common One.'" Meanwhile, as we have seen, the Union League and the prowar publication societies had been busily pushing for a enhanced senses of unconditional loyalty to the nation as a central virtue of federal citizenship. See introduction and Lawson, *Patriotic Fires*.

CHAPTER FIVE

1. Nevins, *Ordeal of the Union*.

2. For a superb one-volume history of the war see McPherson, *Battle Cry of Freedom*. On the draft in the North, see Murdock, *One Million Men*.

3. Sizer argues for a changed tone in the printed discourse: see Sizer, *The Political Work of Northern Women Writers*.

4. See the introduction.

5. Morford, *The Coward*, chap. 1.

6. Including the ridiculous Brooks Cunninghams, who appeared in chap. 3.

7. Note that Morford used a very similar plot device in *Shoulder Straps*, where the true hero revealed his character in response to a runaway carriage.

8. Morford, *The Coward*, 21.

9. This was a sort of bravery that anticipated the ironic, and largely pointless, hero-

ism demonstrated in the postwar short stories of Ambrose Bierce. See Bierce, *Tales of Soldiers and Civilians*. Despite Morford's explanation, readers might have wondered why his hero demonstrated his bravery in a silly "duel" against the ill-fated Cole, rather than in a more pure act of martial patriotism.

10. Anna W. Shirley, "Tried and True," *Harper's New Monthly Magazine* 27 (November 1863): 835–39.

11. Mary E. Dodge, "Netty's Touchstone," *Harper's New Monthly Magazine* 28 (March 1864): 517–19.

12. On the Enrollment Act see Murdock, *One Million Men*; Shannon, *The Organization and Administration of the Union Army*.

13. *Chicago Tribune*, May 16, 1863.

14. *Chicago Tribune*, August 12, 1863.

15. "The Conscription," *The Liberator*, July 24, 1863.

16. "The Conscription Law," *The Liberator*, August 28, 1863.

17. *Chicago Tribune*, August 25, 1863.

18. "The Way to Encourage the Draft," *Dover (NH) Gazette*, July 24, 1863. Editorial reprinted from the *Newburyport Herald*. A few weeks later the *Springfield Republican* ran a short item praising local citizens who had opted to serve when drafted rather than taking advantage of questionable exemptions. As illustrations, the *Republican* pointed out that the son of a local wealthy man appeared on the list of those who had stepped forward to serve, as had several local ministers. *New Haven Daily Palladium*, August 5, 1863, quoting the *Springfield Republican*.

19. Mitchell, *Civil War Soldiers*, 84–85.

20. Sears, *Mr. Dunn Browne's Experiences in the Civil War*, 132–98. Quotations from 133 (July 27, 1863); 148 (August 12, 1863); 149 (August 12, 1863); 155 (August 18, 1863); 191–92 (November 14, [1863]).

21. Rosenblatt and Rosenblatt, *Hard Marching Every Day*, 67 (April 19, 1863); 136 (August 20, 1863); 149–50 (September 12, 1863); 183–84 (December 31, 1863). For the comments of Union soldiers about conscripts and substitutes, see also Wiley, *The Life of Billy Yank*, 286–87; Robertson, *Soldiers Blue and Gray*, 38–39. On the attitudes of Democratic soldiers toward draft evaders, see White, *Emancipation, the Union Army, and the Reelection of Abraham Lincoln*, esp. 111.

22. *All for the Union*, 3–4, 68, 110.

23. *Civil War Letters of General Robert McAllister*, 401 (quotation), 487, 505, 509 (quotation).

24. "Weed on Draft-Shirkers," *Dover (NH) Gazette*, October 2, 1863.

25. *"Look Sharp!"* In other cases cartoonists and satirists did poke fun at those men who hired substitutes to avoid service, unfiltered by explicit charges of hypocrisy. See, for instance, Volck, *Buying a Substitute*. For soldiers' attitudes toward during the election of 1864, see White, *Emancipation, the Union Army, and the Reelection of Abraham Lincoln*.

26. *Lowell Daily Citizen and News*, August 7, 1863, quoting the *Portland Transcript*.

27. *North American and United States Gazette*, March 21, 1863. On immigrants, conscription, and patterns of enlistment see Anbinder, "Which Poor Man's Fight?"

28. "The Draft," *Tri-Weekly Miner's Register* (Central City, CO), May 28, 1863. This

emphasis on local recruiting spoke both to the strong desire to avoid the draft and to community pride in meeting draft quotas.

29. See, for instance, "Let Us Not Be Disgraced by Another Draft," *North American and United States Gazette*, December 15, 1863.

30. *Round Table*, February 6, 1864. For similar examples in the press, calling on draft eligible men to be more involved in bounty funds, see Murdock, *One Million Men*, 157–61.

31. *Boston Daily Advertiser*, August 23, 1864.

32. Artemus Ward [David Farrar Browne], "Circular No. 78." This short "circular" appeared in newspapers across the nation, including *New Haven Daily Palladium*, August 21, 1863; *Leavenworth Daily Bulletin*, September 2, 1863; *Western Reserve Chronicle*, September 9, 1863; *Cape Girardeau Weekly Argus*, September 24, 1863; *Daily Evening Bulletin* (San Francisco), September 19, 1863; *Deseret News*, October 7, 1863; *Freedom's Champion* (Atchison, KS), October 15, 1863; *Yankee Notions* 12 (November 1863): 350; *The Liberator*, September 18, 1863.

33. "The Sick Brigade," *Yankee Notions* 12 (March 1863): 91.

34. "I Am Sick, Don't Draft Me," song sheet.

35. "I Am Not Sick, I'm over Forty-Five," song sheet.

36. Work, *Grafted into the Army*.

37. Conscripts occasionally sought to avoid service by knocking out their front teeth so that they could not bite open bullet cartridges. This strategy rarely worked.

38. "The Curiosities of Exemption," *Chicago Tribune*, August 17, 1863, reprinted from the *Philadelphia North American*.

39. "The Draft," *Daily Miner's Register* (Central City, CO), October 22, 1863. The paper cites the *Kennebec Journal*. Note that this small story had traveled halfway across the country.

40. See "The Draft and Physical Debility," *Daily Miner's Register* (Central City, CO), October 27, 1863, citing the *Army and Navy Journal*. Also republished in *Milwaukee Daily Sentinel*, November 11, 1863. See also John H. Watson, "Exempt," *Frank Leslie's Illustrated Newspaper*, April 30, 1864.

41. Murdock describes a series of "absurd dependent mother claims" that no doubt spurred on the satirists. See *One Million Men*, 78–80.

42. "A Bachelor's Soliloquy on the Conscript Act," *Chicago Tribune*, June 16, 1863. This appeared in various publications. See *San Francisco Bulletin*, July 9, 1863.

43. "A Pathetic Appeal," *Frank Leslie's Budget of Fun* (June 1863).

44. "On Draft," *Yankee Notions* 12 (November 1863): 331.

45. Howard Del, "A Liberal Offer," *Frank Leslie's Budget of Fun* (June 1863).

46. "Cool," *Yankee Notions* 12 (October 1863): 305.

47. "Advice to Tom Tidler," *Vanity Fair*, June 13, 1863.

48. "Precept and Practice," *Frank Leslie's Budget of Fun* (June 1863).

49. *Yankee Notions* 12 (July 1863): 215.

50. "Opposition to the Draft," *Frank Leslie's Budget of Fun* (September 1863).

51. "John C. Smith's Experience of the Draft," *New Haven Daily Palladium*, September 19, 1863.

52. "Holding On to a Substitute," *Comic Monthly* (September 1863): 13.

53. Howard Del, "On Draft," *Yankee Notions* 12 (September 1863): 257.

54. "Attention: Avoid the Draft," *Yankee Notions* 12 (October 1863): 307.

55. "Volunteering or Drafting," *Yankee Notions* 12 (December 1863): 353.

56. "Out of the Draft," *New Haven Daily Palladium*, July 17, 1863, reprinted in *Vermont Watchman and State Journal*, August 21, 1863.

57. *Boston Daily Advertiser*, June 24, 1864. Stories about draftees pulling their teeth to avoid service cropped up regularly throughout the war. For an 1864 example, see *Milwaukee Daily Sentinel*, July 8, 1864.

58. *New Haven Daily Palladium*, July 24, 1863, citing an unnamed Philadelphia paper. Public shame also motivated another draftee, who had been approved for exemption because of an unspecified "peculiar malady" but then withdrew his appeal when he learned that said malady would be published in the local press. Murdock, *One Million Men*, 80, citing the *Philadelphia Public Ledger*, August 17, 1863.

59. "John Morgan's Substitute," *The American Mail-Bag*, 332–42.

60. Amanda Minnie Douglas, *Kathie's Soldiers*, summarized by Marten, *Lessons of War*, 158.

61. Oliver Optic, "Teacher's Desk," *Student and Schoolmate* 11 (December 1862): 428–29. In Marten, *Lessons of War*, 4–5.

62. Mary E. Dodge, "Netty's Touchstone," *Harper's New Monthly Magazine* 28 (March 1864): 517–19. George had elected to "avoid the draft" by enlisting before draft day.

63. "The Narrow Escape," *The American Mail-Bag*, 84–92.

64. *Yankee Notions* 12 (November 1863): 345.

65. W. O. Eaton, "Victim of the Draft," *Yankee Notions* 12 (December 1863): 358–60.

66. "The Draft," *Soldier's Casket* 1 (January 1865): 64. For another commentary on the hypocrisy of the draftee, see Jo Bows, "Suggestions for the Coming Draft," *Yankee Notions* 13 (October 1864): 293.

67. The classic history of conscientious objectors and the Civil War is Wright, *Conscientious Objectors in the Civil War*. Also see Gallman, *Mastering Wartime*; Murdock, *One Million Men*, 207–17.

68. *Daily Evening Bulletin* (Philadelphia), September 16, 1864, quoting the *Friends Review*. This position remained contested terrain among Quakers.

69. "Friendly Aid," *Vanity Fair*, June 8, 1861.

70. Patriotic envelopes, Print Department, Library Company of Philadelphia.

71. "The Draft," *Yankee Notions* 11 (October 1862): 301.

72. "A Prudent Proceeding," *Frank Leslie's Budget of Fun* (September 1863).

73. Duryea, *Civil Liberty*.

74. Stewart, *The Nation's Sins and the Nation's Duty*.

75. Moses Smith, *God's Honor Man's Ultimate Success*.

76. "Clergymen and the Draft," *Vermont Chronicle*, August 11, 1863. This article includes the full text of Potter's sermon, which was later released as a published broadside. The Union army accepted Potter's services but assigned him as a member of the military clergy, not as an ordinary foot soldier. Potter's statement was reprinted in various other northern newspapers. See *The Liberator*, September 4, 1863. For an earlier editorial endorsing the idea of drafting clergymen, but with the presumption that they

would be ministering to the troops, see "The Draft and the Clergy," *Boston Daily Advertiser*, August 14, 1862. For criticism of the whole idea of drafting clergy see "Drafting Clergymen," *The Liberator*, August 14, 1863, quoting the *Boston Pilot*. Murdock notes two northern preachers who entered service after being drafted, Potter and Rev. A. M. Haskell of Salem, Massachusetts. *One Million Men*, 217. General Robert McAllister described a New Jersey minister who came to him in 1865 to enlist because he feared conscription. The general praised the man's patriotism and seemed unbothered that he had been at home for nearly four years. *Civil War Letters of General Robert McAllister*, 570.

77. Mary A. Howe, "Breaking Hearts," serialized in the *American Monthly Knickerbocker* (February, March, April, June 1864).

78. Ella Rodman, "'He' and I," *Peterson's Magazine* 47 (January 1865): 60–65.

CHAPTER SIX

1. The scholarship on northern women and the Civil War is vast. The crucial books include Giesberg, *Army at Home*; Silber, *Gender and the Sectional Conflict*; Silber, *Daughters of the Union*; Creighton, *Colors of Courage*; Attie, *Patriotic Toil*; Venet, *Neither Ballots nor Bullets*; Sizer, *The Political Work of Northern Women Writers*; Schultz, *Women at the Front*; and Richard, *Busy Hands*. The important essay collections include Clinton and Silber, *Battle Scars*; Clinton and Silber, *Divided Houses*; and Cashin, *The War Was You and Me*. For a recent collection of essays on the midwestern home front, with excellent attention to gender, see Aley and Anderson, *Union Heartland*.

2. In addition to those families that became refugees when they fled invading armies, many northern women moved in with family members or friends when their husbands went off to war.

3. For discussions of the wartime economy, see Gallman, *The North Fights the Civil War*; Gallman, *Mastering Wartime*; and Paludan, *A People's Contest*.

4. See, for instance, Dean, *The War*.

5. This theme of wartime characters quietly enduring the absence of loved ones also appears regularly in the children's literature, where boys and girls are instructed to accept the absence of fathers. See "Myself or My Country," *Youth's Companion* 37 (June 9, 1864): 88, cited in Ringel, "Thrills for Children."

6. See the introduction for a further discussion of antebellum prescription.

7. For the classic articulation of some of these ironies see Cott, *The Bonds of Womanhood*.

8. See Coontz, *Marriage, a History*.

9. See Norton, *Liberty's Daughters*; Kerber, *Women of the Republic*; Cott, *The Bonds of Womanhood*.

10. "Patriotism" is itself a term with a gendered history. In an eighteenth-century context, patriotism—insofar as it was rooted in an ideological commitment to the republic—was essentially a male domain. Women were expected to be loyal to their husbands and families, but any true commitment to the nation was presumably reflected in devotion to the men around them and in the willingness to sacrifice those men when called on to do so. I argue that by the outbreak of the Civil War, these northern women

were already thinking of themselves as individual political actors, especially when they were engaged in public discussions about the behavior of women. That is not to say that women routinely parted ideological ways with their fathers or spouses (although some did), but that they understood their decisions as reflecting a personal relationship with the Union and not merely as adjunct to their relations with men. The fact that so many published essays written by both women and men presumed to speak directly to women, offering advice on how they should act, speaks to this larger truth that the printed discourse presumed northern women were political actors capable of contemplating their own patriotic decisions. For a fascinating discussion of "women's patriotism" in both the Union and the Confederacy, see Silber, "The Problem of Women's Patriotism, North and South," in Silber, *Gender and the Sectional Conflict*, 37–68.

11. Gertrude Karl, "Who Are the Brave?," *Sibyl* (October 1861): 987, quoted in Sizer, *The Political Work of Northern Women Writers*, 83.

12. Oliver Wendell Holmes, "'Thus Saith the Lord, I Offer Thee Three Things,'" *Frank Leslie's Illustrated Weekly*, September 13, 1862. This poem was published as a pamphlet in 1862 by the Loyal Publication Society, and later republished in a volume of Holmes's poems.

13. See Fahs, *The Imagined Civil War*, 65–66.

14. Fahs, *The Imagined Civil War*, 120–49; Sizer, *The Political Work of Northern Women Writers*, 84–86. The cases of women playing these roles are numerous, often as an incidental piece of a larger story. For examples of poems emphasizing women waiting and suffering, see Mary A. Lee, "Missing," *Harper's New Monthly Magazine* 27 (June 1863): 119–20; Louise Chandler Moulton, "A Woman Waiting," *Harper's New Monthly Magazine* 27 (November 1863): 815–16. The *Ladies' Repository*, a Cincinnati-based religious journal, ran a steady stream of poems celebrating this sort of quiet suffering by northern women. See, for instance, Ellen E. Mack, "Home 'on Furlough,'" *Ladies' Repository* 22 (July 1862): 400; Luellen Clark, "Our Volunteer," *Ladies' Repository* 22 (July 1862): 434; Mary E. Nealy, "To My Soldier Boy," *Ladies' Repository* 23 (February 1863): 74; Meriba A. Babcock, "Midnight Musings," *Ladies' Repository* 23 (May 1863): 295.

15. See chap. 4.

16. [Rev. D. W. Clark], "An Appeal to Christian and Patriotic Women upon Their Duties in Relation to the War," *Ladies' Repository* 22 (August 1862): 492–97.

17. "Editor's Repository," *Ladies' Repository* 22 (September 1862): 576.

18. Gail Hamilton, "A Call to My Country-Women," *Atlantic Monthly* 11 (March 1863): 345–49. Gail Hamilton was the pen name of Mary Abigail Dodge. On Dodge and this pamphlet, see Sizer, *The Political Work of Northern Women Writers*, 121–30; Silber, *Gender and the Sectional Conflict*, 47–48.

19. [Kirkland], *A Few Words in Behalf of the Loyal Women of the United States*. The author does not mention Hamilton's essay by name, but it is fair to assume that her readers recognized the *Atlantic Monthly* piece. Note that this essay also appears in chap. 3 in a different context. In his earlier essay, Clark had also gotten a shot in at southern women, calling on his readers to "not imitate the bad manners of the women of the South," even while showing their zeal. Clark, "An Appeal to Christian Women."

20. See "The Women of Our Union," *Vanity Fair*, May 4, 1861; Mary E. Nealy, "Woman the Soldier's Friend," *Ladies' Repository* 24 (May 1864); Mrs. Furness, "Our Soldiers," *Atlantic Monthly* 13 (March 1864): 364–71.

21. Clara J. Lee, "What Woman Can Do," *Arthur's Home Magazine* 22 (October 1863): 172.

22. M. E. Rockwell, "Mrs. Gray's Sympathy," *Arthur's Home Magazine* 22 (September 1863): 120–21.

23. Virginia F. Townsend, "Our Soldiers," *Arthur's Home Magazine* 24 (July 1864): 51.

24. Aunt Hattie, "Letters to the Girls," *Arthur's Home Magazine* 21 (February 1863): 121–22.

25. For the original book, see Alcott, *Hospital Sketches*. For an excellent scholarly edition, see Alcott, *Hospital Sketches*, edited with an introduction by Fahs (quotations from 53, 54, 115 of the Fahs edition).

26. "The Narrow Escape," *The American Mail-Bag*. This is a collection of short stories with no authors or original places of publication. I have discovered several in American newspapers, and it seems safe to say that the rest also originated in the United States. Edith's travails with her boyfriend appear in chap. 4.

27. A., "These Are My Sons," *Arthur's Home Magazine* 20 (August 1862): 113–14.

28. Elder, *Love amid the Turmoil*, 265, November 30, 1863. Mrs. Paschal's reading group was discussed in the introduction. The literature aimed at children did seem to include more stories about boys and girls becoming involved in voluntary activities. See, for instance, Mrs. Phebe H. Phelps, "A Box for the Soldier," *Student and School-mate* 13 (March 1864): 71–74, in Marten, *Lessons of War*, 129–32. But many children's authors used the war as a backdrop to teach lessons about good behavior. See Marten, *Lessons of War*.

29. Louise Chandler Moulton, "Kitten," *Harper's New Monthly Magazine* 26 (April 1863): 696–99. As was so often the case in wartime fiction, Kitten's love was not really dead.

30. Louise Chandler Moulton, "One of Many," *Harper's New Monthly Magazine* 27 (June 1863): 120–21.

31. "One of Three," *The American Mail-Bag*, 20–44. Maud ends up winning her sister's lover in the process.

32. See also Belle Z. Spencer, "From a Soldier's Wife," *Harper's New Monthly Magazine* 29 (October 1864): 622–29; Helen Bruce, "The Soldier and the Nurse," *Ladies' Repository* 24 (November 1864): 656. There are other stories where a hospital nurse becomes the centerpiece of a love story, but with the exception of *Hospital Sketches*, the characters who make a decision to become nurses invariably do so after a loved one is killed or wounded.

33. Sophie May, "Begging for the Soldier," *Ladies' Repository* 23 (December 1863): 748–50.

34. On gender and the Philadelphia Sanitary Fair see Gallman, "Voluntarism in Wartime," 93–116.

35. See, for instance, "Ladies, to the Rescue," *Chicago Tribune*, January 12, 1864; Mrs. Furness, "Our Soldiers," *Atlantic Monthly* 13 (March 1864): 364–71; M. E. B.,

"The Great Central Fair," *Arthur's Home Magazine* 24 (August 1864): 96. For a story on children and fair work, see Harriett E. Francis, "Working for the Fair," *Ladies' Repository* (July 1864): 441.

36. See "About Sanitary Fairs," *Round Table*, February 20, 1864; "Raffles and the Fair," *American Knickerbocker Magazine* (March 1864).

37. Katherine F. Williams's story "Tableaux Vivans" concerns a woman's sewing group that stages a grand spectacle to raise money when their donations lag. The overall cause is patriotic, but most of the story focuses on the excitement of "putting on a show" involving lovely costumes. Frank, who had volunteered to write the script, ends up marrying one of the stars. *Harper's New Monthly Magazine* 27 (October 1863): 698–704.

38. Silber, *Gender and the Sectional Conflict*, 46–47, citing the *New York Herald*, September 3, 1864.

39. Nutting, *Three Lessons for This War*.

40. Natalie Heath, "What I Owe the War," *Peterson's Magazine* 40 (September 1861): 200–202.

41. "Rather Suggestive," *Frank Leslie's Budget of Fun*, January 1, 1863.

42. "The Patriotic Young Lady," *Frank Leslie's Illustrated Newspaper*, July 9, 1864.

43. "Red, White and Black," *The American Mail-Bag*, 218–34. As with the other stories in this English publication, the author and original place of publication is not noted.

44. Virginia F. Townsend, "Some Pictures of the Times," *Arthur's Home Magazine* 18 (November 1861): 233–37.

45. Virginia F. Townsend, "Hospital Nurse," *Arthur's Home Magazine* 20 (August 1862): 121–22. See also Fahs, *The Imagined Civil War*, 140. Recall that in "Enlisted! Enlisted!" Townsend portrayed a young girl speaking harshly to her older brother, who promptly enlisted in the Union army. In that story Townsend appeared to be warning girls about the perils of alienating their menfolk in time of war. Townsend, "Enlisted! Enlisted!," *Golden Era*, August 10, 1862. See chap. 4.

46. "What Can Woman Do?" *Chicago Tribune*, April 25, 1861, reprinted from the *New York Post*; "The Best Kind of Recruiting Sergeant," *Vanity Fair*, May 18, 1861; "Good for Charley," *Vanity Fair*, June 15, 1861.

47. "The Female Recruiting Sergeant," *The Tent and Forecastle Songster*, 17–18; "The Northern Girl's Song," *Beadle's Dime Knapster Songster*; Work, *We'll Go Down Ourselves*.

48. Mary W. Janvrin, "The Red, White, and Blue," *Peterson's Magazine* 41 (March 1862): 217–19.

49. "The Loyal Lover," *Arthur's Home Magazine* 19 (April 1862): 204–6. This story harks back to the messages about "duty" discussed in chap. 4. The "good" character, who wins the girl, is not a soldier, nor does he contemplate enlistment or sacrifice for the Union in any substantial way. His great virtue is that his patriotism is unwavering.

50. Kate Sutherland, "The Laggard Recruit," *Arthur's Home Magazine* 19 (January 1862): 9–11. Frank's story is really open to various interpretations. On the one hand, by being slow to volunteer he failed to win the heart of the woman of his dreams. On the other hand, the eventual decision to enlist against his earlier inclinations fails to win

Flora's heart. Perhaps he would have been better off following his actual nature and remaining at home. Several stories in the *New York Ledger* featured young girls choosing one suitor over another because of his patriotism. See Sizer, *The Political Work of Northern Women Writers*, 86, 291n46.

51. Harriet N. Babb, "Jennie Jewitt: The Young Recruiting Officer," *Ladies' Repository* 23 (April 1863): 241–44.

52. Louise Chandler Moulton, "Captain Charley," *Harper's New Monthly Magazine* 27 (August 1863): 407–9.

53. See, for instance, "An Arm for a Heart," *Daily Alta California*, February 15, 1863, reprinted in *The American Mail-Bag*, 57–69. Moulton used the same device only a few months earlier in "Kitten." When Ralph returns home missing an arm, Kitten declares, "God is merciful," almost precisely echoing the words of Charley's mother. Moulton, "Kitten," 699.

54. Morford, *The Days of Shoddy*.

55. Morford, *The Coward*. This novel's examination of cowardice was discussed more fully in chap. 5.

56. "A Hint for the Hour and the Man," *Vanity Fair*, August 2, 1862.

57. *Milwaukee Daily Sentinel*, August 5, 1862.

58. Patriotic Envelopes, Library Company of Philadelphia.

59. For an extended discussion of how the North's "war romances" commonly turned on the heroine's gradual decision to support her lover's military service, see Fahs, *The Imagined Civil War*, 130–33. Numerous stories feature women who, at least at first, balk when the men in their lives discuss enlistment. Some of these are discussed in chaps. 4 and 5.

60. Jane G. Austin, "The Captain's Cousin," *Dollar Monthly Magazine* (November 1863).

61. Mary A. Lowell, "The Soldier's Bride," *Dollar Monthly Magazine* (May 1864).

62. Harry Harewood Leech, "Parlor, Camp and Hospital," *Ballou's Dollar Monthly Magazine* (April 1862). Lu's rejection of the veteran who has lost his arm is a powerful marker of her moral failings.

63. Short stories featuring soldiers who are mistakenly believed to have died in battle, only to return home in the final pages, are too numerous to name.

64. Mathews, *Guy Hamilton*.

65. Jennie L. Eggleston, "One Year Ago," *Ladies' Repository* 22 (September 1862): 528. It is worth noting that the wife is ashamed of herself for fantasizing that her husband would come home without a hand, but otherwise healthy, whereas in several home front short stories the patriotic woman almost seems to be rewarded by the safe return of a man with a missing arm or leg.

66. Mrs. Emily Huntington Miller, "The Soldier's Wife," *Ladies' Repository* 23 (April 1863): 208.

67. "Desertion from the Army," *Chicago Tribune*, February 16, 1863.

68. See Mary E. Nealy, "Woman the Soldier's Friend," *Ladies' Repository* 24 (May 1864): 305. See also Gallman, *Mastering Wartime*; Richard, *Busy Hands*.

69. "Absent without Leave," *Frank Leslie's Illustrated Newspaper*, January 24, 1863.

70. *Frank Leslie's Budget of Fun*, June 1, 1863.

71. Penfield-Bross, "After the War," *Vanity Fair*, June 20, 1863.

72. Ella Rodman, "An Angel of Mercy," *Peterson's Magazine* 47 (June 1865): 416–21.

73. Mary A. Denison, "The Dead Soldier's Ring," *Arthur's Home Magazine* 23 (January 1863): 13–15.

74. "The Opal," *Frank Leslie's Illustrated Newspaper*, April 4, 1863.

75. Caroline Orne, "The Two Young Soldiers," *Dollar Monthly Magazine* (March 1863).

76. It is noteworthy that so many stories imagine women finding their dying lovers or sons on the battlefield or in distant hospitals. As Drew Faust has noted, one of the many challenges in responding to death and dying during the Civil War is that most families were robbed of the opportunity to be present for such scenes. Faust, *This Republic of Suffering*.

77. Almena C. S. Allard, "The Soldier's Dying Wife," *Arthur's Home Magazine* 20 (September 1862): 174–75.

78. Emilie Mozart, "Sacrifice for Country," *Ladies' Repository* 24 (February 1864): 68–70.

79. Lottie Linwood, "Annie Lann: The Soldier's Bride," *Flag of Our Union*, January 21, 1865.

80. Carry Stanley, "The Volunteer's Wife," *Peterson's Magazine* 40 (October 1861): 256–59. For a more extended discussion of the war as an economic challenge for working-class northerners (also free of any patriotic discussion) see Anonymous, *Six Hundred Dollars a Year*.

81. "Helen Christian," *The American Mail-Bag*, 70–83.

82. "The Tuberose," *The American Mail-Bag*, 199–208.

83. Elizabeth S. Phelps, "A Sacrifice Consumed," *Harper's New Monthly Magazine* 28 (January 1864): 235–40.

84. "Tales out of School," *Vanity Fair*, August 16, 1862.

85. Edmund Spencer, "The Last Cold Snap," *Peterson's Magazine* 45 (May 1864): 362–67.

86. "How Private Jake Fay Got Leave of Absence," *Frank Leslie's Budget of Fun* (February 1862).

87. Sarah A. Southworth, "Marcia Grant's Love," *Dollar Monthly Magazine* (January 1865).

88. Mary Kyle Dallas, "John Gant, Coachman," *Golden Era*, December 28, 1862. Dallas was a widely published poet and author. This story was set in New York and was perhaps originally published in an eastern journal. Dallas also submitted occasional "Gossip from Gotham," columns written especially for the *Golden Era*. See July 12, 1863.

89. "The Recruit," *Boston Daily Advertiser*, March 14, 1862.

90. Harriet E. Francis, "The Soldier's Present," *Arthur's Home Magazine* 21 (June 1863): 329–31.

91. Goodwin, *Roger Deane's Work*.

92. [Weston], *Bessie and Raymond*.

93. Novels and short stories set exclusively on the battlefield fell outside the research design of this study. These two books suggest some of the themes that emerged in this

particular genre. For a more extensive discussion of wartime sensational literature see Fahs, *The Imagined Civil War*, 225–55.

94. Anonymous, *The Lady Lieutenant*.

95. [Power], *Miriam Rivers*.

96. And while young women in many stories preferred men who had volunteered, I did not find any stories where a young man chose a spouse because of her energetic voluntarism.

CHAPTER SEVEN

1. These observations are based on my reading of novels and short stories published during the war years and set in the home front. Novels set in slaveholding border states, where white characters wrestled with secession and Union, were more likely to include African American characters, both free and enslaved. For a discussion of how the northern press wrestled with the racial implications of slavery and emancipation during the Civil War, see Fahs, *The Imagined Civil War*, 151–94. Louisa May Alcott's "The Brothers" (also known as "My Contraband") is about a white northern nurse who encounters two southern half-brothers, a wounded Rebel soldier and his biracial sibling. The story is an important contemplation of race and society, although not one that deals directly with northern blacks. Alcott, "The Brothers," *Atlantic Monthly* 12 (November 1863): 584–95.

2. Population data from www.census.gov. See also Gallagher, *The Union War*, 42–43.

3. For useful treatments of the decisions facing African Americans see Kynoch, "Terrible Dilemmas," 104–27; Brian Taylor, "A Politics of Service," 451–80.

4. On antebellum northern black culture, and the press in particular, see Rael, *Black Identity and Black Protest*, esp. 213–16; Horton and Horton, *In Hope of Liberty*, esp. 206–8; Masur, *An Example for All the Land*, 13–21. On African American weekly newspapers published during the Civil War—particularly Boston's *Pine and Palm*, New York's *Anglo-African Weekly*, Philadelphia's *Christian Recorder*, and San Francisco's *Pacific Appeal*—see Brian Taylor, "A Politics of Service." For local studies of black debates over citizenship in two northern cities see Kantrowitz, *More Than Freedom* (Boston), and Masur, *An Example for All the Land* (Washington).

5. *The Liberator*, February 3, 1860, quoted in McPherson, *The Negro's Civil War*, 5.

6. McPherson, *The Negro's Civil War*, 8–18.

7. *Douglass' Monthly*, May 1861.

8. See "Colored Men and the War," *The Liberator*, May 10, 1861, reprinted from the *Boston Daily Atlas and Bee*, April 19, 1861; "Colored Patriotism," *The Liberator*, May 31, 1861; "Black Regiments Proposed," *Douglass' Monthly*, May 1861. See also McPherson, *The Negro's Civil War*, 19–22.

9. *Christian Recorder*, May 4, 1861, and *Pine and Palm*, May 25, 1861, both quoted in McPherson, *The Negro's Civil War*, 29.

10. McPherson, *The Negro's Civil War*, 29–35; Brian Taylor, "A Politics of Service," 459–60; Cullen, "'I's a Man Now,'" 78–79.

11. *Christian Recorder*, April 27, 1861.

12. "Black Regiments Proposed," *Douglass' Monthly*, May 1861; J. W. C. Pennington, "A Word to Colored Politicians," *Anglo-African*, August 10, 1861, cited in Brian Taylor, "A Politics of Service." Taylor's essay offers evidence from the African American weekly press demonstrating that in the first year of the war the opinions of African Americans were decidedly mixed on whether they should offer their services.

13. *Anglo-African*, September 14, 1861, cited in Kynoch, "Terrible Dilemmas."

14. For surveys of these events see Berlin et al., "The Black Military Experience," 190–91; John David Smith, "Let Us All Be Grateful," 1–77. For the classic study, see McPherson, *The Struggle for Equality*.

15. "Something of a Change," *Vanity Fair*, August 10, 1861; "Drafts," *Vanity Fair*, July 26, 1862.

16. Fehrenbacher, *The Dred Scott Case*.

17. See Reidy, "The African American Struggle for Citizenship Rights." See also Kantrowitz, *More Than Freedom*; Samito, *Becoming American under Fire*.

18. "Practical Joke of a Chicago Fire Zouave," *The Liberator*, August 9, 1861, reprinted from the *Chicago Tribune*. The same story appeared in the *Adams Sentinel* (Gettysburg, PA), August 21, 1861.

19. Anna E. Dickinson must have run across this newspaper story at some point. She used almost exactly the same episode in her 1868 novel, *What Answer?*

20. "The Manhood of the Negro," *The Independent*, October 24, 1861; "A Black Citizen of the Disunited States," *Chicago Tribune*, October 31, 1861; "The Manhood of the Negro," *Douglass' Monthly*, November 1861.

21. *The Liberator*, May 9, 1862, reprinted from the *Cincinnati Gazette*. A slightly shorter version of this story was reprinted in *Colonist*, July 1862; *Barker's Review*, April 12, 1862; *Daily National Intelligencer* (Washington), March 21, 1862; and *Newark (OH) Advocate*, April 25, 1862; and no doubt many more northern papers.

22. "Views of an Intelligent Negro," *The Liberator*, December 19, 1862, and *Douglass' Monthly*, January 1863. Both abolitionist papers describe this as a letter from Wilkeson, but they do not indicate whether the *New York Tribune* had previously published it.

23. "The Treatment of Black Men in the Army," *The Liberator*, September 26, 1862.

24. See "Loyal Blacks," *The Liberator*, August 22, 1862, reprinted from the *New York Journal of Commerce*.

25. "Persecution of Negroes," *Douglass' Monthly*, September 1862, reprinted from the *New York Tribune*; "Brutal and Unprovoked Assaults upon Colored People," *Douglass' Monthly*, September 1862. See also McPherson, *The Negro's Civil War*, 69–70.

26. "Another Offer of Colored Men," *The Liberator*, September 12, 1862; "The White Man's War," *The Liberator*, August 8, 1862, reprinted from the *Chicago Tribune*. Also reprinted in *Douglass' Monthly*, September 1862. "The Negro on the Fence," *The Liberator*, September 19, 1862, reprinted from the *Evening Post*.

27. Gallagher, *The Union War*, 97, citing *Harper's Weekly*, August 16, 1862.

28. "Free Negroes in the North," *The Liberator*, May 9, 1862, quoting the *Delhi (NY) Republican*.

29. "Why Should the Negro Fight?," *The Liberator*, August 8, 1862, reprinted from the *Chicago Tribune*.

30. Nasby, *The Nasby Papers*. The small volume collected an assortment of Petroleum Nasby's wartime essays, some of which were dated and most (if not all) were published earlier in the war. This piece seems to date to late 1861.

31. "Citizenship of Colored Americans," *Douglass' Monthly*, February 1863. For summaries of this chain of events, see Reidy, "The African American Struggle for Citizenship Rights," and Berlin et al., "The Black Military Experience," 190–91. See also Samito, *Becoming American under Fire*, 1–4; Emberton, "'Only Murder Makes Men.'" On the legal context of Bates's decision, see Blair, *With Malice toward Some*, 255–56.

32. *Christian Recorder*, February 14, 1863.

33. Frederick Douglass, "Address Delivered in New York," February 6, 1863, in Douglass, *The Frederick Douglass Papers*, 3:569. For a full discussion of Douglass and his responses to military service, see Blight, *Frederick Douglass' Civil War*, 148–74.

34. "The Negro Regiment—Meeting of the Colored Citizens," *The Liberator*, February 20, 1863.

35. "Citizenship of Colored Persons," *Douglass' Monthly*, March 1863.

36. *The Liberator*, March 6, 1863.

37. Frederick Douglass. "Men of Color to Arms!," *Douglass' Monthly*, March 1863, reprinted in *Douglass' Monthly* in April 1863. Douglass's famous proclamation was reprinted in numerous northern publications. See Douglass, "A Call to the Negroes to Arm," *The Liberator*, March 13, 1863; *The Broadside* (Rochester, NY), March 21, 1863. Douglass's speech also appeared in New York's *Anglo-African* (as cited in the letter by John W. Menard to *Douglass' Monthly*, April 1863). On Douglass's wartime rhetoric, see Blight, *Frederick Douglass' Civil War*, esp. 157–59.

38. Mrs. [Mary A.?] Denison, "The Negro's Vision," *The Liberator*, March 13, 1863, reprinted from the *Boston Transcript*.

39. "A Negro Volunteer's Song," *The Liberator*, June 19, 1863.

40. "A Sketch with Color in It," *Vanity Fair*, February 1863.

41. *Frank Leslie's Illustrated Newspaper*, May 22, 1863.

42. John W. Menard, "A Reply to Frederick Douglass, by a Colored Man," *Douglass' Monthly*, April 1863. This letter is followed by a short comment from the editor (presumably Douglass). Menard's letter is dated March 10, 1863. Menard went on to become a leading African American journalist and politician. For other African American voices dissenting from the call to enlist in the first months of 1863, see Brian Taylor, "A Politics of Service," 465–70.

43. "Mr. Brown" et al., "Michigan State Convention," *Anglo-African Weekly*, March 7, 1863. Also cited in Brian Taylor, "A Politics of Service," 467. This is an excellent example of the nationwide conversation within the African American press.

44. Frederick Douglass, "Another Word to Colored Men," *Douglass' Monthly*, April 1863.

45. "A Sermon for the Present Hour," *The Liberator*, May 1, 1863.

46. Blight, *Frederick Douglass' Civil War*, 165. Blight notes that Garnet shifted ground and supported enlistment at a meeting the following week.

47. *Christian Recorder*, May 23, 1863.

48. See, for instance, "Freedom's Trial—Acquiescences of the Whole North in the

Enlistment of Colored Soldiers," *Pacific Appeal*, May 30, 1863; "Will the Negro Fight?," *The Liberator*, June 26, 1863.

49. For contemporary accounts of both engagements, see McPherson, *The Negro's Civil War*, 188–91. The scholarship on African American soldiers during the Civil War is vast. For a useful recent overview see John David Smith, "Let Us All Be Grateful." For broader surveys see Quarles, *The Negro in the Civil War*; Cornish, *The Sable Arm*; McPherson, *The Negro's Civil War*; Glatthaar, *Forged in Battle*; Berlin et al., "The Black Military Experience." On the responses of white soldiers to black troops see Mitchell, *The Vacant Chair*, 55–70; McPherson, *For Cause and Comrades*, 126–28.

50. McPherson, *The Negro's Civil War*, 176.

51. Gerrit Smith, "Denying Suffrage Even to Soldiers!," *Douglass' Monthly*, June 1863.

52. Masur, *An Example for All the Land*, 43–49; McPherson, *The Negro's Civil War*, 180.

53. "Disgraceful Proceedings," *Douglass' Monthly*, June 1863.

54. For a short treatment of the riots, see Spann, *Gotham at War*. For book-length treatments see Cook, *The Armies of the Streets*; Bernstein, *The New York City Draft Riots*. For a particularly famous image of the riots, see *Harper's Weekly*, August 1, 1863, 493.

55. "The Meeting of the Colored Loyalist," *Douglass' Monthly*, June 1863.

56. C. K. W., "Foreshadowings," *The Liberator*, June 5, 1863.

57. "A Negro Mass Meeting," *The Liberator*, June 5, 1863, quoting the New York *Evening Post*.

58. "Enlistment of Colored Regiments," *The Liberator*, July 17, 1863. This is the official fund-raising statement of the Supervisory Committee, dated June 27, 1863. The appeal—with its somewhat self-serving tone—is aimed at white donors, although no doubt many African Americans read it in the pages of *The Liberator*.

59. Bassett (and fifty-four others), *Men of Color*, recruiting broadside, Library Company of Philadelphia.

60. All three speeches and the text of the *Men of Color* broadside were published in *Address of the Hon. W. D. Kelley, Miss Anna E. Dickinson, and Mr. Frederick Douglass*. For a more detailed discussion of these documents and events see Gallman, "In Your Hands That Musket Means Liberty," 95–100. For manhood and African American soldiers, see Cullen, "'I's a Man Now,'" 76–91.

61. *The Liberator*, July 31, 1863. For accounts of the Pennsylvania recruiting effort see *Pacific Appeal* (San Francisco), August 1, 1863.

62. I am assuming that the arguments made by the three speakers offer a window into the issues that most concerned the black men in the audience. Although Dickinson and Kelley were both white orators, they each had substantial experience working with the Philadelphia black community.

63. On African American recruiting in Philadelphia see Frank Taylor, *Philadelphia in the Civil War*, 189–90; Wert, "Camp William Penn and the Black Soldier"; Binder, "Pennsylvania Negro Regiments in the Civil War."

64. J. C. Hagen, "Men of Color," *The Liberator*, July 31, 1863, reprinted from the *New York Christian Inquirer*.

65. "The Duty of Colored Men to Enlist," *New York Times*, August 2, 1863. Note that Seward's letter is paraphrasing Langston's earlier letter.

66. "Duty of Colored Men," *Douglass' Monthly*, August 1863. This editorial notes that Seward's letter had been reprinted without comment in the *National Anti-Slavery Standard*.

67. L. Holmes, "Brief Words on Present Interests," *The Liberator*, November 20, 1863.

68. [Charles Graham Halpine], "Miles O'Reilly on the 'Naygurs,'" *The Liberator*, January 29, 1864. See also Fahs, *The Imagined Civil War*, 219.

69. See Yacovone, "The Fifty-Fourth Massachusetts Regiment"; Reidy, "The African American Struggle for Citizenship Rights," 222–25. For contemporary accounts see "The Pay of Soldiers," *The Liberator*, February 12, 1864; "Colored Soldiers," *The Liberator*, February 12, 1864, citing *Vermont Journal*.

70. Blight, *Frederick Douglass' Civil War*, 167.

71. "The Government and the Colored Troops," *The Liberator*, May 4, 1864, reprinted from the *Boston Journal*. The *Journal*'s story cites the *Anti-Slavery Standard*.

72. *Christian Recorder*, April 2, 1864, cited in Kynoch, "Terrible Dilemmas."

73. "Justice to the Colored Soldiers," *The Liberator*, May 13, 1864. See also "The Pay of Colored Soldiers," *The Liberator*, June 17, 1864, quoting the *Philadelphia Press*; McPherson, *The Negro's Civil War*, 200–208.

74. "Letter from the Army of the Potomac," *The Liberator*, July 15, 1864, quoting the *Boston Journal*.

75. "Ovation to Black Troops," *New York Times*, March 6, 1864.

76. "The Colored People of Philadelphia," *The Liberator*, August 5, 1864, reprinted from the *Christian Recorder*.

77. See Giesberg, *Army at Home*, 92–118.

78. On the First USCT's conflicts with Washington's streetcar lines, see Masur, *An Example for All the Land*, 45.

79. Giesberg notes that African American women engaged in streetcar protests in San Francisco, St. Louis, Cincinnati, New Orleans, New York, and Philadelphia. Giesberg, *Army at Home*, 95, 196n9.

80. Ibid., 99–100.

81. For details on the streetcar battles in Philadelphia see Foner, "The Battle to End Discrimination (Part I)" and "The Battle to End Discrimination (Part II)."

82. McPherson, *The Negro's Civil War*, 260–61.

83. "Color and Cars in Philadelphia," *The Liberator*, August 12, 1864, quoting *Episcopal Recorder*.

84. "Colored People and the Philadelphia City Cars," *The Liberator*, December 23, 1864. See also "Street Cars and the Rights of Citizens," *The Liberator*, January 6, 1865, quoting the *Philadelphia Press*; "Colored Persons in the City Passenger Cars," *The Liberator*, February 17, 1865, quoting the *Philadelphia Press*; "Colored Passengers in Streetcars," *The Liberator*, March 24, 1865, quoting the *Philadelphia Press*. Each of these stories, and many more, appeared in the Philadelphia press and were reprinted in other newspapers. See McPherson, *The Negro's Civil War*, 262–68.

85. Giesberg, *Army at Home*, 102–7, citing "Home Affairs: The Cars and Our People," *Christian Recorder*, June 30, 1865.

86. Dickinson, *What Answer?*

87. In a note at the end of the novel Dickinson explains that the chapter came from a scene she witnessed where a black soldier was ejected from the cars. Dickinson, *What Answer?*, 314.

88. Dickinson, *What Answer?*, 311.

CONCLUSION

1. William Novak has argued against the popular notion that nineteenth-century Americans lived in a world free of regulations. I would argue that Novak's impressive research illustrates that Americans embraced some regulations in the name of a "well-regulated society," but that the sum total of antebellum regulations left most Americans largely undisturbed. Novak, *The People's Welfare*.

2. The purchase of war bonds became both an act of patriotism and a sound investment promising a reasonable yield. For a discussion of the wartime economy and government policies in both the Union and the Confederacy see Engerman and Gallman, "The Civil War Economy."

3. In addition to the previously cited books by Murdock see Murdock, "Was It a 'Poor Man's Fight?,'" and Anbider, "Which Poor Man's Fight?"

4. These are certainly complicated issues, most of which I have written about in other contexts. See Gallman, *The North Fights the Civil War*. The federal government did adopt a heavier hand in limiting free speech and civil liberties, largely—although not exclusively—in the contested border regions. See Neely, *The Fate of Liberty*.

5. This notion of a wartime world above partisan politics was most famously articulated by the Loyal Publication Society's Francis Lieber in April 1863. Lieber, *No Party Now*. For a detailed scholarly examination of the antipartisan impulse see Adam I. P. Smith, *No Party Now*.

6. Woodrow Wilson, "Proclamation 1370."

7. Kennedy, "Inaugural Address."

8. What follows is based on Basler, *The Collected Works of Abraham Lincoln*. Volumes 4–8 cover Lincoln's presidency. These volumes are also available online, at http://quod.lib.umich.edu/l/lincoln/. I used the online versions for follow-up word searches. These paragraphs are a very abbreviated summary of findings in Gallman, "The President as Pedagogue."

9. More than two years into the war, Lincoln responded to a request for assistance from two widows by writing, "My conclusion is that, other claims and qualifications being equal, they have the better right and this is especially applicable to the disabled and the soldier, deceased soldier's family." This was an unusual moment when the president suggested that those who sacrificed were owed some special considerations. July 24, 1863, to Montgomery Blair, *Collected Works*, 6:326.

10. He only used the term "good citizen" on one occasion, and that was in offering his hopes that a young boy would grow up to be a good citizen.

11. Abraham Lincoln to John Phillips, November 21, 1864, *Collected Works*, 8:118; Abraham Lincoln to Willie Smith, February 23, 1864, *Collected Works*, 7:202.

12. Irving, "We Are Coming Father Abraham," song sheet. The song was based on a poem published by James Sloan Gibbons in 1862.

13. "We Are Coming Father Abraham" spawned various updates as the federal government made new calls for volunteers, as well as several parodies of the patriotic anthem. See "Six Hundred Thousand More," song sheet; Root, "Father Abraham's Reply to the 600,000," song sheet; Pond, "How Are You, Greenbacks?" (1863) in *Shoddy Songster (1864)*, 56–57.

14. See, for instance, *All for the Union*, 46; Wiley, *The Life of Billy Yank*, 286; Mitchell, *Civil War Soldiers*, 86–87.

15. For a discussion of citizenship and the Civil War see Samito, *Becoming American under Fire*. Note that after the war Union veterans engaged in a parallel conversation about the rights they had earned through wartime service. See Marten, *Sing Not the War*.

16. For a valuable summary of postwar citizenship within a broader context see Kettner, *The Development of American Citizenship*.

Works Cited

PRIMARY SOURCES

Civil War Periodicals

Adams Sentinel (Gettysburg, PA)
American Monthly Knickerbocker
Anglo-African Weekly (New York)
Arthur's Home Magazine (Philadelphia)
Atlantic Monthly
Ballou's Monthly Magazine
Bangor (ME) Daily Whig and Courier
Barker's Review
Boston Daily Advertiser
Boston Investigator
The Broadside (Rochester, NY)
Burlington (VT) Free Press
Cape Girardeau Weekly Argus
Cass County (MI) Republican
Chicago Tribune
Christian Recorder (Philadelphia)
Cincinnati Daily Press
Cleveland Morning Leader
Colonist
Columbia (PA) Spy
Comic Monthly
Continental Monthly
The Crisis (Columbus, OH)
Daily Alta California
Daily Cleveland Herald
Daily Evening Bulletin
   (San Francisco, CA)
Daily National Intelligencer
   (Washington, DC)
Daily Ohio Statesman (Columbus)
Dayton Daily Empire
Deseret News
Dollar Monthly Magazine
Douglass' Monthly
Dover (NH) Gazette

Evening Star (Washington, DC)
Farmer's Cabinet (New Hampshire)
Flag of Our Union
Frank Leslie's Budget of Fun
Frank Leslie's Illustrated Newspaper
   (New York, NY)
Freedom's Champion (Atchison, KS)
Godey's Lady's Book and Magazine
Golden Era (San Francisco)
Harper's New Monthly Magazine
Harper's Weekly
Daily Patriot and Union (Harrisburg, PA)
Huntington Globe
The Independent
Ladies' Repository (Cincinnati)
Lancaster (PA) Intelligencer
Leavenworth Daily Bulletin
The Liberator
Living Age
Lowell (MA) Daily Citizen and News
Milwaukee Daily Sentinel
Morning Oregonian (Portland)
New Hampshire Statesman
New Haven Daily Palladium
New York Daily Tribune
New York Herald
New York Times
Newark (OH) Advocate
Nick Nax
North American and United States
   Gazette (Philadelphia)
Old Guard
Pacific Appeal (San Francisco)
Pennsylvania Daily Telegraph
   (Harrisburg)

Penny Press (Cincinnati)
Peterson's Magazine (Philadelphia)
Philadelphia Daily Evening Bulletin
Philadelphia Evening Telegraph
Philadelphia Inquirer
Philadelphia Press
Philadelphia Public Ledger
Pittsburg Daily Gazette and Advertiser
Reading (PA) Gazette and Democrat
Ripley (OH) Bee
Rocky Mountain News
  (Cherry Creek, KS)
Round Table
San Francisco Bulletin
Scientific American

Scioto (OH) Gazette
Tri-weekly Miner's Register
  (Central City, CO)
Urban Union (Ohio)
Vanity Fair
Vermont Chronicle
Vermont Watchman and State Journal
Weekly Dakotian (Yankton, SD)
Weekly Mariettian (PA)
Weekly Vincennes (IN) Gazette
Western Reserve Chronicle (Warren, OH)
Wisconsin Daily Patriot
Wisconsin State Register
Yankee Notions

Printed Primary Sources

Adams, William. *Christian Patriotism*. New York: Anson D. F. Randolph, 1863.

Address of the Hon. W. D. Kelley, Miss Anna E. Dickinson, and Mr. Frederick Douglass, at a Mass Meeting, Held at National Hall, Philadelphia, July 6, 1863, for the Promotion of Colored Enlistments. Philadelphia: n.p., 1863.

Alcott, Louisa May. *Hospital Sketches*. Edited with an introduction by Alice Fahs. 1863; reprint, Boston: Bedford St. Martin's, 2004.

The American Mail-Bag, or Tales from the War. London: War and Lock, 1863.

Anonymous. *The Lady Lieutenant: A wonderful, startling and thrilling narrative of the adventures of Miss Madeline Moore, who, in order to be near her lover, joined the Army, was elected lieutenant, and fought in western Virginia under the renowned General McClellan*. Philadelphia: Barclay and Co., 1862.

Anonymous. *Six Hundred Dollars a Year: A Wife's Effort at Low Living, under High Prices*. Boston: Ticknor and Fields, 1867.

"The Army Contractor." Valentine. [S.l.: s.n.], [1861–65?]. McAllister Collection, Library Company of Philadelphia.

Arthur, Timothy Shay. *Home-Heroes, Saints and Martyrs*. Philadelphia: Lippincott, 1865.

Barber, Joseph. *War Letters of a Disbanded Volunteer*. New York: F. A. Brady, 1864.

Basler, Roy P., ed. *Collected Works of Abraham Lincoln*. 8 vols. New Brunswick, NJ: Rutgers University Press, 1953.

Bassett, E. D. (and fifty-four others). *Men of Color*. Recruiting broadside. [July 1863]. Original in the Library Company of Philadelphia.

Beadle's Dime Knapster Songster. New York: Beadle and Co., [c. 1862].

Bellows, Henry. *Unconditional Loyalty*. New York: Anson Randolph, 1863.

Berry, J. Romeyn. *Christian Patriotism: A Sermon Delivered in the Reformed Dutch Church of Kinderhook on Sabbath Morning, June 23, 1861*. Albany, NY: Weed, Parsons, 1861.

Bierce, Ambrose. *Tales of Soldiers and Civilians*. Edited by Donald T. Blume. Kent, OH: Kent State University Press, 2004.

Bishop, Putnam P. *Liberty's Ordeal*. New York: Sheldon and Company, 1864.

A Black Record! Gov. Curtin's Portrait Drawn by a Black Republican Editor: Who Clothed Our Soldiers in Shoddy: Who Plundered Our Brave Volunteers? Philadelphia: Printed at the "Age" Office, [1864]. Pamphlet, Library Company of Philadelphia.

Blondheim, Menahem, ed. *Copperhead Gore: Benjamin Wood's Fort Lafayette and Civil War America*. Bloomington: Indiana University Press, 2006.

Boardman, George Dana. *Civil Government*. Philadelphia: Ringwalt and Brown, 1864.

Brockett, Linus Pierpont, and Mary Vaughan. *Women's Work in the Civil War*. Philadelphia: King and Baird, 1867.

Browne, Charles Farrar. *See* Ward, Artemus.

Bureau of the Census. *Statistics of the United States in 1860*. Washington: Government Printing Office, 1866.

Chesebrough, Amos S. *Christian Politics: A Sermon Preached on Fast Day, April 3, 1863*. Hartford: Case, Lockwood and Company, 1863.

Civil War Letters of General Robert McAllister. Edited by James I. Robertson Jr. New Brunswick, NJ: Rutgers University Press, 1965.

Collier, Robert Laird. *Moral Heroism: Its Essentialness to the Crisis: A Sermon, Preached in the Wabash Ave. M.E. Church, Chicago, Sabbath Evening, August 3, 1862*. Chicago: Tribune Book and Job Steam Printing Office, 1862.

Cornwallis, Kinahan. *Pilgrims of Fashion*. New York: Harper and Brothers, 1862.

Dean, Sidney. *The War: And the Duty of a Loyal People: A Sermon, Preached in the Mathewson Street Methodist Episcopal Church, Providence, R.I. . . . July 27, 1862*. Providence: Pierce and Budlong, 1862.

Devon, W. A. *War Lyrics*. New York: n.p., 1864.

Dickinson, Anna E. *What Answer?* 1868; reprint, New York: Humanity Books, 2003.

Dodge, Mary Abigail. *See* Hamilton, Gail.

Douglass, Frederick. *The Frederick Douglass Papers*. Edited by John W. Blassingame. Series 1, 5 vols. New Haven, CT: Yale University Press, 1985.

Duryea, Joseph T. *Civil Liberty: A Sermon Preached on the National Thanksgiving Day, August 6th, 1863*. New York: J. A. Gray and Green, 1863.

Elder, Donald, ed. *Love amid the Turmoil: The Civil War Letters of William and Mary Vermilion*. Iowa City: University of Iowa Press, 2003.

"A Fancy Soldier." Comic valentine. McAlister Collection, Library Company of Philadelphia.

Foster, Hannah Webster. *The Coquette*. 1789; reprint, New York: Oxford University Press, 1987.

Fransioli, Rev. Joseph. *Patriotism: A Christian Virtue. Sermon Preached by the Rev. Joseph Fransioli at St. Peter's (Catholic) Church, Brooklyn, July 26th, 1863*. Loyal Publication Society, No. 24. New York: Loyal Publication Society, 1863.

Glover, Charles W., et al. "Jeanette and Jeannot, or, The Conscript's Departure." Sheet music. Philadelphia, 1850. Library of Congress, Washington, DC.

Goodwin, [Hannah Bradbury]. *Roger Deane's Work*. Boston: Graves and Young, 1863.

Gould, Benjamin Apthorp. *Investigations in the Military and Anthropological Statistics of American Soldiers*. Cambridge, MA: Harvard University Press, 1869.

Hamilton, Gail [Mary Abigail Dodge]. *Skirmishes and Sketches*. Boston: Ticknor and Fields, 1865.

Haskell, Thomas Nelson. *Christian Patriotism: A Medium of God's Power and Purpose to Bless Our Land: A Sermon, Delivered in the First Presbyterian Church, East Boston, April 30, 1863*. Boston: Hollis and Gunn, 1863.

Holmes, Mary J. *Rose Mather: A Tale*. New York: G. W. Carleton and Co., 1868.

Huntington, Rev. F. D. *Personal Humiliation Demanded by the National Danger*. Boston: E. D. Dutton and Company, 1864.

"I Am Not Sick, I'm Over Forty-Five." Sheet music. No author, c. 1863. Confederate Broadside Collection, Wake Forest University, http://wakespace.lib.wfu.edu /handle/10339/358.

"I Am Sick, Don't Draft Me." Sheet music. No author, c. 1863. American Song Sheets, Library of Congress Rare Books and Special Collections, Library of Congress, http://www.loc.gov/item/amss.cw102600.

Irving, B. "We Are Coming Father Abraham, or, Three Hundred Thousand More." Sheet music. Chicago: H. M. Higgins, c. 1862.

Kennedy, John F. "Inaugural Address." January 20, 1961. American Presidency Project, by Gerhard Peters and John T. Woolley, http://www.presidency.ucsb.edu /ws/index.php?pid=8032.

[Kirkland, Caroline]. *A Few Words in Behalf of the Loyal Women of the United States by One of Themselves*. Loyal Publication Society No. 10. New York: Wm. C. Bryant and Co., May 1863.

Lieber, Francis. *No Party Now, but for All Our Country*. Loyal Publication Society No. 16. New York: Loyal Publication Society, 1863.

Locke, David Ross. *See* Nasby, Petroleum V.

"Look Sharp!" Lithograph. Huntington Library, Huntington, CA.

Mathews, Joanna H. *Guy Hamilton: A Story of the Civil War*. New York: American News Co., 1866.

Mohr, James C., ed. *The Cormany Diaries: A Northern Family in the Civil War*. Pittsburgh: University of Pittsburgh Press, 1982.

Moore, Frank. *Women of the War: Their Heroism and Self-Sacrifice*. Hartford: S. S. Scranton and Co., 1866.

Morford, Henry. *The Coward: A Novel of Society and the Field in 1863*. Philadelphia: T. B. Peterson and Brothers, 1864.

———. *The Days of Shoddy: A Novel of the Great Rebellion in 1861*. Philadelphia: T. B. Peterson and Brothers, 1863.

———. *Over-Sea; or, England, France and Scotland as Seen by a Live American*. Philadelphia: J. B. Lippincott and Co., 1867.

———. *Rhymes of Twenty Years*. Philadelphia: T. B. Peterson and Brothers, 1859.

———. *Shoulder Straps: A Novel of New York and the Army, 1862*. Philadelphia: T. B. Peterson and Brothers, 1863.

Nasby, Petroleum V. [David Locke]. *The Nasby Papers*. Indianapolis: C. O. Perrine and Co., 1864.

Nutting, William J. *Three Lessons for This War, from an Ancient Chronicle: A Sermon, Preached before the Presbyterian Churches of Unadilla, Stockbridge, and Plainfield, Michigan, on Sabbath, July 24, 1864*. Ann Arbor: C. G. Clark, 1864.

"Offering a Substitute. A Scene in the Office of the Provost Marshall." Lithograph. P.2275.17—Recon 6282 1862—15W, Library Company of Philadelphia.

Paddock, Wilber F. *God's Presence and Purpose in Our War*. Philadelphia: Caxton Press of C. Sherman, Son and Co., 1863.

Patriotic envelopes. Print Department, Library Company of Philadelphia.

[Power], M. C. *Miriam Rivers, the Lady Soldier: Or, General Grant's Spy*. Philadelphia: Barclay and Co., 1865.

[Reed, Isaac George]. *The Russian Ball: Or the Adventures of Clementina Shoddy*. New York: Carleton, 1863.

Report of the Commission Appointed to the Governor of Pennsylvania to Investigate Alleged Army Frauds, August, 1861. Harrisburg, 1861.

Robinson, Mary S. *The Brother Soldiers: A Household Story of the American Conflict*. 1866; reprint, New York: N. Tibbals and Sons, 1871.

Root, George F. "Father Abraham's Reply to the 600,000." Sheet music. Chicago: Root and Cady, 1862.

Rosenblatt, Emil, and Ruth Rosenblatt, eds. *Hard Marching Every Day: The Civil War Letters of Private Wilbur Fisk, 1861-1865*. Lawrence: University Press of Kansas, 1983.

Rowson, Susanna. *Charlotte Temple*. 1791; reprint, New York: Oxford University Press, 1987.

Sears, Stephen W., ed. *Mr. Dunn Browne's Experiences in the Civil War: The Civil War Letters of Samuel W. Fiske*. New York: Fordham University Press, 1998.

"Shoddy." New York: Union Valentine Co., n.d. McAllister Collection, Library Company of Philadelphia.

Shoddy Songster: New and Popular Songs: A collection of the most popular songs of the day, comprising sentimental, comic, Negro, Irish, national patriotic, military, social, convivial, and pathetic songs, ballads, and melodies . . . Philadelphia: Simpson and Company, 1864.

Shoddy Songster: New and Popular Songs . . . Philadelphia: Simpson and Co., 1865.

"Six Hundred Thousand More." Sheet music, c. 1862. Hayes Library, Fremont, OH.

Smith, John David, and William Cooper Jr., eds. *A Union Woman in Civil War Kentucky: The Diary of Frances Peter*. Lexington: University of Kentucky Press, 2000.

Smith, Moses. *God's Honor Man's Ultimate Success: A Sermon Preached on Sunday, September 27th, 1863*. New Haven, CT: T. J. Stafford, 1863.

Spear, Samuel. *The Duty of the Hour*. New York: Anson D. F. Randolph, 1863.

Stewart, William Bell. *The Nation's Sins and the Nation's Duty: A Sermon, Preached in the First Presbyterian Church, Pottstown, Pennsylvania, on National Fast Day, April 30, 1863*. Philadelphia: William S. and Alfred Martien, 1863.

Stillé, Charles Janeway. *How a Free People Conduct a Long War: A Chapter from English History*. New York: Loyal Publication Society, 1863.

Tammany Society. *Celebration at Tammany Hall, on Friday, July 4th, 1862. Including the Poem, by Henry Morford, Esq*. New York: Baptist and Taylor, 1862.

———. *Celebration at Tammany Hall, on Saturday, July 4, 1863. Including the Oration, by Hon. Henry C. Murphy, the Poem, by Henry Morford, Esq*. New York: Baptist and Taylor, 1863.

The Tent and Forecastle Songster. New York: Dick and Fitzgerald, [c. 1862].

Turner, Austin Augustus. *Beauties of the Draft*. Library Company of Philadelphia, 5780.F.511 i-p.

Volck, Adelbert. *Buying a Substitute in the North during the War*. Cartoon. Library Company of Philadelphia.

Wadsworth, Charles. *American Patriotism: A Sermon Preached in the Arch Street Church, Sabbath Morning, April 28th, 1861*. Philadelphia: J. W. Bradley, 1861.

Walters, B. Frank. *"Come In out of the Draft, or The Disconsolate Conscript?"* Sheet music. Philadelphia: Lee and Walker, 722 Chestnut St., c. 1863. Library Company of Philadelphia.

The War of the Rebellion: A Compilation of the Official Records of the Union and Confederate Armies. Washington: Government Printing Office, 1880–1901.

Ward, Artemus [Charles Farrar Browne]. *The Complete Works of Artemus Ward*. New York: G. W. Carleton and Company, 1875.

Ware, John Fothergill Waterhouse. *Manhood, the Want of the Day. A Sermon Preached in the Church of the Cambridgeport Parish, March 1, 1863*. Boston: Leonard C. Bowles, 1863.

[Weston], Maria D. *Bessie and Raymond, or, Incidents Connected with the Civil War in the United States*. Boston: E. P. Weston, 1866.

Wetherell, Elizabeth [Susan Warner]. *The Wide, Wide World*. New York: George P. Putnam, 1850.

Wevill, engraver. *Before. After*. Library Company of Philadelphia, [1863?].

Woolf, Benjamin Edward. *Off to the War! An Original Farce for the Times in One Act*. Boston: W. V. Spencer, 1861.

Work, Henry C., composer. *Grafted Into the Army*. Chicago: Root & Cady, [1862].

———. *We'll Go Down Ourselves*. Chicago: Root & Cady, 1862.

SECONDARY WORKS

Books and Dissertations

Aaron, Daniel. *The Unwritten War: American Writers and the Civil War*. New York: Oxford University Press, 1973.

Aley, Ginette, and Joseph Anderson, eds. *Union Heartland: The Midwestern Home Front during the Civil War*. Carbondale: Southern Illinois University Press, 2013.

Anbinder, Tyler. *Nativism and Slavery: The Northern Know Nothings and the Politics of the 1850s*. New York: Oxford University Press, 1992.

Appleby, Joyce. *Liberalism and Republicanism in the Historical Imagination.* Cambridge, MA: Harvard University Press, 1992.

Attie, Jeannie. *Patriotic Toil: Northern Women and the American Civil War.* Ithaca, NY: Cornell University Press, 1998.

Bailyn, Bernard, ed. *Pamphlets of the American Revolution, 1740–1776.* Cambridge, MA: Harvard University Press, 1965.

Barth, Gunther. *City People: The Rise of Modern City Culture in Nineteenth-Century America.* New York: Oxford University Press, 1982.

Bederman, Gail. *Manliness and Civilization: A Cultural History of Gender and Race in the United States, 1880–1917.* Chicago: University of Chicago Press, 1995.

Bernstein, Iver. *The New York City Draft Riots.* New York: Oxford University Press, 1990.

Berry, Stephen W., II. *All That Makes a Man: Love and Ambition in the Civil War South.* New York: Oxford University Press, 2003.

Blair, William A. *With Malice toward Some: Treason and Loyalty in the Civil War Era.* Chapel Hill: University of North Carolina Press, 2014.

Blight, David W. *Frederick Douglass' Civil War: Keeping Faith in Jubilee.* Baton Rouge: Louisiana State University Press, 1989.

Blumin, Stuart M. *The Emergence of the Middle Class: Social Experiences in the American City, 1760–1900.* New York: Cambridge University Press, 1989.

Boyd, Steven R. *Patriotic Envelopes of the Civil War: The Iconography of Union and Confederate Covers.* Baton Rouge: Louisiana State University Press, 2010.

Bray, Robert C. *Reading with Lincoln.* Carbondale: Southern Illinois University Press, 2010.

Brown, Richard D. *The Strength of a People: The Idea of an Informed Citizenry in America, 1650–1870.* Chapel Hill: University of North Carolina Press, 1996.

Casey, Emily A. "The Mightiest Influence on Earth: Americans' Emerging Conception of Parenthood, 1820–1880." PhD diss., University of Florida, 2011.

Cashin, Joan, ed. *The War Was You and Me: Civilians in the American Civil War.* Princeton, NJ: Princeton University Press, 2003.

Civil War History. Special issue, "Civil War Humor," 2 (September 1956).

Clinton, Catherine, and Nina Silber, eds. *Battle Scars: Gender and Sexuality in the American Civil War.* New York: Oxford University Press, 2006.

———. *Divided Houses: Gender and the Civil War.* New York: Oxford University Press, 1992.

Cook, Adrian. *The Armies of the Streets.* Lexington: University Press of Kentucky, 1974.

Coontz, Stephanie. *Marriage, a History: How Love Conquered Marriage.* New York: Penguin, 2005.

Cornish, Dudley Taylor. *The Sable Arm: Black Troops in the Union Army, 1861–1865.* 1956; reprint, Lawrence: University Press of Kansas, 1987.

Cott, Nancy F. *The Bonds of Womanhood: "Woman's Sphere" in New England, 1780–1835.* 2nd ed. New Haven, CT: Yale University Press, 1997.

Creighton, Margaret. *Colors of Courage: Gettysburg's Forgotten History, Immigrants,*

Women, and African Americans in the Civil War's Defining Battle. New York: Basic Books, 2005.

Cullen, Jim. *The Art of Democracy: A Concise History of Popular Culture in the United States*. 2nd ed. New York: Monthly Review Press, 2002.

Denith, Simon. *Parody*. New York: Routledge, 2000.

Diffley, Kathleen. *Where My Heart Is Turning Ever: Civil War Stories and Constitutional Reform, 1861–1876*. Athens: University of Georgia Press, 1992.

Duquette, Elizabeth. *Loyal Subjects: Bonds of Nation, Race, and Allegiance in Nineteenth-Century America*. New Brunswick, NJ: Rutgers University Press, 2010.

Fahs, Alice. *The Imagined Civil War: Popular Literature of the North and South, 1861–1865*. Chapel Hill: University of North Carolina Press, 2001.

Faust, Drew. *This Republic of Suffering: Death and the American Civil War*. New York: Knopf, 2008.

Fehrenbacher, Don E. *The Dred Scott Case: Its Significance in American Law and Politics*. New York: Oxford University Press, 1978.

Gallagher, Gary. *The Union War*. Cambridge, MA: Harvard University Press, 2011.

Gallman, J. Matthew. *America's Joan of Arc: The Life of Anna Elizabeth Dickinson*. New York: Oxford University Press, 2006.

———. *Mastering Wartime: A Social History of Philadelphia during the Civil War*. New York: Cambridge University Press, 1990.

———. *The North Fights the Civil War: The Home Front*. Chicago: Ivan R. Dee, 1994.

———. *Receiving Erin's Children: Philadelphia, Liverpool, and the Irish Famine Migration, 1845–1855*. Chapel Hill: University of North Carolina Press, 2000.

Geary, James W. *We Need Men: The Union Draft in the Civil War*. Dekalb: Northern Illinois University Press, 1989.

Giesberg, Judith. *Army at Home: Women and the Civil War on the Northern Home Front*. Chapel Hill: University of North Carolina Press, 2009.

Glatthaar, Joseph T. *Forged in Battle: The Civil War Alliance of Black Soldiers and White Officers*. New York: Free Press, 1990.

Gray, Wood. *The Hidden Civil War: The Story of the Copperheads*. New York: Viking, 1942.

Greenberg, Amy. *Manifest Manhood and the Antebellum American Empire*. Cambridge: Cambridge University Press, 2005.

Halttunen, Karen. *Confidence Men and Painted Women: A Study of Middle-Class Culture in America, 1820–1870*. New Haven, CT: Yale University Press, 1982.

Hemphill, C. Dallett. *Bowing to Necessities: A History of Manners in America, 1620–1860*. New York: Oxford University Press, 2002.

Henkin, David M. *City Reading: Written Words and Public Spaces in Antebellum New York*. New York: Columbia University Press, 1998.

———. *The Postal Age: The Emergence of Modern Communications in Nineteenth-Century America*. Chicago: University of Chicago Press, 2006.

Hess, Earl J. *Liberty, Virtue, and Progress: Northerners and Their War for the Union*. New York: New York University Press, 1988.

Hoganson, Kristen. *Fighting for American Manhood: How Gender Politics Provoked*

the *Spanish-American and Philippine-American Wars*. New Haven, CT: Yale
University Press, 1998.

Horton, James Oliver, and Lois E. Horton. *In Hope of Liberty: Culture, Community
and Protest among Northern Free Blacks, 1700–1860*. Oxford: Oxford University
Press, 1997.

Howe, Daniel Walker. *What Hath God Wrought: The Transformation of America,
1815–1848*. New York: Oxford University Press, 2007.

Hutcheson, Linda. *A Theory of Parody: The Teachings of Twentieth-Century Art
Forms*. Urbana: University of Illinois Press, 2000.

Ignatiev, Noel. *How the Irish Became White*. New York: Routledge, 1996.

Kantrowitz, Stephen. *More Than Freedom: Fighting for Black Citizenship in a White
Republic, 1829–1889*. New York: Penguin, 2012.

Kelley, Mary. *Private Woman, Public Stage: Literary Domesticity in Nineteenth-
Century America*. Chapel Hill: University of North Carolina Press, 1984.

Kerber, Linda. *Women of the Republic: Intellect and Ideology in Revolutionary
America*. Chapel Hill: University of North Carolina Press, 1980.

Kettner, James H. *The Development of American Citizenship, 1608–1870*. Chapel Hill:
University of North Carolina Press, 1978.

Klement, Frank L. *The Copperheads in the Middle West*. Chicago: University of
Chicago Press, 1960.

Lawson, Melinda. *Patriotic Fires: Forging a New American Nationalism in the Civil
War North*. Lawrence: University Press of Kansas, 2002.

Levine, Lawrence W. *Highbrow/Lowbrow: The Emergence of Cultural Hierarchy in
America*. Cambridge, MA: Harvard University Press, 1990.

Marius, Richard, ed. *The Columbia Book of Civil War Poetry*. New York: Columbia
University Press, 1994.

Marten, James, ed. *Children and Youth during the Civil War Era*. New York: New
York University Press, 2012.

———. *The Children's Civil War*. Chapel Hill: University of North Carolina Press,
1998.

———, ed. *Lessons of War: The Civil War in Children's Magazines*. Wilmington, DE:
Scholarly Resources, 1999.

———. *Sing Not the War: The Lives of Union and Confederate Veterans in Gilded Age
America*. Chapel Hill: University of North Carolina Press, 2011.

Masur, Kate. *An Example for All the Land: Emancipation and the Struggle over
Equality in Washington, DC*. Chapel Hill: University of North Carolina Press,
2010.

Matthews, Glenna. *The Golden State in the Civil War: Thomas Starr King, the
Republican Party and the Birth of Modern California*. New York: Cambridge
University Press, 2012.

McPherson, James M. *Battle Cry of Freedom: The Civil War Era*. New York: Oxford
University Press, 1988.

———. *Crossroads of Freedom: Antietam*. New York: Oxford University Press, 2002.

———. *For Cause and Comrades: Why Men Fought in the Civil War*. New York:
Oxford University Press, 1997.

———. *The Negro's Civil War: How American Blacks Felt and Acted during the War for the Union.* 1965; reprint, New York: Vintage Books, 2003.

———. *The Struggle for Equality: Abolitionists and the Negro in the Civil War and Reconstruction.* Princeton, NJ: Princeton University Press, 1964.

McPherson, James M., with James Hogue. *Ordeal by Fire: The Civil War and Reconstruction.* 4th ed. New York: McGraw Hill, 2010.

Mitchell, Reid. *Civil War Soldiers: Their Expectations and Their Experiences.* New York: Simon and Schuster, 1988.

———. *The Vacant Chair: The Northern Soldier Leaves Home.* New York: Oxford University Press, 1993.

Mott, Frank Luther. *A History of American Magazines, vol. 2: 1850–1865.* Cambridge, MA: Harvard University Press, 1938; 2nd ed., 1957.

Murdock, Eugene C. *One Million Men: The Civil War Draft in the North.* Madison: State Historical Society of Wisconsin, 1971.

———. *Patriotism Limited, 1862–1865: The Civil War Draft and the Bounty System.* Kent, OH: Kent State University Press, 1967.

Neely, Mark E., Jr. *The Fate of Liberty: Abraham Lincoln and Civil Liberties.* New York: Oxford University Press, 1991.

———. *Lincoln and the Triumph of the Nation: Constitutional Conflict in the American Civil War.* Chapel Hill: University of North Carolina Press, 2011.

———. *The Union Divided: Party Conflict in the Civil War North.* Cambridge, MA: Harvard University Press, 2002.

Neely, Mark E., Jr., and Harold Holzer. *The Union Image: Popular Prints of the Civil War North.* Chapel Hill: University of North Carolina Press, 2000.

Nevins, Allen. *Ordeal of the Union.* 8 vols. New York: Scribner, 1947–71.

Nickels, Cameron C. *Civil War Humor.* Jackson: University Press of Mississippi, 2010.

Norton, Mary Beth. *Liberty's Daughters: The Revolutionary Experience of American Women, 1750–1800.* 3rd ed. Ithaca, NY: Cornell University Press, 1996.

Novak, William J. *The People's Welfare: Law and Regulation in Nineteenth-Century America.* Chapel Hill: University of North Carolina Press, 1996.

Paludan, Phillip S. *A People's Contest: The Union and the Civil War.* New York: Harper and Row, 1988.

Poovey, Mary. *Making a Social Body: British Cultural Formation, 1830–1864.* Chicago: University of Chicago Press, 1995.

Quarles, Benjamin. *The Negro in the Civil War.* 1953; reprint, New York: Da Capo, 1979.

Rable, George C. *God's Almost Chosen Peoples: A Religious History of the American Civil War.* Chapel Hill: University of North Carolina Press, 2010.

Rael, Patrick. *Black Identity and Black Protest in the Antebellum North.* Chapel Hill: University of North Carolina Press, 2002.

Ray, Angela G. *The Lyceum and Public Culture in the Nineteenth-Century United States.* East Lansing: Michigan State University Press, 2005.

Richard, Patricia L. *Busy Hands: Images of the Family in the Northern Civil War Effort.* New York: Fordham University Press, 2003.

Robertson, James I., Jr. *Soldiers Blue and Gray*. Columbia: University of South Carolina Press, 1988.

Rose, Anne C. *Victorian America and the Civil War*. New York: Cambridge University Press.

Rose, Margaret A. *Parody: Ancient, Modern, and Post-Modern*. Cambridge: Cambridge University Press, 1993.

Rotundo, Anthony E. *American Manhood: Transformations in Masculinity from the Revolution to the Modern Era*. New York: Basic Books, 1993.

Ryan, Mary. *Cradle of the Middle Class: The Family in Oneida County, New York, 1790–1865*. New York: Cambridge University Press, 1983.

Samito, Christian G. *Becoming American under Fire: Irish Americans, African Americans, and the Politics of Citizenship during the Civil War Era*. Ithaca, NY: Cornell University Press, 2009.

Sandow, Robert M. *Deserter Country: Civil War Opposition in the Pennsylvania Appalachians*. New York: Fordham University Press, 2009.

Schultz, Jane E. *Women at the Front: Hospital Workers in Civil War America*. Chapel Hill: University of North Carolina Press, 2004.

Seitz, Don C. *Artemus Ward: A Biography and Bibliography*. New York: Harper Brothers, 1913.

Shankman, Arnold M. *The Pennsylvania Antiwar Movement, 1861–1865*. Rutherford, NJ: Fairleigh Dickinson University Press, 1980.

Silber, Nina. *Daughters of the Union: Northern Women Fight the Civil War*. Cambridge, MA: Harvard University Press, 2003.

———. *Gender and the Sectional Conflict*. Chapel Hill: University of North Carolina Press, 2008.

Sizer, Lyde Cullen. *The Political Work of Northern Women Writers and the Civil War, 1850–1872*. Chapel Hill: University of North Carolina Press, 2000.

Smith, Adam I. P. *No Party Now: Politics in the Civil War North*. New York: Oxford University Press, 2006.

Smith, Michael Thomas. *The Enemy Within: Fears of Corruption in the Civil War North*. Charlottesville: University of Virginia Press, 2011.

Spann, Edward K. *Gotham at War: New York, 1860–1865*. Wilmington, DE: Scholarly Resources, 2002.

Taylor, Frank. *Philadelphia in the Civil War*. Philadelphia: The City, 1913.

Thomas, Brook. *Civic Myths: A Law-and-Literature Approach to Citizenship*. Chapel Hill: University of North Carolina Press, 2007.

Venet, Wendy Hamand. *Neither Ballots nor Bullets: Women Abolitionists and the Civil War*. Charlottesville: University Press of Virginia, 1991.

Weber, Jennifer L. *Copperheads: The Rise and Fall of Lincoln's Opponents in the North*. New York: Oxford University Press, 2007.

Weigley, Russell Frank. *A Great Civil War: A Military and Political History, 1861–1865*. Bloomington: Indiana University Press, 2000.

———. *Quartermaster General of the Union Army: A Biography of Montgomery C. Meigs*. New York: Columbia University Press, 1959.

White, Jonathan W. *Emancipation, the Union Army, and the Reelection of Abraham Lincoln*. Baton Rouge: Louisiana State University Press, 2014.

Wilentz, Sean. *The Rise of American Democracy: Jefferson to Lincoln*. New York: Norton, 2005.

Wiley, Bell Irvin. *The Life of Billy Yank*. 1952; reprint, Baton Rouge: Louisiana State University Press, 1971.

Wilson, Edmund. *Patriotic Gore: Studies in the Literature of the American Civil War*. New York: Oxford University Press, 1962.

Wilson, Mark R. *The Business of Civil War: Military Mobilization and the State, 1861–1865*. Baltimore: Johns Hopkins University Press, 2006.

Wood, Peter H. *Near Andersonville: Winslow Homer's Civil War*. Cambridge, MA: Harvard University Press, 2010.

Wright, Edward Needles. *Conscientious Objectors in the Civil War*. Philadelphia: University of Pennsylvania Press, 1931.

Young, Elizabeth. *Disarming the Nation: Women's Writing and the American Civil War*. Chicago: University of Chicago Press, 1999.

Zagarri, Rosemarie. *Revolutionary Backlash: Women and Politics in the Early American Republic*. Philadelphia: University of Pennsylvania Press, 2007.

Zboray, Ronald J. *A Fictive People: Antebellum Economic Development and the American Reading Public*. New York: Oxford University Press, 1993.

Articles and Essays

Anbinder, Tyler. "Which Poor Man's Fight? Immigrants and the Federal Conscription of 1863." *Civil War History* 4 (December 2006): 344–72.

Bahde, Thomas. "'Our Cause Is a Common One': Home Guards, Unions Leagues, and Republican Citizenship in Illinois, 1861–1863." *Civil War History* 56 (March 2010): 66–98.

Berlin, Ira, et al. "The Black Military Experience, 1861–1867." In *Slaves No More: Three Essays on Emancipation and the Civil War, edited by Ira* Berlin et al., 187–234. New York: Cambridge University Press, 1992.

Binder, Frederick M. "Pennsylvania Negro Regiments in the Civil War." *Journal of Negro History* 37 (1952): 383–417.

Blumin, Stuart M. "The Hypothesis of Middle-Class Formation in Nineteenth-Century America: A Critique and Some Proposals." *American Historical Review* (April 1985): 299–338.

———. "The Social Implications of U.S. Economic Development." In *The Cambridge Economic History of the United States, vol. 2: The Long Nineteenth Century*, edited by Stanley L. Engerman and Robert E. Gallman, 813–65. New York: Cambridge University Press, 2000.

Cullen, Jim. "'I's a Man Now': Gender and African American Men." In *Divided Houses: Gender and the Civil War*, edited by Catherine Clinton and Nina Silber, 76–96. New York: Oxford University Press, 1992.

Durden, Michelle. "Not Just a Leg Show: Gayness and Male Homoeroticism in Burlesque, 1868 to 1877." *thirdspace: a journal of feminist theory and culture*

3 (March 2004), http://journals.sfu.ca/thirdspace/index.php/journal/article/view /durden/173.

Emberton, Carole. "'Only Murder Makes Men': Reconsidering the Black Military Experience." *Journal of the Civil War Era* 2 (September 2012): 369–93.

Engerman, Stanley, and J. Matthew Gallman. "The Civil War Economy: A Modern View." In *On the Road to Total War: The American Civil War and the German Wars of Unification, 1861–1871*, edited by Stig Forster and Jorg Nagler, 217–48. Washington: German Historical Institute/Cambridge University Press, 1997.

Fischer, Hannah. "American War and Military Operations Casualties: Lists and Statistics." Congressional Research Service Report for Congress, updated July 2005. http://www.history.navy.mil/library/online/american%20war%20casualty .htm.

Fogel, Robert W. "New Sources and New Techniques for the Study of Secular Trends in Nutritional Status, Health, Mortality, and the Process of Aging." *Historical Methods* 26 (1993): 5–43.

Foner, Philip S. "The Battle to End Discrimination against Negroes on Philadelphia's Streetcars (Part I): Background and Beginning of the Battle." *Pennsylvania History* 3 (September 1973): 261–90.

———. "The Battle to End Discrimination against Negroes on Philadelphia's Streetcars (Part II): The Victory." *Pennsylvania History* 4 (December 1973): 368–72.

Friedel, Frank. Introduction to *Union Pamphlets of the Civil War, 1861–1865*, 2 vols., edited by Frank Friedel. Cambridge, MA: Harvard University Press, 1967.

———. "The Loyal Publication Society: A Pro-Union Propaganda Agency." *Mississippi Valley Historical Review* (December 1939): 359–76.

Gallman, J. Matthew. "Entrepreneurial Experiences in the Civil War: Evidence from Philadelphia." In *Economic Development in Historical Perspective*, edited by Thomas Weiss and Donald Schaefer, 205–22. Palo Alto, CA: Stanford University Press, 1994.

———. "How a Free People Conduct a Long War: Citizenship, Ethics, and Conflict in the North." Paper delivered at the meetings of the Society of Civil War Historians, Philadelphia. June 17, 2008.

———. "In Your Hands That Musket Means Liberty: African American Soldiers and the Battle of Olustee." In *Wars within a War: Controversy and Conflict over the American Civil War*, edited by Joan Waugh and Gary W. Gallagher, 87–108. Chapel Hill: University of North Carolina Press, 2009.

———. "The President as Pedagogue: Teaching Citizenship in Time of War." In *A War Worth Fighting: Abraham Lincoln's Presidency and Civil War America*, edited by Stephen Engle. Gainesville: University of Florida Press, 2015.

———. "Snapshots: Images of Men in the United States Colored Troops." *American Nineteenth Century History* (June 2012): 127–51.

———. "Voluntarism in Wartime: Philadelphia's Great Central Fair." In *Toward a Social History of the American Civil War: Exploratory Essays*, edited by Maris A. Vinovskis, 93–116. New York: Cambridge University Press, 1990.

Gallman, J. Matthew, and Susan Baker. "Gettysburg's Gettysburg: What the Battle

Did to the Borough." In *Northerners at War: Reflections on the Civil War Home Front*, edited by J. Matthew Gallman, 43–72. Kent, OH: Kent State University Press, 2010.

Grinspan, Jon. "'Sorrowfully Amusing': The Popular Comedy of the Civil War." *Journal of the Civil War Era* (November 2011): 313–38.

Hacker, J. David. "Economic, Demographic, and Anthropometric Correlates of First Marriage in the Mid-Nineteenth-Century United States." *Social Science History* 32 (Fall 2008): 307–45.

Hattaway, Herman M. "The Civil War Armies: Creation, Mobilization, and Development." In *On the Road to Total War*, edited by Stïg Forster and Jörge Nagler, 173–98. New York: Cambridge University Press, 1997.

Hochfelder, David. "The Communications Revolution and Popular Culture." In *A Companion to 19th-Century America*, edited by William D. Barney, 303–16. Malden, MA: Blackwell, 2001.

Kynoch, Gary. "Terrible Dilemmas: Black Enlistment in the Union Army during the American Civil War." *Slavery and Abolition* 18 (August 1997): 104–27.

Lawson, Melinda. "'A Profound National Devotion': The Civil War Union Leagues and the Construction of a New National Patriotism." *Civil War History* 4 (December 2002): 338–62.

Marten, James. "For the Good, the True, and the Beautiful: Northern Children's Magazines and the Civil War." *Civil War History* 41 (March 1995): 57–75.

Mitchell, Reid. "The Northern Soldier and His Community." In *The Vacant Chair: The Northern Soldier Leaves Home*, 19–38. New York: Oxford University Press, 1993.

Murdock, Eugene C. "Was It a 'Poor Man's Fight'?" *Civil War History* 10 (September 1964): 241–45.

Nagler, Jorg. "Loyalty and Dissent: The Home Front in the American Civil War." In *On the Road to Total War: The American Civil War and the German Wars of Unification, 1861–1871*, edited by Stig Forster and Jorg Nagler, 329–56. Washington, DC: German Historical Institute, 1997.

Nardin, James T. "Civil War Humor: The War in *Vanity Fair*." *Civil War History* (September 1956): 67–85.

Paludan, Phillip S. "'The Better Angels of Our Nation': Lincoln, Propaganda, and Public Opinion in the North during the Civil War." In *On the Road to Total War: The American Civil War and the German Wars of Unification, 1861–1871*, edited by Stig Forster and Jorg Nagler, 357–76. Washington, DC: German Historical Institute, 1997.

Reed, John Q. "Civil War Humor: Artemus Ward." *Civil War History* 2 (September 1956): 87–101.

Reidy, Joseph P. "The African American Struggle for Citizenship Rights in the Northern United States during the Civil War." In *Civil War Citizens: Race, Ethnicity, and Identity in America's Bloodiest Conflict*, edited by Susannah J. Ural, 213–36. New York: New York University Press, 2010.

Ringel, Paul B. "Thrills for Children: *The Youth's Companion*, The Civil War, and the Commercialization of American Youth." In *Children and Youth during the Civil*

War Era, edited by James Marten, 77–91. New York: New York University Press, 2012.

Scholnick, Robert. "'An Unusually Active Market for Calamus': Whitman, *Vanity Fair*, and the Fate of Humor in a Time of War, 1860–1863." *Walt Whitman Quarterly Review* 19 (Winter 2002): 148–81.

Shalhope, Robert E. "Toward a Republican Synthesis: The Emergence of an Understanding of Republicanism in American Historiography." *William and Mary Quarterly* 29 (January 1972): 49–80.

Shannon. Fred A. *The Organization and Administration of the Union Army, 1861-1865*. Gloucester, MA: P. Smith, 1965.

Smith, John David. "Let Us All Be Grateful That We Have Colored Troops That Will Fight." In *Black Soldiers in Blue: African American Troops in the Civil War Era*, edited by John David Smith, 1–77. Chapel Hill: University of North Carolina Press, 2002.

Taylor, Brian. "A Politics of Service: Black Northerners' Debates over Enlistment in the American Civil War." *Civil War History* (December 2012): 451–80.

Welter, Barbara. "The Cult of True Womanhood: 1820–1860." *American Quarterly* 18 (Summer 1966): 151–74.

Wert, Jeffry D. "Camp William Penn and the Black Soldier." *Pennsylvania History* 46 (October 1979): 335–46.

West, Richard S. "Frank Leslie's Budget of Fun." In Alexander Street Press, *Illustrated Civil War Newspapers and Magazines* (online collection), http://lincolnandthecivilwar.com/SubLevelPages/BudgetOfFun.asp.

Wilson, Woodrow: "Proclamation 1370—Conscription," May 18, 1917. *American Presidency Project*, by Gerhard Peters and John T. Woolley, http://www.presidency.ucsb.edu/ws/?pid=65403.

Yacovone, Donald. "The Fifty-Fourth Massachusetts Regiment, the Pay Crisis, and the 'Lincoln Despotism.'" In *Hope and Glory: Essays on the Legacy of the 54th Massachusetts Regiment*, edited by Martin H. Blatt, Thomas J. Brown, and Donald Yacovone, 35–51. Amherst: University of Massachusetts Press, 2001.

Zboray, Ronald J., and Mary S. Zboray. "Books, Reading, and the World of Goods in Antebellum New England." *New England Quarterly* 48 (December 1996): 587–622.

———. "Cannonballs and Books: Reading and the Disruption of Social Ties on the New England Homefront." In *The War Was You and Me: Civilians in the American Civil War*, edited by Joan Cashin, 237–61. Princeton, NJ: Princeton University Press, 2002.

Acknowledgments

I have a folder on my computer called "New Project." It contains the hundreds of files that became the basis for this book. If we are going to get technical about things, this project is no longer really that "new," and the computer that completes the book is not the computer that started it. I have been at this for quite a few years, and my intellectual debts are many. As always, many of the greatest debts are to the scholars who appear in this book's endnotes. I am fortunate to be in a profession where we learn from the folks who have come before, even if they wrote fifty years ago. I have tried to mention the articles and books that have had the most significant impact on my thinking, but those acknowledged debts are certainly incomplete.

I have had the opportunity to share early returns from this research at various colleges and universities. These occasions involved formal comments and informal chats, all of which contributed to the larger project. Thanks are due to the Vermont Humanities Council and the participants at their conference "The Northern Civil War Home Front"; the organizers and participants at the National Archives Symposium "The Civil War: Fresh Perspectives"; Enrico Dal Lago and his colleges at the National University of Ireland, Galway; Kevin Adams and Kent State University; Steve Engle and Florida Atlantic University; Scott Reynolds Nelson, Carol Sheriff, the Virginia Sesquicentennial Commission, and the historians at the College of William and Mary; Tom Pegram and Loyola University of Maryland; C. Dallett Hemphill and Ursinus College; and my own colleagues who commented on a presentation at the University of Florida (UF). Thanks as well to the panelists and audience members for sessions at the meetings of the Policy History Conference and the Society of Civil War Historians.

I have profited from dozens of comments at conferences, in conversations at restaurants or the occasional bar, and through e-mail discussions about various aspects of this book. Particular thanks to Sean Adams, Bruce Baker, Steve Berry, Bill Blair, Vernon Burton, Richard Carwardine, Catherine Clinton, Steve Engle, Eric Foner, Judy Giesberg, Lesley Gordon, Bill Link, Jim Marten, Mark Neely, Louise Newman, Taylor Patterson, Lyde Cullen Sizer, Sarah Traphagen, Liz Varon, and Joan Waugh for the formal comments, informal chats, and answered queries. A particular thanks to Dora Costa, Elizabeth Duquette, Andra Gillespie, Brian Taylor, Richard West, and Ronald Zborsky, who all took the time to answer an e-mail from a complete stranger.

Many friends have taken time from their own work to read portions of this manuscript. Thanks to Jeff Adler, Judy Giesberg, Dallett Hemphill for reading chapters at crucial points in the process. And special thanks to Bill Link, Jim Marten, Liz Varon, and Joan Waugh, who read the entire book (in some cases more than once). Each of these wonderful scholars made this a better book, and it would be much better still if I had successfully followed every suggestion. I would also like to thank Lyde Cullen Sizer, who gave the manuscript a very close reading for UNC Press and who provided many valuable suggestions.

Gathering material for this project has been unusual because so much material has become available in digital form even as I was plugging away on my research. Later in the project I spent hundreds of hours doing research at my desk or wherever a coffee shop offered Internet access, but I laid the groundwork for this book by reading real books, pamphlets, and journals in their original musty form. Thanks to the wonderful archivists at the Library Company of Philadelphia; the Rutherford B. Hayes Library in Fremont, Ohio; and the Huntington Library in San Marino, California. And thanks to Allison Fredette and Chris Ruehlen for taking time from their own UF studies to help me run down useful sources. When it came time to assemble the many illustrations reproduced here, I turned to a wide array of archives. Thanks to Shelley Arlen at the University of Florida, Nicole Joniec at the Library Company of Philadelphia, Brian Moeller and Alan Jutze at the Huntington Library, Jaclyn Penny at the American Antiquarian Society, Max Goldberg at Brandeis University, Suzanne Smailes at Wittenberg University, and Susan Severtson and John Adler at HarpWeek.

The transition from "New Project" to possible book unfolded in dozens of conversations with David Perry, who was then the editor-in-chief of the University of North Carolina Press, and Gary Gallagher, who edits the press's superb Civil War America series. I brought this project to UNC Press because I wanted to work with David and Gary, and I wanted to add my name to the astonishing list of authors in the Civil War America series. David offered his characteristic wisdom in those early days, then steered the book through to signed contract, before he retired to offer us all a model for how to live a full life outside this business. Gary has been the ideal friend and critic to guide this book from the first ideas to its current incarnation. He is a superb scholar and the best editor around. I am proud to add my name to the long list of historians who owe him so much. Thanks as well to Mark Simpson-Vos and the talented staff at UNC Press who managed such a seamless transition after David's retirement.

Acknowledgments

Index

Christian Recorder, 227, 234–35, 240; on streetcar battles, 248; on treatment of African Americans, 247–48

Cincinnati and segregated streetcars, 248

Cincinnati Gazette, 101, 231

"Circular No. 28" (Ward), 170–71

Citizenship, 1, 14–15, 64, 186–87; and bounties, 140–42; and conscription, 140, 162, 165, 169, 170; defined, 29; and duty, 10, 130; and enlistment, 125–27, 137–38; expectations of, 35; and ministers, 183–84; and newspapers, 134; obligations, and African Americans, 226–31; prescriptions for, 220; as reciprocal relationship, 257; and recruiting posters, 129; and recruiting, 169; in twentieth century, 255; and wartime, 84–85, 253; in wartime, 118

Citizen-soldiers, 8–9, 26

Civil liberties, 126

Clark, D. W.: "An Appeal to Christian and Patriotic Women upon their Duties in Relation to the War," 192–93, 195

Cleveland Morning Leader, 19

Colored Orphan Asylum (New York City), 241

"Come In out of the Draft," 144

Comic Monthly, 97; and conscription, 175; and swells, 38–39, 41–42, 44–45

Comic valentines, 11, 80, 97, 99–100

Commission seekers, 89–90, 184–85

Commonwealth, 195

Communities: and conscription, 139; and recruiting, 252

Commutation fee, 163. *See also* Conscription

Companionate marriages, 221

Confederacy: and attitudes towards black soldiers, 240; and contrabands, 228; and government seizure of goods, 251

Confederate women, perceptions of, 131, 194, 206

Confidence men, 5, 12–13; and Nathaniel Hawthorne, 70

Congregationalists, 184

Congressmen and conscription, 179

Conscription, 15–16, 129, 143–57; and bounties, 139–41; and community quotas, 139; and commutation fees, 163; constitutional arguments regarding, 125–27; decision to adopt, 139; federal, 158–87; federal draft law, 134; and Abraham Lincoln, 125–27; and market forces, 252; medical exemptions, 171; options to avoid service, 139; and patriotism, 157; and provost marshals, 172; and satire, 170–84; and self-mutilation, 152–53, 177; and substitutes, 140–41, 175, 177; and swells, 41, 44, 46

Continental Monthly, 101

Contrabands, 106, 225–26, 259

Contract fraud, 94–95

"Contractor's Plaint, The," 101

"Cool Captain, The," 137

Copperheads, 2, 126–27, 130–31; and conscription, 150–51; in literature, 101; and Union soldiers, 258

Cormany, Rachel, 23

Corning, Erastus, 126

Cornwallis, Kinaham: *Pilgrims of Fashion*, 103–4

Coward, The (Morford), 19–20, 115–16, 159–62, 206

Cowards and cowardice, 15–16, 21, 31, 101, 159–62, 210; and African Americans, 241; and conscription, 143–57, 165–67, 177–79; defined, 134; and Frederick Douglass, 236, 238; explanations for, 159–62; fears of cowardice and enlistment, 138; and Abraham Lincoln, 126; and Henry Morford, 19; and shoulder straps, 82; and swells, 46

Craft, Ellen and William, 223

Crisis, The (Columbus, Ohio), 104, 105

Cropper, William, 227
Cross-dressing women, 218–20
Curtin, Andrew G., 93

Daily Advertiser (Boston), 119
Daily Evening Bulletin (Cleveland), 22
Daily Evening Bulletin (Philadelphia), 20, 114
Daily Evening Bulletin (San Francisco), 153
Daily National Intelligencer (Washington, D.C.), 23, 114
Dallas, Mary Kyle, 105
Danbury (CT) Times, 152
Davis, Jefferson, 241
Days of Shoddy, The (Morford), 19, 91–93, 137, 206
"Dead Soldier's Ring, The," 212
Del, Howard, 42, 173, 207; and conscription, 149–50; on draft evaders, 153
Delmonico's (New York restaurant), 73–74, 76
Democratic Party, 2; and Abraham Lincoln, 126
Democratic Society for the Diffusion of Political Knowledge, 9
Denison, Mary A.: "The Negro's Vision," 236
Dickinson, Anna Elizabeth, 188, 244–45, 249–50
Disbanded Volunteer. *See* Barber, Joseph
"Discarded Lieutenant's Lament, The," 87–88
Dissent, 2
Dodge, Mary Abigail. *See* Hamilton, Gail
Dodge, Mary E.: "Netty's Touchstone," 162
Dollar Monthly Magazine, 208. See also *Ballou's Dollar Monthly Magazine*
Douglass, Frederick, 223, 226, 245; "Another Word to Colored Men," 239; and black enlistment, 227, 235–36, 238, 239; "A Call to the Negroes to Arm," 236; "Men of Color to Arms!" 236; and William Seward, 246; sons

in Union Army, 236; and unequal pay issue, 246
Douglass' Monthly, 231–32, 239–41
Dover (NH) Gazette, 104, 119
Draft: quotas, 141; and silly women, 57, 59–60; state militia, 139–57. *See also* Conscription
"Draft at Monkeytown, The," 143
Draft evaders: and Canada, 149–50; mocked, 143–57; and national reporting, 22
Draft riot, New York City, 162, 177, 241
"Dream of the Army Contractor, The," 95–96, 98, 100
Dred Scott v Sanford, 228–29, 231, 234–35, 258
Dunn Browne. *See* Fiske, Samuel W.
Durden, Michelle, 35
Duryea, Joseph T., 181, 183
Duty, 14–15, 26, 64, 209; and citizenship, 125–57; and war, 12, 117, 122; and women, 217
"Duty of the Hour, The," 133

Eaton, W. O.: "Victim of the Draft," 179
Economic growth, 4
Economic strains of war, and women, 213–14
Economy, wartime, 189
Editors: of newspapers, 10; and publication decisions, 18
Elections: of 1860, 226; of 1862, 1; of 1863, 2, 158; of 1864, 2, 158, 167
Elevator (San Francisco), 248
Ellsworth, Elmer, 67
Elyria (OH) Democrat, 153
Emancipation Proclamation, 2, 158, 210, 225, 234, 237–38; and enlistment, 245
"Emigrant Volunteer's Wife, The" (Furman), 137
England, and World War I, 255
"Enlisted! Enlisted!" (Townsend), 138
Enlistment: angry motivations for in fiction, 138–39, 215; cultural expecta-

tions regarding, 254; decisions, 8–9, 84–85, 135–39; decisions discussed in fiction, 135–37; motives for, 125; numbers, 7–8; three-month recruits, 65–66; Union Army, 65–67. *See also* Recruiting posters and broadsides

Enrollment Act of 1863, 158, 162–63, 252. *See also* Conscription; Federal conscription

Envelopes. *See* Patriotic envelopes

Etiquette manuals, 12, 15

European governments and conscription, 163

Evening Journal, 167

Evening Star (Washington, D.C.), 20

Fahs, Alice, 191

Farming and women, 189, 196, 209

Federal conscription, 134, 158–87

Federal government in antebellum America, 251

Federal income tax, 252

"Female Recruiting Sergeant, The," 203

Female volunteers, 216

Feminized war, 191

Fern, Fanny, 67

"Few Words in Behalf of the Loyal Women of the United States by One of Themselves, A" (Kirkland), 131–32, 193–95

Fields, James T., 24

Fifteenth Amendment, 258

Fifty-Fifth Massachusetts Colored Volunteers, 241

Fifty-Fourth Massachusetts Colored Volunteers, 236, 239; pay dispute, 246

Fisk, Wilbur, 165–6

Fiske, Samuel W., 134, 164–65

"Flag Mania," 29–30

Fogel, Robert, 8

Fools. *See* Swells

Fort Lafayette (Wood), 70–71

Fort Sumter aftermath, 13, 29–30, 33–34, 65–66; and Frederick Douglass, 226; and patriotic women, 52

Fort Wagner, Battle of, 250

Fourteenth Amendment, 258

Francis, Harriet E., 215

Frank Leslie's Budget of Fun, 7, 18, 38, 46–47, 73–76, 105, 113, 199, 211; and conscription, 17; on draft avoidance, 153; readership, 22; and Russian Ball, 121; satire on women, 56, 59; and shoddy, 112

Frank Leslie's Illustrated Newspaper, 153, 238; circulation, 7; on conscription, 141; on Henry Morford, 20; and Russian Ball, 118; satire on women, 55, 59

Frauds, 14. *See also* Shoddy; War contractors and contracting

Frémont, John C., 94; and Western Department, 113

Friends Review, 179–80

"Frightened Conscript, The," 150

Furloughed soldiers, 81–82; and African American soldiers, 248; and women, 214

Furman, Mrs. S. K.: "The Emigrant Volunteer's Wife," 137

Garnet, Henry Highland, 231, 239, 246

Garrison, William Lloyd, 163

Gender: and conscription, 177; and enlistment, 137–38, 142, 143; and patriotism, 131; prescription and, 190; stereotypes, 15, 199; and war meetings, 31–33

General Orders No. 2, 86

German immigrants, 5

Gettysburg, Pa., 189; Battle of, 115

Godey's Lady's Book, 24, 57, 112; readership, 21

Golden Era (San Francisco, Calif.), 22, 105, 134, 143

Goodwin, Hannah Bradbury: *Roger Deane's Work*, 216

Government contracting, 102

"Grafted into the Army," 172

"On Negro Emigration" (Nasby), 233–34
"On War Contractors," 101
"Opal, The," 212
Opdyke, George, 97, 113, 167
Optic, Oliver, 178; *The Student and Schoolmate*, 131
O'Reilly, Miles, 246. *See also* Halpine, Charles Graham
Orne, Caroline: "The Two Young Soldiers," 212
"Our Departed Braves," 87
"Our Duty" (Arthur), 130–31
Overland Campaign, 3

Pacific Appeal (San Francisco), 248
Pamphlets and pamphleteers, 9–10, 130–33, 181, 253, 257
Patriotic envelopes, 11, 67–68, 253; and Quakers, 181, 207–8
Patriotism: and bounty funds, 139–42; and gender, 284–85 (n. 10); and secession, 134
"Peaceable Man, A." *See* Hawthorne, Nathaniel
Pease, H. Ives, 97–98, 100, 102
Penfield-Bross (artist), 211
Pennington, J. W. C., 227
Pennsylvania, 242; 1863 invasion of, 181
People's Contest, 25–26, 259
Peter, Frances, 23
Peterson, T. B., 19
Peterson's Magazine, 23, 24, 90, 196, 199, 213; readership, 21
"Petroleum's Ball," 112
Phelps, Elizabeth S.: "A Sacrifice Consumed," 214
Philadelphia, 197, 242, 244; and African Americans, 245; and segregated streetcars, 248–50
Philadelphia Inquirer, 23, 87, 114
Philadelphia Press, 19, 119, 248–49
Photography and soldiers' portraits, 75; changing technology, 67
Phunny Fellow, readership, 22
Pilgrims of Fashion (Kinaham), 103–4

"Plundermongering," 101
Poems, 10, 67, 167. *See also specific poems*
Pope, John, and Pope's Order, 86–87
Population growth, 4
Port Hudson, 240
Portland Transcript, 167, 169
Postal service, 21
Potter, William J., 183–84; "The Voice of the Draft," 183
Poverty, 185; and Civil War, 121; and shoddy aristocracy, 109; and women, 213–14
Prescriptive literature, 6, 11, 128–29, 253
Press corps and cartoonists, 46–49
Prince of Wales, 119
Prisoners of war in fiction, 142
Publications: audiences of, 18, 20; wartime, 3. *See also specific types of publications*
Punch, 130
Putnam's, 21

Quakers, 179–82, 207–8; and citizenship, 179–80; and conscription, 179–80
Quartermaster's Department, 102

Reconstruction, 249; debates over citizenship, 258
"Recruit, The," 215
Recruiting, 129, 130, 252; and African Americans, 224
Recruiting posters and broadsides, 10, 65–67, 129, 242, 253; and citizenship, 129
"Red, White and Black," 199, 206
"Red, White and Blue, The" (Janvrin), 204–5
Refugees, southern, 189
Religion, 132–33. *See also* Ministers; Sermons
Republican ideals, 13, 202, 253
Republican mothers, 190
Republican Party, 1, 158, 188, 226
Rhodes, Elisha Hunt, 166–67
Richmond, Va., 91

Robinson, Mary S.: *The Brother Soldiers: A Household Story of the American Conflict*, 135
Rock, John, 226
Rockwell, M. E.: "Mrs. Gray's Sympathy," 195
Rodman, Ella: "'He' and I," 185–86
Rodman, Ella: "Angel of Mercy," 212
Roger Deane's Work (Goodwin), 216
"Romance, A—The Conscript" (Ward), 150
Rose Mather: A Tale (Holmes), 33–34
Round Table, 169
Russian Ball, The, 118–22
Russian Ball, The: Or the Adventures of Clementine Shoddy, 119, 121–22

"Sacrifice Consumed, A" (Phelps), 214
"Sacrifices for Country" (Mozart), 213
St. Louis, Mo., 94, 135–36
St. Thomas's Episcopal Church (Philadelphia), 249
Salem Register, 143
San Francisco and segregated streetcars, 248–49
San Francisco Bulletin, 88–89, 119
Sanitary fairs, 197–98
Saratoga, 114, 115
Satire and satirists, 13–14, 25; and wartime culture, 11. *See also specific authors*
Scientific American, 97
Second Confiscation Act, 234
"Sermon for the Present Hour, A" (Johnson), 239
Sermons, 6, 10, 12, 181, 183, 198, 253; and manhood, 131; on patriotism, 132–33; published, 132–33
Seward, William, 231, 245–46
Shakespeare, 20
Shirley, Anna W.: "Tried and True," 161
Shoddy, 253; article on, 24; defined, 92, 113; and Irish immigrants, 113; and Henry Morford, 19; in political debate, 167; and women, 92, 104–8

"Shoddy" (Pease), 97–98, 102
Shoddy aristocracy, 14–15, 91–122, 129; and women, 192, 198; term coined and defined, 103–5
Shoddyocracy, introduced as new term, 107
Shoulder Straps (Morford), 19–20, 82–86
Shoulder straps, 14, 69–90, 129, 184–85, 253–54; in *The Coward*, 160; and Henry Morford, 19, 115; and swells, 3
"Shows Why He Should Not Be Drafted" (Nasby), 149
"Sick Brigade, The," 171
Slavery, 4, 25, 223–24; as political concern, 226–34, 259
Smith, Gerrit, 163, 226, 240, 241
Smith, Moses, 183–84
Society for the Diffusion of Political Knowledge, 10
Society of Friends. *See* Quakers
"Soldier on Leave, The," 81–82
Soldiers, demographics of, 189
"Soldier's Bride, The" (Lowell), 208, 211
Soldier's Casket, 179
"Soldier's Dying Wife, The" (Allard), 212–13
"Soldier's Wife, The" (Miller), 209
"Song of the Draft, The," 144
"Song of the Eleventh-Hour Patriot, The," 142
"Song of the Exempts," 149
"Song of the Home Guard, The," 71–72
"Song of the Shoddy," 97
Songs, 67, 191; and songbooks, 10
Southworth, Sarah A.: "Marcia Grant's Love," 214–15
Spear, Samuel, 133
Springfield Republican, 134, 164–65
Stanley, Carry: "The Volunteer's Wife," 213
Stanton, Edwin M., 94
Stanton, Elizabeth Cady, 188
State Central Committee of Colored Men (Michigan), 239
State militia draft, 139–57, 159, 232

Stearns, George L., 246

Stephans, Bobbett-Hooper, 228

Stewart, William Bell, 183–84

Still, William, 248–49

Stillé, Charles Janeway, 1, 3, 9, 10, 131, 132, 259; *How a Free People Conduct a Long War*, 1, 3, 131, 133

Stowe, Harriet Beecher: *Uncle Tom's Cabin*, 223

"Strategy," 138

Streetcars, and African Americans, 248–49

Student and Schoolmate, The (Optic), 131

Substitutes, 252; and conscription, 177

Supervisory Committee on Enlistments for Colored Regiments, 242

Supreme Court of the United States, 228

Sutherland, Kate: "The Laggard Recruit," 205

Swells, 13–14, 35–46, 76, 129, 253; and conscription, 41, 44, 46, 176; and draft evasion, 153; and manhood, 41, 60; and sexuality, 35; and women, 39, 41–42, 44

"Swell's Soliloquy on the War, The," 37–38

Tammany Hall, 19, 115

Taney, Roger, 228, 231

Technology and publications, 6, 25

"These Are My Sons," 196

Thirteenth Amendment, 258

Ticknor & Fields, 24

Tilton, Theodore, 167

Tomes, Robert, 108

Townsend, Virginia F., 131, 137–38, 195, 201–2; "Enlisted! Enlisted!," 138; "Home Pictures of the Times," 201–2; "Hospital Nurse," 202

Transportation changes, 21

Travel guides, 253

Tricksters, 5

"Tried and True" (Shirley), 161

Tri-Weekly Miner's Register, 169

True womanhood, 60, 109, 185, 190, 208, 217–18; and "Cult of True Womanhood," 5

"Tuberose, The," 214

Turner, A. A.: "Beauties of the Draft," 153

Twain, Mark, 22

Twentieth United States Colored Troops, 247

"Two Young Soldiers, The" (Orne), 212

"Uncle Sam," 255, 257

Uncle Tom's Cabin (Stowe), 223

Unconditional Loyalty (Bellows), 10

Union Army: and black soldiers, 224; demographic estimates of, 93, 263 (n. 24); treatment of freedmen, 232; and war contracting, 93–94, 251–52

Union League (Philadelphia), 9, 249

Union Leagues, 9, 253, 257

Union soldiers and conscription, 164–67

United States, financing of the Civil War by, 252

United States Christian Commission, 188

United States Colored Troops (USCT), 240, 244–45, 249–50; and unequal pay and treatment, 246–47

United States Sanitary Commission, 1, 188, 197–99

United States War Department, 102

Urban guides, 5, 12–13

Valentines, comic, 11, 80, 97, 99–100

Vallandigham, Clement, 126–27

Vanity Fair, 7, 29, 30, 85, 87, 132, 214; and African Americans, 237–38; and commission seekers, 89–90; and conscription, 144, 174; contract fraud, 95–96; and Democratic sympathies, 18, 19; on draft evasion, 153, 155; and duty, 129–30; and Home Guard, 71–73, 82; national distribution, 22; and Quakers, 180–81; and satirical commentary on women, 52–53, 55, 57; and shoddy, 97; and shoulder straps, 71–73, 76–77, 80; and swells,

Wool, John E., 87

Woolf, Benjamin Edward, 30–31

Work, Henry Clay, 172; "We'll Go Down Ourselves," 202–3

Working class: characters in fiction, 215, 267 (n. 80); women, 188

World War I and American mobilization, 255, 257

World War II, 255, 257

"Wounded" (Arthur), 128

Yankee Notions, 7; and children, 61; and conscription, 149–50, 171, 175–76; and Quakers, 181; satire on women, 57; and swells, 38–40, 46

Youth. *See* Children and youth